THE PE

FOUNDER EDI

Ed.

CICERO'S LETTERS TO HIS FRIENDS · I

CICERO, MARCUS TULLIUS (106–43 B.C.), Roman orator and statesman, was born at Arpinum of a wealthy local family. He was taken to Rome for his education with the idea of a public career and by the year 70 he had established himself as the leading barrister in Rome. In the meantime his political career was well under way and he was elected praetor for 66. His ambitious nature enabled him to obtain those honours which would normally only have been conferred upon members of the Roman aristocracy, and he was duly elected consul for 63. One of the most permanent features of his political life was his attachment to Pompey. As a politician his notable quality was his consistent refusal to compromise; as a statesman his ideals were more honourable and unselfish than those of his contemporaries. Cicero was the greatest of the Roman orators, possessing a wide range of technique and an exceptional command of the Latin tongue. He followed the common practice of publishing his speeches, but he also produced a large number of works on the theory and practice of rhetoric, on religion, and on moral and political philosophy. He played a leading part in the development of the Latin hexameter. Perhaps the most interesting of all his works is the collection of 900 letters published posthumously. These not only contain a first-hand account of social and political life in the upper classes at Rome, but also reflect the changing personal feelings of an emotional and sensitive man.

D. R. SHACKLETON BAILEY was born in 1917 and educated at Lancaster Royal Grammar School and at Gonville and Caius College, Cambridge, where he was a Fellow from 1944 to 1955 and again, as Deputy and Senior Bursar, from 1964 to 1968. From 1948 to 1968 he was University Lecturer in Tibetan and from 1955 to 1964 Fellow and Director of Studies in Classics at Jesus College, Cambridge. From 1968 to 1974 he was Professor of Latin at the University of Michigan and has been Professor of Greek and Latin at Harvard University since 1975. He is a Doctor of Letters (Cambridge, 1957), a Fellow of the British Academy (1958), and a member of the American Philosophical Society (1977). Among his classical publications are *Propertiana* (1956), *Towards a Text of Cicero ad Atticum* (1960), *Ciceronis Epistulae II.ii* (1961), *Cicero's Letters to Atticus* (1965–1970), *Cicero* (1971), *Two Studies in Roman Nomenclature* (1976), *Cicero, Epistulae ad Familiares* (1977).

CICERO

CICERO'S LETTERS TO HIS FRIENDS

VOLUME ONE

Translated by
D. R. Shackleton Bailey

PENGUIN BOOKS

Penguin Books Ltd, Harmondsworth, Middlesex, England
Penguin Books, 625 Madison Avenue, New York, New York 10022, U.S.A.
Penguin Books Australia Ltd, Ringwood, Victoria, Australia
Penguin Books Canada Ltd, 2801 John Street, Markham, Ontario, Canada L3R 1B4
Penguin Books (N.Z.) Ltd, 182–190 Wairau Road, Auckland 10, New Zealand

—

This translation first published 1978

—

—

Printed in the United States of America by
Offset Paperback Mfrs., Inc., Dallas, Pennsylvania
Set in Monotype Bembo

CONTENTS

INTRODUCTION

THE collection of Cicero's 'Letters to Friends' (*Epistulae ad Familiares*) did not originally appear as such. Our manuscripts have it in sixteen 'Books'. Some of these consist entirely or mainly of letters to or from a single correspondent: Lentulus Spinther in 'Book' I, Appius Claudius Pulcher in 'Book' III, Caelius in 'Book' VIII, Terentia in 'Book' XIV, Tiro in 'Book' XVI. 'Book' XIII consists of letters of recommendation, 'Books' X–XII of correspondence relating to the struggle with Antony in 44–43. The other 'Books' show more or less of internal cohesion. The evidence suggests that they were arranged and published separately or in groups during the Augustan period by a single editor, who was in all probability Cicero's faithful secretary, Tiro; he is also likely to have produced the now lost collections of letters to individual correspondents other than Atticus known to have existed in antiquity, Caesar, Pompey, Octavian and others, as well as those surviving to Quintus Cicero and Marcus Brutus. At what time the collection of sixteen 'Books' came into being is unknown. The title 'Letters to Friends' seems to be no older than the Renaissance.

The 'friends' are a motley group. Some of them, as Trebatius Testa, Caelius, and Papirius Paetus, really were familiars, to whom Cicero could write as informally, though not as intimately, as to Atticus or to his brother. With powerful aristocrats like Cato, Lentulus Spinther, and Appius Pulcher he was on no such easy footing, and his letters to them are in as elaborate a style as his published works. The high sentiments, stately flatteries, and courteously veiled rebukes might have transposed naturally into eighteenth-century English, but put a modern translator at a disadvantage. In contrast with both types are a series of official or semi-official documents, including two dispatches from Cilicia, both models of elegant, straightforward language.

The letters are arranged and numbered as in my edition of the Latin texts (Cambridge, 1977), partly chronologically, partly by grouping according to correspondent or genre, and are translated from its text.

BIBLIOGRAPHICAL NOTE

THIS translation follows my recently published text and commentary, nos. 16–17 in the Cambridge Classical Texts and Commentaries series (Cambridge University Press, 1977). My *Cicero* (Gerald Duckworth, 1971) may be of use as a biographical and historical companion to the Correspondence. As a general history of the period T. Rice Holmes, *The Roman Republic* (3 vols., Oxford University Press, 1923), can still be recommended. Mommsen's *History of Rome*, however outmoded its ideological bias, keeps its fascination as a work of genius. Among contributions by living scholars R. Syme's *Roman Revolution* (Oxford University Press, 1939) is an established classic (largely, however, concerned with the period after Cicero's death). Anything by E. Badian and P. A. Brunt is worth reading. For penetrating analysis of the problems and determinants underlying late-republican politics I know nothing to equal the work of Christian Meier, especially *Res Publica Amissa* (Wiesbaden, Steiner, 1966) and *Caesars Bürgerkrieg* (1964; republished in *Entstehung des Begriffs Demokratie*, Frankfurt am Main, Suhrkamp Verlag, 1970); unfortunately it has not been translated.

Gaston Boissier's *Cicéron et ses amis* (1865; Engl. tr. 1897) can never be superseded as a delightful and sympathetic account of the man and his milieu. The straightforward biographies tend to be soporific. The only modern commentary on the whole Correspondence, that of Tyrrell and Purser (7 vols., 1904–33), is a mine of honest misinformation. On the other hand, J. Carcopino's *Les Secrets de la correspondance de Cicéron* (2 vols., 1947; Engl. tr. 1951), a farrago of garbled facts and false inferences, is more worthy of an unscrupulous prosecuting attorney than of a serious scholar.

NOTE

THIS translation (in two volumes) of *Cicero's Letters to his Friends* is a companion to *Cicero's Letters to Atticus* (Penguin Classics) in which appears a full Introduction to Cicero's correspondence.

CICERO'S LETTERS TO HIS FRIENDS

I (V. I)

METELLUS CELER TO CICERO

Cisalpine Gaul, c. 12 January 62

Q. Metellus Celer, son of Quintus, Proconsul, to M. Tullius
Cicero greetings.

I hope you are well!

In view of our reciprocal sentiments and the restoration of
our friendly relations I had not expected that I should ever be
held up by you to offensive ridicule in my absence, or that my
brother Metellus[1] would be attacked at your instance in person
or estate because of a phrase.[2] If his own honourable character
did not suffice for his protection, the dignity of our family and
my zeal on behalf of you and your friends and the commonwealth should have been support enough. Now it seems that
he has been beset, and I deserted, by those whom it least
behoved.

So I wear the black of mourning[3] – I, in command of a
province and an army conducting a war![4] Well, you and your
friends have managed it so, without reason or forbearance. It
was not like this in our forbears' time, and it will not be sur-

1. Q. Caecilius Metellus Nepos. Since entering office as Tribune on
10 December 63 he had demonstrated hostility to Cicero and his
handling of the Catilinarian crisis. See next letter.

2. Probably the one reported in para. 7 of Cicero's reply ('that one
who had punished others' etc.).

3. Customary when (e.g.) a close relative faced prosecution on a
capital charge. Many Romans put on mourning for Cicero when
threatened by Clodius in 58. Metellus Nepos had been suspended from
office by the Senate.

4. Against Catiline.

prising if you all come to be sorry.[5] I did not think to find your own disposition so changeable towards me and mine. In the meantime neither domestic unhappiness nor any man's ill-usage shall turn me away from the commonwealth.

2 (V. 2)

CICERO TO METELLUS CELER

Rome, mid January 62

From M. Tullius Cicero, son of Marcus, to Q. Metellus Celer, son of Quintus, Proconsul, greetings.

I hope all is well with you and the army.[6]

You write that you had not expected ever to be held up to offensive ridicule by me, in view of our reciprocal sentiments and the restoration of friendly relations. What that means, I cannot precisely tell. But I suspect you have heard a report to the effect that, while arguing in the Senate that there were very many who regretted my saving of the commonwealth, I remarked that relatives of yours, to whom you could not say no, had prevailed upon you to suppress what you had decided you ought to say in the Senate in commendation of myself. In making this observation, I added that you and I had made a division of duty in the preservation of the commonwealth: my part was to guard Rome from domestic plots and the enemy within the gates, yours to protect Italy from armed force and underground conspiracy.[7] This partnership of ours in so vital

5. Perhaps a hint of what might happen when Pompey returned from the East.

6. It was usual to include the army in this formula when writing to a commanding general.

7. As Praetor in 63 Celer had raised troops in northern Italy and cut off Catiline's retreat to Gaul.

and splendid a task had been impaired by relatives of yours, who feared you might make me some gesture of mutual good-will in response to the ungrudging warmth of my tributes to yourself.

When in the course of my remarks I explained how eagerly I had been looking forward to your speech and how egregiously I had been astray, my speech caused some amusement and a moderate amount of laughter ensued – not directed at you, but rather at my mistake, and at the artless candour with which I admitted my desire to be praised by you. Really there could be nothing but compliment to you in my saying that at the very height of my glory I still hankered for some testimonial from *your* lips.

As for your reference to 'our reciprocal sentiments', I do not know how *you* define reciprocity in friendship. *I* conceive it to lie in good-will equally received and returned. If I were to say that I forwent a province[8] for your sake, you would think *me* less than sincere. It suited my purpose to do so, and I draw more pleasure and profit every day from my decision. What I do say is, that having announced the relinquishment of my province at a public meeting, I lost no time in planning how to transfer it to you. Of the lottery among the board of Praetors I say nothing. I only invite you to surmise that I was privy to all my colleague's actions in the matter. Be pleased to recall what followed, how promptly I called the Senate together on the day the lottery had taken place, and at what length I spoke about you. You said to me yourself that my speech was flattering to you to the point of being less than complimentary to your

8. Macedonia and Cisalpine Gaul had been assigned by the Senate as consular provinces for 62. Cicero enlisted support against Catiline from his unreliable colleague C. Antonius by letting him have Macedonia instead of drawing lots. Later he announced that he would not take a province at all, leaving Cisalpine Gaul to be allotted to one of the eight Praetors. He goes on to imply that Antonius, instigated by himself, had manipulated the lottery in Celer's favour.

colleagues. Moreover, the senatorial decree[9] passed that day contained a preamble which, as long as the document survives, will plainly testify to the friendly office I did you. Then, after you left Rome, I would ask you to recollect my speeches in the Senate with reference to yourself, my deliverances at public meetings, and the letters I sent you. When you have put all this together, I leave to your own judgement whether your conduct on the occasion of your recent visit[10] to Rome adequately 'reciprocated' mine at all these points.

You refer to 'the restoration of friendly relations'. I fail to understand why you should speak of a restoration of relations which have never been impaired.

You write that your brother Metellus should not have been attacked by me because of a phrase. Now in the first place I would ask you to believe that your sentiment here, your fraternal spirit redolent of good feeling and natural affection, has my warm approval. Secondly, if in any matter I have opposed your brother on public grounds, I ask you to forgive me – in public spirit I call no man my superior. But if I have defended my existence as a citizen in face of a savage onslaught on his part, you should be content that *I* do not protest to *you* about your brother's ill-usage. When I learned that he was planning and preparing his entire programme as Tribune with a view to my destruction, I addressed myself to your lady wife Claudia[11] and your sister Mucia[12] (her friendly disposition towards me as a friend of Cn. Pompeius had been plain to me in many connections) and asked them to persuade him to give up his injurious design. And yet, on the last day of the year, as I am

9. The decree (c. October 63) will have appointed Celer to a command in north Italy prior to his taking over the governorship of his province. Cicero's name would appear in the preamble with a complimentary reference to Celer's services as Praetor.

10. This visit must have taken place at the end of 63 while Celer was still Praetor.

11. See Glossary of Persons under 'Clodia'.

12. Actually half-sister, married to Pompey.

sure you have heard, he put upon me, Consul and saviour of the commonwealth, an insult which has never been put on any holder of any magistracy, no matter how disloyal: he deprived me of the power to address an assembly before retiring from office. This affront, however, redounded greatly to my honour. In face of his refusal to let me do more than take the oath,[13] I swore in loud tones the truest and finest oath that ever was, and the people likewise in loud tones swore that I had sworn the truth.

Even after receiving so signal an insult I sent common friends to Metellus that very same day to urge him to change his attitude. He replied that his hands were no longer free; and in fact he had declared at a public meeting a little while previously that one who had punished others without a hearing ought not to be given the right to speak himself. What sense of responsibility, what civic virtue! To judge the preserver of the Senate from massacre, of Rome from arson, of Italy from war, worthy of the same penalty as was inflicted by the Senate with the approbation of all honest men upon those who had designed to set fire to Rome, slaughter magistrates and Senate, and kindle a terrible conflict![14] Accordingly, I stood up to your brother Metellus face to face. On the Kalends of January we had a political disputation in the Senate which let him feel that he had to deal with a man of courage and resolution. In a speech on 3 January he named me in every sentence with threats; he had thoroughly made up his mind to bring me down by hook or by crook – not through due process of law, but by aggressive violence. If I had not offered a spirited and manly resistance to his indiscretions, nobody could have believed that my record

13. The usual oath taken by a retiring magistrate, that he had observed the laws during his term of office. Cicero neatly adapted it to the occasion by swearing that he alone had saved Rome and the Republic.

14. The Senate had decreed a public Thanksgiving in honour of Cicero's services almost in these terms.

as a courageous Consul was aught but a freak of chance.

If you were unaware of Metellus' intentions towards me, you must recognize that your brother has kept you in the dark about matters of the highest consequence. On the other hand, if he told you something of his plans, you ought to appreciate how mild and easy-going I show myself in not expostulating with you on this very subject. And if you recognize that I was not upset by a 'phrase' of Metellus but by the bitter hostility of his purpose and attitude towards me, I must ask you now to note my forbearance – if that is the right word for laxity and weakness in the face of the most severe provocation. I have never once spoken in the Senate for a motion against your brother; on all such occasions I have kept my seat and supported those who appeared to me to make the most lenient proposal. I will add something else: although I could not be expected, after what had passed, to be active in the matter, I was not sorry to see my enemy relieved[15] (because he was your brother) by a senatorial decree, and I even assisted, so far as in me lay, to bring this about.

Thus I made no attack upon your brother, but repelled *his* attack on me; and my disposition towards you, so far from being 'changeable', has been eminently stable, so much so that my feelings remained the same even when friendly actions on your part were no longer forthcoming. Even now, though you have written to me in almost menacing terms, this is the answer I have to make: I not only pardon your irritation, I highly commend it – my own experience of the power of a brother's affection is my monitor. In return, I ask you to be fair in your judgement of a similar feeling on my part, and to take the view that, if I have been the victim of a bitter, savage, and un-provoked attack by a member of your family, it was not incumbent on me to give way – that, on the contrary, I was entitled in such a situation to your support and that of the army you command.

15. Perhaps the decree allowed Nepos to leave Italy, as in fact he did.

I have ever wanted you to be my friend, and have tried to let you see that I am a very good friend of yours. My sentiments remain the same, and shall, as long as you so desire. I shall sooner give up my resentment against your brother out of affection for you than abate a jot of the good-will between us out of animosity towards him.

3 (V. 7)

CICERO TO POMPEY

Rome, April 62

From M. Tullius Cicero, son of Marcus, to Cn. Pompeius Magnus,[16] son of Gnaeus, Imperator, greetings.

I hope all is well with you and the army, as it is with me.

Like the rest of us I was immeasurably delighted with your dispatch,[17] in which you have held out the bright prospect of a peaceful future; such a prospect as I have ever been promising to all and sundry in reliance on your single self. I must tell you, however, that it came as a severe blow to your old enemies, nowadays your friends;[18] their high hopes dashed, they despond.

Your personal letter to me evinces but little of your friendly

16. Pompey's cognomen 'Magnus' ('the Great'), conferred by his victorious troops in 81 and confirmed by Sulla, was used officially, and in a formal address like this it would have been discourteous to omit it. Otherwise Cicero does not normally use it simply as a name, without further implications.

17. To the magistrates and Senate, no doubt announcing the writer's return to Italy in the near future. He actually arrived at the end of the year.

18. Who these were is disputed. Probably Caesar and perhaps Crassus were in mind, also subversives generally who hoped to see Pompey take their part against the senatorial establishment.

sentiments towards me, but you may be sure that it gave me pleasure all the same. My chief joy is apt to lie in the consciousness of my services to others. If these fail of a like response, I am perfectly content that the balance of good offices should rest on my side. I have no doubt that if my own hearty goodwill towards you does not suffice to win your attachment, the public interest will join us in confederacy.

Not to leave you in ignorance of the particular in which your letter has disappointed me, let me speak plainly, as becomes my character and our friendly relations. My achievements[19] have been such that I expected to find a word of congratulation upon them in your letter, both for friendship's sake and that of the commonwealth. I imagine you omitted anything of the sort for fear of giving offence in any quarter.[20] But I must tell you that what I have done for the safety of the country stands approved in the judgement and testimony of the whole world. When you return, you will find that I have acted with a measure of policy and a lack of self-regard which will make you well content to have me as your political ally and private friend – a not much lesser Laelius to a far greater Africanus.[21]

19. These had been described in a lengthy letter sent to Pompey the previous December.

20. i.e. to people like Caesar who condemned the execution of the Catilinarian conspirators.

21. Scipio Africanus the Younger, destroyer of Carthage in 146. His lifelong friend was C. Laelius, called Sapiens ('the Wise'). Both figure in Cicero's Dialogues.

4 (v. 6)

CICERO TO P. SESTIUS

Rome, mid or late December 62

From M. Cicero to P. Sestius, son of Lucius, Proquaestor, greetings.

When your secretary Decius called on me and asked me to do my best to ensure that no successor to you is appointed for the present, despite my estimation of his honesty and loyalty to yourself, I hardly believed him. I remembered how you had written to me earlier on, and here was this sensible fellow telling me that you had completely changed your mind! But after your Cornelia met Terentia and I had a word with Q. Cornelius,[22] I took care to attend whenever there was a meeting of the Senate; and I had a deal of trouble to make Tribune Q. Fufius and the others to whom you had written believe me rather than your letters. The whole question has been deferred till January, but we are carrying our point without difficulty.

You wrote to me some time ago about Crassus' house, wishing me luck in my bargain. Stimulated by your felicitations I actually bought the house some time after I received them, for HS3,500,000.[23] So take notice that I am so deeply in debt that I should be glad to join a plot, if anyone would have me. But some of them bar me out of prejudice – they hate me as a plot-breaker and make no bones about it. Others do not

22. Cornelia, daughter of L. Scipio Asiaticus, Consul in 83, was Sestius' wife. Q. Cornelius may have been a client of her family.

23. A very large sum, though there is evidence that much larger amounts were sometimes paid for houses in Rome. Cicero's purchase, situated on the Palatine above the Forum, was considered ostentatious (cf. *Letters to Atticus* 16 (1.16).8).

trust me. They fear a trap, and won't believe that the man who got the capitalists out of a tight corner can be short of cash! To be sure there's plenty of money to be had at $\frac{1}{2}\%$;[24] and my exploits have at least got me the reputation of being a good risk.

I have inspected your house and all the new building, and heartily approve.

The lack of friendship towards me on Antonius' part is universally remarked; notwithstanding which, I have defended him in the Senate in the most weighty and conscientious style. The House was strongly impressed by what I said and the fact that I said it.

Please write to me more often.

5 (V. 5)

CICERO TO C. ANTONIUS

Rome, c. 23 December 62

From M. Cicero to C. Antonius, son of Marcus, Imperator, greetings.

I had not intended to write you any letters except of recommendation – not that I had any reason to suppose they carry any particular weight with you, but because I did not wish to show the persons who asked for them that our connection was less close than formerly. However, T. Pomponius[25] knows my zeal and friendly offices on your behalf better than any man; he is a well-wisher of yours and a very devoted friend of mine. Since he is setting out to join you, I think I ought to write a few lines, especially as Pomponius himself would be disappointed if I did not.

24. Monthly.
25. Cf. *Letters to Atticus* 12 (I.12) and 13 (I.13). Atticus no doubt took the letter with him to Greece.

Nobody could fairly wonder if I were to expect great favours from you, for everything has been forthcoming on my side which might conduce to your interest, honour, and prestige. To the fact that I have received nothing from you in return you are the best witness; that in some measure you have even shown a disposition to the contrary I have heard from many sources – I dare not say 'learned' in case I might be using the very word which they tell me you often bring up against me (untruly).[26] But I had rather you heard of the stories which have reached me from Pomponius (he has been no less vexed by them than I) than from a letter of mine. The Senate and People of Rome stand witness to my conspicuously friendly disposition towards you. Of your gratitude yourself can judge, of your debt to me let the world judge.

What I have already done for you was done at first out of good-will and later for consistency's sake. But I assure you that the future will make far larger demands on my zeal, loyalty, and energy. I shall persevere with all my might, provided I do not seem to be throwing my trouble away. But if I find that it gets me no thanks, I shall not let myself be taken for an idiot – even by you. Pomponius will inform you of what I mean and explain its nature.[27] As for Pomponius himself, I recommend him to you, though I am confident that you will do all you can for his own sake. Still, I will ask you to show any regard for me that you may retain in Pomponius' affair.[28] You can do nothing that will oblige me more.

26. 'Learned' (*comperisse*) was the word used by Cicero when reporting to the Senate what he had discovered about Catiline's plot. His enemies took it up against him, no doubt with the implication that the 'intelligence' had been manufactured or doctored by Cicero himself. The word 'untruly' (*falso*) seems to be in denial of such an implication.

27. Antonius might, and in the event did, have to face charges when he returned to Rome, and Pompey was rumoured to intend getting him recalled.

28. The money owed to Atticus by the town of Sicyon (cf. *Letters to Atticus* 13 (1.13).1).

6 (XIV. 4)

CICERO TO HIS FAMILY

Brundisium, 29 April 58

From Tullius to his dear Terentia and Tullia and Marcus greetings.

I send you letters less often than I have opportunity, because, wretched as every hour is for me, when I write to you at home or read your letters I am so overcome with tears that I cannot bear it. If only I had been less anxious to save my life! Assuredly I should have seen no sorrow in my days, or not much. If fortune has spared me for some hope of one day recovering some measure of well-being, my error has not been so total. But if these present evils are to stay, then, yes, I want to see you, dear heart, as soon as I can, and to die in your arms, since neither the Gods whom you have worshipped so piously nor the men to whose service I have always devoted myself have made us any recompense.

I have stayed in Brundisium for thirteen days with M. Laenius Flaccus, a very worthy gentleman. He has disregarded the danger to his own property and status in his concern for my safety, and refused to be deterred by the penalties of a wicked law[29] from carrying out the established duties of hospitality and friendship. I pray that one day I may be able to show him my gratitude. Grateful I shall always be. I am leaving Brundisium on 29 April and making for Cyzicus by way of Macedonia.

Ah, what a desperate, pitiful case is mine! What now? Shall I ask you to come – a sick woman, physically and spiritually exhausted? Shall I *not* ask then? Am I to live without you? Perhaps I should put it like this: if there is any hope of my

29. See *Letters to Atticus* 49 (III.4).

return, you must build it up, and help in the campaign. On the other hand if all is over, as I fear, then come to me any way you can. Be sure of one thing: if I have you, I shall not feel that I am utterly lost. But what is to become of my Tulliola? You at home must take care of that – I have nothing to suggest. But assuredly, however matters turn out, the poor little girl's marriage and good name must be a primary consideration. Then there is my son. What will he do? I hope that *he* will always be with me, my darling child. I cannot write any more now. Grief clogs my pen.

How you have fared I do not know – whether you still have something left, or, as I fear, have been stripped of all. Yes, I trust that Piso[30] will always be faithful. You need not worry about the freeing of the household. In the first place, the promise made to your people was that you would treat each case on its merits (Orpheus, in fact, is loyal so far, none of the others very noticeably so). The position of the other slaves is that if it turned out that my property was no longer mine, they would be my freedmen, provided they could make good their claim to the status; whereas, if I still had a hold on them, they would remain my slaves except for just a few. But these are minor matters.

You urge me to hold my head high and hope for restoration. I wish the facts may give ground for reasonable hope. Meanwhile, as matters wretchedly stand, when am I going to get your next letter? Who will bring it to me? I should have waited for it at Brundisium if the sailors had let me, but they did not want to lose the fair weather.

For the rest, dearest Terentia, bear up with all the dignity you can muster. It has been a good life, a great career. The good in me, nothing bad, has brought me down. I have done nothing wrong, except that when I lost the good things of life I did not lose life itself. But if it was more for our children's happiness that I should live, let us bear what remains, intolerable though it be. And yet, while I tell you to be strong, I cannot tell myself.

30. Tullia's husband, C. Calpurnius Piso Frugi.

I am sending Clodius Philhetaerus back, because he is hampered by eye-trouble. He is a faithful fellow. Sallustius is the most forward of all. Pescennius is full of kindly feeling towards me; I think he will always be attentive to you. Sicca had told me that he would stay with me, but has left Brundisium.

Take care of your health as best you can, and believe that your unhappiness grieves me more than my own. My dear Terentia, loyalest and best of wives, my darling little daughter, and Marcus, our one remaining hope – goodbye.

29 April, from Brundisium.

7 (XIV. 2)

CICERO TO HIS FAMILY

Thessalonica, 5 October 58

From Tullius to his dear Terentia and his dear Tulliola and Marcus greetings.

You are not to suppose that I write letters of any length to anyone, unless somebody has written a lot to me and I feel I ought to reply. In fact I have nothing to write about, and at the present time I find it the most intractable of tasks. To you and our Tulliola I cannot write without many tears, for I see that you are very unhappy – you, for whom I wished all the happiness in the world. I ought to have given it to you, and should have done so if I had not been such a coward.

I have a great affection for Piso, as he deserves. I have written encouraging him as best I could and thanking him as was proper. I gather that you pin hopes on the new Tribunes. That will hold good, if Pompey is friendly; but I am still afraid of Crassus.

I see that courage and love shines in all you do, nor does that surprise me. But it is a heartbreaking situation when my distresses are relieved at the cost of so much distress to you. P. Valerius (he tries to help) has written to me an account, which I wept bitterly to read, of how you were taken from the Temple of Vesta to the Tabula Valeria.[31] Ah, my beloved, my heart's longing! To think that you, dearest Terentia, once everybody's refuge in trouble, should now be so tormented! There you are, plunged in tears and mourning, and it is my fault! In saving others, I ruined you and me.

As for what you say about the house, or rather the site on which it stood, indeed I shall not feel myself truly restored until that is restored to me. But these things are not in our hands. What grieves me is that in your unhappy and impoverished state you should be contributing to any necessary outlay. If the thing goes through, we shall win all. But if fortune stays my enemy, are you going to throw away what poor little you have left? My darling, I beg you, where expense is concerned, let others bear it who can, if only they will; and do not overstrain that frail health of yours, if you love me. For you are before my eyes night and day. I see you are shouldering every burden. I fear you may not have the strength. Yet clearly everything depends on you. So in order that we may win the prize of your hopes and efforts, take good care of your health.

I do not know whom I should write to, except those who write to me or who are mentioned in letters from home. Since it is your joint wish, I shall not go further away. But I hope you will send me letters as often as possible, especially if we have grounds for reasonable hope.

Goodbye, my absent loves, goodbye.

Dispatched 5 October, from Thessalonica.

31. In the Comitium, called after a painting set up by M. Valerius Messala (nothing to do with P. Valerius) to commemorate a victory in the first Punic War. The Tribunes met there officially and it seems that Terentia had been summoned before them in connection with a financial matter. Her half-sister Fabia was a Vestal Virgin.

8 (XIV, 1)

CICERO TO TERENTIA

Dispatched from Dyrrachium, 25 November 58

From Tullius to his dear Terentia and to dear Tulliola and to dear Marcus greetings.

Many folk write to me and everybody talks to me about you, what amazing courage and fortitude you show, how no trials of body or spirit wear you out. Ah me, to think that my brave, loyal, true, gentle wife should have come by such misery because of me! And to think that our Tulliola should be suffering so much grief on account of her papa, who used to give her so much pleasure! As for Marcus, what can I say? Bitter sorrow and suffering has been his portion since the earliest dawn of intelligence. If I thought all this was the work of fate, as you say, I should find it a little easier to bear. But I am to blame for everything. I thought I was loved by people who were only jealous of my success, while I refused to follow those who sought my friendship. If only I had relied upon my own judgement instead of paying so much attention to the talk of friends, whether fools or knaves, how happy I might have been! As things are, since our friends tell us to hope, I shall take care not to let my health betray your efforts. I well understand the magnitude of the task, and how much easier it would have been to stay at home than it is to return. However, if we have all the Tribunes on our side, if Lentulus[32] is as zealous as he seems, and if we also have Pompey's and Caesar's good-will, we ought not to despair.

As to my household, I shall do as you tell me our friends think best. As to my place of residence, the epidemic has now dis-

32. P. Cornelius Lentulus Spinther.

appeared, but while it lasted it did not touch me. Plancius, who is untiring in his good offices, is anxious to have me with him, and keeps me here. I wanted to stay in some less frequented place in Epirus out of the way of Piso[33] and his soldiers, but Plancius still keeps me here. He hopes it may turn out that he leaves for Italy in my company. If I live to see that day, and return to my family's embraces, and get all of you and my own self back again, I shall feel that your devotion to me and mine to you have been sufficiently rewarded.

Piso's kindness, manliness, and affection for us all is quite superlative. I pray it may bring him happiness; certainly it will bring him honour. As regards my brother Quintus, I meant no criticism of yourself; but I wanted you all to be as close to one another as possible, especially as you are so few. I have thanked the persons you wished me to thank, and written that my information came from you.

Dearest, you tell me that you are going to sell a row of houses. This is dreadful. What in the name of heaven, *what* is to happen? And if no change of fortune comes to my relief, what is to become of our poor boy? I cannot go on, the tears overcome me, and I would not wish to draw yours. Just this I will say: if my friends are loyal, money will not be lacking; if not, you cannot achieve results with *your* money. For pity's sake, pitiable that we are, don't let our unfortunate boy be utterly ruined! If he has something to keep him above penury, he only needs a modicum of ability and a modicum of luck to gain the rest.

Take care of yourself and send me couriers, so that I know what is doing and what you and the children are doing. To be sure, I have not long to wait now. Give my love to Tulliola and Marcus. Goodbye to you all.

33. L. Calpurnius Piso Caesoninus, Consul in 58 and incoming governor of Macedonia. Distinguish from Cicero's son-in-law in the next paragraph.

I have come to Dyrrachium[34] because it is a Free City, and anxious to serve me, and the nearest point to Italy. But if I find there are too many people about for my liking, I shall go somewhere else and send you word.

Dispatched 25 November, Dyrrachium

9 (XIV. 3)

CICERO TO TERENTIA

Dyrrachium, 29 November 58

From Tullius to his dear Terentia and Tullia and Marcus greetings.

I have received three letters from Aristocritus, and almost blotted them out in tears. I am overwhelmed with grief, dearest Terentia; and my own distresses do not torture me more than yours and my family's. But my wretchedness is greater than yours (and yours is bitter enough) because, while we both share the disaster, the blame for it is mine and mine only. It was my duty either to avoid the impending danger by taking a Commissionership[35] or to oppose it by careful provision or to fall bravely. Nothing could have been more miserable, dishonourable, and unworthy of me than *this*. So I am overwhelmed by shame as well as grief. Yes, I am ashamed to have been found wanting in the courage and carefulness that the best of wives and most enchanting of children had the right to expect of me. Night and day I have before my eyes the sorry spectacle of my family in grief and mourning and the frailty

34. Para. 6 is a postscript added at Dyrrachium. The letter proper was written before Cicero left Thessalonica in mid November (cf. *Letters to Atticus* 67 (III.22)).

35. See Glossary of Terms under 'Legate'.

of your health. The hope of restoration held out to me is very slender. Many are hostile, almost all are jealous. To drive me out was a feat, but to keep me out is easy. However, as long as my family continues to hope, I shall do my part, for I would not wish to seem responsible for *every* fiasco.

You need not be concerned for my safety. That is no problem now, for even my enemies want me to stay alive in my present wretchedness. However, I shall do as you advise. I have thanked the friends you named and given the letters to Dexippus, and I have written that my information about their good offices came from you. Our dear Piso's extraordinary devotion and activity on my behalf is evident to me and everyone talks of it. The Gods grant that I may enjoy the blessing of such a son-in-law in person with you and our children! Our last hope now lies in the new Tribunes – and in the first few days; for if novelty is lost, we are finished. I am therefore sending Aristocritus to you straight away, so that you can write me an immediate account of the initial stage and a conspectus of the whole business. To be sure, Dexippus also has my orders to hurry back straight away, and I have written to my brother asking him to send couriers at short intervals. I am staying in Dyrrachium at the present time expressly so that I get the quickest possible news of what goes on. Also I am quite safe, having always been a patron of this town. When my enemies are reported to be on their way, it will be time to go to Epirus.

As regards your offer to join me if I wish, well, I know that a large share of this burden rests upon your shoulders, and so I want you to stay in Rome. If you and the others succeed in your efforts, it is for me to join you. If not – but there is no need to go on. I shall be able to decide what to do from your first letter, or at latest from your second. All I ask is that you write me the most comprehensive and detailed accounts – though it is results rather than letters I should be expecting now.

Take care of your health, and rest assured that nobody in the world is more precious to me than you, or ever has been.

Goodbye, dearest Terentia. I seem to see you, and my weeping exhausts me. Goodbye.

29 November.

10 (V. 4)

CICERO TO METELLUS NEPOS

Dyrrachium, mid January 57

From M. Cicero to Q. Metellus, Consul, greetings.

Letters from my brother Quintus and my friend and connection T. Pomponius had so raised my hopes that I counted on your assistance no less than on your colleague's.[36] Accordingly, I wrote to you at once in terms proper to my present position, both expressing my gratitude and soliciting your assistance in the future. Later it was conveyed to me, not so much by letters from home as by the talk of travellers passing this way, that your attitude had changed. That is why I did not venture to importune you with letters.

Now my brother has sent me the text of your speech in the Senate[37] in which you express yourself in the gentlest terms. It has emboldened me to write to you and to beg you, with whatever urgency your own sentiments make acceptable, to preserve those near to you[38] along with myself rather than attack me on account of *their* high-handed cruelty. In giving up a grudge of your own for the sake of the public interest you

36. Lentulus Spinther.

37. On 1 January 57. In his defence of Sestius (para. 75) in 56 Cicero says that Metellus declared himself as ready to give up his personal enmity (dating from 63–62) in deference to the Senate and in the public interest.

38. i.e. P. Clodius. It has recently been ascertained that he was half-brother to the Metelli, not cousin, as hitherto supposed.

have won a victory over yourself. Are you prevailed upon to support the grudges of others against that interest? If you will find it in your heart to help me, I give you my word that I shall be at your disposition in all things. If the violence which has overcome me and the commonwealth together shall prevent magistrates and Senate and People from assisting me, may I say a word of warning? When you would fain call back the time for saving *all*, you may call in vain, because there will be none to save.[39]

11 (V. 3)

METELLUS NEPOS TO CICERO

Hither Spain, latter half of 56

From Q. Metellus Nepos to M. Cicero, greetings.

The insults heaped upon my head by an unmannerly in-dividual[40] in speech after speech are softened by your acts of friendship. From such a person they are of small account, and I despise them accordingly; and, welcoming the change of roles, I take *you* for my brother. Of him I do not even want to think, though I saved him twice over in spite of himself.[41]

As for my concerns, not wanting to trouble you and my other friends with a spate of letters, I have written in detail to

39. Cicero evidently did not care to put his meaning directly, but Metellus was to understand that (a) he, Cicero, could be saved without ruining Clodius, and (b) if rescue did not come soon it would be too late. The final words, though general in form, point to Cicero himself (not Clodius). His letters from exile hint more than once at suicide if hopes of return did not materialize.

40. Clodius.

41. During his Consulship the previous year, when he thwarted Milo's attempts to bring Clodius to trial.

Lollius,[42] telling him my wishes with regard to the administration of my province and asking him to inform and remind you all accordingly.

If you can, I hope you will keep your friendly sentiments towards me as in the past.

12 (I. 1)

CICERO TO LENTULUS SPINTHER

Rome, 13 January 56

From M. Cicero to P. Lentulus, Proconsul, greetings.

In all that is due to a friend, or rather a benefactor, my efforts on your behalf seem adequate to everyone except myself; for me they are never enough. Your services to me have been so great that my life turns sour when I think that I am failing to achieve in your case[43] what you achieved in mine, never relaxing short of complete success. The relevant facts are as follows: The king's representative, Hammonius, is openly working against us with money. His intermediaries are the creditors who played the same role when you were in Rome.

---

42. Probably L. Lollius, formerly fellow-Legate of Nepos under Pompey. They captured Damascus together in 65 or 64.

43. This refers to the affair of the exiled King of Egypt, Ptolemy XII, nicknamed 'the Piper', father of the famous Cleopatra. In September 57 the Senate had commissioned Lentulus, as proximate governor of Cilicia, to restore him to his throne. But in January the custodians of the Sibylline prophecies produced an oracle forbidding the employment of a 'host'. This was no doubt also a move against Pompey, who came more and more to be suspected of wanting to handle the restoration himself. The business dragged on until August (see Letter 18 (1.7)). In the end Lentulus did nothing, and Ptolemy was reinstated by the enterprising governor of Syria, A. Gabinius, in 55.

The king's well-wishers (there are not many of them) all want to see the business handed over to Pompey, whereas the Senate is approving the religious subterfuge;[44] not for religion's sake, but out of ill-will and the odium aroused by the royal largesse. I never stop urging and begging Pompey, even going so far as to take him pretty frankly to task and warning him to steer clear of a major scandal. But truth to tell, he leaves no opening for appeals or warnings on my part, since both in day-to-day conversation and publicly in the Senate he has pleaded your cause as eloquently, impressively, zealously, and vigorously as anybody could possibly have done, with the fullest acknowledgement of your services to himself and his affection for you. You write that Marcellinus is annoyed with you. He promises that he will be your most ardent champion in all respects, except this affair of the king. We take what he offers, but there is no diverting him from his determination to refer the religious point to the Senate, as he has already done on a number of occasions.

Up to the Ides this is the record (I am writing on the morning of the Ides): The resolution put forward by Hortensius, myself, and Lucullus[45] gives way to the religious objection as regards an army; we cannot gain our point in any other way. But in accordance with the decree which was passed on your own motion it gives you authority to restore the king, if you can do so without prejudice to the public interest. While an army is precluded by the religious obstacle, the Senate would thus retain you as the person responsible. Crassus proposes a Commission of Three, from which he does not exclude Pompey, since he provides that persons holding military command[46]

44. The aforesaid Sibylline oracle.
45. M. Terentius Varro Lucullus. His brother Lucius had died earlier in the year. He and the orator Hortensius, both senior Consulars, were Spinther's principal backers in the Senate along with Cicero.
46. Pompey at this time held proconsular *imperium* in virtue of his extraordinary office as controller of grain supplies.

shall be eligible. Bibulus[47] proposes a Commission of Three to be selected from those *not* holding command. He is supported by the other Consulars excepting Servilius,[48] who is against *any* restoration, Vulcatius,[49] who is for authorizing Pompey on Lupus'[50] motion, and Afranius, who supports Vulcatius. The last circumstance intensifies suspicion as to Pompey's wishes – support for Vulcatius by Pompey's intimates did not go unmarked. It is a hard struggle, and things are going against us. Energetic lobbying by Libo and Hypsaeus, which is no secret, and the interest shown by all Pompey's friends have led to the opinion that Pompey is anxious for the assignment. Those who are against him are no friends to you either, because of what you have done for him.

I carry less weight in the matter because of my obligations to you, and my private influence is nullified by the prevailing suspicion – they think they are obliging Pompey. We are dealing with a business that was inflamed in secret long before you left Rome by the king himself and by Pompey's close friends and familiars, and has subsequently been stirred up in public by the Consulars. It has now gained a highly invidious notoriety. My loyalty will be recognized by all, and my affection for you by your absent self and present friends. If others whose loyalty should have been beyond reproach were not falling short, we would not be in such difficulties.

47. Bitterly hostile to Pompey at this period.
48. P. Servilius Vatia Isauricus, Consul in 79.
49. Consul in 66. The contemporary spelling seems to have been 'Volcacius'.
50. The Tribune (see Glossary of Persons). On his motion see the next letter.

13 (I. 2)

CICERO TO LENTULUS SPINTHER

Rome, 15 January 56

From M. Cicero to P. Lentulus, Proconsul, greetings.

Nothing was settled in the Senate on the Ides of January because a large part of the day was taken up by an altercation between Consul Lentulus[51] and Tribune Caninius.[52] I spoke at length that day myself, and I think I made a very considerable impression on the Senate when I dwelt on your attachment to that Order. We therefore thought best to make only short speeches on the day following, feeling that we had regained the House's good-will – I had clear evidence of that both during my address and in approaches and appeals to individuals. Accordingly three proposals were put forward: first Bibulus', that the king be restored by a Commission of Three, second Hortensius', that he be restored by you without an army, and third Vulcatius', that he be restored by Pompey. There was a demand that Bibulus' motion should be split. So far as it concerned the religious issue it was agreed, opposition on this point being now out of the question, but on the Commission of Three it was heavily defeated. Hortensius' motion stood next, when Tribune Lupus began to insist that, having himself consulted the House earlier concerning Pompey, he had the right to take a vote before the Consuls. His speech was received with loud protests from all sides – it was unfair and without precedent. The Consuls did not give way, but neither did they put up much of a fight. They wanted the sitting talked out, which is what happened, because it was plain to them that Hortensius'

51. Marcellinus.
52. L. Caninius Gallus (see Glossary of Persons).

motion would get a thumping majority despite much open canvassing in support of Vulcatius – which again was not to the liking of the Consuls, who had wished Bibulus' motion to win the day. The argument was prolonged till nightfall, and the House rose.

I happened to be dining with Pompey that evening. It was a better moment than had ever come my way before, because we had just had our most successful day in the Senate since your departure. So I talked to him, and I could flatter myself that I led his mind away from all other notions and focused it upon upholding your position. When I listen to him talking, I quite acquit him of all suspicion of selfish aims. But when I look at his friends of all classes, I see what is now plain to everyone, that this whole business has for a long while past been bedevilled by certain individuals, not without the connivance of the king himself and his advisers.

I am writing this on 15 January before daybreak. The Senate is to meet today. At the meeting, as I hope, we shall maintain our position, so far as practicable in the general ambience of treachery and unfair play. As for the role of the People,[53] I think we have so managed that no proceedings in that quarter are possible without violation of the auspices and the laws, in fact without violence. Yesterday a senatorial resolution[54] in very impressive terms went through on these matters, and although Cato[55] and Caninius cast vetoes, it was placed on record. I think you have been sent a copy. On other matters I shall write to tell you whatever takes place, and shall use all my care, pains, diligence, and influence to ensure that things go as much as possible on the right lines.

53. i.e. the popular legislative assembly.
54. See Glossary of Terms.
55. C. Porcius Cato.

14 (I. 4)

CICERO TO LENTULUS SPINTHER

Rome, 17 (?) January 56

From M. Cicero to P. Lentulus, Proconsul, greetings.

We were holding up magnificently in the Senate on 15 January. Already on the previous day we had smashed that motion of Bibulus on the Commission of Three, and the only battle left to fight was Vulcatius' motion. However, our opponents dragged the proceedings out on various pretexts, because we were carrying our point in a full House, which showed little difference of opinion and no little irritation against those who were trying to put the king's affair out of your hands and into someone else's. We found Curio[56] bitterly hostile to us that day, Bibulus much fairer, almost friendly even. Caninius and Cato undertook not to bring forward any legislation before the elections. As you know, the Senate is debarred by the lex Pupia from meeting before the Kalends of February, and throughout February there can be no sitting until embassy business has been completed or deferred.[57] However, the belief of the Roman People is that the religious pretext was trumped up by your ill-wishers and detractors, and then adopted by others not so much to stand in *your* way as to stop anyone from wanting to go to Alexandria for the sake of a military command. Everyone judges that the Senate has taken proper account of your honour, since everybody knows that your opponents

56. The elder, Consul in 76.
57. All days in January after the 15th were 'comitial' days, on which it was illegal for the Senate to meet except by special dispensation. Another law (lex Gabinia) provided that during February the hearing of deputations from abroad should take precedence over other business.

prevented a decision. If they now make any move, nominally through the People but in reality by a criminal act of tribunician freebooting, sufficient means have now been taken to ensure that they can do nothing without violating the auspices and the laws, or indeed without the use of force.

I do not think it would be appropriate for me to describe my own zeal or the ill-usage of certain persons. There is no occasion for me to parade myself, for if I were to sacrifice my life in defence of your honour, I should not appear to have balanced a fraction of what I owe you; nor yet to complain of the wrongs done you by others, which I cannot do without heartfelt distress. I can offer you no guarantee against violence, especially in the present weakness of our officers of state, but, violence apart, I can say with confidence that you will maintain your high standing through the zealous good-will of the Senate and People of Rome.

15 (I. 5 a)

CICERO TO LENTULUS SPINTHER

Rome, c. 5 February 56

From M. Cicero to P. Lentulus, Proconsul, greetings.

It was my dearest wish that my gratitude to you should be abundantly demonstrated, first to yourself, and then to the world. But I am deeply sorry that conditions since your departure have been such as to give you in your absence a trial both of my loyalty and good-will towards you and of other people's. I see from your letter how keenly you are aware that the same brand of loyalty has been forthcoming on behalf of your honour as *I* experienced when my existence as a citizen was at stake. While I was striving my utmost in the king's matter, by dint of thought, zeal, hard work, and personal influence, Cato's abominable bill[58] suddenly made its appearance to hamper our efforts and divert our attention from the lesser concern to a grave alarm. However, although no unwelcome possibility can be ruled out in such an imbroglio as this, my main fear is treachery; as for Cato, we shall of course oppose him in any circumstances.

With regard to Alexandria and the king's business, I can promise you this much, that your absent self and your friends here present will be more than satisfied with my conduct. But I am afraid that the king's business will either be snatched out of our hands or let drop, and I find it hard to judge which of the two I like less. But if the worst comes to the worst, there is a third possibility, which neither Selicius nor I find inadmissible – namely not to let the matter go by the board, and at the same time not to let it be assigned *in the teeth of opposition from our side* to the person[59] to whom it has almost been assigned (so people think) already; throughout taking care on the one hand not to lose any possible success by default, and on the other to avoid the appearance of a rebuff in any failure.

As a wise and high-minded man, you must regard your status and honour as depending entirely upon your own qualities and achievements and your moral dignity. If any of the gifts which fortune has showered upon you is abstracted by the treachery of certain persons, you will judge that they more than yourself will be the sufferers. I am losing no opportunity of acting and planning in your interests. In all matters I am availing myself of Q. Selicius' services. None of your friends in my judgement surpasses him in shrewdness or loyalty or affection for you.

58. To deprive Lentulus of his province. It had been promulgated by C. Cato as Tribune.
59. Pompey.

16 (I. 5 b)

CICERO TO LENTULUS SPINTHER

Rome, shortly after 9 February 56

From M. Cicero to P. Lentulus, Proconsul, greetings.

I expect you have heard what is happening and has happened here from plenty of informants, both by letter and word of mouth. It is my business, I think, to write to you about matters of surmise and forecast.

Pompey appeared to me much shaken after his rough reception – noise and abuse – when he spoke for Milo[60] at the public meeting on 7 February, and Cato's bitter and vehement attack in the Senate, which was received by his enemies in portentous silence. He seems to me to have quite given up the Alexandrian business. Our position is intact, because the Senate has taken nothing from you except what cannot, on account of the same religious scruple, be given to anybody else.

What we are now hoping and working for is that when the king realizes that his plan of a restoration by Pompey is impracticable and that unless he is brought home by you he will be left totally in the lurch, he will go to you. Without the smallest doubt he *will* do this, if Pompey makes a sign, however slight, to show his approval. But you know how slow and uncommunicative Pompey is. However, I am letting nothing slip which might have a bearing on this question. As for the other outrages threatened in Cato's proposal, I hope we shall have no difficulty in resisting them. I do not find any of the Consulars to be your friend except Hortensius and Lucullus. The rest are either more or less overtly ill-disposed or undisguisedly in

60. Arraigned by Clodius before a popular assembly. Letter 7 (II.3). 2 of the letters to his brother Quintus gives a full account.

dudgeon. You must keep your courage and spirit high and be of good hope that, when we have crushed this irresponsible fellow's attack, you will flourish in your old dignity and repute.

17 (I. 6)

CICERO TO LENTULUS SPINTHER

Rome, March (?) 56

From M. Cicero to P. Lentulus, Proconsul, greetings.

You will learn what is toward from Pollio,[61] who has taken not only part but the leading part in every transaction. In the keen distress which I feel in your affairs hope is naturally my greatest comforter, since I have a strong inkling that the evil disposition now current will be worn down by the countermeasures of your friends and by mere lapse of time, which is weakening the devices of your enemies and betrayers.

I have a second comforter ready to hand in the recollection of my own experience, which I see mirrored in yours. True, your standing is injured in a smaller concern than that which brought mine so low. None the less, the similarity is so close that I hope you forgive me if I decline to fear contingencies which you never thought formidable. Only show yourself the man I have known you since your nails were tender,[62] as the Greeks say. Trust me, the wrong men do you will add lustre to your greatness. Expect from me at every turn the uttermost in zealous service; I shall not disappoint your good opinion.

61. Probably C. Asinius Pollio, though he was only about 21 at this time.
62. i.e. 'from childhood'. In Greek the expression can also mean 'from the finger-tips inward', i.e. 'all through'.

18 (I. 7)

CICERO TO LENTULUS SPINTHER

Rome, late June or July 56

From M. Cicero to P. Lentulus, Proconsul, greetings.

I have read your letter, in which you say you are glad to be kept informed through me on all points at such frequent intervals and to see such plain evidence of my good-will towards you. As for the latter, I must needs hold you in the highest regard, if I choose to be such as you have chosen to think me. As for the former, it is a pleasure to talk to you by letter as often as possible, separated as we are by distance of place and time. If I do so more rarely than you expect, the reason will be that my letters are such as I should not care to hand to the first comer. Whenever I find reliable persons, to whom I can safely entrust them, I shall not let the opportunity slip.

You wish to know how this person and that has behaved and felt towards you. It is difficult to speak of individuals. I only venture now to report in the light of ascertained fact what I have often intimated to you in the past, that certain persons, particularly those most bound in duty to help you and best able to do so, have been jealous of your standing, and that despite differences of circumstance there has been a remarkably close parallel between your present experience and mine in days gone by. Those whom you offended in the public interest have been your open adversaries, whereas those whose prestige, position, and purposes you supported have shown themselves less mindful of your manly conduct than hostile to your credit. In this crisis, as I have already informed you in detail, I have found Hortensius most anxious to serve you. Lucullus has shown good-will, and among those in office L. Racilius' loyalty and courage have been outstanding. My own role as champion and defender of your honour may perhaps with most minds count rather as a fulfilment of obligation than as an expression of opinion in view of the magnitude of your services to me. Aside from those mentioned, I cannot honestly report any good-will or service or friendly disposition on the part of any of the Consulars. You know, of course, that Pompey was not much in the Senate during the period in question. He talks to me about you very frequently, not only when I prompt him but of his own accord. I could easily see how much your latest letter pleased him. For my part, I was not only pleased but struck with admiration at your forbearance, or rather your excellent good sense. Bound to you as he was for your signally handsome behaviour to himself, he was inclined to suspect an estrangement on your side due to the notion some people entertained about his own aspirations. Now by that letter you have kept this eminent man's friendship. I always thought he wished you to emerge with credit, even during that highly suspicious episode of Caninius; and now that he has read your letter, I am clear that his one thought is for you and the honours and advantages to come to you.

So please regard what I am about to write as written with his approval and authority after frequent consultation between us. No decree of the Senate exists under which the restoration of the King of Egypt[63] is taken out of your hands. The recorded resolution, which as you know was vetoed, against the king's restoration by any person whomsoever, should be regarded as an ebullition of bias and spite rather than as the firm policy of the Senate, and its authority is to be measured accordingly. I therefore say that *you*, as governor of Cilicia and Cyprus, are in a position to judge what you can do and achieve. Should circumstances appear to furnish a fair prospect of your controlling Alexandria and Egypt, your honour and the Empire's will be

63. Literally 'the Alexandrian King', Cicero's usual way of referring to Ptolemy. So too Caelius at the end of Letter 81 (VIII. 4).

well served if you proceed to Alexandria with a naval and military force, after first settling the king at Ptolemais[64] or some other place in the vicinity; then, when you have established order in the city and stationed troops to secure it, let Ptolemy come back to his throne. In this way he will be restored by you, as the Senate originally resolved he should be, and he will be restored without a 'host', which according to our pious politicians is how the Sybil wants it done.

But both Pompey and I approve this view with the qualification that we realize your policy will be judged by results. If all turns out as we wish and pray, there will be universal praise for your good judgement and courage. If anything goes wrong, those same voices will say you acted ambitiously and rashly. That being so, it is not as easy for us as for you, almost within sight of Egypt as you are, to judge what you can accomplish. Our feeling is that if you are certain you can take over the kingdom, you should lose no time; but if this is doubtful, you ought not to make the attempt. I do guarantee that if you bring it off satisfactorily, many will applaud you in your absence, and everyone when you return. But I recognize that a setback would be dangerous because of the Senate's contrary resolution and the religious aspect. Well then, I am urging you forward to a certain success and at the same time I am warning you back from a doubtful conflict; and I return to my starting-point: your entire action will be judged by results, rather than by your own policy.

If the above way of proceeding seems to you too risky, we suggest the following: provided the king fulfils his engagements to your friends who have lent him money in your province and sphere of command, you should help him with auxiliary troops and supplies. The nature and situation of your province enable you either to support his restoration by lending

64. Cicero will have meant Ptolemais Hormos, an important Nile port at the southern entrance of the Fayum (not Ptolemais in Cyrenaica or Ptolemais in Phoenicia (Acre)).

CICERO'S LETTERS TO HIS FRIENDS

him assistance or to hinder it by withholding the same. In this context nobody will perceive so readily and accurately as yourself just what is best in the particular circumstances of the case and time. I thought you ought to know *our* views from me rather than another.

You felicitate me on the state of my affairs, on Milo's friendship and Clodius' irresponsibility and impotence. Well, it does not at all surprise me to see a fine artist delighting in his own masterpieces. And yet the perverseness (I prefer not to use a stronger word) of folk is beyond belief. With good-will they could have kept me in the common cause; instead, their jealousy has estranged me. For I must tell you that their venomous backbiting has pretty well succeeded in turning me away from my old, long-established principles and brought me to the point, not indeed of forgetting my honour, but of paying some belated attention to my vital interest. The two could have run perfectly well in harness, if our Consulars had known the meaning of good faith and responsibility. But the majority are such fribbles that they are less pleased by my steadfastness in public affairs than irritated by my distinction. I write this to you the more frankly because you supported my public credit and standing almost from their earliest beginnings long ago as you do today – and that there *is* a today I owe to you. I can also write so because I find that it is not my birth, as I always used to think, that has aroused ill-will. For the evils of envy have been similarly manifest in your case, *crème de la crème* as you are. In your case, however, they were willing enough to see you figure among the leaders of the community, but as for any higher flight – no, no! I am glad that your lot has been different from mine; for it is one thing to lose some prestige and quite another to be left alone when one's existence is at stake. However, thanks to your noble self, I am not overmuch dissatisfied with *my* lot, for you saw to it that what I forfeited in worldly prosperity should appear more than made up to my future reputation and memory.

Your services to me and my affection for you alike prompt me to a word of admonition. Use all diligence and effort to win all the glory that has fired your imagination since you were a lad. Never let any man's injustice bend the greatness of spirit which I have always admired and loved in you. Yours is a great reputation, your liberality is loudly commended, your Consulship has left a fine memory. You cannot fail to see how much all this will gain in definition and brilliance by an access of credit from provincial office and command. All the same, while I want you to do what may properly be done by military means in the exercise of military authority, I also want you to plan well beforehand your future in Rome. Prepare for that, think of it, train for it. Realize – it is what you have always hoped for, so I do not doubt that you are aware now that you have achieved it – that without any difficulty you can hold the greatest and highest place in our society. I trust you will not think this exhortation on my part a piece of unnecessary verbiage. I offer it because I feel I should advise you in the light of our common experience to consider whom to trust, and of whom to beware, throughout the rest of your natural life.

You enquire as to the political situation. There is bitter conflict but the two sides are unequally matched. The party[65] superior in resources, armed force, and power has actually contrived, so it seems to me, to gain moral ascendancy as well, thanks to the stupidity and irresolution of their adversaries.[66] Accordingly they have secured from the Senate with very few opposing voices all that they did not expect to obtain even through the People without civil disorder. Caesar[67] has been voted a grant to pay his troops and ten Legates; and the ap-

65. i.e. the dominant coalition between Pompey, Caesar, and Crassus known as the 'First Triumvirate'.

66. M. Cato and his friends – the 'Optimates'.

67. Now in process of conquering Gaul north of the Roman provinces.

pointment of a successor under the lex Sempronia[68] has been blocked without difficulty. I tell you this rather briefly because the present political situation is little to my liking; but I tell it all the same, so that I can advise you to learn before you meet with any setback a lesson that I myself have learned from experience rather than books (devoted to every class of literature as I have been since childhood): we must not consider our security without regard to honour, nor honour without regard to security.

It is very kind of you to offer me your congratulations on my daughter's engagement to Crassipes. I hope and pray that the connection will bring us pleasure. Mind you instruct our dear Lentulus,[69] most promising and excellent young man that he is, in the accomplishments to which you have always applied yourself, but especially in the imitation of his father; he can have no finer education. I have a special regard and affection for him because he is your son and worthy to be yours, and because he is and has always been fond of me.

19 (I. 8)

CICERO TO LENTULUS SPINTHER

Rome, February (?) 55

From M. Cicero to P. Lentulus, Proconsul, greetings.

On all matters that concern you – proceedings, decisions,

68. Under this law of C. Sempronius Gracchus the Senate was bound to name two provinces for the Consuls of the following year (55) before their election. These they would take over in 54. Had one of the two Gauls been named, an extension of Caesar's command, which was due to expire that year, would have been precluded.

69. P. Lentulus Spinther the Younger. So Cicero regularly refers to his own son as 'Cicero' ('Marcus' in this translation).

Pompey's undertaking[70] – you will have an excellent informant in M. Plaetorius, who has taken, not only part, but the leading part in them. He has performed on your behalf every friendly service that affection, sagacity, and industry could render. You will likewise learn from him the whole state of public affairs, which are not easy to explain in writing. They are at all events in our friends'[71] control, so firmly that no change in the position seems likely for a generation to come.

For my part I follow my prescribed course, the course which you advised and which gratitude and expediency dictate; that is to say, I attach myself to the interests of the personage[72] whom you thought proper to attach to yourself where my interests were concerned. But you realize how hard it is to put aside one's political views, especially when they are well and firmly founded. However, as I cannot honourably oppose him, I adapt myself to his wishes. Nor in so doing am I belying my real feelings, as some may perhaps imagine. My inclination, indeed my affection for Pompey is strong enough to make me now feel that whatever is to his advantage and whatever he wants is right and proper. Even his opponents would in my opinion make no mistake if they gave up fighting, since they cannot be a match for him.

I have another consolation. Everyone agrees that I of all people am entitled either to support Pompey's every desire or to hold my peace or simply (and this is my chief wish) to return to my literary studies. That, you may be sure, is what I shall do, if the claims of Pompey's friendship allow me. As for what I had promised myself after attaining the highest state dignities and passing through the most severe ordeals – a lofty platform in the Senate, a position of independence in public life – there is an end to all that, not for me in particular, but for all and

70. Its nature is unknown. Pompey and Crassus were now Consuls.
71. The 'Triumvirs', or perhaps only Pompey and Caesar.
72. Pompey.

sundry. The choice lies between undignified support for a clique and fruitless opposition.

I am writing all this to you chiefly because I want you now to give thought to your own position. The whole face of things has changed – the Senate, the courts, the whole body politic. Tranquillity is what we have to pray for, and this the present holders of power seem likely to provide, if certain persons can submit with a modicum of patience to their domination. The old exalted notion of a Consular playing his firm and courageous part in the Senate must be dismissed from our minds. It has disappeared through the fault of those who lost the Senate the sympathies of a very friendly class and a very eminent individual.[73]

But to return to matters bearing more directly on your own position, I know that Pompey is very much your friend. While he is Consul, so far as I can judge, all you wish will be yours. In that connection he will have me close at his elbow, and I shall not neglect anything which may concern you. I have no fear of his finding me importunate – he will be glad even for his own sake to see that I know the meaning of gratitude.

I hope you will rest assured that the least of your concerns means more to me than all of mine put together. Such being my feelings, I could not be assiduous enough to satisfy my own mind; as for results, the reason why I fail to satisfy myself is that I cannot adequately repay, or even imagine myself repaying, any part of what I owe you.

There is a report that you have had a highly successful campaign.[74] We are waiting for a dispatch from you, as to which I have already had a talk with Pompey. Once it arrives, I shall be zealously to the fore in canvassing officers of state

73. i.e. the Knights (cf. *Letters to Atticus* 21 (II.1).5) and Pompey.
74. No doubt against the 'Free Cilicians' of the Taurus or Amanus mountains, at whose expense Cicero himself was to win laurels in 51. Lentulus seems to have mounted another campaign in 54 (see next letter, para. 1).

and members of the Senate;[75] and in other matters which concern you my efforts may go beyond my capacity, but they will fall short of my obligations.

20 (I. 9)

CICERO TO LENTULUS SPINTHER

Rome, December 54

From M. Cicero to Lentulus, Imperator, greetings.

I am glad to have your letter, which shows that you appreciate my *piety* towards you – I won't say my good-will, for even this solemn, sacred word 'piety' seems to me inadequate for what I owe you. When you write that you are grateful for my efforts on your behalf, it must be out of the overflowing affection of your heart. *Grateful*, because I do what it would be rank villainy to leave undone? But you would have a much better and clearer impression of my sentiments towards you, if we had been together and in Rome all this time we have been separated. Take what you say you have in view (nobody can do it better than you, and I am eagerly looking forward to the prospect) – speeches in the Senate and general activity and conduct of public affairs, as to which I shall tell you my opinion and position presently and answer your enquiries – well, at least I should have found in you the wisest and most affectionate of guides, while you would have found in me an adviser of experience perhaps not altogether negligible, and of undeniable loyalty and good-will. For your sake, it is true, I am duly delighted to think of you as Imperator, governing your province after a successful campaign at the head of a victorious

75. For a public Thanksgiving in honour of Lentulus' success. He finally celebrated his Triumph in 51.

army. But at least you could have enjoyed the due fruits of my gratitude fuller and fresher on the spot; and when it came to repaying certain people, some of them hostile to you, as you know, because you championed my restoration, others jealous of the grandeur and glory of the achievement – what a companion in arms I should have made you! To be sure, that inveterate enemy of his friends[76] who recompensed your signal favours by turning the feeble remnants of his violence against you[77] has done our work for us. The exposure of his recent operations[78] has robbed him of all independence in the future, let alone prestige. I could have wished that you had gained your experience in my case and not in your own as well, but I am glad in a bad business to think that you have not paid so very heavy a price for a lesson in the unreliability of mankind which *I* learned to my bitter sorrow.

This seems a good opportunity for me to give an exposition of the whole topic by way of a reply to your enquiries. You write that you have heard by letter that I am in good relations with Caesar and Appius, and you add that you have nothing to say against that. But you intimate that you would like to know my reasons for defending Vatinius and speaking to his character. To give you a clear explanation I must trace the principles of my political conduct a little further back.

To begin with, thanks to your public endeavours, dear sir, I conceived myself as restored, not only to my family and friends, but to my country. I owed *you* an affection wellnigh transcending reason and the most complete and signal personal devotion. To our country, which had lent you no slight assistance in your campaign for my restoration, I felt myself to owe

76. L. Domitius Ahenobarbus, now Consul along with Ap. Claudius Pulcher (see my commentary).

77. We do not know how Domitius had attacked Lentulus.

78. The scandalous electoral compact revealed by C. Memmius in September 54; see *Letters to Atticus* 91 (IV.17).2.

as a matter of gratitude at least the loyalty which I had formerly rendered only as the common duty of a Roman, and not as due in respect of any special favour to myself. The Senate heard these sentiments from my own lips during your Consulship, and you perceived them in the talks and discussions we had together. Yet even in those early days there was much to give me pause. I saw how your efforts to complete my rehabilitation met with covert ill-will in some quarters and doubtful support in others. In the matter of my memorials[79] those who ought to have helped you did not; similarly with respect to the criminal violence with which I and my brother were driven out of our homes.[80] I must add that even in those items to which, necessary as they were to me after the ruin of my private fortune, I attached minimal importance, I mean the indemnification of my losses by authority of the Senate, they showed a less forthcoming attitude than I had expected. I saw all this – it was plain enough; but any bitterness was outweighed by gratitude for what they had done.

And so, notwithstanding my regard for Pompey, to whom by your own declaration and testimony I owed a very great deal – a regard founded not only upon his goodness to me but on affection and what I might call life-long predilection – I made no account of his wishes and held firmly by all my old political sentiments. When Pompey came into town to speak to character on behalf of P. Sestius[81] and Vatinius said in evidence that I had made friends with C. Caesar because of his success and good fortune, I said in Pompey's presence that I thought M. Bibulus' sad plight (as Vatinius regarded it) preferable to any man's Triumphs and victories. At another point in Vatinius' evidence I said that the same people who had not allowed

79. No doubt including the one referred to on p. 62.
80. See *Letters to Atticus* 75 (IV.3).2.
81. Tried on charges of violence in February 56, Cicero defending. He was acquitted.

Bibulus to leave his home had forced me to leave mine.[82] My whole cross-examination was nothing but a condemnation of Vatinius' career as Tribune. On this topic I spoke throughout with the greatest frankness and spirit, dwelling on the use of violence, the auspices, and the grants of foreign kingdoms. And I did so not only at this trial but in the Senate, consistently and often. On the Nones of April in the Consulship of Marcellinus and Philippus the Senate actually adopted a proposal of mine that the question of the Campanian land should be referred to a full House on the Ides of May. Was not that invading the innermost citadel of the ruling clique? And could I have shown myself more oblivious of my past vicissitudes or more mindful of my political record?

That speech of mine caused a sensation, not only where I had intended but in quite unexpected quarters.[83] After the Senate had passed a decree in accordance with my motion, Pompey (without giving me any indication of displeasure) left for Sardinia and Africa, and joined Caesar at Luca on the way. Caesar there complained at length about my motion – he had been stirred up against me by Crassus, whom he had seen previously at Ravenna. Pompey by general admission was a good deal upset. I heard this from various sources, but my principal informant was my brother. Pompey met him in Sardinia a few days after leaving Luca. 'You're the very man I want,' he told him. 'Most lucky our meeting just now. Unless you talk seriously to your brother Marcus, you are going to have to pay up on the guarantee[84] you gave me on his behalf.' In short, he remonstrated in

82. As Consul in 59 Bibulus had spent most of the year shut up in his house. The remarks quoted here do not in fact occur in the extant speeches *pro Sestio* and *in Vatinium*.

83. Probably Caesar and Pompey are respectively indicated.

84. Pompey spoke metaphorically, Q. Cicero having in 57 made himself responsible for his brother's future political behaviour if restored from exile.

strong terms, mentioning his services to me, recalling the many discussions he had had with my brother himself about Caesar's legislation and the pledges my brother had given him concerning my future conduct, appealing to my brother's personal knowledge of the fact that his own support for my restoration had been given with Caesar's blessing. He asked him to commend to me Caesar's cause and prestige, with the request that I should refrain from attacking them if I would not or could not defend them.

Though my brother conveyed all this to me, Pompey also sent Vibullius with an oral message, asking me not to commit myself on the Campanian question till his return. Then I took stock. It was like a dialogue between me and my country. Would she not allow me, after all I had suffered and gone through for her sake, to behave with propriety and gratitude towards my benefactors and to honour my brother's pledge? Would she not let her loyal citizen, as I had always shown myself, be also a man of honour?

Now all the time I was acting and speaking in a manner liable to annoy Pompey, I received reports of how certain folk,[85] whose identity you should by now be able to guess, were talking. Fully as the course I was now following accorded with their past and present political sentiments, they were none the less expressing satisfaction at Pompey's disappointment with me and at the prospect that Caesar would be my sworn enemy in future. This was wounding enough; but much more so was their behaviour to my enemy[86] – the enemy, I should rather say, of law, justice, and tranquillity, of Rome and all honest men. This individual they chose to embrace and caress, petting and cosseting him before my very eyes. It was not enough to raise my spleen, because that organ has entirely disappeared, but enough at any rate to let them think they were raising it. At this point I surveyed the whole range of my

85. 'Optimates' like Hortensius, Bibulus, and Domitius.
86. Clodius.

affairs, so far as I could with only human wit to guide me, cast up my accounts in full, and arrived at the grand total of my cogitations. That is what I shall try to set out for you in brief.

If I had seen the state in the control of rascals and villains, as we know happened in Cinna's time and at some other periods of its history, no reward, or danger either (and while rewards count for little with me, even the bravest of us are influenced by dangers), would have driven me on to their side, no matter how much they might have done for me personally. But the leading man in Rome was Cn. Pompeius. The power and glory he enjoyed had been earned by state services of the highest importance and by the most signal military achievements. From early manhood I had rejoiced in his success, and as Praetor and Consul had come forward to promote it. On his side, he had individually helped me with his influence and voice in the Senate, and in conjunction with yourself by planned effort in my cause. His only enemy in Rome was also mine. All these points considered, I did not feel I need fear the reputation of inconsistency if in certain speeches I changed my tack a little and rallied in sentiment to the support of this great figure, my personal benefactor.

In this determination I could not but embrace Caesar, as you will recognize, for his interest and prestige were bound up with Pompey's. Here the old friendship which, as you are aware, existed between Caesar and myself and my brother Quintus counted for much, and no less Caesar's own gracious and generous attitude, which soon became plainly apparent to us in his letters and friendly acts.[87] Moreover, patriotic considerations had great weight with me. It was not, I felt, the will of our country that there should be a struggle with these men, especially after Caesar's great achievements; I felt she was keenly anxious to avoid such a struggle. But the weightiest element in thus persuading me was the pledge concerning

87. In the spring of 54 Q. Cicero left for Gaul to take up an appointment as Caesar's Legate.

myself which Pompey had given to Caesar and which my brother gave to Pompey.

I had besides to note in our community the phenomena which our favourite Plato has characterized so wonderfully – the tendency for the members of a political society to resemble its leaders.[88] I remembered that from the very first day of my Consulship sure foundations were laid for the strengthening of the Senate, so that no one ought to have been surprised either at the courage or the moral power of that Order as revealed on the Nones of December following.[89] Equally I remembered that after my retirement from office down to the Consulship of Caesar and Bibulus, so long as my views carried any considerable weight in the Senate, all honest men were pretty much of one mind. Later, while you were governor of Hither Spain and the state had no Consuls, only traffickers in provinces[90] and servile instruments of sedition, accident may be said to have flung my person as a bone of contention into the midst of civil conflict and strife. At that crisis the consensus in my defence of the Senate, of all Italy, of all honest men was truly remarkable, a thing transcending belief. I will not say what happened – the blame is complex and many shared in it – only this briefly, that it was generals, not an army, that I lacked. Granted that those who failed to defend me[91] were to blame, no less so were those who left me in the lurch;[92] and if those who were afraid should be in the dock, those who only pre-

---

88. Cf. *Laws*, 711 C. But Cicero's words are in fact an almost exact translation of a passage in Xenophon's *Education of Cyrus* (VIII.8.5).

89. The day on which the Senate voted for the execution of the Catilinarian conspirators.

90. According to Cicero's version of events the Consuls of 58, Piso and Gabinius, were bribed by Clodius with appointments to the provincial governorships of Macedonia and Syria respectively.

91. Not the mass of the 'honest men' but Pompey (cf. *Letters to Atticus* 171 (IX.5).2).

92. The 'optimate' leaders.

tended to be afraid are yet more deserving of censure.[93] At any rate there must be applause for my refusal to let my countrymen, whom I had preserved and who were desirous of saving me, be thrown leaderless against armed slaves – for my decision to let the potential power of honest[94] men united (had they been allowed to fight for me before I fell) be demonstrated rather when the opportunity came to raise me from the dust. You saw their spirit when you took action on my behalf; more, you confirmed and maintained it. In that campaign – so far from denying, I shall always remember and gladly proclaim it – you found certain very high-born personages more courageous in securing my reinstatement than they had shown themselves in preventing my exile. Had they chosen to hold to that policy, they would have recovered the respect of the community at the same time as they restored me to its membership. Your Consulship had put fresh heart into the honest men, roused from their apathy by your resolute and praiseworthy initiatives, especially when Cn. Pompeius joined the cause. Even Caesar, now that the Senate had recognized his splendid achievements by signal and unprecedented honours and marks of esteem, was moving towards a position of support for the authority of the House. No bad citizen would have had a loophole through which to injure his country.

Now pray mark the sequel. That embodiment of mischief, that pilferer of the secrets of women's worship, who treated the Good Goddess[95] with as little respect as his three sisters, escaped scot-free. A Tribune[96] was ready to bring the agitator to trial and punishment at the hands of honest men. He was saved by

93. In Cicero's obstinately held opinion the behaviour of certain of his friends (especially Hortensius) at the crisis of March 58 amounted to deliberate treachery (cf. *Letters to Atticus* 52 (III.7).2 etc.).

94. See Glossary of Terms.

95. See *Letters to Atticus* 12 (I.12).2.

96. Probably Racilius; cf. Letter 5 (II.1).3 of Cicero's letters to his brother Quintus.

the votes of those who thereby lost Rome what should have been a splendid example to posterity of the chastisement of sedition. Subsequently the same group allowed a memorial[97] – not my memorial, for the funds employed were not victory-spoils of mine, I merely signed the contract for the work – allowed the *Senate's* memorial to be inscribed with the name of a public enemy in letters of blood. These people desired my restoration, and for that I am deeply beholden. But I could have wished that they had not merely taken a doctor's interest in the life of the patient, but a trainer's in his strength and physical appearance. Certain persons in my case have followed the example of Apelles, who applied the utmost refinement of his art to perfecting the head and bust of his Venus, but left the rest of the body a mere sketch – they made a finished job of the *capital*[98] section only, leaving the rest unfinished and rough.

In this connection I disappointed the expectations of the jealous as well as the hostile. Once upon a time they were told, and believed, a false story about one of the boldest and most stout-hearted men who ever lived, whose equal in grandeur and resolution of spirit I do not know, Q. Metellus,[99] son of Lucius. He, so they like to say, was a broken man after his return from exile. A likely tale! Had he not gone quite readily into banishment, endured it with notable cheerfulness, and been at no great pains to return? Was he broken as the result of an episode in which he had emerged superior to all his contemporaries, even the eminent M. Scaurus, in resolution and integrity? Be that as it may, they formed the same notion about me as they had been given, or surmised for themselves,

97. Cf. p. 56. It may have been a building started at the end of Cicero's Consulship to commemorate the suppression of the Catilinarian conspiracy. Clodius seems to have effaced the inscription and substituted one bearing his own name.

98. Cicero plays on two meanings of *caput*, 'head' and 'status as a citizen'.

99. Numidicus (see Glossary of Persons).

about Metellus. They thought I should be a humbled man
henceforth – whereas my country was making me actually
prouder than I had ever been in my life! Had she not declared
that she could not do without me – one single citizen? Metellus,
after all, was brought back by the bill of a single Tribune, I by
the whole state under the leadership of the Senate and with all
Italy in attendance. The relevant law was promulgated by
almost[100] the entire body of magistrates, moved by yourself as
Consul at the Assembly of the Centuries with the enthusiastic
support of all classes and individuals. In a word, all the forces
of the commonwealth were mobilized to that one end.

Not that after this experience I made any pretensions, or
make any today, to which the most jaundiced critic could fairly
take exception. I merely endeavour to serve my friends, or
even my acquaintances, with time and counsel and hard work.
My way of life perhaps irritates those who look at its outward
show and glitter, but cannot see the care and toil behind. One
stricture, of which they make no secret, is that in my speeches
in favour of Caesar I am more or less deserting the good old
cause. Well, I have just advanced my reasons, but to these I
would add another, not the least important, which I had begun
to explain. Dear sir, you will not find again among our honest
men that league of sentiment which you left behind you.
Established in my Consulship, thereafter disturbed from time
to time, shattered before you became Consul, and then restored by you in its entirety, it has now been forsaken by those
who should have been its champions. Their faces, though faces
can easily play the hypocrite, declare as much; more, they have
shown it to be so by many a vote in Senate and courtroom –
these men who in the world as we used to know it were called
Optimates.

Accordingly, men of sense, of whom I hope I am and am
considered to be one, have now completely to recast their views

100. See my edition. One Praetor (Clodius' brother Appius) and two
Tribunes stayed out.

and sympathies. To cite Plato again, a very weighty authority with me; he tells us to push our political efforts as far as may be acceptable to our countrymen, but never to use force against parent or fatherland.[101] He gives his reason for keeping out of public affairs as follows: finding the people of Athens almost in its dotage, and seeing them without government either of persuasion or compulsion, he did not believe them amenable to persuasion and regarded compulsion as a sacrilege.[102] My situation was different. I was not dealing with a nation in its dotage, nor did I have a free choice whether or not to engage in public life, being inextricably involved. But I congratulated myself on having a cause to champion both expedient to myself personally and commendable to any honest man.[103] An added incentive was Caesar's quite remarkable, in fact amazing, generosity towards my brother and myself. He would have deserved my support however he was faring, but in so brilliant a career of success and victory I should think him worthy of homage even if he were not the good friend to us that he is. For I would have you believe that, apart from yourself and your fellow-architects of my restoration, there is no man to whose good offices I acknowledge myself so deeply beholden – and am glad to do so.

After this exposition your enquiries as to Vatinius and Crassus are easily answered – about Appius, as about Caesar, you say you have no criticism to offer, and I am glad my action has your approval. To take Vatinius then, Pompey originally arranged a reconciliation between us immediately after his election to the Praetorship,[104] although I had made some very

101. In *Crito*, 51c.

102. Cf. Plato, *Epist.* 5. 322a, b.

103. The maintenance of Caesar in his command, championed by Cicero in his speech 'On the Consular Provinces' (summer of 56; Caesar's personal generosity came later).

104. Early in 55. M. Cato's candidature was defeated by bribery and violence.

strong speeches in the Senate against his candidature – not so much to damage *him* as in support and compliment to Cato. Subsequently Caesar made a tremendous point of my undertaking his defence.[105] As for why I spoke for his character, I appeal to you not to ask me that question about Vatinius or any other defendant, otherwise I shall ask you a similar question when you come home. For that matter I can ask it while you are still abroad. Just call to mind the men for whom *you* have sent testimonials from the ends of the earth – don't be afraid, I do the same myself for the same people and shall so continue. To resume, I had another incentive to defend Vatinius, to which I referred in my speech at the trial. I said I was doing what the Parasite in the *Eunuch* recommends to the Captain:[106]

> When she says 'Phaedria', you must straight away
> Say 'Pamphila'. Should she want Phaedria in
> To dinner, you must counter 'Why not ask
> Pamphila for a song?' If she commends
> His handsome looks, you praise the girl's. In short,
> Give tit, my friend, for tat. The pin will prick.

So I drew the parallel. Certain high-born gentlemen, to whom I owed a debt of gratitude, were over-fond of an enemy of mine. In the Senate they would sometimes take him aside for a serious talk, sometimes salute him in hearty, hail-fellow-well-met style; this before my eyes. Well then, since they had *their* Publius, I hoped the gentlemen of the jury would allow *me* another Publius, with whom to sting those personages just a little in return for the mild provocation I had received! Nor did I merely *say* this; I often do it, Gods and men approving.

So much for Vatinius. Now as to Crassus: I was on very good terms with him, having in the interests of general harmony expunged by what I might call a deliberate act of oblivion all

105. In 54, when Vatinius was accused of bribery. Cicero's witness to character seems to have been given in a second trial.

106. Terence, *The Eunuch*, 440 ff. Phaedria is a male character, Pamphila female.

the grave wrongs he had done me. I should have stomached his sudden defence of Gabinius,[107] whom he had attacked on the days immediately preceding, if he had gone to work without abusing me. But when I argued with him politely, he insulted me. I flared up. It was not, I think, just the irritation of the moment, which might not have carried me so far, but my suppressed resentment at the many injuries he had done me. I thought I had dissipated all that, but a residue was still there without my being aware of it, and now it all suddenly came to the surface. Here again certain persons, the same whom I so often indicate without naming names, expressed the greatest satisfaction at my plain speaking, and told me that now at last they felt I was restored to Rome the man I used to be; and outside the House too this fracas brought me many congratulations. And yet they went around saying how pleased they were to think that Crassus would be my enemy henceforward, and that his associates would never be my friends. These backbitings were brought to my knowledge by very worthy folk; and when Pompey pressed me as strongly as I have ever known him do to make it up with Crassus and Caesar wrote a letter making it plain that this quarrel has greatly upset him, why, I took account of my circumstances and of my heart as well. And Crassus, as though to make all Rome witness of our reconciliation, set out for his province virtually from my doorstep. He offered to dine with me, and did so at my son-in-law Crassipes' place in the suburbs. Accordingly I took up his cause at his urgent request and defended it in the Senate,[108] as you say you have heard. Good faith required no less.

·   You now know my reasons for defending each particular

107. When Gabinius restored Ptolemy the Piper to his throne in 55 Cicero attacked him in the Senate. According to Dio Cassius (XXXIX. 60.1) the Consuls, Pompey and Crassus, came to his defence, calling Cicero 'exile', but no doubt the insult came from Crassus, not Pompey.
108. In January 54 (cf. letter 25.).

cause or case, and the general position from which I take such part in politics as I may. I should like it to be clear to you that my attitude would have been just the same if I had had a completely open and untrammelled choice. I should not be in favour of fighting such formidable power, nor of abolishing the pre-eminence of our greatest citizens, even if that were possible. Nor should I be for sticking fast to one set of opinions, when circumstances have changed and the sentiments of honest men are no longer the same. I believe in moving with the times. Unchanging consistency of standpoint has never been considered a virtue in great statesmen. At sea it is good sailing to run before the gale, even if the ship cannot make harbour; but if she *can* make harbour by changing tack, only a fool would risk shipwreck by holding to the original course rather than change and still reach his destination. Similarly, while all of us as statesmen should set before our eyes the goal of peace with honour to which I have so often pointed, it is our aim, not our language, which must always be the same.

Therefore, as I have just stated, my politics would be exactly what they now are, even if my hands were completely free. But since I am attracted to this standpoint by favours from some quarters and pushed to it by injuries from others, I am by no means loath to take and express the political views which I deem most conducive to the public welfare as well as my own. I take this line the more openly and frequently because my brother Quintus is Caesar's Legate, and because Caesar has always received my slightest intervention, even purely verbal, on his behalf with such display of gratitude as to make me feel that he is deeply obliged to me. I use all his influence, which is very powerful, and his resources, which you know to be very large, as though they were my own. In fact, I do not think I could have foiled the designs of evil men against me in any other way than by adding to the means of defence which have always been at my disposal the good-will of the powers that be.

Had I had you with me here, my belief is that I should have followed this same course. I know your natural temperance and moderation. I know that your warm friendship towards myself has no cast of malice towards others, that on the contrary you are as frank and straightforward as you are high-minded and unselfish. I have seen certain persons behave to you as you could once see them behaving to me. Surely my motives would have been yours. But when eventually I can avail myself of your presence, you will be my director in all things, with the same care for my standing as you had for my existence as a citizen. As for me, you may be sure of finding in me a partner and companion in all things, in your every act, opinion, and desire. No object in all my life will be so precious to me as to make you happier every day in the services you have rendered me.

You ask me to send you the products of my pen since you left Rome. There are some speeches, which I shall give to Menocritus – don't be alarmed, there are not very many of them! I have also composed – I am tending to get away from oratory and go back to the gentler Muses who please me best, as they always have from my youth – composed, as I was saying, three volumes in the form of an argument and dialogue *On the Orator*, in the manner (so at least I intended) of Aristotle. I think your son will find them of some use. They do not deal in the standard rules, but embrace the whole theory of oratory as the ancients knew it, both Aristotelian and Isocratic. I have also written a poem in three books *On my Vicissitudes*. I should have sent you this before, if I had thought right to publish it, for it is, and will be to all eternity, evidence of your services and of my gratitude. But I was inhibited by the thought, not so much of those who might feel themselves aspersed (*that* I have done sparingly and gently), but of my benefactors – if I had named them all, there would have been no end to it. All the same I shall see that you get these volumes too, if I can find a reliable bearer. All this part of my daily life I submit to you. Everything I may achieve in the way of literature and study, my old delights, I shall be most happy to bring to the bar of your judgement. You have always cared for these things.

What you say about your domestic concerns and the commissions you give me lie so close to my heart that I desire no reminder; a *request* I can scarcely take without real pain. You say you were unable to settle my brother Quintus' business, because sickness prevented you from crossing over to Cilicia[109] last summer, but that you will now use your best efforts to settle it. The fact is that my brother considers with good cause that once he has annexed this property his fortunes will have been placed on a firm foundation, thanks to you. I hope you will keep me abreast, as intimately and as often as you can, of your own affairs and of your (and my) dear boy's studies and exercises. And I would have you believe that you are to me the dearest and most valued friend that ever man had, and that I shall make it my business to prove this, not only to you, but to all mankind, indeed to all posterity.

Appius was in the habit of saying in private, and later said publicly in the Senate, that, if passage was given to a curiate law, he would draw lots for a province with his colleague; but if there was no curiate law, he would come to an arrangement with his colleague and supersede you. A curiate law, he contended, was something a Consul should have, but did not absolutely need. Since he had a province by decree of the Senate, he would hold military authority under the lex Cornelia until he re-entered the city boundary. What your various friends may write to you I do not know – I understand that opinions differ. Some think you have the right to stay in your province because you are being superseded without a curiate law; others that, if you go, you are entitled to leave a governor

109. i.e. Cilicia proper, as distinct from the whole Roman province so called. It has been suggested that Quintus wanted to buy a property adjoining one of his two estates near Arpinum, of which the owner was in Cilicia and so amenable to Lentulus' influence.

in charge. For my part, I am less certain of the legal position (though even that is not so very dubious) than of the advisability of your handing over the province to your successor without delay. Your high standing and prestige, your independence, in which I know you take especial satisfaction, are involved, particularly as you cannot rebuff Appius' exorbitance without incurring some suspicion of a similar fault. I regard myself as no less bound to tell you my sentiments than to defend whatever course you adopt.

After writing the foregoing I received your letter about the tax-farmers. I cannot but commend your sense of justice, but could have wished that you had had the good luck, as it were, to avoid offending the interests or sentiments of that class, which you have always favoured in the past. *I* shall steadily defend your rulings. But you know their way, you know how strongly hostile they were to the great Q. Scaevola himself. Despite what has happened, I hope you will do everything in your power to reconcile, or at any rate mollify, their feelings towards you. That is difficult I grant, but I think it is what a wise man like yourself ought to do.

21 (I. 10)

CICERO TO L. VALERIUS

Rome, 54 (?)

From M. Cicero to L. Valerius, Counsellor, greetings (I don't see why I should not make you a present of the title, especially in these days, when effrontery can stand substitute for good counsel).[110]

110. *sapientia*, 'wisdom' or 'good sense', has a special application to the science of the jurist with which Cicero likes to make play when writing to his legal friends Valerius and Trebatius.

I have written to thank our friend Lentulus on your behalf in suitable terms. But I wish you would stop using my letters and revisit us after all this while, and elect to spend your time here, where you will be a *kent* man,[111] rather than over yonder, where I suppose nobody *kens* but you. To be sure some travellers tell that you are grown arrogant, because you don't 'respond';[112] others complain of your incivility, because you 'respond' in bad form.[113] However, I hope I shall soon be cracking my joke with you face to face. So mind you come back as quickly as you can, and don't go to your beloved Apulia. We want some pleasure in your safe return.[114] If you go there after such an Odyssey, you won't recognize any of your folk.[115]

111. Literally 'where you will be in some number (account) ... where you seem to be the only man of sense' (legal learning; with a play on *sapere*). Robbed of *doubles entendres* the sense amounts to 'better be in Rome, where jurists have their place, than in Cilicia, where Roman law is unknown'. For 'ken' as a term in Scottish law (Valerius seems to have come from Apulia) see the *Oxford English Dictionary*.

112. *respondere* is technically used of a jurisconsult's 'opinions' – legal rulings given in response to questions. It is also used of answering a question or a greeting. Not to answer such would be the reverse of polite. Cicero is fond of playing on the various uses of this verb (see note in my C.U.P. edition of the *Letters to Atticus*, Vol. I, p. 222).

113. *male respondere* = 'reply insultingly' or alternatively 'give bad (mistaken) legal advice'. Cicero really seems to have had a poor opinion of Valerius professionally; see p. 130.

114. *salvum venisse gaudere*, 'to be glad you have arrived safely', is a polite formula (cf. *Letters to Atticus* 114 (v.21).1), to which Cicero here gives a special twist. Valerius' friends in Rome would *not* be glad if he buried himself down in Apulia.

115. In the *Odyssey* (as Cicero may not have precisely remembered) the returning hero recognizes his family and friends but they do not recognize him.

22 (V. 12)

CICERO TO LUCCEIUS

Cumae (?), *c. 12 April 55*

From M. Cicero to L. Lucceius, son of Quintus, greetings.

Although I have more than once attempted to take up my present topic with you face to face, a sort of shyness, almost awkwardness, has held me back. Away from your presence, I shall set it out with less trepidation. A letter has no blushes.

I have a burning desire, of a strength you will hardly credit but ought not, I think, to blame, that my name should gain lustre and celebrity through your works. You often promise me, it is true, that you will comply with my wish; but I ask you to forgive my impatience. The quality of your literary performances, eagerly as I have always awaited them, has surpassed my expectation. I am captivated and enkindled. I want to see my achievements enshrined in your compositions with the minimum of delay. The thought that posterity will talk of me and the hope, one might say, of immortality hurries me on, but so too does the desire to enjoy in my lifetime the support of your weighty testimony, the evidence of your goodwill, and the charm of your literary talent.

As I write these words, I am not unaware of the heavy burden weighing upon you of projects undertaken and already commenced. But seeing that you have almost finished your account of the Italian War and the Civil War,[116] and remembering that you told me you were embarking on subsequent events, I feel I should be failing myself if I did not suggest two alternatives for your consideration. Would you prefer to weave

116. i.e. from the beginning of the war between Rome and her Italian allies in 91 down to Sulla's final victory over the Marians in 81.

my affairs along with those of the rest of the period into a single narrative, or might you not rather follow many Greek precedents, as Callisthenes with the Phocian War, Timaeus with the War of Pyrrhus, and Polybius with that of Numantia, all of whom detached their accounts of these particular wars from their continuous histories? Just so, you might deal with the domestic conspiracy apart from wars against external enemies. From my point of view there seems little to choose, so far as my credit is concerned. But there is my impatience to be considered; and here it does make a difference, if, instead of waiting until you reach the place, you immediately seize upon that entire subject and period. Furthermore, if your whole mind is directed upon a single theme and a single figure, I can already envisage the great gain in general richness and splendour.

Not that I am unconscious of the effrontery of what I am about, first in laying such a burden upon you (pressure of work may refuse me), and secondly in asking you to write about me eulogistically. What if the record does not appear to you so eminently deserving of eulogy? But the bounds of delicacy once passed, it is best to be frankly and thoroughly brazen. Therefore I ask you again, not mincing my words, to write of this theme more enthusiastically than perhaps you feel. Waive the laws of history for this once. Do not scorn personal bias, if it urge you strongly in my favour – that sentiment of which you wrote very charmingly in one of your prefaces, declaring that you could no more be swayed thereby than Xenophon's Hercules by Pleasure.[117] Concede to the affection between us just a little more even than the truth will license.

117. Prodicus the Sophist's allegory of the Choice of Hercules is retailed by Xenophon in his *Memoirs of Socrates* (II.1.21). Cicero refers to it in his treatise *On Duties* (I.118). – This passage ought not to be taken too literally. It is an exhibition of false modesty – Cicero did not really believe that the wine of his achievements needed any bush – and a compliment to Lucceius, as showing how much store Cicero set upon his praise.

If I prevail upon you to undertake the task, I persuade myself that the material will be worthy of your ready and skilful pen. I fancy a work of moderate length could be made up, from the beginning of the plot down to my return from exile. In it you will also be able to make use of your special knowledge of political changes, in explaining the origins of the revolutionary movement and suggesting remedies for things awry. You will blame what you judge deserving of reproof and give reasons for commending what you approve; and if, according to your usual practice, you think proper to deal pretty freely, you will hold up to censure the perfidy, artifice, and betrayal of which many were guilty towards me. Moreover, my experiences will give plenty of variety to your narrative, full of a certain kind of delectation to enthrall the minds of those who read, when you are the writer. Nothing tends more to the reader's enjoyment than varieties of circumstance and vicissitudes of fortune. For myself, though far from desirable in the living, they will be pleasant in the reading; for there is something agreeable in the secure recollection of bygone unhappiness.[118] For others, who went through no personal distress and painlessly survey misfortunes not their own, even the emotion of pity is enjoyable. Which of us is not affected pleasurably, along with a sentiment of compassion, at the story of the dying Epaminondas on the field of Mantinea, ordering the javelin to be plucked from his body only after he had been told in answer to his question that his shield was safe, so that even in the agony of his wound he could meet an honourable death with mind at ease? Whose sympathies are not aroused and held as he reads of Themistocles' flight and death?[119] The actual chronological record of events exercises no very powerful fascination upon us; it is like the recital of an almanac. But in the doubtful and various fortunes of an outstanding individual we often find

118. Cf. Virgil's *forsan et haec olim meminisse iuvabit*.
119. The manuscripts say 'and return'. But Themistocles never returned from his exile.

surprise and suspense, joy and distress, hope and fear; and if they are rounded off by a notable conclusion, our minds as we read are filled with the liveliest gratification.

So I shall be especially delighted if you find it best to set my story apart from the main stream of your work, in which you embrace events in their historical sequence – this drama, one may call it, of what I did and experienced; for it contains various 'acts', and many changes of plan and circumstance. Nor am I apprehensive of appearing to angle for your favour with the bait of a little flattery when I declare that you of all others are the writer by whom I desire my praises to be sung. After all, you are not ignorant of your own worth; a man like you knows better than to see sycophancy in admiration rather than jealousy in its absence. Nor am I myself so foolish as to ask any author to immortalize my name but one who in so doing will gain glory for his own genius. Alexander the Great did not ask Apelles to paint his portrait and Lysippus to sculpt his statue in order to curry favour with these artists, but because he believed the work would redound to his own fame as well as theirs. Those artists, however, only made a physical likeness known to people unacquainted with the original; and even in default of such memorials famous men would lose none of their celebrity. Agesilaus of Sparta, who would not allow representations of himself in paintings or sculpture, is no less pertinent to my case than those who took pains over the matter. Xenophon's one little volume in eulogy of that king has achieved far more than all the portraits and statues under the sun.

There is a further reason why a place in your works as compared with those of other writers will bring my mind a more lively satisfaction and my memory more signal honour. You will confer upon me the benefit not only of your literary skill, as Timaeus did upon Timoleon or Herodotus upon Themistocles, but of your authority as a famed and admired public man, tried and notably approved in public affairs of the greatest moment. Not only shall I gain a herald, such as Alexander when he visited Sigeum said Homer was to Achilles, but a witness – the weighty testimony of a great and famous man. For I am of one mind with Naevius' Hector, who delights, not in praise merely, but, he adds, 'from one that praisèd is'.[120]

Suppose, however, I am refused; that is to say, suppose something hinders you (for I feel it would be against nature for you to *refuse* any request of mine), I shall perhaps be driven to a course often censured by some, namely to write about myself – and yet I shall have many illustrious precedents. But I need not point out to you that this *genre* has certain disadvantages. An autobiographer must needs write over-modestly where praise is due and pass over anything that calls for censure. Moreover, his credit and authority are less, and many will blame him and say that heralds at athletic contests show more delicacy, in that after placing garlands on the heads of the winners and loudly proclaiming their names, they call in another herald when it is *their* turn to be crowned at the end of the games, in order to avoid announcing their own victory with their own lips. I am anxious to escape these drawbacks, as I shall, if you take my case. I beg you so to do.

In case it may surprise you that I urge you so earnestly and at such length *now*, when you have repeatedly promised me that you will compose the record of my public career, its policies and events, and spare no pains, my motive is, as I wrote in the first place, impatience. I cannot wait to see the world learning about me in my lifetime from your books and to enjoy my modicum of glory myself before I die.

If it is not troubling you too much, please write back and tell me what you intend to do. If you undertake the case, I will prepare notes on all points.[121] If you put me off, I shall talk to

---

120. Cf. p. 231. The verse is from Naevius' (lost) play *Hector's Departure*.
121. i.e. factual statements for Lucceius to embellish.

you personally. Meanwhile, do not be idle. Give a thorough polish to the work you have in hand. And love me well.

23 (V. 17)

CICERO TO P. SITTIUS

Rome (?), 56 (?)

From M. Cicero to P. Sittius, son of Publius, greetings.

It is not from unmindfulness of our friendship, or any interruption in my normal habit, that I have not sent you a letter at an earlier time. A period of prostrating calamity for our country and for myself was followed by one in which your own misfortunes, as painful as they were undeserved, made me reluctant to write. But the interval has now grown long enough; and recalling more closely your manly and lofty spirit, I thought it would be consonant with my general practice to write you these lines.

My dear Sittius, in the days when you first became the object of a slanderous attack in your absence, I defended you; and when your closest friend[122] was brought to trial and his ordeal was conjoined with the charge against yourself, I championed you and your cause as diligently as I was able. Then latterly, shortly after my return to Rome, finding the matter had been handled otherwise than I should have wished if I had been on the spot, I none the less did everything I could to save you. But the public prejudice due to the grain shortage,[123] enemies –

122. P. Cornelius Sulla.
123. Evidently a reference to the grain crisis in September 57, just after Cicero's return from exile, when Pompey was given charge of supplies for five years. Why Sittius was blamed is unknown.

your friends' enemies as well as your own – the unfairness of the whole court proceedings, and many other disorders in the body politic proved more powerful than truth and the merits of the case. Then I did not fail your son Publius; my time, my advice, my trouble, my testimony were at his disposal.

Thus I may claim to have observed faithfully and strictly all the obligations of friendship; and these include another which I do not deem it right to leave unfulfilled, and that is to urge and beg you to remember that you are both a human being and a man: as the former, to bear with philosophy the working of chance, universal and unpredictable, which none of us can avoid and which none can by any means guarantee; and, as the latter, to offer stout resistance to pain and misfortune, and to bear in mind that such misadventures as a result of unjust trials have befallen many gallant and excellent men in our own and in other imperial states. I wish it were not true to add that you are deprived of a commonwealth in which no man of sense finds anything to give him pleasure.

As for your son, I am afraid that if I say nothing you may feel that I have withheld the tribute due to his merit; whereas if I write down all I feel, my letter may exacerbate the pain of your separation. Your wisest course, however, is to deem that wherever you may be, his filial affection, manliness, and diligence belong to you and are beside you. What we envisage in our minds is no less our own than what we see with our eyes. So his exemplary character and profound affection should be a great source of comfort to you; so too should be the thought of myself and those others who value you, and always shall, by your character, not your worldly fortune; and so above all should be your own conscience. You will reflect that you have deserved nothing of what has happened, and you will add the thought that wise men are troubled by dishonour, not by chance, and by their own fault, not by others' ill-usage.

Prompted by the memory of our old friendship and the

merit and attention of your son. I shall ever be ready both to comfort and to alleviate your plight. If you care to write me a few words, I shall not let you feel that you have written them for nothing.

24 (VII. I)

CICERO TO M. MARIUS

Rome, late August 55

From M. Cicero to M. Marius greetings.

If some bodily distress or the frailty of your health has kept you from coming to the show,[124] I give credit to chance rather than to your own good sense. On the other hand, if you thought these objects of public wonderment unworthy of your notice, and chose not to come though your health would have permitted, why, I rejoice both at your freedom from physical distress and at your health of mind, in that you have disregarded these spectacles at which others idly marvel – always provided that you have reaped the fruits of your leisure. You have had a wonderful opportunity to enjoy it, left almost on your own in that delightful spot.[125] And after all, I don't doubt that throughout the period of the show you have spent the mornings browsing over your books in that bedroom of yours with its window that you let into the wall to overlook the bay of Stabiae. Meanwhile those who left you there were watching the public

124. Given by Pompey in his second Consulship to inaugurate his stone theatre (the first built in Rome) and the temple of Venus Victrix. Pliny the Elder and Cassius Dio write of their magnificence.
125. Elsewhere Cicero writes of Marius as his neighbour at Pompeii. But Marius' villa may have been two or three miles to the south above modern Castellammare di Stabia.

pantomimes half-asleep.[126] As for the rest of the day, you have been spending it in such diversions as you have provided to suit your own taste while we have had to endure what Sp. Maecius[127] presumably thought proper.

To be sure, the show (if you are interested) was on the most lavish scale; but it would have been little to your taste, to judge by my own. To begin with, certain performers honoured the occasion by returning to the boards, from which I thought they had honoured their reputation by retiring.[128] Your favourite, our friend Aesopus, gave a display which everyone was willing should be his finale. When he came to take an oath[129] and got as far as 'if I knowingly swear false', he lost his voice! I need not give you further details – you know the other shows.[130] They did not even have the sprightliness which one mostly finds in ordinary shows – one lost all sense of gaiety in watching the elaborate productions. These I don't doubt you are very well content to have missed. What pleasure is there in getting a *Clytemnestra* with six hundred mules or a *Trojan Horse* with three thousand mixing-bowls[131] or a variegated display of cavalry and infantry equipment in some battle or other? The public gaped at all this; it would not have amused you at all.

126. The weather in high summer was naturally oppressive. Valerius Maximus (11.6.4) says that streams of running water were channelled through the theatre to mitigate the heat.

127. Spurius Maecius Tarpa selected the plays to be produced at the show. He may have been Chairman (*magister*) of the Guild of Poets established in the third century: cf. Horace, *Satires*, 1.10.38, *Art of Poetry*, 386.

128. The common phrase *honoris causa*, 'by way of compliment', is echoed in another sense, 'for the sake of (their) repute'.

129. Perhaps as part of his role. Others suppose that actors had to take an oath before starting their performance (but why?).

130. i.e. comedies and mimes.

131. The first of these two tragedies was by Accius. Grammarians ascribe a *Trojan Horse* both to Livius Andronicus and to Naevius. The bowls are thought to have figured as part of the spoils of Troy.

If you were listening to your man Protogenes[132] during those days (so long as he read you anything in the world except my speeches), you have certainly had a good deal better time of it than any of us. As for the Greek[133] and Oscan[134] shows, I don't imagine you were sorry to miss *them* – especially as you can see an Oscan turn on your town council,[135] and you care so little for Greeks that you don't even take Greek Street to get to your house! Or perhaps, having scorned gladiators,[136] you are sorry not to have seen the athletes! Pompey himself admits that they were a waste of time and midday oil![137] That leaves the hunts, two every day for five days, magnificent – nobody says otherwise. But what pleasure can a cultivated man get out of seeing a weak human being torn to pieces by a powerful animal or a splendid animal transfixed by a hunting spear? Anyhow, if these sights are worth seeing, you have seen them often; and we spectators saw nothing new. The last day was for the elephants. The groundlings showed much astonishment thereat, but no enjoyment. There was even an impulse of compassion, a feeling that the monsters had something human about them.[138]

As for me, these past days, during the plays (in case you

132. No doubt a reader (*anagnostes*).

133. Probably Greek plays performed in Greek, as distinct from Latin adaptations of Greek originals; cf. *Letters to Atticus* 410 (XVI.5).1.

134. i.e. *Fabulae Atellanae*, a type of coarse farce with stock characters, like a Punch and Judy show.

135. 'Oscan' standing for 'Campanian'. *Graffiti* found in Pompeii show that a M. Marius stood for election as Aedile.

136. i.e. some gladiatorial show (apparently a private allusion). The explanation that Marius had defied Clodius' gangs does not suit what is known of him.

137. *operam et oleum perdere* was a proverbial expression for a waste of time and money, *oleum* referring to 'midnight oil'. Here it is humorously applied to the oil used by athletes in anointing themselves.

138. Pliny's account (*Natural History*, VIII.21) that the whole crowd of spectators rose and cursed Pompey is evidently exaggerated.

picture me as a free man, if not a happy one), I pretty well ruptured my lungs defending your friend Caninius Gallus.[139] If only my public were as accommodating as Aesopus', upon my word I should be glad to give up my profession and spend my time with you and other congenial spirits. I was weary of it even in the days when youth and ambition spurred me forward, and when moreover I was at liberty to refuse a case I did not care for. But now life is simply not worth living. I have no reward to expect for my labours, and sometimes I am obliged to defend persons who have deserved none too well of me at the request of those who *have* deserved well.

Accordingly, I am looking out for any excuse to live as I please at long last; and you and your leisured manner of existence have my hearty commendation and approval. I resign myself to the rarity of your visits more easily than I otherwise should, because, even if you were in Rome, I am so confoundedly busy that I should not be able to enjoy the entertainment of your company, nor you of mine (if any entertainment it holds). When and if I slacken my chains (for to be loose of them entirely is more than I can ask), then, no question about it, I shall teach you the art of civilized living, to which you have been giving your undivided attention for years! Only you must go on propping up that frail health of yours and looking after yourself, so that you can visit my places[140] in the country and run around with me in my little litter.

I have written at unusual length, out of an abundance, not of spare time, but of affection for you, because in one of your letters you threw out a hint, if you remember, that I might

139. The charge may have referred to his activities as Tribune in 56 (cf. p. 39 etc.). As an adherent of Pompey's he will have been one of a number of defendants for whom Cicero appeared at this period at the behest of Pompey and Caesar, some of them old enemies of his own.

140. Possibly 'our places'; Marius too may have had more than one villa in the area. Cicero at this period had one at Pompeii and one at Cumae.

write something to prevent you feeling sorry to have missed the show. If I have succeeded in that, so much the better; but if not, I console myself with the thought that henceforth you will come to the shows and visit us, and that you won't forgo any prospect of pleasure to yourself on account of my letters.

25 (V. 8)

CICERO TO CRASSUS

Rome, January 54

From M. Cicero to M. Licinius Crassus, son of Publius, greetings.

I do not doubt that all your friends have apprised you in their letters of the zeal which I put forward on the Ides (?)[141] for the defence, or even enhancement, of your position. It was too ardent and too conspicuous to go unrecorded. Against the Consuls and many of the Consulars I joined issue with a vehemence which I have never before displayed in any cause, thus taking upon myself the standing role of protagonist on behalf of all that tends to your honour, and discharging more than amply the service which has long been owing to our old friendship, but which the many variations of circumstance had caused me to intermit.

But indeed I never lacked will to cultivate your friendship and contribute to your advancement. Only certain persistent fellows, whom it hurts to hear others well spoken of, estranged you from me more than once, and at times changed my attitude to you. But now the occasion has arisen which I prayed for,

141. Of January (but the reading is conjectural). The debate in the Senate concerned the allocation of funds etc. to Crassus as governor of Syria.

but scarcely hoped to see: in the full tide of your prosperity I have had the chance to show myself mindful of our mutual sentiments and loyal to our friendship. Yes, I have succeeded in making plain, not only to your entire domestic circle but to the community at large, that I am your very good friend. Your wife, the paragon of her sex, and your two sons, whose filial affection, high character, and popularity do them honour, rely on my counsels and promptings and my active support. And the Senate and People of Rome now know that in all matters affecting you during your absence my devoted and indefatigable service and the influence I command are absolutely and unreservedly at your disposal.

Day-to-day events, past and current, are presumably conveyed to you by your domestic correspondents. As for me personally, I very much hope you will thoroughly persuade yourself that I have not *happened* to embrace your cause and work for your greatness through any accident or sudden whim, but have always made it my aim ever since my entry into public life to be on the closest terms with you. Since those days I recall no failure of attention on my part or of good-will and generosity in the highest measure on yours. If in the meanwhile certain infringements, surmised rather than real, have affected our relations, these are mere figments of the imagination; let them be utterly eradicated from our memories and our lives. Between two men such as you are and I desire to be, whose lot has fallen on the same political ground, I would hope that alliance and friendship will conduce to the credit of both.

You yourself, therefore, will decide the place in your esteem which you think appropriate for me, and I trust your decision will take account of my standing in the world. On my side, I profess and promise you my signal and exemplary devotion in every kind of service tending to your dignity and glory. Many may be my rivals, but by the verdict of every beholder, and of your sons above all, I shall comfortably win the race. For both young men I have a particular regard, but, while both have my good-will equally, I am the more attached to Publius because ever since he was a boy, but especially at the present time, he pays me attention and regard as though to a second father.

Please believe that this is no ordinary letter; it will have the force of a covenant. Be sure that the promises and undertakings I give you will be religiously respected and carried out to the letter. Having taken up the defence of your position while you are abroad, I shall persevere therein, not only for our friendship's sake but to maintain my own reputation for consistency. Accordingly, I have thought it enough at present to assure you of my unsolicited activity wherever I myself see an opportunity to promote your wish, your interest, or your dignity; and to add that, should any suggestion reach me from you or yours, I shall take care you do not suppose any written word of your own or any representations from your folk to have been lost upon me. So please write to me yourself on all matters, large, small, or in between, as to a most sincere friend, and advise your people to make use of my service and counsel, my public and personal influence, in all concerns – no matter whether public or private, business or domestic, your own or your friends' or your guests' or your clients'. My labour shall go to fill, so far as may be, the void created by your absence.

26 (VII. 5)

CICERO TO CAESAR

Rome, April 54

From Cicero to Caesar, Imperator, greetings.

Please observe how fully I am persuaded that you are my *alter ego*, not only in my own concerns but in those of my friends also. I had intended to take C. Trebatius with me wherever I might go, in order to bring him home again the richer by any and every benefit and mark of good-will in my power to bestow. But Pompey has stayed on longer than I expected, and my own departure seems prevented, or at any rate delayed, by a certain hesitation on my part of which you are not uninformed.[142] So observe my presumption: I now want Trebatius to look to you for everything he would have hoped for from me, and I have assured him of your friendly disposition in terms really no less ample than I had previously been wont to use respecting my own.

But a remarkable coincidence has supervened, as though in evidence of the correctness of my opinion and in guarantee of your kindness. Just as I was talking rather seriously to our friend Balbus at my house on the subject of this very Trebatius, a letter comes in from you concluding as follows: 'I shall make M. Curtius' son[143] king of Gaul. Or, if you please, make him over to Lepta,[144] and send me somebody else on whom to bestow my favours.' Balbus and I both raised our hands to heaven. It came so pat as to seem no accident, but divine intervention.

I send you Trebatius accordingly. I thought it right to do so of my own accord in the first instance, but at your invitation in the second. In embracing his acquaintance with all your usual courtesy, my dear Caesar, I should wish you to confer upon his single person all the kindnesses which I could induce you to wish to confer upon my friends. As for him, I will answer that

142. In 55 Pompey received a five-year command in Spain and in the autumn of 54 he appointed Cicero as his Legate (cf. *Letters to his Brother Quintus* 21 (III.1).22, *Letters to Atticus* 93 (IV.19).2). But neither he nor Cicero went there. The 'hesitation' is generally referred to apprehensions about Clodius' designs.

143. *M. Curti filium*, conjectured for *M. itfiuium* in the manuscripts. The person referred to is clearly the M. Curtius whom Cicero had asked Caesar to appoint Military Tribune in the following year (*Letters to his Brother Quintus* 18 (II.14).3).

144. See Glossary of Persons. This is his first appearance in the Letters and Caesar's reason for mentioning him is unknown.

you will find him – I won't use that old-fashioned expression[145] of which you rightly made fun when I wrote to you about Milo, I'll say it in plain Latin, in the language of sensible men: there is no better fellow, no more honest and honourable gentleman alive. Add to which, he is a leading light in Civil Law; his memory is extraordinary, his learning profound.

I do not ask on his behalf for a Tribunate or Prefecture or any other specific favour. It is your good-will and generosity I bespeak; though if in addition you have a mind to decorate him with suchlike ambitious trinkets, I say nothing to deter you. In fine, I put him altogether, as the phrase goes, out of my hand into yours – the hand of a great conqueror and a great gentleman,[146] if I may become a trifle fulsome, though that's hardly permissible with you. But you will let it pass, I see you will.[147]

Take care of your health and keep that warm corner in your heart for me.

27 (VII. 6)

CICERO TO TREBATIUS

Cumae or Pompeii, latter May 54

From Cicero to Trebatius greetings.

Every letter I write to Caesar or to Balbus carries as a kind of statutory bonus a recommendation of yourself, and not the standard sort but phrased with some special indication of my

145. Or 'old saw'. What this was, or why Cicero wrote to Caesar about Milo, we do not know.

146. Literally 'pre-eminent both in victory' (i.e. with the sword) 'and loyalty' (to its pledges).

147. The good nature apparent in Caesar's letter will tolerate even flattery of himself.

regard for you. Now what you have to do is to put aside this foolish hankering after Rome and city ways, and by dint of perseverance and energy achieve the purpose with which you set out. I and your other friends will excuse you, as the 'rich and noble dames that dwelt in Corinth, lofty citadel'[148] excused Medea. She persuaded them 'hands thick in plaster' not to censure her for living abroad:

Helping self and helping country many a rover wide doth roam.
Naught accounted in his staying sitteth many a stay-at-home.

Which latter case would certainly have been yours, if I had not thrust you forth.

But I shall be writing more anon. Now you, who have learned how to enter caveats[149] for others, enter one for yourself against the tricks of those charioteers in Britain.[150] And since I have started to play Medea, always remember what she says: 'He who cannot help his own case, be he *wise*, his *wisdom's* vain.'[151]

Take care of your health.

148. The quotations are from a Latin version by Ennius of Euripides' *Medea*.

149. *cavere* ('beware,' 'look out for') was also used in a legal sense, of a jurisconsult advising a client or prescribing a form of procedure. I have had to resort to paraphrase.

150. Caesar's second expedition to Britain was now in preparation. He describes how the Britons used their war-chariots in *Bell. Gall.* IV.33.

151. The Euripidean original may be the line quoted in letter 317, which is not in our text of the Greek play. On 'wisdom' see n.110.

28 (VII. 7)

CICERO TO TREBATIUS

Rome, end of June (?) 54

From Cicero to Trebatius.

I am continually putting in a word for you, but with what effect I am anxious to hear from yourself. My greatest hope is in Balbus, to whom I write about you very earnestly and often. What surprises me is that I don't get a letter from you whenever one comes in from my brother Quintus. I hear there is not an ounce of either gold or silver in Britain. If that is true, my advice is to lay hold of a chariot and hurry back to us at full speed! But if we can gain our end even without Britain, contrive to make yourself one of Caesar's intimates. My brother will give you valuable assistance, and so will Balbus; but your greatest asset, believe me, is your own honourable character and hard work. You are serving under a very generous chief, your age is just right, your recommendation is certainly out of the ordinary. So the one thing you have to be afraid of is seeming to do yourself less than justice.

29 (VII. 8)

CICERO TO TREBATIUS

Rome, August (middle or late) 54

From Cicero to Trebatius.

Caesar has written to me very civilly, regretting that he has so far been too busy to get to know you very well, but assuring me that this will come. I told him in my reply how greatly he would oblige me by conferring upon you all he could in the way of good-will, friendly offices, and liberality. But your letter gave me an impression of undue impatience; also it surprised me that you make so little account of the advantages of a Tribunate, especially one involving no military service. I shall complain to Vacerra and Manilius.[152] I dare not say a word to Cornelius.[153] He is responsible if you play the fool, since you give out that it was from him you learned your *wisdom*. Now why don't you press this opportunity, this chance? – you'll never find a better.

As for what you say about that Counsellor Precianus,[154] I go on commending you to him, for he writes himself that he has given you reason to be grateful. Let me know how that matter stands. I am looking forward to Britannic letters from you all.

30 (VII. 9)

CICERO TO TREBATIUS

Rome, middle or late October 54

From Cicero to Trebatius.

It's a long time since I had news of you. You don't write, and the last two months I have not written to you myself. As you were not with my brother Quintus, I could not tell where to send a letter or whom to give it to. I am anxious to know what you are doing and where you will be spending the winter – with Caesar, I hope; but I have not ventured to write any-

152. Two of Trebatius' fellow-jurisconsults.

153. Q. Cornelius Maximus is mentioned in the *Digest* as Trebatius' teacher in law.

154. Unknown. Possibly *Preciano* means 'in the Precius business'.

thing to him on account of his recent loss.[155] I did write to Balbus though. Mind you don't let yourself down. Better later back to us, so you come fatter! There is no occasion for you to hurry, especially now that Battara[156] is no more. But you are well able to make your own plans. I am anxious to know what you have decided.

There is a certain friend of yours called Cn. Octavius (or is it Cn. Cornelius?), 'mother Earth's son, a fine old family'.[157] Knowing me to be a friend of yours, he showers me with invitations to dinner. So far he has not succeeded in getting me all the way, but I am obliged just the same.

31 (VII. 17)

CICERO TO TREBATIUS

Rome, October or November 54

From Cicero to Trebatius greetings.

On the strength of your letter I gave thanks to my brother Quintus, and can at last commend yourself in that you now seem to have fairly made up your mind. Your letters in the first few months disturbed me not a little, for they gave me an impression (if you will forgive me for saying so) at times of irresponsibility in your hankering for Rome and city ways, at times of indolence, at times of timidity in face of the labours of

155. Julia, Caesar's only child and Pompey's wife, died in September 54.

156. Who he was and what Cicero means is unknown. The suggestion that 'Battara' was a nickname for Vacerra (see previous letter) does not seem very likely.

157. Perhaps quoted from a play, though this is not certain. 'Son of Earth' (*terrae filius*) = 'a nobody'. The name which Cicero was, or pretended to be, unable to remember was in fact 'Octavius'; cf. p. 93.

army life, and often too, most uncharacteristically, of something not unlike presumption. You seemed to think you had brought a note of hand to the Commander-in-Chief instead of a letter – such a hurry you were in to take your money and get back home! It did not seem to occur to you that people who *did* go with notes of hand to Alexandria have thus far been unable to get a penny![158]

Were I thinking in terms of my own convenience, I should wish you to be with me of all things, for I gained no small pleasure from our intercourse and no small profit from your advice and services. But since from youth upwards you have confided yourself to my friendship and patronage, I have always felt a responsibility not only for your protection but for your promotion and betterment. Accordingly, as long as I expected to go myself on a provincial assignment, I made you certain unsolicited offers, which you doubtless remember. When that plan changed, I hit on another. Observing that Caesar extended to me the most flattering courtesies and held me in particular regard, knowing too his extraordinary generosity and punctilious loyalty to his engagements, I commended you to his care in the fullest and most emphatic terms I could find. He took my words in the same spirit, and has often intimated to me by letter and made clear to you by word of mouth and by act that he has been greatly impressed by my recommendation. Now that you have come by such a patron, if you credit me with any good sense or good-will towards you, don't let him go. Should anything occur to ruffle you, should you find him less prompt than you expected through pressure of affairs or some untoward circumstance, be patient and wait for the final outcome. That it will be agreeable to yourself I will guarantee.

158. Ptolemy the Piper had borrowed large sums with which to bribe Roman politicians to further his restoration to his throne; that achieved, he was in no hurry to pay his debts. Cicero's defence of C. Rabirius Postumus in the following winter had to do with this matter.

I must not urge you at greater length. I will only point out that if you let slip this opportunity of securing the friendship of a most eminent and generous personage in a wealthy province at just the right time of your life, you will never find a better. In this opinion, as you jurists say in your books, Q. Cornelius concurs.

I am glad that you have not gone to Britain. You are quit of the fatigues, and I shall not be listening to your accounts of it all! Please send me full details as to where you will be spending the winter, in what expectations or under what conditions.

32 (VII. 16)

CICERO TO TREBATIUS

Rome, late November 54

From M. Cicero to Trebatius greetings.

You remember the words at the end of the *Trojan Horse*:[159] 'Their wisdom comes too late.' But yours, you old fox, does not come too late. First you sent those snappish letters, which were silly enough. Then you showed yourself none too keen a sight-seer in the matter of Britain, for which I frankly don't blame you. *Now* you seem to be snug in winter quarters, and so you have no mind to stir. '*Wisdom* everywhere befitteth; that shall be thy sharpest arm.'[160]

If I were by way of dining out, I should not have disappointed your friend Cn. Octavius; though I did say to him after several invitations 'Do please tell me, who *are* you?' But really, in all seriousness, he is a pretty fellow. A pity you did not take him with you!

Let me know plainly what all of you are about and whether

159. Cf. n. 131.
160. From an unknown play.

you will be coming to Italy this winter. Balbus has assured me that you are going to be a rich man. Whether he uses the word in plain Roman style, meaning that you will have plenty of cash, or after the manner of the Stoics when they say that all are rich who can enjoy the sky and the earth, remains to be seen. Travellers from Gaul complain of your arrogance – they say you don't *respond*[161] to enquiries. Still you have one satisfaction; everybody agrees that there is no greater legal pundit than yourself in all Samarobriva.[162]

33 (VII. 10)

CICERO TO TREBATIUS

Rome, December 54

From M. Cicero to Trebatius greetings.

I have read your letter, from which I understand that our friend Caesar is impressed with you as a jurist. You may congratulate yourself on having got to your present part of the world, where you can pass for a man of some *wisdom*! Had you gone to Britain as well, I daresay there would have been no greater expert than you in the whole vast island. But really (you won't mind my jokes – after all, you challenged me), I am half inclined to be jealous of you, actually sent for by a personage whom affairs, not arrogance, make inaccessible to the rest of mankind.

But you say nothing in your letter about *your* activities, which I assure you interest me no less than my own. I am terribly afraid you may have a chilly time of it[163] in winter

161. Cf. n. 113.

162. Caesar's winter headquarters.

163. With innuendo. *frigere*, 'to be cold,' often = 'have nothing to do' or 'be coldly received' ('a frost').

quarters. So I advise you to install a good stove. Mucius and Manilius[164] concur. After all, you are not too well supplied with army greatcoats![165] To be sure, I hear that things are warm enough for you all out there just now,[166] and truly that intelligence made me very nervous about you. However, you are a much safer campaigner than counsel. Keen swimmer[167] as you are, you had no mind for a dip in the Ocean and you didn't care to watch those charioteers,[168] though in the old days we could never do you out of a blindfold gladiator. But enough of badinage.

How pressingly I have written to Caesar on your behalf, you know; how often, I know. But to tell the truth, I had temporarily given it up, because in dealing with so generous a man and so warm a friend of mine I did not want to risk appearing to lack confidence in his good-will. All the same, in my last letter I thought it time for a reminder, and wrote accordingly. Please let me know the result, and inform me at the same time of your whole situation and all your plans. I am anxious to learn of your present doings and future prospects. How long do you think this absence of yours will continue? For I do assure you that the only thing that consoles me and makes our

164. Famous lawyers of the past bore these names, M'. Manilius (Consul in 149) and (along with other members of his family) Q. Mucius Scaevola the Pontifex. Trebatius of course would catch the echo. But primarily Cicero must be referring to contemporaries (cf. p. 93 'Q. Cornelius concurs'). Manilius is obviously the lawyer mentioned on p. 90. For a contemporary Mucius Scaevola see Glossary of Persons. If he was, as may be presumed, a friend of Trebatius, Cicero might bring him in for the sake of the legal associations of his name even though he was not himself a jurist.

165. *saga.* Cicero pretends to assume that the unsoldierly Trebatius would be short of them.

166. The tribe of the Eburones in north-east Gaul rose against the Romans and destroyed two legions in the winter of 54–53.

167. Horace in his *Satires* (II.1.8) alludes to Trebatius' partiality for swimming, as well as for wine.

168. See n. 150.

separation easier to bear is the knowledge (if it be so) that you are the gainer thereby. If that is *not* the case, we are arrant fools, both of us – I for not hauling you back to Rome, you for not hastening hither. I'll be bound that a single meeting of ours, serious or jocose, will be worth more than all our Aeduan brethren,[169] to say nothing of the enemy. So please inform me on all points as soon as possible.

> By comfort or by counsel or by act
> I'll help.[170]

34 (VII. 11)

CICERO TO TREBATIUS

Tusculum (?), January 53

From Cicero to Trebatius.

If you had not already left Rome, you would surely be leaving now. Who wants a lawyer with all these *interregna*?[171] The advice I should give to all defendants in civil suits is to ask every Interrex for two adjournments.[172] Aren't you proud of your pupil in Civil Law?

But look here, what are you up to? Is anything happening? I notice that you now crack jokes in your letters. That looks well,

169. As the first Gaulish tribe to form an alliance with Rome the Aedui had been addressed by the Senate as 'brothers and kinsmen' (Caesar, *Bell. Gall.* 1.33.2; cf. *Letters to Atticus* 19 (1.19).2).

170. From Terence's *Self-Tormentor* (86).

171. See Glossary of Terms. The year 53 opened with no curule magistrates, disorders in Rome having made it impossible to elect them. Consuls were finally elected in July.

172. This would mean that the hearing would be postponed until a new Interrex came into office, and the process could be repeated indefinitely.

better than the statues[173] in my place at Tusculum! But I want to know what it means. You say that Caesar is consulting you. I had rather he consulted your interests! If that is happening, or you think it is going to happen, put up with your soldiering and stay right on. While missing you, I shall comfort myself with the hope of your advancement. But if all that is in the nature of moonshine, then rejoin us. Something will turn up here one of these days, and even if it doesn't, I'll be bound that a single conversation of ours will be worth more than all the Samarobrivas in Gaul. Furthermore, if you come back soon, there won't be any talk; whereas if you are away for a long while to no purpose, I am afraid of Laberius, even of our friend Valerius.[174] A Britannic counsellor would make a marvellous figure of fun! I am not laughing at all this, though maybe you are, but cutting jokes with you in my usual style about an extremely serious matter. Joking aside, my advice to you as a most sincere well-wisher is this: if as a result of my recommendation you are likely to receive in Gaul the recognition that is your due, then bear your homesickness and advance your standing and means; but if the outlook there is bleak, come back to us. You will doubtless achieve all your aims even so by your own energies and my wholehearted zeal for your welfare.

35 (VII. 12)

CICERO TO TREBATIUS

Rome, February 53

From Cicero to Trebatius.

I was wondering why you had stopped sending me letters.

173. A play on two senses of *signum*, 'sign' and 'statue'.
174. See Glossary of Persons. Not impossibly this Valerius is to be identified with an author of mimes called Catullus, mentioned by Martial and others.

Now my friend Pansa intimates that you have turned Epicurean. A remarkable camp yours must be! What would you have done if I had sent you to Tarentum[175] instead of Samarobriva? I was uneasy about you even in the days when you were maintaining the same position as my crony Velleius (?).[176]

But how are you going to be a champion of Civil Law if everything you do is done for your own sweet sake and not for the community?[177] And what becomes of the trust formula 'in accordance with honest practice proper between honest men'? Who is honest that does nothing except for his own interest? What rule will you lay down for division of goods held jointly, seeing that nothing can be joint among people whose only yardstick is their own pleasure? How will you think it proper to swear by Jupiter Stone,[178] when you know that Jupiter can't get angry with anybody? And what is to become of the good folk of Ulubrae,[179] if you decide that it is wrong to take part in public affairs?[180]

Well, if you are really forsaking us, I'm put out. But if it suits your book to humour Pansa, you have my forgiveness. Only write me at long last, and tell me what you are doing and what you want me to do or see to on your behalf.

175. A notorious centre of luxury and pleasure.

176. C. Velleius is the Epicurean spokesman in Cicero's dialogue *On the Nature of the Gods*, but the reading is doubtful. There is probably an allusion to some litigation in which Trebatius had been involved as legal adviser.

177. In this passage Cicero facetiously sets out to prove that Epicurean dogmas are incompatible with the vocabulary of Roman Civil Law.

178. The man swearing this most solemn of Roman oaths flung a stone, praying that if guilty of deliberate perjury he should be cast out like the stone.

179. A small place near the Pontine Marshes (see p. 102). Trebatius had become its patron, no doubt by legal services.

180. As held by Epicurus.

36 (VII. 13)

CICERO TO TREBATIUS

Rome, 4 March 53

From M. Cicero to Trebatius greetings.

Did you really suppose me so unreasonable as to be angry with you because I thought you lacking in perseverance and too eager to leave Gaul? And do you imagine that this was the reason why I have not sent you a letter for some considerable time? The agitation visible in your first letters caused me distress, not annoyance; and there was no reason whatsoever for the intermission of mine other than my complete ignorance of your whereabouts. And now do you still persist in making false charges against me and refuse to accept my explanation? Hark ye, my good Testa: is it money that is swelling your head or the fact that you are consulted by the Commander-in-Chief? Upon my soul, you are such a coxcomb that I believe you would rather be consulted by Caesar than covered in gold! But if it's both together, I wonder who is going to put up with you except myself, who can put up with anything.

But to come back to the point, I am heartily glad that you are tolerably content to be out there. That gives me as much pleasure as the other gave me distress. My only apprehension is that your professional skill may stand you in poor stead, for out there, as I hear,

> No claim in form of laws lay they; with steel
> Their due they seek.[181]

You yourself are used to being called in to 'a using of force'. But you don't have to worry about that limiting clause in the

181. From Ennius' *Annals* (Vahlen,[2] 272).

injunction, 'provided you have not been the first to enter by armed force' – I know you are no ruffling blade to start a quarrel![182] However, to give you a caveat from your own legal arsenal, I advise you to keep clear of the Treviri – I hear they are *capital* customers, like their Roman namesakes. If you want a Board of Three, better try the Masters of the Mint![183] But we'll have our joke some other time. Please write to me in full detail about everything over there.

Dispatched 4 March.

37 (VII. 18)

CICERO TO TREBATIUS

The Pomptine Marshes, 8 April 53

From Cicero to Trebatius greetings.

I have received several letters from you in a batch, dispatched at different times. In every respect but one they made pleasant reading. They show that you are now bearing your army life with a stout heart, and that you are a man of fortitude and resolution. For a little while I missed these qualities in you, not however putting down your restlessness to weakness of spirit but to your pain at being parted from us. So carry on as you have begun. Tolerate your service with a stout heart. Depend upon it, you will be well rewarded. I shall follow up my

182. The joke, implying that Trebatius was not a man to risk his skin if he could help it, is based on procedural technicalities arising under Roman law of property. I forbear to discuss its details here.

183. Another complex joke with a pun on 'Treviri', a Gaulish tribe, and *tres viri* (probably pronounced identically), 'Board of Three'. Two Roman Boards of Three are involved, *tres viri capitales*, who were police functionaries (but in general usage *capitalis* = 'dangerous', 'deadly'), and *tres viri monetales*, in charge of the Roman mint.

recommendation, but at the right time. Rest assured that I am as anxious as yourself for you to derive the maximum of advantage from this separation of ours. And since the caveats you legal gentlemen enter are none too dependable, I am sending you a little caveat in Greek under my own hand.[184] On your side, please give me an account of the war in Gaul – the less adventurous my informant, the more I trust the information.

However, to get back to your letters: all very nice, except for one feature, which surprises me. Is it not unusual to send several identical letters in one's own handwriting?[185] As for the palimpsest, I applaud your thrift. But I wonder what could have been on that scrap of paper which you thought proper to erase rather than not write these screeds. Your forms of procedure perhaps?[186] I scarcely suppose that you rub out my letters in order to substitute your own. Or do you mean to imply that nothing is happening, that you are neglected, without even a supply of paper? Well, that is your own fault for taking your modesty away with you instead of leaving it behind with us.

When Balbus sets out to join you, I shall commend you to him in plain Roman style. If you get no further letter from me for some time, don't be astonished. I am going to be away through April. I am writing this in the Pomptine country,

184. What this was is doubtful. Some think a letter of advice on how to behave to Caesar, written in Greek for greater security. Rather perhaps an epigram or other literary *jeu d'esprit*.

185. Important letters were sometimes dispatched in two or more copies by separate messengers to ensure delivery. The sender would naturally use an amanuensis for such copies, though otherwise it was considered polite to write in one's own hand. Cicero jestingly implies that Trebatius' letters were so similar to one another as to be virtually copies. The quaint notion that Roman etiquette required letters sent as aforesaid *not* to be verbally identical is baseless.

186. With the usual implication that Trebatius did not know his legal business. Forms of procedure (*formulae*) drawn up by him would be expendable.

having turned in for the night at M. Aemilius Philemo's[187] house, from which I have already heard the hubbub created by my clients, those, that is, whom you have procured for me – it is common knowledge that a vast crowd of frogs in Ulubrae[188] have bestirred themselves to pay me their respects.

Take care of your health.

8 April, Pomptine Marshes.

P.S. I have torn up a letter of yours received from L. Arruntius – which did not deserve it, for it contained nothing that could not safely have been read out at a public meeting. However, Arruntius said that you had so requested, and you had added a note to the same effect. Well, no matter. I am much surprised that you have not written since then, especially in view of the startling developments.[189]

38 (VII. 14)

CICERO TO TREBATIUS

Rome, May or June 53

Cicero to Trebatius.

Vettius Chrysippus, Cyrus the architect's freedman, has made me think that you have some recollection of my existence; he has given me your kind regards. Very grand we have become! Was it too much trouble to give him a letter for me, and him practically one of my own household? If, however, you have forgotten how to put pen to paper, you will have fewer clients in future to lose their cases! If *I* have slipped your mind, I'll make shift to come to Gaul myself before I fade out

187. A freedman of Lepidus', the future Triumvir.
188. See n. 179.
189. In Gaul (revolts in north and north-east).

of it completely. But if it is apprehension of the summer campaign that is sapping your energies, you must think up an excuse, as you did in the matter of Britain.

One thing I was greatly pleased to hear from the same Chrysippus, that you are on close terms with Caesar. But I must say, I would rather have learned how you are getting on from your own letters as often as possible; it would have been more fitting. No doubt that is the way it would be, if you had cared to study the rules of friendship as thoroughly as those of court procedure.

But all this is badinage in your own style – and a little in mine too. I am very fond of you, and not only want you to be fond of me but am confident that you are.

39 (VII. 15)

CICERO TO TREBATIUS

Rome, June (?) 53

From Cicero to Trebatius.

'Lovers are contrary folk.' How true that is may be seen from the fact that I used to be distressed because you were unhappy in Gaul, whereas now I feel a prick when you write that you are well-content with life there. I used to be vexed that you were not pleased with the result of my recommendation, and now it hurts me to find that you can enjoy anything without me. However, I prefer that we put up with your absence than that you miss the advantages which I hope for on your account.

I cannot tell you how pleased I am to hear that you have struck up a friendship with C. Matius. He is a very charming, cultivated person. Make him as fond of you as possible. Take my word for it, nothing you can bring back from this province of yours will give you more pleasure.

Take care of yourself.

40 (XVI. 13)

CICERO TO TIRO

Cumae, 10 April 53

From Tullius to Tiro greetings.

I shall feel you have given me all I could ask, once I see you fit and well. I am writing in great anxiety for Andricus, whom I sent to you, to arrive. If you care for me, see that you get well and join us when you are thoroughly strong again.

Goodbye.

10 April.

41 (XVI. 14)

CICERO TO TIRO

Cumae, 11 April 53

From Tullius to Tiro greetings.

Andricus arrived a day later than I expected him, so I had a miserable, apprehensive night. I am none the wiser from your letters as to how you are, but still it made me feel better. I have nothing to amuse me, no literary work – I cannot touch it before I see you.

Give orders for the doctor to be promised whatever fee he asks. I have written to Ummius to that effect. I hear you are in distress of mind, and that the doctor says your sickness is due to this. If you care for me, rouse your dormant love of literary work and the things of the spirit, which makes you very dear to me. Now you need health of mind to recover health of body, and I ask you to gain it for my sake as well as your own. Keep Acastus, so that you are better looked after. Preserve yourself for me. My promise[190] is almost due now. If you come, I will even settle up right away.

Again, goodbye.

11, noon.

42 (XVI. 15)

CICERO TO TIRO

Cumae, 12 April 53

From Tullius to Tiro greetings.

Aegypta arrived today, 12 April. He told me that you are quite free of fever and in pretty good shape, but said you had not been able to write to me. That made me anxious, all the more so because Hermia, who ought also to have arrived today, has not come. You cannot imagine how anxious I feel about your health. If you relieve my mind on this score, I shall relieve yours of every worry. I should write more if I thought you could read with any pleasure at the present time. Put your clever brain, which I value so highly, to the job of preserving yourself for us both. Look after yourself carefully, I repeat.

Goodbye.

P.S. Hermia has arrived and I have received your letter, shakily written, poor fellow – no wonder, when you are so seriously ill. I have sent you Aegypta to be with you. He is not

190. To give Tiro his freedom.

uncivilized and I think he is fond of you. Also a cook for your use.

Goodbye.

43 (XVI. 10)

CICERO TO TIRO

Cumae, 17 April 53

From Tullius to Tiro greetings.

Indeed I want you to join me, but I am afraid of the journey. You have been very seriously ill, you are worn out, what with lack of food and purges and the disease itself. Serious illnesses often have serious repercussions, if there is any imprudence. And then, right on top of the two days you will have on the road travelling to Cumae, there will be five days for the return journey. I want to be at Formiae on the 28th. Let me find you there, my dear Tiro, well and strong.

My (or *our*) literary brain-children have been drooping their heads missing you, but they looked up a little at the letter which Acastus brought. Pompey is staying with me as I write, enjoying himself in cheerful mood. He wanted to hear my compositions, but I told him that in your absence my tongue of authorship is tied completely. You must get ready to restore your services to my Muses. My promise will be performed on the appointed day (I have taught you the derivation of 'faith').[191] Now mind you get thoroughly well. I shall be with you soon.

Goodbye.

17th.

191. *fides*, supposed to be derived from *fit* ('is done').

44 (XVI. 16)

Q. CICERO TO M. CICERO

Transalpine Gaul, May (end) or June (beginning) 53

From Quintus to his brother Marcus greetings.

My dear Marcus, as I hope to see you again and my boy and my[192] Tulliola and your son, I am truly grateful at what you have done about Tiro, in judging his former condition to be below his deserts and preferring us to have him as a friend rather than a slave. Believe me, I jumped for joy when I read your letter and his. Thank you, and congratulations!

If Statius' loyalty gives me so much pleasure,[193] how highly you must value the same qualities in Tiro, with the addition of literary accomplishments and conversation and culture, gifts worth even more than they! I have all manner of great reasons to love you, but this is a reason – the very fact that you so properly announced the event to me is a reason. I saw all that is you in your letter.

I have promised Sabinus'[194] boys all assistance, and shall be as good as my word.

192. Perhaps a mistake for 'your'.

193. Quintus will not have forgotten his brother's annoyance when Statius was freed; cf. *Letters to Atticus* 38 (II.18).4, 39 (II.19).1.

194. Sabinus is very likely Titurius Sabinus, one of Caesar's Legates who had lost his life and his army in the revolt of the Eburones. 'Boys' could mean either 'children' or 'slaves'.

45 (II. I)

CICERO TO CURIO[195]

Rome, 53 (first half)

From M. Cicero to Curio greetings.

I am sorry to be under suspicion of neglecting a friendly duty, but I am not so much put out by your accusation as I am pleased by your exigency – especially as I am innocent of the offence alleged against me, whereas when you show that you miss my letters, you demonstrate your affection for me. I am well aware of it to be sure, but it is delightful and gratifying to me none the less. Now *I* have let nobody set out without a letter whom I thought likely to reach you. After all, I can challenge all comers as an active correspondent. From *you*, on the other hand, I have heard only two or three times at most, and very short letters at that. So if you are a stern judge to me, I shall convict you on the same charge. Unless you want that to happen, you should take a lenient view of my case.

But there's enough about letters; I don't doubt I can give you your fill of them, especially if you are going to appreciate my efforts in that direction. I have been sorry that you have been so long away from us, because I have missed your most delectable company; but at the same time I am glad, because in your absence you have attained all your objectives with the greatest *éclat* and because in all your affairs fortune has seconded my prayers. One short admonition, which my transcendent affection for you compels me to offer: your spirit and talents are so eagerly expected that I don't scruple to beg and adjure you to shape yourself, before you come back to us, into one capable of matching and living up to the expectation you have

195. In 53 the younger Curio was serving as Proquaestor under the governor of the province of Asia, C. Claudius Pulcher.

aroused. No forgetfulness will ever wipe out the memory of your services[196] to me, and so I ask you to remember, whatever further success and honour may come your way, that you would never have attained them, if in the days of your boyhood you had not listened to my sincere and affectionate advice. So your feelings towards me should be such that my declining years may rest happily upon your affection and your youth.

46 (II. 2)

CICERO TO CURIO

Rome, 53 (first half)

From M. Cicero to C. Curio greetings.

I have lost a weighty witness to the great affection I bear you in your illustrious father;[197] with his own fine record and with you for a son, he would have been the most fortunate of men had it been granted him to see you before he passed away. However, I hope our friendship needs no testimony. May the Gods prosper you in your inheritance! In me you may be sure of having one to whom you are as dear and as delightful as you were to your father.

196. Rendered no doubt during Cicero's exile; cf. p. 113.
197. Curio the Elder, Consul in 76. Cicero's relations with him had been chequered and never warmly friendly.

47 (II. 3)

CICERO TO CURIO

Rome, 53 (first half)

From M. Cicero to C. Curio greetings.

Rupa[198] was ready and willing to announce a show in your name, but I and all your friends thought that no step should be taken in your absence by which you would be committed on your return. I shall write to you later at greater length to give my views, or else, since you might then think of arguments to counter them, I shall take you unprepared and advance my opinion against yours face to face. In that way, if I do not convert you, I shall at least leave my sentiments on record in your mind; so that if the time comes (as I hope it never will) when you begin to repent your own counsel, you may remember mine. All the same, to put it in a few words, do realize that you are returning at a juncture in which your gifts of nature, application, and fortune will count for more in winning you the highest political prizes than will shows. Nobody admires the capacity to give shows, which is a matter of means, not personal qualities; and everybody is sick and tired of them.[199]

But I am doing what I said I was not going to do, starting to explain my reasons. So I defer the whole argument till your return. Be sure that the highest anticipations have been formed – all is expected of you that may be expected of the highest qualities and talents. If you are prepared to meet those hopes worthily, and I am confident you are, you will give us, your

198. An agent (not necessarily freedman) of Curio's. When an eminent man died his son(s) sometimes gave a show in his honour.

199. Curio did not take this advice, but gave a show of memorable splendour.

friends, and all your countrymen, and your country, the greatest of shows[200] – and many of them. One thing you will surely find, that no one is dearer or more delightful to me than yourself.

48 (II. 4)

CICERO TO CURIO

Rome, 54 (middle)

From Cicero to C. Curio greetings.

That there are many different categories of letters you are aware. But the most authentic, the purpose in fact for which letter-writing was invented, is to inform the absent of what it is desirable for them to know, whether in our interest or their own. Letters of this kind I suppose you do not expect from me, since you have your domestic correspondents and messengers to tell you about your affairs, and there is nothing very new to report about mine. That leaves two categories which give me great pleasure; one familiar and jocular, the other serious and grave. Which would be the less fitting for me to use I don't know. How can I joke with you in these times, when upon my word I don't think a Roman who can laugh deserves the name? As for something in more serious vein, what is there for Cicero to write seriously about to Curio except public affairs? But on that subject my predicament is that I dare not write what I think and do not care to write what I don't think.

Well then, having no topic left, I shall resort to my usual conclusion and urge you to strive for glory. You have a formidable adversary ready and waiting – public expectation, which is really amazingly high. This you will easily overcome, but in one way only, and that is by determining to work hard at

200. The Latin word for 'show' also means 'gift'.

those pursuits which bring the kind of credit you have set your heart on. I should write more in this strain, if I were not sure that you are your own sufficient spur. Even this little I have said, not to kindle *your* enthusiasm, but to demonstrate *my* affection.

49 (II. 5)

CICERO TO CURIO

Rome, 53 (middle)

From Cicero to C. Curio greetings.

The state of things here I dare not tell even to you in a letter. As I wrote once before, wherever you are, you are in the same boat; but all the same I congratulate you on your absence. On the one hand, you do not see what we are seeing; on the other, you are in a place where your merit shines high before the eyes of a multitude, Roman citizens and natives. The report of it comes to us, not by doubtful and various gossip, but in a single loud, concerted voice.

On one point I hardly know whether to congratulate you or to take alarm – the extraordinary eagerness with which your return is awaited. It is not that I doubt your capacity to live up to public expectation, but I am seriously afraid that when you do come home, you may no longer have anything to work for. Such is the decay, almost to extinction, of all our institutions. But perhaps even such remarks as this ought not to be entrusted to a letter, so I leave others to tell you the rest. But whether you see any ray of hope for the commonwealth or none, you must prepare and train and plan as befits a man and a Roman whose mission it is in sad times and evil manners to raise his country from the depth of affliction to her ancient dignity and freedom.

50 (II. 6)

CICERO TO CURIO

Rome, July (?) 53

From M. Cicero to C. Curio greetings.

As I dispatch this letter by the hand of my dear Milo's friend, Sex. Villius,[201] no news has yet come in of your approaching Italy. But your arrival is thought not to be far off, and reports agree that you have set out from Asia on your way to Rome. So, considering the importance of the matter in hand, I feel no scruples on the score of undue haste, for I am very anxious that you should get this letter at the earliest possible moment.

If obligations between us were all on your side, and my services to you had been such as you are apt to proclaim them rather than as I myself appraise them, I should approach you with some diffidence when the time came for me to ask an important favour. It is not easy for a man of sensibility to ask a great deal of someone who he thinks has reason to be grateful to him. He will be afraid of presenting the appearance of a creditor demanding payment rather than of a petitioner seeking a kindness. But in fact your benefactions to me are great and notorious, rendered the more conspicuous by the strange turns of fortune through which I have passed. And it is the mark of a liberal spirit to wish to owe more where one already owes much. Therefore I do not hesitate to write to you with a request of the highest consequence, one that lies very near to my heart. After all, I am not afraid of succumbing under the load of your good offices, past number though they may be. Whatever

201. His full name seems to have been Sex. Villius Annalis and he can be identified with the Villius mentioned by Horace (*Sat.* 1.2.64) as a lover of Milo's wife Fausta.

favour you may confer upon me, I feel confident that my mind has the capacity to accept it and the power to make a generous return, such as will add lustre to your gift.

Well then, I have firmly concentrated all my efforts, all my time, care, diligence, and thought, my whole mind in short, on winning the Consulship for Milo. In so doing, as I see it, I have to look not only for the reward of friendly service but for the credit of gratitude displayed to a benefactor. I do not believe any man's life and fortune ever meant as much to himself as Milo's success means to me. On this, I have decided, everything for me now depends. It is evident to me that your single self, if you will, can lend such effectual assistance to our campaign that we shall need nothing else. We have so much on our side – the good-will of the honest men, acquired from his Tribunate through his championship of my cause, as I expect you appreciate; that of the common people, through the magnificence of his shows and the generosity of his nature; that of the younger generation and the electorally influential, through his own outstanding influence and activity in that sphere; and my own interest on his behalf, which may not be powerful, but is at any rate approved and right and due, and therefore perhaps not without some influence. What we need is a leader and a counsellor, one to govern and harness, as it were, the favourable currents of which I have spoken; and if we could choose from all the world, we should find no one comparable to you.

You may judge from the very depth of my concern on Milo's behalf whether I am a man who does not forget, a man of gratitude and honour. If so, if in short you consider me worthy of your kindness, then I appeal to you to come to my help at this anxious time, and to dedicate your efforts to a cause in which my credit, indeed I might more properly say my virtual existence, is involved. As for T. Annius[202] himself, I promise you that if you will take him to your heart you will

202. Milo's full name was T. Annius Milo or T. Annius Milo Papianus.

have no bolder, steadier, more resolute, or more sincere friend. As for me, you will add lustre and prestige to my name; and I shall readily recognize the same concern for my credit as you once showed for my existence as a citizen.

I should continue further, if I did not know how well you see my mind as I write this letter, that you realize what a load of obligation I carry and how in this candidature of Milo's I must needs labour and strive, and even fight, my hardest. Knowing that, I put the whole matter in your hands; Milo's cause and I myself are all yours to do with as you will. Only understand that, if you do as I ask, I shall owe you more almost than I owe Milo himself; for my restoration, in which he was my chief helper, meant less to me than the satisfaction I shall take in repaying a sacred debt of gratitude. That I am sure your single support will enable me to attain.

51 (V. 18)

CICERO TO T. FADIUS

Rome (?), 52 (after end of March)

From M. Cicero to T. Fadius greetings.

I, your would-be comforter, stand in need of comfort myself; for nothing this long while past has distressed me so deeply as your mishap.[203] However, I not only urge but earnestly beg and entreat you in the name of our mutual affection to take a firm hold of yourself and play the man. Remember the lot of mankind in general and the times in which *we* have been born. Your merit has given you more than fortune has taken from you. Few self-made men have attained what you have attained, whereas many of the highest birth

203. Fadius had been found guilty on a bribery charge, probably in connection with his election to the Praetorship.

have lost what you have lost. Moreover, the future of our laws, law courts, and political conditions in general is likely to be such that whoever makes his exit from this commonwealth under the lightest penalty may be accounted highly fortunate. *You* have your property and your children. You also have me and others closely attached to you in friendship and good-will. You will have ample opportunity to spend your time with me and all those dear to you. Yours is the only trial out of so many in which the verdict is criticized, as depending on a single dubious vote[204] and given, it is thought, to please a powerful personage.[205] For all these reasons you should take this trouble as easily as may be. My disposition towards you and your children will ever remain what you wish and what is right and proper.

52 (VII. 2)

CICERO TO M. MARIUS

Rome, January (?) 51

From M. Cicero to M. Marius greetings.

I shall execute your commission[206] with care. But shrewd business man that you are, you have selected the very person whose interest it is that the article should sell for as high a price as possible! Very wise of you, though, to set a limit on what I am to pay! Now if you had left me a free hand, my regard for you being what it is, I should have come to an arrangement with my co-heirs. As matters stand, now that I know your

204. Or possibly 'wavering'. The circumstances of Fadius' conviction are known only from this letter.

205. Presumably Pompey.

206. Marius had asked Cicero to buy on his account something (perhaps an article of *virtu*) at the auction of an estate to which Cicero was one of the heirs.

price, I'll put up a dummy bidder rather than see the thing go for less! But joking apart, I'll do your business with all proper care.

I am sure you are pleased about Bursa,[207] but you need not have been so diffident in your congratulations. You say you suppose I don't rate the triumph very high, because he's such a low creature. Well, I ask you to believe that this trial gave me more satisfaction than the death of my enemy.[208] To begin with, I prefer to get my revenge in a court of law than at sword-point. Secondly, I prefer my friend to come out of it with credit than with ruin.[209] I was especially pleased at the display of good-will towards me on the part of the honest men in the face of an astonishing amount of pressure from a very grand and powerful personage.[210] Lastly, and this may seem hard to credit, I detested this fellow far more than Clodius himself. I had been Clodius' adversary, whereas I had defended the other in court.[211] Clodius had a great object in view – he knew that the entire state would be jeopardized in my person; and he acted, not all on his own, but with the assistance of those whose power depended on my downfall.[212] Whereas this little ape selected me for attack just because he felt like it, giving certain ill-wishers of mine to understand that he was ready to be set on me at any time. Therefore I tell you to rejoice and be glad. It is a great victory. No braver Romans ever lived than those jury-men who dared to find him guilty in spite of all the power of the very personage who had empanelled them. They would

207. i.e. his condemnation on a charge of violence brought by Cicero himself (whose role as prosecutor in this case was for him most unusual).

208. Clodius, of whom Bursa had been a leading supporter. He was killed by Milo on 18 January 52.

209. Apparently the meaning is that Milo, who was in banishment for Clodius' murder, had been vindicated by Bursa's conviction.

210. Pompey.

211. Nothing more is known about this.

212. The 'Triumvirs'. It suits Cicero's argument here to ignore Clodius' personal reasons for attacking him in 58.

never have done that if they had not felt my grievance as their own.

What with the multitude of *causes célèbres* and the new legislation I am kept so busy here that I offer up a prayer against intercalation every day, so that I may be able to see you as soon as possible.

53 (XIII. 42)

CICERO TO CULLEOLUS

Rome (?), 61 or 60

From M. Cicero to L. Culleolus, Proconsul, greetings.

My friend L. Lucceius, who is the last man in the world to fail in appreciation of a kindness, has expressed to me the most profuse gratitude to yourself for your most handsome and liberal promises to his agents. Since your words have so deeply obliged him, you can imagine how beholden he will feel when you have actually performed what you have promised, as I look forward to your doing. To be sure the people of Byllis have expressed their readiness to meet Lucceius' claims at Pompey's discretion. But we urgently need your good-will, influence, and official authority in addition. Let me again request of you that they be forthcoming. I am particularly gratified that Lucceius' agents are aware, and Lucceius himself has gathered from the letter you sent him, that no man's word and influence counts for more with you than mine. Allow me to beg you yet again to let him find by experience that this is really so.

54 (XIII. 41)

CICERO TO CULLEOLUS

Rome (?), 61 or 60

Cicero to Culleolus greetings.

I want you to feel thoroughly assured that in doing what you have for L. Lucceius you have accommodated one who never forgets a favour. He is very much beholden to you for it, and Pompey expresses his gratitude in the warmest terms whenever we meet, as we often do. I will add what I feel sure will be highly agreeable to you, that I have personally been deeply gratified by your kindness to Lucceius. As for the future, I have no doubt that you will continue in your generosity, your earlier concern for our sakes being now supported by regard for your own consistency. However, let me again entreat you to be so good as to add at the conclusion some enhancing, crowning touches to your original promise and subsequent performance. You have my solemn guarantee that both Lucceius and Pompey will be deeply obliged and that your favour will be excellently placed.

I wrote to you a few days ago at some length about the political situation and about what is afoot here and my thoughts thereupon. I gave the letter to your boys.

Goodbye.

55 (XIII. 60)

CICERO TO C. MUNATIUS[213]

Rome (?), after 57

From Cicero to C. Munatius, son of Gaius, greetings.

213. Nothing known.

L. Livincius Trypho is to be sure a freedman of my close
friend L. Regulus, whose misfortune[214] has made me even more
anxious to serve him – *feel* more kindly than I always did I
cannot. But I am fond of his freedman for his own sake. He
rendered me great service at that crisis of my life in which it was
easiest for me to discern the good-will and loyalty of my
fellows.[215] I recommend him to you as men who gratefully
remember what is done for them ought to recommend their
benefactors. You will oblige me greatly if Trypho finds that,
when he exposed himself to many dangers in the cause of my
restoration (frequently taking ship in the depth of winter), he
earned *your* gratitude as well as mine in virtue of your kindly
disposition towards me.

56 (I. 3)

CICERO TO LENTULUS SPINTHER

Rome, January (?) 56

From M. Cicero to P. Lentulus, Proconsul, greetings.

For many years I have been on friendly terms with A.
Trebonius,[216] who has important business concerns, both
extensive and in good order, in your province.[217] In the past he
has always been very well regarded in the province on account
of his personal distinction and of recommendations from
myself and his other friends; and he now trusts that this letter
from me will put him in your good graces in view of your
affection for me and the close relations between us. May I

214. Exile.
215. Cf. *Letters to Atticus* 62 (III.17).1.
216. Distinguish from Caesar's assassin, C. Trebonius.
217. Cilicia.

earnestly request you not to disappoint him, and commend to you all his business affairs, his freedmen, agents, and household? May I ask you in particular to confirm T. Ampius'[218] decisions with respect to his property, and to treat him in all matters in such a way as to let him understand that my recommendation has been more than formal?

57 (XIII. 6)

CICERO TO VALERIUS ORCA[219]

Rome (?), late 56 or 55

From M. Cicero to Q. Valerius Orca, son of Quintus, Proconsul, greetings.

I trust you are well, as I am.

I expect you have not forgotten that I spoke to you in P. Cuspius' presence when I accompanied you as you were leaving Rome for your province, and likewise that I subsequently asked you at considerable length to regard any friends of his whom I recommended to you as friends of mine. With the great friendship and courtesy you always show me, you gave me your promise in the kindest and most handsome fashion.

Cuspius, who makes a point of serving all his friends, takes a remarkably close and benevolent interest in certain individuals from your province – the reason being that he was twice in Africa in charge of important company business. It is my habit to second his friendly endeavours on their behalf with such means and influence as I can command. I have therefore deemed it proper in this letter to set before you the general position as regards my recommendation of Cuspius' people. In

218. Lentulus' predecessor.
219. Governor of the province of Africa.

future letters I shall simply affix the symbol on which you and I agreed, along with an intimation that the person concerned is one of Cuspius' friends.

Let me, however, assure you that the recommendation which I desire to put on record in this letter is of the most serious character. P. Cuspius has been extraordinarily urgent to have me give L. Julius[220] a most particular recommendation to you. He is so earnest in the matter that I hardly think it will be enough for me to use the phrases which we normally employ when we are making a very pressing request. He demands novelties, and supposes me to possess a special skill in this *genre*. I have promised him to produce from the secret stores of my art something quite amazing in the way of a recommendation. As I am unable to keep my word, I hope that *you* will use practical means to make him think that the style of my letter has worked wonders. To effect this you have only to bring out for the occasion all the manifold generosity that it lies within your good nature and your present power to provide, not only in a practical way but in words and even in looks. How much these things can do in a province I can guess, though unfortunately without experience.[221]

That the person whom I am recommending is very worthy to be your friend I believe not only because Cuspius tells me so, though that ought to be enough, but because I know his good judgement in choosing men and friends.

I shall soon be assessing the efficacy of this letter and, I feel sure, expressing my thanks to you. On my side I shall zealously and conscientiously attend to whatever I suppose to be relevant to your wishes and interests.

Take care of your health.

220. Perhaps L. Julius Calidus, a friend of Atticus and in his day a celebrated poet.
221. At this time Cicero's experience of provincial government was confined to the subordinate office of Quaestor, which he had held in Sicily in 75.

58 (XIII. 6 a)

CICERO TO VALERIUS ORCA

Rome (?), some time after the preceding

From M. Cicero to Q. Valerius, son of Quintus, Proconsul, greetings.

P. Cornelius, the bearer of this letter, has been recommended to me by P. Cuspius. Doubtless you have readily gathered from what I have told you how anxious I am, and ought to be, to serve Cuspius. Let me particularly ask you to ensure that as a result of this recommendation he thanks me as warmly, as soon, and as often as circumstances admit.

Goodbye.

59 (XIII. 40)

CICERO TO Q. ANCHARIUS[222]

Rome (?), 55 (late) or 54

From M. Cicero to Q. Ancharius, son of Quintus, Proconsul, greetings.

Let me warmly recommend to you L. and C. Aurelius, sons of Lucius, with whom and with that very worthy gentleman their father I am on the most familiar terms. They are highly accomplished young men, very close to me, and thoroughly deserving of your friendship. If any recommendation of mine has carried weight with you (and I know that many have carried a great deal), please accord it to this. If you deal with them in

222. L. Piso's successor as governor of Macedonia.

handsome and complimentary style, you will attach two excellent and most appreciative young men to yourself and greatly oblige me.

60 (XIII. 75)

CICERO TO T. TITIUS

Rome (?), 52 (end) or 51 (beginning)

From M. Cicero to T. Titius, son of Titus, Legate,[223] greetings.

Although I do not doubt that my original recommendation carries sufficient weight with you, I am none the less complying with the request of my very good friend C. Avianius Flaccus, whose well-wisher in all things I not only am but assuredly ought to be. I spoke of him to you in person at some length, and you answered me in the kindest way; also I have already written to you about him in detail. However, he thinks it is to his advantage that I should write to you as often as I can. So please forgive me if, in deferring to his wishes, I may seem less mindful than I should be of your dependability.

My request is the same as ever. I want you to accommodate Avianius with regard to his shipments of grain, both as to place and time of disembarcation. In both respects his wishes were met, likewise at my intercession, for the three years during which Pompey presided over the business.[224] The long and short of it is that you have the opportunity to oblige me greatly, if you will let Avianius, since he thinks that I am his good friend, know that you are mine. That will oblige me very much indeed.

223. Evidently serving in a grain-exporting province, probably Sicily, and perhaps identical with the recipient of Letter 187 (v.16).

224. Pompey's five-year term as High Commissioner for grain supplies expired in the autumn of 52. The concessions to Avianius appear to have come into operation in 55.

61 (XIII. 51)

CICERO TO P. CAESIUS[225]

Date uncertain

From Cicero to P. Caesius greetings.

May I most particularly recommend to you a Roman Knight, a man of quality in every sense of the word, and a very good friend of mine, P. Messienus, and request you in the name of my friendship with yourself and your father to take him under your patronage and protect his interests and reputation? You will attach to yourself an honourable man, worthy to be your friend, and you will greatly oblige me.

62 (XIII. 76)

CICERO TO THE MAGISTRATES AND TOWN COUNCIL OF FABRATERIA VETUS (?)

Date uncertain

From M. Cicero to the Board of Four and Councillors greetings.

I am attached to Q. Hippius by so many bonds that no relationship could be closer than ours. Otherwise I should not be departing from my practice of never troubling your worships. You yourselves can best testify that, although persuaded of your readiness to grant any request I might make, I have never cared to impose upon you. Therefore let me beg

225. Nothing is known about him or Messienus. There may be a connection with the Caesii of Arpinum (see Glossary of Persons).

of you most earnestly, as a compliment to myself, to give C. Valgius Hippianus the handsomest of treatment, and to come to a settlement with him so that he can hold his property purchased from your corporation in the district of Fregellae[226] free of all dues and charges. If you grant me this request, I shall feel myself beholden to your worships for a most important favour.

63 (XIII. I)

CICERO TO C. MEMMIUS

Athens, June (end) or July (beginning) 51

From M. Cicero to C. Memmius greetings.

I was not quite sure whether it would have been in a way distressing to me to see you in Athens[227] or a pleasure. I should have felt pain in the injustice[228] of which you are the victim, but happiness in the philosophy with which you bear it. However, I would rather I *had* seen you. The measure of distress is not very much diminished when you are out of my sight, and, had I seen you, the pleasure I might have had would assuredly have been greater. So I shall not hesitate to try to see you as soon as I can fairly conveniently do so. In the mean-

226. The town of Fregellae, not far from Arpinum, was destroyed after its revolt in 125 and Fabrateria Nova founded in its place. But the latter was governed by two magistrates (*duoviri*). This letter may therefore have been addressed to the governing body of the old town, Fabrateria Vetus, which had four magistrates and may have been granted some of the Fregellane territory.

227. On his way to his province of Cilicia in 51 Cicero stopped in Athens from 24 June to 6 July. With this letter cf. *Letters to Atticus* 104 (V.11).6.

228. Condemnation for electoral bribery in 52.

while, allow me to raise with you now a matter which can be raised, and I imagine, settled, in correspondence. And first I would ask you not to do anything on my account which you would rather not. I hope you will grant me a favour which, as you will see, matters a good deal to me and not at all to you, but only if you are satisfied beforehand that you will do it gladly.

I have all manner of ties with Patro the Epicurean, except that in philosophy I strongly disagree with him. But in the early days in Rome I was one of those whose acquaintance he particularly cultivated (that was when he was also paying attentions to you and all connected with you). Recently too he gained all he wanted in the way of personal advantages and honoraria with myself as pretty well the chief among his protectors and friends. He was originally recommended to my care and regard by Phaedrus, of whom as a philosopher I had a great opinion when I was a boy, before I knew Philo, and whom ever afterwards I respected as a man, honourable, amiable, and obliging.

Well, Patro wrote to me in Rome, asking me to make his peace with you and to beg you to let him have those ruins (or whatever they are) of Epicurus' house. I did not write to you, not wanting your building plans to be interfered with by a vicarious request of mine. When I arrived in Athens he again asked me to write to you to the same effect. This time I consented, because all your friends were agreed that you had given up your building. If that is so, and your interests are now quite unaffected, I hope you will take a lenient view of any little vexation which the untowardness of certain people may have caused you (I know the breed!), out of the great goodness of your heart or even by way of compliment to me. For my part, if you wish to know my personal sentiments, I don't see why he should make such a point of it nor why you should object – except that, after all, it is much less allowable in *you* to make a fuss about nothing than in him. However, I am sure you know

Patro's case and how he puts it. He pleads that he owes a responsibility to his office and duty, to the sanctity of testaments, to the prestige of Epicurus' name, to Phaedrus' adjuration, to the abode, domicile, and memorials of great men. If we wish to find fault with his insistence in this matter, we are at liberty to deride his whole life and philosophical principles. But really, since we have no deadly enmity towards him and others who find these doctrines to their taste, perhaps we ought not to be hard on him for taking it so much to heart. Even if he is wrong, it is silliness rather than wickedness that is leading him astray.

However, to make an end (I must come to it some time), I love Pomponius Atticus like a second brother. Nothing is more precious and delightful to me than to have him as a friend. Nobody is less of a busybody, less inclined to importune, but I have never known him request anything of me so pressingly as this – not that he is one of the sect,[229] for he is a person of the most comprehensive and refined culture,[230] but he has a great regard for Patro, and had a deep affection for Phaedrus. He is confident that I should only have to signify a wish for you to grant the point, even if you intended to build. But now, if he hears that you have put aside your building project and that I have still not obtained the favour, he is going to think, not that you have been disobliging to me, but that I have not troubled to oblige *him*. May I therefore ask you to write to your people and tell them that the relevant decree of the Areopagus[231] (*hypomnematismos* as they call it) may be rescinded with your blessing?

However, I go back to where I started. Before you decide to comply with my request I want you to be satisfied that you will

229. A notable statement. Atticus' Epicurean leanings were not taken very seriously by those who knew him.

230. The Epicureans by their own profession were not, and Cicero often jeers at their supposed ignorance and stupidity.

231. The ancient Athenian court and council.

do so gladly for my sake. None the less, you may be sure that I shall be extremely grateful if you do what I ask.

Goodbye.

64 (III. 1)

CICERO TO APPIUS PULCHER

Rome, 53 (end) or 52 (beginning)

From Cicero to Appius, Imperator,[232] greetings.

If our country could tell you for herself how she does, you would find her no better a source of information than your freedman Phanias. He is so sensible and, what is more, so inquisitive, in a good sense of the word. So he will make all plain to you. That will help me to be brief, and will be wiser from other standpoints. As to my good-will towards you, there too Phanias can be your informant, but I think that I also have a word to say. Please assure yourself that you are very dear to me. Your natural gifts, your obliging and kindly disposition, attract me in many ways; furthermore, from what you write and others say, I know that you are very appreciative of anything I have been able to do for you. Since that is so, I must evidently contrive to make up for what has been sacrificed in the long period of suspension of our intercourse by the acceptability, the frequency, and the magnitude of the services I render you; and since you so wish, I flatter myself that I shall succeed – by grace of Minerva.[233] If by any chance I

232. As governor of Cilicia Appius had concluded a successful campaign.

233. More literally 'with Minerva's good-will' (*non invita Minerva*), i.e. 'not against the grain'. Minerva (Athene) represents intellect and natural aptitude. But Cicero uses the expression here for the sake of the following allusion to a statue of the goddess which he was apparently hoping to acquire from Appius (a famous art-collector). Cf. Letter 373 (XII.25).1.

obtain the Goddess from your collection,[234] I shall style her not Polias only, but Appias.[235]

I was not previously very well acquainted with your freed-man Cilix, but after handing me your affectionate and friendly letter, he followed up its kind expressions with words of his own to quite remarkable effect. I enjoyed listening to his account of your disposition towards me and of what you say about me from day to day. In fact within a couple of days he has become my friend – but not so much so that I shall not miss Phanias sorely. When you send him back to Rome, as I imagine you will shortly be doing, please give him your commissions on all matters on which you would like action or attention from me.

Allow me to recommend to you warmly Counsellor L. Valerius,[236] but with the proviso that the quality of his counsel is not guaranteed – I want to make a better caveat[237] for him than he generally drafts for his clients. I have a strong regard for him; he is one of my inner circle of familiar friends. He expressed gratitude to you, it is true, but he also writes that a letter from me will carry great weight with you. May I par-ticularly request that he be not disappointed therein?

Goodbye.

234. Or 'your people'.
235. 'Polias' ('of the city') and 'Poliouchos' ('guarding the city') were cult-titles of Athene; *Minerva custos urbis* is the Latin equivalent. The statue, whether or not the one dedicated by Cicero in the Capitol on the eve of his exile (see Volume Two, n. 930), represented the god-dess in this guise (the vulgate 'Pallas' here is not supported by our only valid manuscript). 'Appias' is, of course, a title invented by Cicero on the spur of the moment to make a pleasantry.
236. See Letter 21 (I.10).
237. See n. 149.

65 (III. 2)

CICERO TO APPIUS PULCHER

Neighbourhood of Rome, February or March 51

From M. Cicero, Proconsul, to Appius Pulcher, Imperator, greetings.

Contrary to my own inclination and quite unexpectedly[238] I find myself under the necessity of setting out to govern a province. My only consolation in a multitude of various annoyances and preoccupations lies in the reflection that you could not have a more friendly successor than me, and that I could not take over the province from anyone more anxious to consign it to me in as orderly and unembarrassed a state as possible. If you on your side expect the same of my disposition towards yourself, you may be sure you will never be disappointed. Let me particularly pray and request you, bearing in mind the close bond between us and your characteristic consideration for others, to watch and provide for my interests in every way you can – and there will be many ways.

You see that I am obliged under a senatorial decree to take the province. If you hand it over to me free from all embarrassments, so far as you find that possible, I shall run my lap (so to speak) of tenure the more easily. It is for you to decide what you can do in this way, but you have my urgent request to take any steps which may occur to you as helpful.

238. A law passed during Pompey's third Consulship (52) enjoined a five-year interval between the holding of a Consulship or Praetorship and the consequent governorship of a province. To fill the resulting gap the Senate called upon former Consuls and Praetors who had not previously held provincial command, of whom Cicero was one. Cilicia was assigned to him for a term of one year. His reluctance seems to have been entirely sincere.

I will not use more words. Your kindness will not expect a lengthy discourse, our friendship does not permit it; nor does the case call for words, it speaks for itself. I should only like you to feel assured that, if I find you have been thoughtful for what concerns me, my gratitude will bring you deep and lasting satisfaction.

Goodbye.

66 (III. 3)

CICERO TO APPIUS PULCHER

Brundisium, shortly after 22 May 51

From Cicero to Appius Pulcher greetings.

On my arrival at Brundisium on 22 May your Legate Q. Fabius Vergilianus was there to meet me. He conveyed to me your admonition to the effect that a larger military force is needed for the defence of this province. The considerations you raise had occurred not only to me, whom they especially concern, but to the whole Senate, which declared almost without exception in favour of a levy in Italy to reinforce my troops and those of Bibulus.[239] However, Consul Sulpicius said he would not allow it. I protested at length, but in face of the Senate's unanimous desire for me to leave without delay I had no choice but to comply, as I have done.

Let me now repeat the request I made in the letter which I gave your couriers in Rome. I hope you will do whatever can be done by an outgoing governor to ease matters for a successor to whom he is bound by close ties of friendship. Bearing in mind the perfect harmony of sentiment which exists between us, employ your care and diligence in this regard, so that all may understand that I could have had no more benevolent

239. Consul in 59, now appointed governor of Syria.

predecessor and that you could not have handed over your province to a better friend.

I understood from the dispatch which you desired to be read aloud in the Senate, of which you sent me a copy, that you had given large numbers of soldiers their discharge. Fabius, however, has explained that you had proposed to do this, but that at the time he left you numbers were still up to complement. If that is so, I shall be very grateful if you make the minimum of reductions in the meagre forces under your command. I think the decrees passed by the Senate on this subject have been sent to you. For my part, my regard for you is such that whatever you do will have my approval, but I feel sure that you on your side will take such measures as you see to be most convenient for me.

I am waiting for my Legate C. Pomptinus at Brundisium, and expect him to arrive before the beginning of June. When he does, we shall sail at the first opportunity.

67 (III. 4)

CICERO TO APPIUS PULCHER

Brundisium, 4 (?) June 51

From Cicero to Appius Pulcher, greetings.

On 4 June I received a letter from you at Brundisium in which you write that you have commissioned L. Clodius[240] to discuss certain matters with me. I am eagerly expecting him, so as to learn as soon as possible what word he brings from you. You have, I hope, already had evidence in plenty of my good-will and desire to serve you, but I shall demonstrate it most conspicuously where I can most clearly show how precious to me are your good name and dignity. Your warm regard for myself

240. Appius' 'Prefect of Engineers' (see Glossary of Terms).

had been made plain to me by Q. Fabius Vergilianus, by C. Flaccus, son of Lucius, and especially by M. Octavius, son of Gnaeus.[241] I had previously deduced it from many indications, above all the charming gift of your volume on Augury[242] with its affectionate dedication to me.

All that I can do for you to the uttermost limits of friendly service shall be done. My esteem for you has increased from day to day ever since you began to have a regard for me. To that has accrued my associations with connections of yours, for two of whom, belonging to different generations, I have the greatest esteem, namely Cn. Pompeius, your daughter's father-in-law, and your son-in-law, M. Brutus; further our association in the same College, especially now that you have approved it in so flattering a fashion, has in my eyes added a tie of no small importance to the linking of our sentiments.

Well, when I have met Clodius, I shall write to you further in the light of what he has to say, and I shall do my best to see you as soon as possible. Your statement that you are staying on in order to meet me gives me pleasure, I won't deny it.

68 (III. 5)

CICERO TO APPIUS PULCHER

Tralles, 27 or 28 July 51

From Cicero to Appius Pulcher greetings.

I arrived at Tralles on 27 July. There to meet me was L. Lucilius with your letter and messages. You could not have sent me any friendlier or, as I suppose, better qualified or more

241. The first two certainly, and the third presumably, were on Appius' staff.

242. Cicero had been elected to the College of Augurs, of which Appius was a member, in 53.

sensible informant to tell me what I want to know. I was glad to read your letter, and I have listened carefully to Lucilius. Well, since you feel as you do (you write that, while the remarks in my letter about our services to one another gave you pleasure, you saw no need to go back so far into the past), and since reminders of services rendered are in truth superfluous between firm and tried friends, I shall leave that topic on one side. Nevertheless I shall thank you as I ought. From my own observation and from your letter I find that in all matters you have been studiously thoughtful of me, and that you have, as it were, predetermined and prepared everything so as to give me an easier and freer run. When I tell you that I am most grateful for this friendly behaviour on your part, it follows that I wish you to believe that I shall be, and now am, most sedulous for you yourself and all connected with you in the first place, and for the rest of the world in the second, to know how sincerely I am attached to you. Those who are still not altogether convinced on this point must, I think, be unwilling rather than unable to perceive our sentiments. But perceive them they surely will, for the persons involved are not obscure, nor are the issues trivial. But I want all this to come out better in the doing than in the saying or writing.

My itineraries seem to have raised some doubt in your mind as to whether you will be seeing me in the province. This is how the matter stands: When I spoke with your freedman Phanias at Brundisium, I told him in the course of conversation that I should be glad to go first to whatever part of the province I thought you preferred. Then he told me that you wished to leave by boat, and that it would therefore be very much to your convenience if I made my approach by sea and landed at Side. I said I would do so, and so I should have done, if our friend L. Clodius had not told me at Corcyra that this would not answer at all, and that you would be at Laodicea awaiting my arrival. That was a much shorter and more convenient route for me, especially as I supposed you preferred it. Later your plans changed. It will be easiest for you to decide what can be done now; I shall simply explain my own intentions. I expect to reach Laodicea on 31 July. I shall stay only a very few days, to collect the sum due on my Treasury draft. Then I shall proceed to join the army, so that I should expect to be in the neighbourhood of Iconium about the Ides of August. But if at such a distance from the places and circumstances I am at all out in what I write now, as soon as I start making progress I shall send you by letter, as quickly and as often as possible, full details of my dates and routes. I dare not and ought not to impose upon you, but I do think it important for both of us that we should meet before your departure, if you can conveniently manage it. If chance robs us of the opportunity, I shall still try to serve you in every way just as though I had seen you. On my own affairs I shall not send you any commissions by letter until I have given up hope of being able to discuss them with you personally.

You say you asked Scaevola[243] to take charge of the province in your absence pending my arrival. I saw him at Ephesus and he was on a familiar footing with me during the three days I spent in the city; but I heard nothing from him about any instructions from you. I certainly regret that he was unable to comply with your wish – for I do not believe him to have been unwilling.

69 (III. 6)

CICERO TO APPIUS PULCHER

Camp near Iconium, 29 August 51

From M. Cicero to Appius Pulcher greetings.

When I compare my conduct with yours, for all my desire

243. Probably another of Appius' Legates.

to give you no less credit than myself in the maintenance of our friendship, I feel much more satisfied with the former. At Brundisium I enquired of Phanias, of whose loyalty to you and place in your confidence I thought I had good evidence and knowledge, what part of the province he thought you would wish me to enter first as your successor. He replied that I could do nothing more agreeable to you than if I came by ship to Side. Although this mode of arrival was less dignified and in many ways less convenient to me, I promised so to do. Then, when I met L. Clodius in Corcyra, a person so close to you that in talking to him I felt I was talking to yourself, I told him that I should be sure to enter the province where Phanias had asked. He thanked me, but requested me emphatically to go straight to Laodicea, saying that you wanted to be on the borders of the province, so as to leave as quickly as possible; in fact, he said, if your successor were someone whom you were less desirous to see, you would have left before he arrived. That fitted in with the letter I had received in Rome, from which it seemed to me evident that you were in a hurry to leave. I replied to Clodius that I should do as he suggested, and should in fact be much better pleased than if I had had to do what I promised Phanias. Accordingly I altered my plan, and immediately dispatched a letter to you in my own hand. From your letter I see that it reached you in quite good time.

With my conduct, as described, I am well satisfied; nothing could have been more friendly. Now consider yours. Not only did you fail to be where you could see me soonest, you withdrew where I could not even follow you within thirty days, that being, I believe, the period prescribed for your departure by the lex Cornelia. Those who do not know our mutual sentiments might well regard your conduct as that of a person indifferent (to use no harsher word), avoiding his successor, whereas mine would appear that of the closest of friends. And yet before I entered the province a letter from you was delivered to me in which you held out assured hope of meeting me, although you intimated that you were leaving for Tarsus. Meanwhile malicious persons, as I believe (a widespread human failing, many have it), finding, however, a plausible theme for talk, tried to influence my mind in your disfavour, unaware how firmly it is anchored. They said you were holding assizes in Tarsus, making many decisions both administrative and judicial, although you already had reason to think that your successor had arrived – unusual procedure even when a governor expects to be superseded within a short time.

Their talk had no effect upon me. Indeed I can assure you that I considered any such action on your part as relieving me of trouble. My year of office seems all too long, and I am glad it has been reduced almost to eleven months, if a month's work has been taken off my hands in my absence. But I must candidly own that I am disturbed to find three cohorts missing from my exiguous force, and those the most nearly up to strength, and to be ignorant of their whereabouts. What vexes me most, however, is not to know where I shall see you. That is why I have been slow in writing, since I have been expecting you in person from day to day. Meanwhile I have not even had a letter to tell me what you are doing or where I am to see you. I am therefore sending to you Prefect of Reserves[244] D. Antonius, a gallant officer, one of the best I have, to take over the cohorts, if you have no objection, so that I can get something done before the season is over. Our friendship and your letter had led me to hope that I should have the benefit of your advice in that connection, nor have I given up hoping even now. But unless you write to me when and where I am to see you, I am quite unable even to make a guess.

I shall take good care to make it clear that I am your very good friend to well-wishers and ill-wishers alike. You appear to have given some handle to the latter for misconstruction of your attitude towards myself. I shall be grateful if you will put

244. *evocati*, an élite body of veterans, retained or re-enlisted after completing their service.

this straight. And to enable you to judge where you can meet me without breach of the lex Cornelia, I entered the province on 31 July, am travelling to Cilicia through Cappadocia, and am breaking camp near Iconium on 29 August. You will now decide on the basis of dates and route where and on what day you can most conveniently meet me, if you think a meeting with me is called for.

70 (III. 8)

CICERO TO APPIUS PULCHER

In camp near Mopsuhestia, 8 October 51

From Cicero to Appius Pulcher greetings.

So far as I can gather from your letter you will read this of mine after you get to Rome, when provincial tittle-tattle will have grown stale. None the less, as you have written to me at such length about what evil-minded folk have been saying, I feel I ought to reply briefly to your letter.

Its first two paragraphs, however, I must in a sense leave unanswered, since they contain nothing precise or positive, except that I am supposed to have indicated by looks and silences that I was no friend of yours, and that this was perceptible in proceedings before my Tribunal and at certain dinner-parties. That this is all nothing I can see; but since it *is* nothing, I cannot even make out what is being said. This I do know, that you might truthfully have been told of many notorious utterances of mine, both official and private, in which I praised you highly and implied the close relations between us in unmistakable terms.

As for the matter of delegates, how could I have acted with greater propriety or fairness than by reducing the outlays of penurious communes, at their own request moreover, without any derogation to your dignity? This whole matter of deputations travelling on your behalf lay outside my ken. When I was at Apamea, the leading men in a number of communes submitted to me that excessive sums were being voted for delegates, although the communes concerned were in a state of bankruptcy. I had many factors here to consider. First, I did not suppose that so intelligent and furthermore (to use the fashionable expression) so urbane a man as yourself would take any pleasure in such deputations. I made this point at considerable length from my Tribunal, at Synnada I think it was. I said that in the first place the Senate and People of Rome did not need a testimonial from the townsfolk of Midaium (the community concerned) in praise of Appius Claudius; his praises sang themselves. I further remarked that I had often seen deputations coming to Rome on this or that person's account, but did not remember them ever being given a time or place to deliver their encomia. While approving their zeal and gratitude to you for what you had done for them, I said that the whole plan seemed to me very far from necessary. If, however, they desired to manifest their loyalty in that way, those who travelled at their own expense would have my commendation, and those who claimed expenses authorized by law would have my permission; unlimited expenses I should not allow.

What is there to censure? To be sure, you add that certain persons thought my edict was framed as though on purpose to stop these deputations. At this point, I do not consider myself so much wronged by those who so contend as by those whose ears are open to such a contention. I drew up my edict in Rome, and made no addition except what the tax-farmers asked me to transfer *verbatim* from your edict into mine, when they waited upon me at Samos. The section directed to reducing the expenses of the communes was very carefully worded. It contains some novelties beneficial to the communes, in which I take much satisfaction, but the passage which has given rise to the suspicion that I went out of my way to cross you is common form. I was not so irrational as to suppose that these deputations were in a private interest, sent as they were to express gratitude to you, no private individual, for a matter not private to themselves but public, and in no private conclave but before the parliament of the world; that is to say, the Senate. And when I laid down that no one should leave without my authority, I did *not* eliminate persons unable to follow me to my camps or to the other side of the Taurus – this is the most ludicrous point in your letter. Why should they have to follow me to my camps or to cross the Taurus, when I so managed my journey from Laodicea to Iconium that the magistrates and deputations of all districts our side of the Taurus and of their appertaining communes could meet me? Or did they start appointing deputations after I had crossed the mountains? Certainly they did not. When I was at Laodicea, and at Apamea, and at Synnada, and at Philomelium, and at Iconium (I spent time in all these towns), all deputations of this sort had already been nominated. All the same, I wish you to know that I made no ruling for the reduction or cancellation of such expenditure on deputations except at the request of the leading men of the communes, to save charging expenditures of a far from necessary kind on the proceeds of the sale of taxes and those very harsh imposts (you will know to what I refer), the poll tax and the door tax.[245] As for me, having undertaken not only in justice but in mercy to relieve these wretched, ruined communes, ruined in the main by their own magistrates, I could not turn a blind eye to this unnecessary expenditure.

If such talk about me has been carried to you by others, you should not have believed them. If, on the other hand, you favour the practice of attributing to others the thoughts that enter your own mind, you introduce into friendship a far from gentlemanly mode of conversation. Had I ever had it in mind to derogate from your good name in the province, I should not ★ ★ ★ your son-in-law, nor should I have consulted your freed-

245. See *Letters to Atticus* 109 (v.16).2.

man at Brundisium or your Prefect of Engineers at Corcyra as to where you wished me to go. So, following the advice of learned men who have written excellent books on the conduct of friendship, you can dismiss this whole line of language – 'they contended . . . *I* argued to the contrary,' 'they said . . . *I* denied it.'

Perhaps you suppose that nothing has ever been said to *me* about *you*? For example, that after desiring me to go to Laodicea you yourself crossed the Taurus? That at one and the same time I held assizes at Apamea, Synnada, and Philomelium, and you at Tarsus? I will not continue, or I might seem to be following your example in the very point on which I am reproaching you. One thing I *will* say as I think: if the sayings you attribute to others are your own sentiments, you are very much to blame; but if others do talk to you in this strain, you are still in some degree to blame for listening. My attitude throughout our friendship will be found consistent and responsible. If I am credited with cunning, may I point out that I always upheld your interests in your absence, even though I had no thought that I should one day stand in need of your support in similar circumstances? Would I now give you an excellent justification for deserting my absent self? That would be artful dodging indeed!

One sort of talk, in which things are very frequently said which I imagine you would prefer unsaid, I put in a special category, I mean unfavourable comment on one or other of your Legates or Prefects or Military Tribunes. Even so, I can assure you that no such criticism has so far been uttered in my hearing in more severe terms or reflecting upon a larger number of persons than what Clodius said to me on the subject at Corcyra, when he spoke with especial emphasis of his regret that you should have been so unfortunate in the rascality of others. Since such talk is frequent and does not in my opinion damage *your* reputation, I have not repressed it very vigorously, though I have never encouraged it.

Anyone who believes that *bona fide* reconciliations are impossible does not convict my bad faith, but exposes his own; and he thinks as badly of you as of me. Whereas anyone who is dissatisfied with my administration here and considers himself injured by a certain dissimilarity between my administration and yours, the fact being that both of us have acted properly but on different principles, why, I do not care to have him as a friend. You, as a great nobleman, were more open-handed here than I have been. I may have kept a rather tight hand on the purse-strings – though your own bountiful and kindly instincts were a little cramped in your second year by something unpropitious in the times. I have always been naturally rather conservative in generosity at other people's expense and am influenced by the same temporary conditions as influence others. So folk ought not to be surprised that to be 'sweet to myself, I must be sour to them'.[246]

I am obliged for your information about affairs in Rome for its own sake, and also because you intimate that you will attend to all my commissions. On one of them I make a special request; please see that this charge of mine is not increased or its period extended, and please ask our friend and colleague[247] Hortensius, if he has ever voted or acted for my sake, to give up this two-year proposal. Nothing could be more hostile to me.

You ask my news. I left Tarsus for the Amanus on the Nones of October, and am writing this the following day from camp in the territory of Mopsuhestia. If I do anything, I shall write to you, and I shall never send a letter to my home without adding one to be forwarded to you. As for your question about the Parthians, I do not think there *were* any Parthians. There were Arabs,[248] some of them with Parthian equipment, and they are said to have all withdrawn. We are told that there is not a single enemy in Syria.

246. From an unknown Latin play.
247. As Augur.
248. See p. 185.

I hope you will write to me as often as you can about your affairs and my own and about the whole state of the common-wealth, as to which your information that our friend Pompey is to go to Spain has aggravated my concern.

71 (III. 7)

CICERO TO APPIUS PULCHER

Laodicea, soon after 11 February 50

From Cicero to Appius Pulcher greetings.

I shall be writing to you at greater length when I get more time. I am writing this in haste, Brutus' boys having met me at Laodicea and told me that they are in a hurry to get back to Rome. So I have given them no letters except this to you and one to Brutus.

Envoys from Appia have handed me a roll from you full of highly unreasonable complaints concerning their building, which is said to have been stopped by a letter of mine. In the same missive you ask me to set them free to proceed with the building as soon as possible before they run into winter, and at the same time you complain with much asperity of my having forbidden them to levy special taxes until I had examined the case and given permission. That, you say, was one way of stopping them, since I could not make any examination until I returned from Cilicia for the winter.

Allow me to answer all these points, and observe the justice of your expostulation. To start with, I had been approached by persons who claimed that they were being subjected to taxation on an intolerable scale. Was it so unfair that I should write instructing them not to proceed until I had investigated the facts of the case? Oh, but I could not do this before winter – that's what you say in your letter. As though it was for me to go to them to investigate, and not for them to come to me! 'At such a distance?' you ask. Come, when you gave them your letter asking me not to stop them building before winter, did you not suppose they would come to me? To be sure they managed this absurdly enough – they did not bring me the letter, which was meant to enable them to do the job during the summer, until after midwinter. But you must understand that the objectors to the taxes are in a large majority over those who want them levied – and that none the less I shall do what I think you wish. So much for the good folk of Appia.

I have heard from my marshal Pausanias, Lentulus' freed-man, that you complained to him about my not having gone to meet you. I treated you with contempt, it seems, and my arrogance is quite monstrous! The facts are that your boy arrived about the second watch[249] with a message that you would join me before daybreak in Iconium. As there were two roads and he said it was uncertain which of them you were taking, I sent A. Varro, a close friend of yours, by one and my Prefect of Engineers, Q. Lepta, by the other to meet you, in-structing both to hasten back from you to me so that I could go to meet you. Lepta came hurrying back to tell me that you had already passed the camp. I went to Iconium immediately. The rest you know.[250] Was it likely that I should not turn out to meet *you* – Appius Claudius, Commander-in-Chief, entitled by traditional practice to the courtesy, and, what is most to the purpose, my friend – I who am in the habit of carrying my desire to please in many such matters further than my own rank and dignity require? But I say no more. Pausanias also told me of the following remark of yours: 'Well, of course! Appius went to meet Lentulus, Lentulus went to meet Ampius;[251] but Cicero go to meet Appius, oh no!' Really! These absurdities from *you* – a man of excellent sound sense, as I judge, much

249. About 9 p.m.
250. We do not. But it seems unlikely that a meeting took place.
251. See n. 218.

learning also, great knowledge of the world, and, let me add, urbanity, which the Stoics very rightly rank as a virtue! Do you suppose that any Appiety or Lentulity[252] counts more with me than the ornaments of merit? Even before I gained the distinctions which the world holds highest, I was never dazzled by aristocratic names; it was the men who bequeathed them to you that I admired. But after I won and filled positions of the highest authority in such a fashion as to let me feel no need of additional rank or fame, I hoped to have become the equal (never the superior) of you and your peers. And I may add that I have never observed a different way of thinking in Cn. Pompeius or P. Lentulus, one of whom I judge the greatest man that ever lived, the other greater than myself. If *you* think otherwise, you might do worse than pay rather particular attention to what Athenodorus, son of Sandon, has to say on these points – in order to understand the true meaning of *noblesse*.

But to come back to the point. I want you to believe that I am not only your friend, but your very good friend. Naturally I shall do all I can in a practical way to enable you to decide that this is really so. As for yourself, if your object is not to appear bound to work for my interests while I am away as heartily as I worked for yours, why, I hereby relieve you of that preoccupation –

> Others stand by me
> to do me grace, and before all wise Zeus.[253]

But if you are a fault-finder by nature, you will not make me any the less your well-wisher; all you will achieve is to leave me less concerned about your reactions.

I have written rather frankly, in the consciousness of my own

252. i.e. nobility, as though Appius was the name of a family. In fact it was a personal name (*praenomen*), but one almost exclusive to the patrician Claudii. Both nouns are, of course, coined by Cicero.

253. *Iliad*, 1.174 f. 'Wise Zeus' seems to indicate Pompey.

friendliness and good-will, an attitude which, as I have adopted it of deliberate choice, I shall maintain so long as *you* wish.

72 (III. 9)

CICERO TO APPIUS PULCHER

Laodicea, shortly after 20 February 50

Cicero to Appius Pulcher greetings.

Well, at long last I have read a letter worthy of Appius Claudius, full of courtesy, friendliness, and consideration! It would seem that the sight of Rome has given you back your old urbanity.[254] For I was very sorry to read the letters you sent me *en route* before you left Asia, one concerning my alleged orders to stop deputations leaving, the other about my holding up the building in Appia; and so, in the consciousness of my unswerving good-will towards you, I wrote back in some irritation. But having read the letter you gave to my freedman[255] Philotimus, I find and understand that, whereas there are many in this province who would sooner we did not feel towards one another as we do, you had only to approach Rome, or rather to see your friends there, to learn from their lips how loyal I was to you during your absence, how attentive and steadfast in fulfilling all friendly offices towards you. So you can imagine how much I appreciate the promise you make in your letter to repay me in kind, should anything arise involving my own position – though you say such repayment is hardly possible. On the contrary, you will do it easily enough; for there is nothing beyond the power of zeal and good-will, or rather affection.

254. A sort of play on words: *urbis* (= Rome), *urbanitatem*.
255. In fact, Terentia's.

The confident, in fact assured, hope of a Triumph expressed in your letter, although it only conforms to my own judgement and the frequent intimations of my correspondents, has given me the greatest happiness. That was not because I may find it the easier to gain one myself (an Epicurean point of view!),[256] but because your dignity and greatness are, I do assure you, intrinsically dear to me. Now you are better placed than others to know of persons setting out for this province, because practically all of them call on you for your commissions; so I shall be deeply obliged if you will send me a letter as soon as you have won the prize which you expect and for which I pray. If the dilatory deliberations of the 'long bench',[257] to use Pompey's expression, cost you too a day or so (surely no more), your dignity will take no harm. But, if you care for me and wish me to care for you, send me a letter, so that I may rejoice at the earliest possible moment.

I hope too that you will discharge what remains of your promised gift[258] to me. I am anxious to instruct myself in augural law for its own sake, and am marvellously delighted, believe me, with your friendly gestures and gifts. I note that you would like something of the kind from me, and certainly must consider in what form I can best reciprocate your favour. It would hardly be in character in so industrious a writer as I am (to your amazement, as you often say) to let myself appear negligent through failure to write, especially where the charge of negligence would be aggravated by one of ingratitude.

But that we shall see. Now as to this other promise of yours, look to it, I beg you, as a man of your word and as our friendship (I won't say 'now established', for it is already inveterate) claims; do all you can to have me decreed a Supplication in

256. Friendship according to Epicurus (and Cicero himself in his younger days; cf. *Pro Roscio Amerino* 111) was founded on self-interest.

257. This probably means the Board of Tribunes.

258. The work on Augury. Evidently Cicero had received only the first section.

terms as complimentary, and with as little delay, as possible. I
sent my dispatch later than I should have wished (there were
tiresome difficulties of navigation, and I believe it will arrive
just as the Senate goes into recess),[259] but I did so on your
authority and advice. And after all, I think I was right not to
send it as soon as I was saluted Imperator, but to wait for further
achievements and the end of the season's campaigning. This
then will be your concern, as you promise; and please regard
me and all things and persons that are mine as entirely commended to your care.

73 (III. 10)

CICERO TO APPIUS PULCHER

Laodicea, April (first half) 50

Cicero to Appius Pulcher greetings.

The first news of the reckless behaviour of the trouble-
makers[260] gave me a severe shock, for nothing could have
happened more against my expectations. But having had time
to take stock, I believe that, except in one respect, everything
will be plain sailing. I set my hopes chiefly upon yourself, but
in no small measure upon your family and friends; and many
reasons occur to persuade me that this ordeal will actually
enhance your reputation. But I certainly am disheartened to see
that this piece of malice has robbed you of a perfectly secure
and well-earned Triumph.[261] If you estimate that at what I have

259. The Senate often rose for a vacation in April.

260. A charge of lèse-majesté (see Glossary of Terms) had been laid
against Appius by P. Cornelius Dolabella, of whose engagement to
Tullia Cicero was informed three months later.

261. In order to answer the charge Appius had to cross the ancient
city boundary and thereby give up his *imperium;* having given up his
imperium he could not be decreed a Triumph.

always judged to be its proper importance, you will do wisely; and you will celebrate a well-earned Triumph in virtue of the chagrin of your defeated enemies. For it is abundantly clear to me that your energy, resources, and sagacity will give them good cause to repent their insolence. As for me, I call all the Gods to witness this my solemn pledge, that in this province of which you were governor I shall do what in me lies for your honour (I prefer to say 'honour' rather than 'safety'). On your behalf I shall solicit like an intercessor, and work like a blood-relation. My influence with the communes, which I flatter myself hold me in affection, and my authority as Commander-in-Chief shall be at your service. I want you to demand all things of me, and to expect no less. My good offices shall surpass anything you can imagine.

Q. Servilius gave me a very short letter from you. To me, however, it appeared too long, for I felt it an injury to be *asked*. Sorry I am that a time should have come in which you will be able to perceive the extent of my regard for yourself, and for Pompey (whom I esteem, as I ought, more than any man alive), and for Brutus – not that you would not have seen it in our day-to-day intercourse, as see it you will; but since such a time *has* come, I shall acknowledge any omission on my part as an offence against others and against my own honour.

Pomptinus, to whom you behaved with such truly remark-able loyalty and kindness,[262] as I myself am witness, does not fail to remember you with the regard that is your due. Import-ant private business obliged him to leave me, greatly to my regret. He was at Ephesus, just taking ship, when he heard that your interests were at stake, and at once returned to Laodicea. Such is the zeal which you can command in countless quarters. With that before my eyes, I simply cannot doubt that your present anxiety will bring you greater honour. And if further you secure the appointment of Censor, and discharge that

262. Cf. *Letters to Atticus* 92 (IV.18).4.

office as you should and can,[263] you will clearly be a tower of enduring strength, not only to yourself, but to all connected with you. Only strive with might and main to prevent any extension of my tenure, so that, when I have done what is fitting for you here, I may have the opportunity to serve you as I wish in Rome.

What you write to me about the backing you get from all persons and classes gives me no surprise at all and a great deal of pleasure. My friends tell the same story in their letters. I am truly happy to see that one whose friendship is to me no less a pleasure than an honour should receive what is his due; happy also to find that brave and active men still inspire in our community that almost universal good-will which has always been vouchsafed to myself as the only reward of my toils and vigils.

I am, however, very much astonished to find a young man whom I have twice most strenuously defended on capital charges[264] so foolhardy and so wholly oblivious of his own fortunes and interests as to provoke your enmity. It is especially surprising when one considers the superabundance of assets and resources on your side and the many deficiencies (to put it mildly) on his. My friend M. Caelius had previously informed me of his silly, childish talk;[265] and you too wrote to me about it at some length. I should have been more likely to break off an old tie with a self-constituted enemy of yours than to form a new one. And indeed you ought not to have any doubts about my sentiments towards you; they are plain to everyone in the province, and were no less so in Rome.

And yet your letter *does* imply a certain suspicion, a doubt in

263. Cicero politely assumes that if Censors are elected Appius will be one of them (as in fact happened).

264. Their nature is unknown.

265. Clearly with reference to a marriage with Tullia. Caelius' letter has not survived.

your mind. Present circumstances make it inopportune for me to reproach you on that account, but necessary to exculpate myself. Now when did I ever stop the dispatch of a deputation to Rome to sing your praises? If I hated you openly, could I have taken any step which would have harmed you less? If secretly, could I have done anything to make hostility more obvious? Suppose I were as treacherous as those who tell such tales against me, I surely should not have been so stupid as to make a parade of enmity if I wished to hide my malice, or to show the utmost will to hurt you in a fashion which did not hurt you at all. I do remember being approached by certain folk, from the Annexed Territory[266] if I am not mistaken, who alleged that excessive sums were being voted for deputations. I did not so much order as advise them to vote such sums as far as possible in accordance with the lex Cornelia. But that I did not insist even on that point can be proved from the public accounts of the communes, in which each one entered whatever amount it desired as a grant to your delegates.

But what lies these irresponsibles have foisted upon you! Not only were these expenses ruled out for the future, they say, but refunds were demanded and exacted from the agents of those who had already left, and many did not go at all for this reason. I should complain and remonstrate with you, if I did not prefer and think more proper, as I have said above, to exculpate myself rather than to arraign you in your present circumstances. So of you and your belief in these tales I shall say nothing; but a little I *shall* say about myself, to show why you ought not to have believed them. If you know me as an honourable man, worthy of the studies and culture to which I have devoted myself since childhood, as one who in matters of great moment has shown no petty spirit and no contemptible intelligence, then you ought not to suppose me capable of meanness or paltriness in friendship, much less of treachery, guile, and

266. A district of Phrygia adjoining Bithynia, annexed by the king of Pergamum about 184. Hence the name Phrygia Epiktetos.

falsehood. But suppose you choose to think of me as a crafty dissembler, how do these allegations square with such a character? Would a person of this stamp spurn the good-will of one so prosperous? Would he attack in a province the reputation of a man whose credit he defended at home? Would he display hostility just where he could inflict no hurt? Would he elect to practise bad faith in a form at once blatantly declaratory of his spite and quite innocuous to its object? And then, why should I have borne you so implacable a grudge, knowing as I did from my brother that you were no enemy of mine even when circumstances almost compelled you to act like one?[267] After the reconciliation which we mutually sought, did you once during your Consulate solicit an action or a vote from me unsuccessfully? When I accompanied you on your outward journey as far as Puteoli, you gave me certain commissions. Was there one in which my assiduity did not surpass your expectation?

If it is especially characteristic of a crafty fellow to measure all things by the yardstick of his own interest, what, may I ask, could be more in mine, more advantageous and convenient to me than connection with a personage of the highest birth and rank, whose riches, talents, children, and relations by blood and marriage would be a source of pride and strength to me? Yet it was no craftiness which led me to seek those advantages in soliciting your friendship, rather I might call it sound judgement. And then there are other bonds whose constraint I am most happy to feel – similarity of pursuits, the charm of personal intercourse, the enjoyment of a way of life, the give-and-take of conversation, the more recondite studies we share. These are bonds! I speak of our private lives. But let us not forget that some things between us interest the world at large. Our reconciliation was so publicized that any slip, however accidental, cannot but create a suspicion of bad faith. We are

267. During the conflict between Cicero and Appius' brother P. Clodius.

colleagues in an exalted priestly office. Remember that any violation of friendship between such was held a sacrilege in the good old days; indeed no priest could be co-opted who was on terms of enmity with any member of the College.

Reasons in plenty, and of no light weight! But suppose I leave them aside, and only ask whether one man ever thought, ever could or should think, more of another than I think of your daughter's father-in-law, Cn. Pompeius? And well I may. If services count, it was through him that I consider I regained country, children, citizenship, rank, my very being; if the pleasures of private intercourse count, were two Roman Consulars ever faster friends? If the tokens of affection and regard count, has he not made me the confidant of all his secrets and projects? Has he not chosen me of all others to represent his interests in the Senate during his absences? Has he not desired for me all manner of high distinctions? Can I forget how readily and graciously he accepted my efforts on Milo's behalf, which sometimes ran counter to his own policies, how anxious he was to ensure that I was not touched by the public feeling aroused at that time? How he protected me by his dispositions, his authority, even his armed forces?[268] His firm and lofty mind in those days would not let him lend credence to ill-natured talk about me even from the highest quarters, let alone some denizen of Phrygia or Lycaonia, as you did in the matter of the delegates. Well, Pompey's son[269] is your son-in-law; and apart from that connection I am well aware how dear and delightful a friend you are to him. What then should be my feelings towards you? Add that he has sent me a letter, which, even if I had been your enemy, as I am so sincerely your friend, would have disarmed my resentment and rendered me

268. According to existing accounts Cicero was intimidated rather than protected by Pompey's troops at Milo's trial. But *Letters to Atticus* 174B (IX.7B).2 shows that he asked Pompey for a bodyguard and presumably obtained it.

269. Cn. Pompeius the Younger.

obedient to the wishes, the very nod, of the man to whom I owe so much.

But that will do. Perhaps I have already used more words than were needed. Now let me tell you what I have arranged and set in motion[270] ★ ★ ★. All this I am doing and shall continue to do, more for your honour than for your protection. For shortly, I hope, we shall hear of you as Censor. I think the duties of that office, calling as they do for courage and policy of the highest order, more deserve your careful and diligent consideration than these steps I am taking on your behalf.

74 (III. 11)

CICERO TO APPIUS PULCHER

Camp on the Pyramus, 26 June (?) 50

From Cicero to Appius Pulcher, Censor (I hope), greetings.

Two letters from you were delivered to me in camp on the river Pyramus at the same time, sent on to me from Tarsus by Q. Servilius. One of them was dated the Nones of April; the other seemed to me more recent, but bore no date. I shall therefore reply first to the former, in which you write of your acquittal on the charge of lèse-majesté. I had been informed of this long before by letters and oral messages and general report – it was in all mouths; not that anyone expected a different result, but tidings concerning distinguished reputations seldom lack advertisement. Your letter, however, added to my pleasure in the event. It spoke more distinctly and fully than the common talk, and I had a more vivid sense of congratulating you as I heard your news from yourself. So in my mind I embraced you from afar and kissed the letter, congratulating myself as

270. The details which followed may have been omitted in the copy of the letter preserved by Cicero.

well as you. For I feel the tribute paid by the whole people and
the Senate and the jury to talent, energy, and virtue as paid also
to me, flattering myself perhaps in fancying that I possess these
qualities.

What surprises me is not that your trial should have ended so
gloriously, but that your enemies should have shown such
perverseness.[271] You may ask what difference it makes – corruption or lèse-majesté. None at all, as to the substance.
Corruption you have not touched, and as for the majesty of the
state, you have enhanced it. Still there is something indetermi-
nate about a lèse-majesté charge, in spite of Sulla's ordinance
penalizing random declamation against individuals, whereas
corruption is clearly defined – there must be rascality on one
side of the case or on the other. For obviously the fact, whether
improper disbursements have or have not taken place, cannot
be unknown. And what suspicion has ever attached to *your*
rise up the official ladder? How I regret that I was not there!
The laughs I should have raised!

However, two points in your letter about the lèse-majesté
proceedings have given me a great deal of pleasure. One is your
remark that Rome herself was your advocate. To be sure, the
country ought to protect men like yourself, no matter how
plentiful the supply of brave and honest citizens. But as matters
stand now, when at every grade of rank and age there is so
sore a scarcity, our forlorn community could ill afford not to
cling to such champions. The other point is your enthusiastic
praise for the staunchness and good-will shown by Pompey and
Brutus. I am delighted to learn of this sterling loyalty on their
part – not only as they are connections of yours and very good
friends of mine, but because one of them stands as the greatest

271. It is to be inferred from what follows that Dolabella had threatened to prosecute Appius for electoral corruption if he failed to get a
conviction on the lèse-majesté charge; and he was as good as his word.
The alleged corruption probably had to do with Appius' election as
Censor.

man that any century or people has produced, while the other has for some time past been a leading figure among his contemporaries and is shortly, I hope, to become so in the community at large. As to the censures to be passed upon venal witnesses by the communities to which they belong, if steps have not already been taken through Flaccus, they will be taken by me on my way home through Asia.

Now I come to the other letter. Your detailed survey, marked by so much good sense, of the crisis which affects us all and the whole political situation is most welcome. The dangers, it appears, are less serious than I feared, and the resources to deal with them greater, since, as you tell me, the entire forces of the state have rallied to Pompey's leadership. At the same time I well see your ready and forward spirit in the defence of the constitution, and am most sincerely gratified by your attention, in that in the middle of such grave preoccupations of your own you wished me none the less to learn the state of the commonwealth from *your* pen. As for the work on Augury, keep it until both of us have time to spare – when I wrote demanding the fulfilment of your pledge, I imagined you at the capital without a care in the world. As it is, I shall none the less expect the edition of your complete speeches in lieu of the work on Augury, as you yourself promise.

D. Tullius, to whom you gave a message for me, has not come my way. In fact none of your people is with me at the moment – except for all *my* people, who are all yours! I am at a loss to know which letter of mine you have in mind when you refer to 'a rather irritable letter'. I wrote to you twice exculpating myself in detail and mildly reproaching you because you had been quick to believe what you heard about me – a friendly sort of expostulation, so *I* thought; but if it displeases you, I shall eschew it in future. But if the letter was, as you say, not well-expressed, you may be sure I did not write it. Just as Aristarchus denies the authenticity of any Homeric line which he does not like, so I would request you (being in jocular vein), if you find any piece of writing not well-expressed, not to believe I wrote it.

Goodbye – and in your Censorship, if Censor, as I hope, you now are, keep your ancestor[272] much in mind.

75 (III. 12)

CICERO TO APPIUS PULCHER

Side, 3 or 4 August 50

From Cicero to Appius Pulcher greetings.

I shall begin by offering you my congratulations, putting first things first, and then turn to myself.

Indeed I do congratulate you heartily on the corruption trial – not on your acquittal, which was a foregone conclusion, but on the circumstance that even behind the screen of a secret ballot no lurking malice dared to assail you. The better citizen you are, the greater public figure, the braver friend, the more distinguished for ability and energy, the more remarkable the fact. A thing quite out of tune with modern times and men and manners! Nothing for a long while past has so amazed me.

As for me, please for a moment put yourself in my shoes, imagine you are I; and if you have no difficulty in finding what to say, I won't ask you to forgive my embarrassment! I should indeed wish that the arrangement[273] made by my family without my knowledge may turn out well for my dear Tullia and myself, as you are charming and kind enough to desire. But that the thing should have come about just when it did – well, I hope and pray some happiness may come of it, but in so

272. Ap. Claudius Caecus ('The Blind'), whose famous Censorship beginning in 312 produced the Appian Way and the Claudian Aqueduct.

273. Tullia's engagement to Dolabella.

hoping I take more comfort in the thought of your good sense
and kind heart than in the timeliness of the proceeding! And so
how to get out of the wood and finish what I have begun to
say I cannot tell. I must not take a gloomy tone about an event
to which you yourself wish all good luck; but at the same time
I can't but feel a rub. On one point, though, my mind is easy –
you will not fail to realize that what has been done has been
done by others. I had told them not to consult me since I should
be so far away, but to act as they thought best. But as I write, the
question obtrudes itself: What should I have done if I had been
on the spot? Well, I should have approved in principle; but as
for the timing, I should have taken no step against your wishes
or without consulting you.

You perceive what a pother I am in all this while, at my wits'
end to know how to defend what defend I must without offending you. Lift the load from my back. I don't think I have ever
pleaded a more awkward case. But of this you may be sure:
though my long-standing zeal to serve you appears to admit
of no enhancement, yet, had I not already settled all matters
with the utmost regard for your honour, I should have
championed it after the announcement of this connection, not
indeed more zealously, but more ardently, openly, and emphatically. Letters from my people reached me on my voyage
home after the end of my year of office, on 3 August, when I
put into Side. Q. Servilius was with me. I told him then and
there (he seemed upset) that he might expect more from me on
all fronts. In a phrase, I am no whit the friendlier disposed
towards you than I was before, but I *am* much more anxious to
show my friendly disposition to the world. Our old variance
used to be a stimulus, leading me to guard against any suspicion
that the reconciliation was not sincere on my side. Now my
new connection makes me sedulous to avoid any semblance of
a falling off in the profound regard I entertain for you.

76 (III. 13)

CICERO TO APPIUS PULCHER

Rhodes (?), August 50

From Cicero to Appius Pulcher greetings.

In the days when your achievements were under discussion I worked for your distinction[274] as though I had a presentiment that in time to come I should need your support in similar circumstances. But in all candour, you have more than repaid me. From every quarter letters have come telling me how you took upon yourself the load of service, leaving nothing for others to do. From a man like yourself I should have been well content with the support of your moral influence and speech and vote; but in addition to these you contributed your trouble and advice, visiting my house and meeting my domestic circle. To me these efforts mean far more than the prize for which they are undertaken. The badges of merit have often been obtained without the thing itself, but merit alone can enlist such zealous support from men like you.

The gain I promise myself from our friendship is – friendship itself. Nothing rewards more richly, especially in the context of those pursuits to which both of us are dedicated. For I profess myself both your ally in public affairs, on which our views are identical, and your comrade in daily life, which we live in these accomplishments and pursuits. I wish matters had so fallen out that you could feel as much regard for my connections as I feel for all of yours – and yet some presentiment tells me not to despair even of that. But this is no concern of yours, the onus lies on me. I should only like you to believe what you will find to be the fact, that this unexpected development has rather

274. A *supplicatio*, such as the Senate had just voted Cicero.

added something to the warmth of my sentiments towards you, which seemed to admit of no addition, than in any degree diminished it.

As I write these words I trust you are already Censor. My letter is the shorter on that account and the more sober, as addressed to a director of public morals.

77 (VIII. I)

CAELIUS RUFUS TO CICERO[275]

Rome, c. 26 May 51

From Caelius to Cicero greetings.

Redeeming the promise I made as I took my leave of you to write you all the news of Rome in the fullest detail, I have been at pains to find a person to cover the whole ground so meticulously that I am afraid you may find the result too wordy. However, I know how curious you are and how much everybody abroad likes to be told of even the most trifling happenings at home. But I do hope you won't find me guilty of uppishness in my performance of this office because I have delegated the work to someone else. It is not that I shouldn't be charmed to give time to remembering you, busy though I am and, as you know, the laziest of letter-writers. But I imagine the volume[276] I am sending you makes my excuses easily enough. I don't know how anyone could have so much time on his hands as to observe all these items, let alone record them. It's all here – the Senate's decrees, the edicts, the gossip, the rumours. If this specimen does not happen to appeal to you,

275. The eighth Book of the *Letters to Friends* consists entirely of letters from M. Caelius Rufus. They abound in problems of reading and interpretation.

276. i.e. roll of papyrus.

CICERO'S LETTERS TO HIS FRIENDS

please let me know, so that I don't spend money merely to bore you. If there is any major political event which these hirelings could not cover satisfactorily, I shall be careful to write you a full account of the manner of it and of consequent views and expectations.

At the moment we are not looking ahead to anything in particular. Those rumours about elections in Transpadane Gaul[277] were rife only as far as Cumae;[278] when I got back to Rome, I did not hear so much as a whisper on the subject. Moreover, Marcellus[279] has so far not referred the question of appointing new governors in the Gallic provinces to the Senate, and has put it off, so he told me himself, till the Kalends of June. That to be sure has elicited the same sort of talk as was going round about him when we were in Rome.[280]

If you found Pompey, as you wanted to do, be sure to write and tell me what you thought of him, how he talked to you, and what disposition he showed.[281] He is apt to say one thing and think another, but is usually not clever enough to keep his real aims out of view.

As regards Caesar,[282] rumours arrive in plenty about him and they are not pretty – but only of the whispering sort. One says he has lost his cavalry (which I think is certainly a fabrication), another that the Seventh Legion has taken a beating and that

277. Cf. *Letters to Atticus* 95 (v.2).4.

278. Caelius seems to have accompanied Cicero on his outward journey as far as Pompeii, and is referring to his own return journey to Rome.

279. M. Claudius Marcellus, Consul this year. The date on which Caesar should hand over his province was a main issue in Roman politics during the two years preceding the Civil War. After a vast amount of scholarly debate it is still doubtful when his command legally ended.

280. Perhaps that he was slow and inefficient; cf. p. 185.

281. Cf. *Letters to Atticus* 100 (v.7).

282. Now contending with the aftermath of the great Gallic revolt of 52.

Caesar himself is under siege in the country of the Bellovaci, cut off from the rest of his army. But nothing is confirmed as yet, and even these unconfirmed reports are not bandied about generally but retailed as an open secret among a small coterie – you know who. But Domitius claps hand to mouth before he speaks.

On 24 May our pavement gossips[283] had spread it around that you were dead (their funeral, I hope!). All over town and in the Forum there was a great rumour that Q. Pompeius had murdered you on your road. Knowing that Q. Pompeius is operating boats at Bauli with so little to eat that my heart bleeds for him, I was unperturbed, and prayed that if any dangers *are* hanging over you we may be quit of them for the price of this lie. Your friend Plancus[284] is at Ravenna. Despite a massive largesse from Caesar, he is the same dismal vulgarian.[285]

Your work on politics[286] is all the rage.

78 (VIII. 2)

CAELIUS RUFUS TO CICERO

June, early 51

From Caelius to Cicero greetings.

Yes, I tell you, it's true. He[287] has been acquitted (I was there

283. More literally 'loungers around the Rostra (in the Forum)'.

284. Bursa. Ravenna was in Caesar's province.

285. The word-play is untranslatable. After Caesar's liberality Plancus might be rich (*beatus*) and well provided (*bene instructus*); but he was not happy (*beatus*) and well educated (*bene instructus*). The latter deficiency is ridiculed in Letter 217 (IX.10).

286. The six Books *On the Republic*.

287. M. Valerius Messalla Rufus, Consul in 53, and a friend of Cicero. His uncle Hortensius had just successfully defended him on a charge of electoral malpractice; cf. *Letters to Atticus* 105 (V.12).2.

when the verdict was announced), and that by all three categories – but by one vote in each.[288] Just be thankful, sry you.
No, really; nothing so contrary to expectation, no such universal
scandal, has ever been seen. Even I, who as a friend was
wholeheartedly on his side and had prepared myself for the
sad event, was dumbfounded when this happened, and felt as
though I had been cheated. You can imagine how others
reacted. Naturally they howled abuse at the jury and made it
plain that *this* was going beyond all patience. So now he's left
in what looks like a more perilous predicament than ever, to
face the lex Licinia.[289] On top of this, Hortensius walked into
Curio's theatre[290] the day after the acquittal, presumably to let
us share in his jubilation. You should have heard the 'din and
hubbub, roar of thunder, tackle whistling in the gale'.[291] It was
all the more noticed because Hortensius had come to old age
without a single experience of the bird. But he had enough of
it then to last anyone a lifetime, and rued his victory.

About politics I have nothing to tell you. Marcellus' initiatives have subsided, not from lack of energy, but, in my
opinion, from policy. The consular elections are anybody's
guess. *I* have got one nobleman to contend with and one acting-
nobleman[292] – M. Octavius, son of Gnaeus, and C. Hirrus are
standing with me. I am telling you this because I know how
eagerly you will wait for the result of our elections on Hirrus'

288. At this period Roman juries were made up of equal numbers of
Senators, Knights, and Paymaster Tribunes. The votes of each category
were counted separately, but the verdict went by a majority of the
whole jury.

289. A recently passed measure concerned with illegal associations.
Messalla was in fact prosecuted and found guilty under it.

290. A wooden theatre of remarkable construction built by Curio in
53 for the show given in honour of his dead father.

291. From the *Teucer* of Pacuvius.

292. Literally 'playing the nobleman'. Hirrus' family was senatorial
but not 'noble'.

account.[293] As soon as you hear I am designate, please see to the matter of the panthers.[294] I recommend Sittius' bond to your kind attention.[295] I gave my first Abstract of Affairs in Rome to L. Castrinius Paetus, my second to the bearer of this letter.

79 (VIII. 3)

CAELIUS RUFUS TO CICERO

Rome, mid June 51

From Caelius to Cicero greetings.

Well? Have I won? Am I sending you letters often, which as you were leaving you told me I should never bother to do for you? Yes – if those I dispatch get to their destination. I am all the more punctilious about it, because when I have no work on hand there is simply nowhere for me to amuse my leisure. When you were in Rome and I had any free time, I was sure of employment the most agreeable in the world – to pass it in your company. I miss that not a little. It is not merely that I feel lonely; Rome seems turned to desert now that you are gone. I am a careless dog, and when you were here I often used to let day after day go by without coming near you. Now it's a misery not to have you to run to all the time.

Above all else my fellow-candidate Hirrus sees to it that I miss you day and night. Just imagine his chagrin – this competitor of yours, this would-be Augur – at finding my prospects of election better than his own, imagine his efforts to pretend it's otherwise! Upon my word, it's for your sake rather than

293. Hirrus had earned Cicero's displeasure by standing against him for the Augurate.

294. For the 'games' which Caelius would have to give as Aedile.

295. Money was owing to Sittius (probably not the addressee of 23 (V.17)) in Cicero's province. Perhaps Caelius was his creditor.

my own that I want you to get the news you are praying for concerning him as soon as may be. As for *my* sake, if I do get elected, it might suit my book to be in company with the richer of the pair.[296] But *this* would be too delicious! If it happens, we shall never be short of a laugh for the rest of our days. Yes, it's worth a sacrifice. But it is a fact that the mislikes which a good many people feel for Hirrus keep him down without notably buoying M. Octavius up.[297]

With regard to the freedman Philotimus' duty and Milo's property,[298] I have been at pains to ensure that Philotimus behaves with complete propriety to the satisfaction of the absent Milo and of those close to him, and that with good faith and care on his part no harm comes to your reputation.

Now I have a favour to ask. If you are going to have time on your hands, as I expect you will, won't you write a tract on something or other and dedicate it to me, as a token of your regard? You may ask what put that into my tolerably sensible head. Well, I have a desire that among the many works that will keep your name alive there should be one which will hand down to posterity the memory of our friendship. I suppose you will want to know what sort of book I have in mind. With your command of the whole range of knowledge you will think out the most appropriate subject quicker than I; but in general terms, let it be something of relevance to me, with a didactic character so as to have a steady circulation.

296. Hirrus, a very wealthy man. A poor Aedile might draw credit from the outlay of a richer colleague, and Caelius had hoped to share expenses (cf. p. 172).

297. People could vote for as many candidates as there were places to fill (two in this instance) but were probably not obliged to vote for more than one. In that case a refusal to vote for Hirrus would not automatically be a vote for Octavius.

298. See *Letters to Atticus* 101 (v.8).2.

80 (II. 8)

CICERO TO CAELIUS

Athens, 6 July 51

From M. Cicero, Proconsul, to M. Caelius greetings.

Really! Is this what you think I asked you to do – to send me pairings of gladiators, court adjournments, Chrestus'[299] pilfering, all the trivia which nobody would dare tell me when I am in Rome? Let me show you how highly I value your judgement – and right I am, for I have never known a better *politique* than you! I do not even particularly want you to tell me day-to-day political developments in matters of major consequence, unless I am affected personally. Others will be writing, I shall have plenty of oral informants, even common report will transmit a good deal. So I do not expect things past or present from *your* pen. What I want from so far-sighted a fellow as yourself is the future. From your letters, having seen, as it were, an architect's drawing of the political situation, I shall hope to know what kind of building is to come. Not that I have any complaint so far. There has been nothing which you could foresee any better than the rest of us – myself especially, after spending several days with Pompey discussing nothing but public affairs. Of what passed between us I cannot and should not write, but of this much you may be sure: Pompey is a very good patriot, ready in spirit and plan for every contingency against which we have to provide. So court him; believe me, you will be welcomed. He now sees good citizens and bad exactly where we are wont to see them.

I have spent ten clear days in Athens, much in the company of our friend Caninius Gallus.[300] I leave today, 6 July, after

299. Unknown. 'Chrestus' is a common slave-name.
300. Perhaps in exile.

dispatching these few lines. I hope you will take all my interests under your special care, none more than the matter of my tenure here, which I do not want extended. This means everything to me. As to when, how, and through whom to proceed, you will be the best judge.

81 (VIII. 4)

CAELIUS RUFUS TO CICERO

Rome, 1 August 51

From Caelius to Cicero greetings.

I really envy you. So many surprises landing on your doorstep every day! First Messalla acquitted; then convicted. C. Marcellus elected Consul. M. Calidius defeated, and prosecuted by the two Gallii. P. Dolabella a Quindecimvir.[301] One thing I *don't* envy you – you missed a really beautiful sight, Lentulus Crus' face when he heard his defeat. He had gone down to the hustings in the highest fettle, thought to be a certainty. Even Dolabella had little opinion of his own chances. In fact I may say that but for the sharper eyes of your humble servant, Lentulus would have carried the day with his opponent practically conceding victory.

One thing I expect will *not* have surprised you, the conviction of Tribune-Elect Servaeus. C. Curio has announced himself as a candidate for the vacancy, much to the alarm of folk who don't know him and his easy ways. But as I expect and hope and as himself declares, he will be for the Senate and the honest men. At the moment he is absolutely frothing with this sentiment. Its origin and cause is that Caesar, who doesn't usually care how much money he spends to get the friendship

301. The Quindecimviri (Board of Fifteen) were official custodians of the Sibylline prophecies.

of any guttersnipe, has shown his indifference to Curio in no uncertain manner. À propos of which I feel this is a highly amusing coincidence, and others have noticed it – so much so that Curio, who does nothing except on impulse, is credited with deep cunning in evading the designs of certain persons who had set themselves to oppose him as Tribune, I mean Lollius (?), Antony, and other sturdy fellows of the same stamp.[302]

The interval between this letter and its predecessor has been the wider because the postponements of the elections kept me rather busy and made me wait for the outcome from day to day, in order to inform you when everything was over. I have waited until the Kalends of August. The Praetorian elections have been held up by various accidents. What is going to happen in my own I don't know. As regards Hirrus, the election of the Plebeian Aediles has produced an amazing current of opinion. M. Coelius Vinicianus was suddenly brought down (with loud shouts to follow as he lay) by that silly statement of his which we laughed at together at the time and the notice of legislation about a Dictator.[303] After that came a universal hue and cry that *now* Hirrus must not be elected. I trust that it won't be long before you hear the news you have been hoping for about me and the news for which you have hardly dared to hope about him.

In the political arena we had stopped expecting anything

302. As I have interpreted this difficult passage, Curio was given credit for checkmating the plans of his pro-Caesarian opponents by standing at a by-election instead of waiting till the following year. Lollius was a former satellite of Clodius. The manuscript reading *laelios* would presumably refer to D. Laelius, Tribune in 54, who is inappropriate.

303. As Tribune in 53 Hirrus had called for Pompey to be made Dictator. From this passage it is inferred that Coelius did likewise, and that his rout in the elections to the Plebeian Aedileship was now taken as a bad sign for Hirrus. How something that happened two years previously could 'suddenly' bring Coelius down is anybody's guess.

fresh. But when the Senate met in the Temple of Apollo[304] on 22 July, and was asked to consider the matter of pay for Pompey's troops, a question was raised about the legion which Pompey lent to C. Caesar[305] – whose was it, and how long would Pompey let it remain in Gaul. Pompey was forced to say that he *would* withdraw the legion, but not immediately under prompting and clamour from his critics. Then he was interrogated about the replacement of C. Caesar, as to which (i.e. on the provinces generally) it was determined that as soon as Pompey returned to Rome a debate should be held on the replacement of provincial governors in his presence (Pompey was about to go to Ariminum to visit his army and went immediately). I think the debate will be on the Ides of August. Presumably something will be decided, or there will be a scandalous veto. For in the course of the discussion Pompey threw out the remark that everyone ought to obey the Senate. For my own part though, I am looking forward to nothing in the world so much as to Consul-Elect Paulus making the first speech.[306]

I am reminding you about Sittius' bond, not for the first time, because I am anxious to make you realize my strong personal concern in that matter. Likewise about panthers – please send for some from Cibyra and have them shipped to me. Another thing, we have had word of the death of the king of Egypt,[307] and it is now taken as certain. Please write to me at length,

304. In the Campus Martius, outside the ancient city boundary, which Pompey, as holding *imperium*, could not enter except by special dispensation.

305. At the beginning of 53 (cf. Caesar, *Bell. Gall.* VI.1).

306. Consuls-Elect spoke first. Paulus (the contemporary spelling was 'Paullus'), a friend of Cicero, had previously been regarded as a firm 'optimate'. In office he took a passive line, allegedly bribed by Caesar. Caelius seems to have had some inkling of his change of front.

307. Ptolemy the Piper. His successors, Ptolemy XIII and Cleopatra, being too young to rule, a regency was established. Caelius was presumably one of the late king's creditors.

advising me how to act and telling me of the state of the kingdom and who is in charge of it.
Kalends of August.

82 (VIII. 9)

CAELIUS RUFUS TO CICERO

Rome, 2 September 51

From Caelius to Cicero greetings.

'So that's how you handled Hirrus, is it?' I hear you saying My dear sir, if you only knew how easy it was, how completely effortless, you would be ashamed to remember that he ever dared to parade as your competitor. After the defeat he's making us all laugh, playing the good citizen and delivering anti-Caesarian speeches in the Senate, denouncing the waiting game, and taking the Consuls to task in no uncertain terms.[308] This defeat has made a completely different man of him. On top of this, he that never showed his face in the Forum and has little experience of law-courts has taken to appearing in freedom suits[309] – but not often after midday.

I told you earlier that there would be a debate on the provinces on the Ides of August, but Consul-Elect Marcellus' trial[310] has upset this timetable. The matter was put off to the Kalends. They had not even been able to get a quorum. I am dispatching this letter on 2 September, and up to that date nothing has been even in main part accomplished. It looks to me

308. For their dilatory handling of the question of Caesar's command.
309. Cases to determine whether a person was free or slave. A man of Hirrus' rank might gain popularity by appearing on behalf of such humble folk.
310. C. Marcellus, Consul in 50, was prosecuted by his unsuccessful competitor M. Calidius for electoral malpractice after the elections, but was acquitted.

as though the entire question will be relegated to next year, and, as far as I can prophesy, you will have to leave a deputy-governor behind you. There is no way clear to the appointment of a successor, because the Gauls, for which a veto is in readiness, are being linked with the other provinces. I am sure of this. That is another reason why I am writing to you, so that you prepare yourself for this outcome.

In almost every letter I have written to you I have mentioned the subject of panthers. It will be little to your credit that Patiscus has sent ten panthers for Curio and you not many times as many.[311] Curio has given me those same animals and another ten from Africa – in case you imagine that country estates[312] are the only form of present he knows! If you will but keep it in mind and send for beasts from Cibyra and write to Pamphylia likewise (they say the hunting is better there), the trick will be done. I am all the more exercised about this now because I think I shall have to make all my arrangements apart from my colleague.[313] Do be a good fellow and give yourself an order about it. You generally like to be conscientious, as I for the most part like to be careless. Conscientiousness in this business is only a matter of saying a word so far as you are concerned, that is of giving an order and commission. As soon as the creatures are caught, you have the men I sent in connection with Sittius' bond to look after their feeding and transport to Rome. Indeed, if you hold out any hope when you write, I think I shall send some more men over.

M. Feridius, a Roman Knight, is going to Cilicia on personal business. He is the son of a friend of mine, and is a worthy and energetic young man. May I recommend him to you and re-

311. i.e. 'for me'.

312. Apparently with reference to some incident otherwise unrecorded. Curio's plan for a redistribution of land in Campania (cf. p. 186), even if already formed and known to Caelius, would hardly have been known to Cicero.

313. M. Octavius.

quest you to admit him to your circle? He hopes that by a kindness which you can render with ease and propriety[314] some lands held in tenancy by communes will receive exemption from tax. You will be obliging worthy people, who do not forget a service.

I wouldn't have you think that Favonius[315] was passed over by the groundlings. All the best people didn't vote for him. Your friend Pompey is openly against Caesar being elected Consul while he retains his province and army. But speaking in the Senate he himself said that no decree should be passed at present, while Scipio proposed that the question of the Gallic provinces should be brought before the House on the Kalends of March, with no other item attached. His speech cast a gloom over Cornelius Balbus, and I know he has remonstrated with Scipio. Calidius gave an excellent performance in his own defence; as prosecutor he was pretty unimpressive.

83 (VIII. 5)

CAELIUS RUFUS TO CICERO

Rome, mid September 51

From Caelius to Cicero greetings.

How worried *you* may be about the prospects of peace in your province and the adjacent areas I don't know, but for my part I am on tenterhooks. If we could so manage that the size of the war should be proportionate to the strength of your forces and could achieve as much as requisite for glory and a Triumph while avoiding the really dangerous and serious clash,

314. The lands may have been owned by Feridius senior and let to local civic corporations.

315. This satellite of Cato had been defeated in the elections to the Praetorship.

CICERO'S LETTERS TO HIS FRIENDS

it would be the most desirable thing in the world. But I know that as matters stand any move by the Parthians will mean a major conflict; and your army is hardly capable of defending a single pass. Unfortunately nobody allows for this; a man charged with public responsibility is expected to cope with any emergency, as though every item in complete preparedness had been put at his disposal. Furthermore, I do not see any prospect of your being relieved because of the controversy about the Gallic provinces. Although I expect you have settled in your own mind what you are going to do in this contingency, I thought that, since I see it coming, I ought to inform you, so that you take your decision the further ahead. You know the routine. There will be a decision about Gaul. Somebody will come along with a veto. Then somebody else will stand up and stop any move about the other provinces, unless the Senate has free licence to pass decrees on all of them. So we shall have a long, elaborate charade – so long that a couple of years or more may drag by in these manoeuvres.

If I had anything fresh to tell you about the political situation, I should follow my usual practice and describe in detail both what had happened and what consequences I expected to follow. The fact is that everything has stuck in a kind of trough. Marcellus still goes on pressing his point about the provinces, but so far he has not succeeded in getting a muster of the Senate. This year thus passed, Curio will be Tribune, and the same performance about the provinces will come on the boards. You don't need me to tell you how easy it will be then to hold everything up, and how well this will suit Caesar and those who think of themselves and care nothing about the country.[316]

316. Neither the text nor the general sense is certain. Caelius can hardly mean that Curio in office would play Caesar's game (as in fact he did), for at this time he expected quite otherwise. But Curio was unpredictable and might fish in troubled waters. Perhaps *he* might be the one to 'stand up and stop any move about the other provinces'.

84 (VIII. 8)

CAELIUS RUFUS TO CICERO

Rome, early October 51

From Caelius to Cicero greetings.

Although I have some matters of public import to tell you, I have nothing that I think you will be so pleased to read as the following. Learn that your heart's darling, C. Sempronius Rufus,[317] has been nailed for malicious prosecution to loud applause. The case? He charged his own prosecutor, M. Tuccius, with assault under the lex Plotia after the Roman Games, his idea being that, if no priority prosecution came up,[318] he himself would have to stand trial this year – and what would happen then he knew all too well.[319] He thought he might as well make this little present to his accuser as to anybody. So down he went, with no assistant-prosecutor, and charged Tuccius. As soon as I hear of it I hurry unsummoned up to the defence benches. I get on my hind legs and without a syllable on the matter in hand, I make a thorough job of Sempronius, even including Vestorius and the story of how he claimed to have done you a favour in letting Vestorius keep ★★★.[320]

317. This man was in Cicero's bad books; cf. *Letters to Atticus* 95 (v.2).2.

318. Why Rufus' prosecution of Tuccius should have had priority is controversial. The Roman Games ended on 19 September.

319. Nothing more is known of Tuccius or his charge, but Caelius' forecast that Rufus would be convicted was probably correct, since he was in exile in 44 (*Letters to Atticus* 368 (XIV.14).2).

320. The nature of Cicero's involvement in this affair being obscure (cf. *Letters to Atticus* 95 (v.2).2), the corrupt text seems incurable.

Now the Forum is full of another great tussle.[321] M. Servilius, having completed a career of general derangement and left nobody anything to sell, was handed over to me – a most unpopular client. Pausanias prosecuting, me defending, on a charge of receiving, Praetor Laterensis dismissed the case *prima facie*. Then Q. Pilius, our friend Atticus' connection, charged him with extortion. It became at once a *cause célèbre* and a verdict of guilty was eagerly canvassed. Tossed up on the crest of this wave, Appius minor lays information concerning money received by Servilius out of his father's property, alleging that HS3,000,000 had been deposited to rig the prosecution.[322] The folly of it surprises you? It would surprise you more if you had heard him speak, the admissions he made about himself and his father – the former idiotic, the latter shocking.

He sends the jury to consider their verdict, the same jury that had assessed the damages. The votes were equally divided. Laterensis, not knowing his law, announced the verdict of each category and, to finish up, 'I shall not call in' – the usual form.[323] He then left the courtroom, and everyone began to look on

321. The facts up to this point may be made out as follows: C. Claudius Pulcher, governor of Asia in 55–53, had been charged with extortion after his return (the case seems to have been slow in getting to court). He had paid over a sum to M. Servilius (probably a former member of his staff) to obtain an acquittal by collusion with the prosecution. He was, however, found guilty and went into exile without leaving enough assets to pay the damages assessed by the court. Pausanias, representing the provincials, then tried to prosecute Servilius on a charge of 'receiving' (i.e. receiving money extorted from the province), but the Praetor, M. Juventius Laterensis, refused leave to proceed, presumably on the ground of insufficient evidence.

322. Appius minor seems to have been allowed to revive Pausanias' charge under particular provisions of the lex Julia, with priority over Pilius' general charge under the same law, since the former stemmed from a previous trial.

323. Of acquittal. An even vote was normally considered as a verdict of acquittal, but the lex Julia, whether by accident or design, seems to have required a majority; an even vote meant that the trial was void.

Servilius as acquitted. Laterensis, having read the hundred-and-first section of the law, which states 'the verdict of the majority of such members of the jury shall be lawful and binding', made his entry in the record – not 'acquitted', but the verdicts of the several categories. Appius again laid his charge; on which Laterensis said that he had arranged matters with L. Lollius and would ★ ★ ★.[324] So now Servilius is neither acquitted nor convicted, and will be handed over to Pilius the worse for wear, to be tried for extortion. Appius, having sworn good faith,[325] none the less did not have the courage to contest the right to prosecute and gave way to Pilius. He himself has been prosecuted for extortion[326] by the Servilii, and on top of this has been charged with assault by a satellite of his own, ★.[327] A well-matched pair!

As regards public affairs, for a long while nothing was done pending a decision on the Gallic provinces. But eventually, after many postponements and much grave debate, during which it became quite clear that Cn. Pompeius was in favour of his[328] leaving his command after the Kalends of March, the Senate passed a decree, of which I send you a copy, and recorded resolutions.

Decree of the Senate: Resolutions

On this 29th day of September in the Temple of Apollo. Present at drafting the following: L. Domitius Ahenobarbus, son of Gnaeus, of

324. Laterensis' reaction to Appius' demand for a fresh trial is concealed under a corrupt text, but whatever it was it resulted in the lapse of Appius' charge.
325. As a preliminary to claiming the right to prosecute the extortion case in preference to Pilius. Such contests were settled by vote of the jury.
326. Presumably for misconduct in Asia during his father's governorship.
327. The name, possibly Statius or Suettius, is doubtful.
328. Meaning Caesar.

the tribe Fabia; Q. Caecilius Metellus Pius Scipio, son of Quintus, of the tribe Fabia; L. Villius Annalis, son of Lucius, of the tribe Pomptina; C. Septimius, son of Titus, of the tribe Quirina; C. Lucilius Hirrus, son of Gaius, of the tribe Pupinia; C. Scribonius Curio, son of Gaius, of the tribe Pomptina; L. Ateius Capito, son of Lucius, of the tribe Aniensis; M. Eppius, son of Marcus, of the tribe Teretina.

Forasmuch as M. Marcellus, Consul, did address this House touching the consular provinces, it was thus resolved: that L. Paulus and C. Marcellus, Consuls, having entered upon their office, should on or after the Kalends of March falling in their year of office bring the matter of the consular provinces before the Senate, and that from the Kalends of March onwards they bring no other business before the Senate either previously or in conjunction therewith; further that for the said purpose they may hold a meeting of the Senate upon any comitial day and pass a Decree, and that in bringing the said matter before the Senate they may without forfeit incurred bring persons belonging to the panel of 300 jurors from their several juries to this House being members thereof; further, if there be need that proposals touching this matter be brought before People or Plebs, that Ser. Sulpicius and M. Marcellus, Consuls, the Praetors, and Tribunes of the Plebs, whosoever of them see fit, bring such proposals before People or Plebs; and that if they do not so do, then their successors bring such proposals before People or Plebs. Resolved.

On this 29th day of September in the Temple of Apollo. Present at drafting the following: L. Domitius Ahenobarbus, son of Gnaeus, of the tribe Fabia; Q. Caecilius Metellus Pius Scipio, son of Quintus, of the tribe Fabia; L. Villius Annalis, son of Lucius, of the tribe Pomptina; C. Septimius, son of Titus, of the tribe Quirina; C. Lucilius Hirrus, son of Gaius, of the tribe Pupinia; C. Scribonius Curio, son of Gaius, of the tribe Pomptina; L. Ateius Capito, son of Lucius, of the tribe Aniensis; M. Eppius, son of Marcus, of the tribe Teretina.

Forasmuc has M. Marcellus, Consul, did address the senate touching the provinces, it was thus resolved: that in the judgement of the Senate no person having power of veto or impediment should let or hinder that matters touching the commonwealth be brought before the Senate on the first possible occasion and that a Decree of the

Senate be passed; and that whosoever offers such bar or impediment shall in the judgement of the Senate have acted against the commonwealth. If any person shall cast his veto against this Decree of the Senate, it is the Senate's pleasure that a Resolution be recorded and that the matter be brought before the Senate on the first possible occasion.

The above Decree of the Senate was vetoed by the following Tribunes of the Plebs: C. Coelius; L. Vinicius; P. Cornelius; C. Vibius Pansa.

It is likewise the Senate's pleasure as touching soldiers serving in the army of C. Caesar that the cases of any such who have completed their terms of service or who can show cause wherefore they be discharged be brought before this House to the end that their cases be taken under consideration and cognizance. If any person shall cast his veto against this Decree of the Senate, it is the Senate's pleasure that a Resolution be recorded and that the matter be brought before this House on the first possible occasion.

The above Decree of the Senate was vetoed by the following Tribunes of the Plebs: C. Coelius; C. Vibius Pansa.

It is likewise the Senate's pleasure as touching the province of Cilicia and the eight remaining provinces now governed by former Praetors with propraetorian rank that such persons as have held the office of Praetor but have not previously held command in any province, being eligible under the Senate's Decree[329] for dispatch to provinces with propraetorian rank, shall be dispatched to the aforesaid provinces as by lot determined. If the number of persons qualified under the Senate's Decree for such appointment be less than the number required to proceed to the aforesaid provinces, then persons having been members of the Board of Praetors standing next in order of seniority, such persons having previously held provincial office, shall proceed to provinces as by lot determined. If their number be in-

329. Voted in 53 to impose a five-year interval between the holding of a Consulship or Praetorship and the assumption of a province. The rule did not become effective until the following year when it was enacted by law (see n. 238).

CICERO'S LETTERS TO HIS FRIENDS

sufficient, then members of each Board of Praetors in succession, not having previously held provincial office, shall be admitted to the lot, until the requisite number be completed. If any person cast his veto against this Decree of the Senate, let a Resolution be recorded.

The above Decree of the Senate was vetoed by the following Tribunes of the Plebs: C. Coelius; C. Pansa.

Moreover, certain remarks of Cn. Pompeius have been noted, and have greatly raised public confidence. He said that before the Kalends of March he could not in fairness take a decision about Caesar's provinces, but that after this date he would have no hesitation. Asked what would be the position if vetoes were cast at that point, he replied that it made no difference whether C. Caesar was going to disobey the Senate or was putting up someone to prevent the Senate from passing a decree. 'And supposing,' said another questioner, 'he chooses to be Consul[330] *and* keep his army?' To which Pompey, as gently as you please: 'And supposing my son chooses to take his stick to me?' These utterances of his have produced an impression that Pompey is having trouble with Caesar. So it looks to me as though Caesar is now ready to settle for one of two propositions – either to stay where he is and forgo his candidature this year,[331] or, if he can secure election, to retire from his command. Curio is making ready for all-out opposition to him. What he may be able to accomplish I don't know, but it is clear to me that he cannot come to grief even if he achieves nothing, his sentiments being sound.

Curio is behaving handsomely to me, and has made me a somewhat onerous present in the shape of the African panthers which were imported for his show. Had he not done that, one might have let the thing go. As it is, I have to give it. So, as I have asked you all along, please see that I have a few beasts from your part of the world. And I commend Sittius' bond to

330. i.e. to get himself elected.
331. This can only mean 'the current electoral year', i.e. 50.

your kind attention. I have sent out my freedman Philo and a Greek, Diogenes, and given them a message and a letter for you. Please look after them and the object of their errand. How important that is to me I have explained in the letter which they will deliver to you.

85 (II. 9)

CICERO TO CAELIUS RUFUS

Camp near Mopsuhestia (?), about 8 October 51

From M. Cicero, Proconsul, to M. Caelius, Curule Aedile-Elect greetings.

First my due and joyful congratulations on your present dignity and also on what may be expected to follow.[332] That they are rather late in coming is not the result of any negligence on my part but of my ignorance of all that goes on. I am in a region where news comes in very slowly, because of its remoteness and the banditry in the country. And not only do I congratulate you, I cannot find words to express my gratitude for the manner of your election, which has given us, as you wrote to me,[333] something to laugh at for the rest of our lives. When I first heard the news, I was transformed into the man himself[334] (you know whom I mean), and found myself playing all those *jeune premier* roles which he is so fond of performing.[335] It's

332. After election to the Curule Aedileship Caelius could look forward to higher things in due course – the Praetorship, even the Consulship. Or perhaps Cicero is simply referring to his entry into office.

333. See p. 166.

334. Hirrus.

335. The point of this passage is not entirely clear. It has been supposed that Hirrus was fond of quoting or reciting from Latin comedies;

hard to put into words, but I saw you in imagination and it was as though I was talking to you: 'Well done, egad! A famous piece of work!' The thing came to me so unexpectedly that I went on to that bit that goes 'A quite amazing thing today . . .' Then, all of a sudden, 'I walked on air. Glee! Glee!' And when I was taken to task for almost losing my wits with excess of jubilation, I defended myself: 'Joy overmuch, I judge . . .' In short, in laughing at him I almost came to *be* the man.

But more of this and much else, to you and concerning you, as soon as I get a minute to spare. My dear Rufus, you are fortune's gift to me. You raise me in men's eyes, you punish not only my enemies but my enviers, making some of them sorry for their villainies and others for their ineptitudes.

86 (II. 10)

CICERO TO CAELIUS RUFUS

In camp near Pindenissum, 14 November 51

From M. Cicero, Imperator, to M. Caelius, Curule Aedile-Elect greetings.

Just see how letters fail to reach me! For I cannot believe that you have sent none since you were elected Aedile, after so important and felicitous an event – expected as regards yourself, but as regards Hillus (I can't pronounce my 'r's[336]) by me quite unforeseen. And yet it is a fact that no letter of yours has come to my hand since those magnificent elections, which sent me into transports of delight. It makes me afraid that the

but why from these particular roles? Had he a propensity to pose as a dashing young gallant (he must have been in his thirties)? The authorship of the first two quotations is unknown. The third comes from Caecilius, the fourth from Trabea.

336. Neither, we gather, could Hirrus.

same may be happening to *my* letters – I have never sent a letter home without another for you, than whose friendship nothing in life is dearer to me or more agreeable.

But back to business (I *can* pronounce my 'b's!).[337] Your prayer is answered. You say you would have liked me to have just enough trouble to provide a sprig of laurel,[338] but you are afraid of the Parthians, because you have little confidence in the forces at my disposal. Well, so it has turned out. On the news of war with Parthia I marched to the Amanus, relying on certain narrow passes and the mountainous character of the country, at the head of an army tolerably well provided with auxiliary forces and fortified by a certain prestige attaching to my name among those who knew me not. There is a good deal of talk in this part of the world – 'Is that the man to whom Rome . . .?', 'whom the Senate . . .?' (you can fill in the gaps). By the time I reached the Amanus, the range of mountains which Bibulus and I share between us, divided at the watershed, our friend Cassius had driven the enemy back from Antioch in a successful action (a very pleasing piece of news to me) and Bibulus had taken over the province.

Meanwhile I harried the people of the Amanus, who are perpetually at war with us, with my entire force. Many were killed or taken prisoner, the rest scattered. Their strongholds were taken by surprise assaults and burned. So in due recognition of a victorious campaign I was saluted 'Imperator' at Issus, where, as I have often heard you say, Clitarchus told you that Darius was defeated by Alexander. I then led my army into the most hostile part of Cilicia, where I am laying siege to the town of Pindenissum, a very strong place indeed, with ramps, casemates, and towers. The siege is now in its twenty-fifth day; judged by scale and difficulty it is a major operation,

337. Literally 'there is nothing wrong with my speech'; i.e. the topic of Hirrus dismissed (*ad rem redeamus*), Cicero has no more trouble with his 'r's.

338. i.e. a Triumph; cf. p. 173.

one to bring me great glory in everything but the name of the town. If I take it, as I hope to do, *then* I shall send an official report. I am telling you all this now, so that you may be hopeful that you are getting what you prayed for.

However, to return to the Parthians, we can feel tolerably pleased with the final result of this summer's operations. Next summer is an alarming prospect. So keep alert, my good Rufus. First try to get my successor appointed. But if, as you write and I suppose, that is going to be rather sticky, see that my tenure is not extended, which is easy. On politics, as I wrote to you earlier, I expect from your letters the present and still more the future. So *please* write everything to me in full detail.

87 (VIII. 10)

CAELIUS RUFUS TO CICERO

Rome, 17 November 51

From Caelius to Cicero greetings.

We have been uncommonly alarmed by dispatches from C. Cassius and Deiotarus. Cassius has written announcing that Parthian forces are this side of the Euphrates, Deiotarus that they are advancing through Commagene into our province. For my part, the principal fear I had as regards yourself (knowing the extent of your military resources) was that this flare-up might endanger your reputation. If your military resources had been greater, I should have felt anxious about your personal safety, but, being as meagre as they are, I thought they augured retreat, not battle. I was nervous about the way such news would be received and how far the necessity would be appreciated. Nervous I still am, and I shall not stop worrying until I hear you are on Italian soil.

However, the news about the Parthian crossing has given rise to a variety of talk. One man is for sending Pompey out, another says Pompey ought not to be moved away from Rome. Another school of thought would like to send Caesar with his army, another the Consuls. But nobody wants to see persons not holding office appointed by senatorial decree. Moreover, the Consuls are afraid that the decree for their military appointment may not be carried, and that they will be insultingly passed over and the business handed to somebody else. For that reason they don't want the Senate to meet at all, carrying this attitude so far as to suggest a lack of conscientiousness in the public service. However, whatever their motive – whether negligence or inertia or the fear I have suggested – it is respectably cloaked under the current opinion that they are uncovetous men who don't want a province.

No dispatch has come in from you, and but for the subsequent arrival of Deiotarus' letter people were beginning to believe that Cassius had invented the war so that his own plunderings would be attributed to hostile devastations – he was supposed to have let Arabs into the province and reported them to the Senate as Parthian invaders. So let me advise you to let us have a full and carefully worded account of the state of affairs out there, whatever it is, so that there is no talk of your having played into somebody's hands or kept silent about what we ought to know.

Now we are at the end of the year – I am writing this letter on 17 December. It's quite plain to me that nothing can be done before the Kalends of January. You know Marcellus, how slow and ineffective he is, and Servius too – a born procrastinator. How do you imagine they are behaving, how do you rate their capacity to put through something they don't care about,[339] when they are handling what *does* interest them[340] so slackly as to give an impression of disinclination? When the

339. Superseding Caesar.
340. The eastern command.

new men come into office, if the Parthian war is on, that question will monopolize the first months. On the other hand, if there is no war out there, or if it is on a scale which you two[341] or your successors can handle with small reinforcements, I envisage that Curio will make his weight felt in two directions: first he'll try to take something away from Caesar, then to give something to Pompey, any little *douceur*, however trifling. Paulus, moreover, talks unconscionably about a province.[342] Our friend Furnius[343] means to oppose his appetite. More I cannot conjecture.

So much I know. Other possibilities I do not see. That time brings many novelties and changes plans I am well aware, but whatever happens, it will take place within this framework. One addition to C. Curio's programme: the Campanian land.[344] They say that Caesar is not worried, but that Pompey is strongly opposed, not wishing to have the land lying unoccupied for Caesar to play with when he gets back.

As regards your departure from Cilicia, I cannot promise to procure the appointment of a successor, but at least I will guarantee that there will be no prorogation. It will be for you to judge whether you want to maintain your attitude, if circumstances and the Senate bring pressure to bear and we cannot decently refuse. *My* obligation is to remember your parting adjuration not to let it happen.

341. Cicero and Bibulus.

342. He wanted a province after his Consulship despite the law requiring a five-year interval (how he justified this is unknown). Cicero thought he might get Cilicia (*Letters to Atticus* 115 (VI.I).7).

343. Now Tribune-Elect.

344. Curio, still at any rate ostensibly playing an 'optimate' game, was now proposing to interfere with Caesar's agrarian legislation, as Cicero had thought to do in 56.

88 (VIII. 6)

CAELIUS RUFUS TO CICERO

Rome, February 50

From Caelius to Cicero greetings.

Doubtless the news will have reached you that Appius has been charged by Dolabella. I must say that the feeling against him is not what I anticipated. Appius has behaved rather sensibly. The moment Dolabella approached the bench,[345] he crossed the city boundary and gave up his claim to a Triumph, thereby blunting sharp tongues and looking readier for the fray than his prosecutor had expected. His hopes are now mainly pinned on you. I know you don't dislike him. How far you want to put him under obligation rests with you. If you had not had a quarrel with him in the past, you would have a freer hand altogether. As it is, if you demand the letter of the law, the standard of abstract justice without compromise, you will have to be careful not to let it look as though the reconciliation on your side was less than suitably candid and sincere. Moreover, you can safely go the other way, if you want to do him any favours, for nobody is going to say that connection and friendship deterred you from your duty. It comes to my mind that between the preliminary application and the laying of the charge[346] Dolabella's wife left him. I remember the commission you gave me as you were leaving,[347] and I don't suppose you

345. i.e., the Praetor's tribunal, for permission to proceed – the first step in a prosecution.

346. The second step, perhaps involving a detailed specification of the charge; but the procedure is not exactly known.

347. Cicero's parting commission may have been general – to keep an eye open for an eligible match for Tullia.

have forgotten what I wrote to you.[348] Now is not the time to enter into further details. The only advice I can give you is this: even if you are not against the idea in principle, don't show your hand in any way just now. Wait and see how he comes out of this case finally. It would not be good for your reputation if the thing leaks out; and if any hint is forthcoming, it would get more publicity than would be decent or expedient.[349] And *he* won't be able to keep quiet about a development which will chime so conveniently with his own hopes and will be all the more in the public eye as he carries his business through – particularly as he's a fellow who would hardly hold his tongue about such a matter even if he knew that talking would be the ruin of him.

Pompey is said to be greatly exercised on Appius' behalf. They even think he will send one of his sons over to you. Here we are acquitting everybody. To be sure there are screens to protect every dirty scandal. Our Consuls are paragons of conscientiousness – up to date they had not succeeded in getting a single decree through the Senate except about the Latin Festival![350] Our friend Curio's Tribunate is an utter frost. But the stagnation of everything here is indescribable. If I didn't have a battle on with the shopkeepers and inspectors of conduits, a coma would have seized the whole community. Unless the Parthians liven you up a bit over there, we are as dead as dormice – though even without the Parthians Bibulus has somehow or other contrived to lose the odd cohort in the Amanus, so it is here reported.[351]

À propos of what I wrote above about Curio being frozen

348. Caelius' letter, referred to here and in Letter 73 (III.10; see p. 151), may have raised Dolabella's name for the first time.

349. As Appius' prosecutor, Dolabella would be 'in the news', and his engagement to Tullia would attract the more attention on that account.

350. Fixing its date, a matter of no political consequence.

351. Cf. *Letters to Atticus* 113 (V.20).5.

up, he's warm enough now – being pulled to pieces most ardently. Quite irresponsibly, because he hadn't got his way about intercalation, he has gone over to the democrats and started talking in favour of Caesar. He has brandished a Road Bill (not unlike Rullus' Agrarian Bill)[352] and a Food Bill, which tells the Aediles to distribute.[353] He had not done this when I wrote the earlier part of this letter.

If you do take any steps to help Appius, be a good fellow and put in a word with him for me. I recommend you to keep your hands free about Dolabella. That is the right line both from the standpoint of the matter I am talking about and from that of your dignity and reputation for fair dealing.

It will be little to your credit if I don't have any Greek[354] panthers.

89 (II. 14)

CICERO TO CAELIUS RUFUS

Laodicea, mid March (?) 50

From M. Cicero, Imperator, to M. Caelius, Curule Aedile, greetings.

M. Fabius is a man of fine character and culture, and on very close terms with me. I have a quite exceptional regard for him, for his brilliant intellect and scholarly attainments go along with unusual modesty. I want you to take up his case[355] as

352. Successfully opposed by Cicero in 63. The resemblance probably lay in the wide powers proposed for the commissioners who were to execute the bill.
353. i.e. making the Aediles responsible for the regular distributions of free or subsidized grain.
354. i.e. Asiatic as opposed to African.
355. Cf. Letter 114 (IX.25).

though it was an affair of my own. I know you great advocates – a man must commit murder if he wants your services. But in the present instance I take no excuse. If you care for me, you will put everything aside when Fabius wants your services.

I am eagerly and longingly awaiting news of Rome, and especially want to know how you are. Because of the severity of the winter it is a long time since any news reached us.

90 (II. 11)

CICERO TO CAELIUS RUFUS

Laodicea, 4 April 50

M. Cicero, Imperator, to M. Caelius, Curule Aedile, greetings.

Would you ever have thought that I could find myself short of words – and not only the kind of words you orators use, but even this vernacular small change? The reason is that I am on tenterhooks to hear what is decreed about the provinces. I have a marvellous longing for Rome, and miss my family and friends, you especially, more than you would believe. I am sick and tired of the province. I think I have gained a reputation here such that rather than seek to add to it I should beware of fortune's turns. Besides the whole thing is unworthy of my powers. I am able to bear, am used to bearing, greater loads in the service of the state. Then again, the threat of a great war hangs over us; this I believe I escape if I leave by the appointed day.

About the panthers, the usual hunters are doing their best on my instructions. But the creatures are in remarkably short supply, and those we have are said to be complaining bitterly because they are the only beings in my province who have to fear designs against their safety. Accordingly they are reported to have decided to leave this province and go to Caria. But the matter is receiving close attention, especially from Patiscus. Whatever comes to hand will be yours, but what that amounts to I simply do not know. I do assure you that your career as Aedile is of great concern to me. The date is itself a reminder – I am writing on Great Mother's Day.[356] On your side, please send me an account of the whole political situation as full as you can make it. I shall consider what I hear from you as my most reliable information.

91 (VIII. 1)

CAELIUS RUFUS TO CICERO

Rome, mid April 50

From Caelius to Cicero greetings.

Your Supplications[357] have given us a nasty headache – short, but sharp. We found ourselves in a very knotty situation. Curio was most anxious to oblige you, but, finding his comitial days taken away from him on all sorts of pretexts, he said he could not possibly allow Supplications to be decreed.[358] If he did, he would appear as losing by his own fault the advantage offered him by Paulus' lunacy,[359] and would be thought to be betraying the public interest. So we got down to a compromise. The Consuls gave an assurance that they would not

356. 4 April, the first day of the festival of Cybele. Her games, as well as the Roman ones, seem to have been the responsibility of the Curule Aediles.

357. Caelius, like Vatinius, prefers the plural.

358. Because the celebrating of a Supplication would take up 'comitial days' on which he could pursue his legislative programme.

359. Probably with reference to further deferment of the question of Caesar's command for which Paulus, now in Caesar's interest, had been in some degree responsible.

make use of these Supplications for the present year. You really have cause to thank both the Consuls, Paulus to be sure more than his colleague. Marcellus merely replied to Curio that he was not building any hope on these Supplications, whereas Paulus said definitely that he would not announce them for this year.

It was reported to us that Hirrus proposed to speak at some length. We got hold of him. Not only did he not do so, but when the question of sacrificial victims[360] was under discussion and he could have held up the business by demanding a count, he kept quiet. He merely assented to Cato, who after speaking of you in flattering terms declared himself against the Supplications. Favonius joined them to make a third. So you must thank them all according to their various characters and habits of conduct: Cato and his associates, because they merely signified their sentiments but did not put up a fight for their opinion, though it was in their power to obstruct; Curio, because he turned aside from his programme for your sake. Furnius and Lentulus[361] canvassed and worked shoulder to shoulder with me as though it was their own affair, which was right and proper. I can also say a good word for Cornelius Balbus, who worked assiduously. He spoke strongly to Curio, telling him that if he acted in any other way he would be doing Caesar an ill turn; moreover, he called his good faith[362] in question. Domitius, Scipio, and co. had indeed voted in favour, without wanting the business to go through. So they kept interrupting in order to provoke a veto. Curio riposted very neatly that he had all the greater pleasure in *not* casting a veto because he could see that some of the supporters of the motion did not want it to take effect.

As for the political situation, all conflict is directed to a single

360. In decreeing the Supplication the Senate would also specify the number and quality of the animals to be sacrificed as thank-offerings.
361. Spinther.
362. Towards Caesar, whom Curio was now supporting.

question, that of the provinces. As things stand so far, Pompey seems to be putting his weight along with the Senate in demanding that Caesar leave his province on the Ides of November. Curio is resolved to let that happen only over his dead body, and has given up the rest of his programme. Our friends (well you know them) do not dare to push the matter to extremities. This is the tableau, the *tout ensemble*: Pompey pretends that he is not attacking Caesar, but making a settlement which he thinks fair to him; he says that Curio is out to make strife. At the same time he regards the idea of Caesar being elected Consul before he hands over his province and army with strong disfavour and positive apprehension. He gets a pretty rough reception from Curio, and his whole third Consulate is being hauled over the coals. Mark my words, if they use all means to suppress Curio, Caesar will come to his Tribune's[363] rescue. If, as seems probable, they are afraid to do that, Caesar will stay as long as he pleases.

The various speeches made in the Senate are in the abstract of city news. Pick out the worthwhile items for yourself. You can pass over a lot, such as who was hissed at the games and the quantity of funerals and other nonsenses. Most things in it are of use. Anyway, I prefer to err on the generous side – better you should hear what doesn't interest you than that some matter of consequence be left out.

I am glad you are attending to the Sittius business. But since you suspect that the persons I sent are not altogether trust-worthy, please act as though you were my agent.

363. Literally 'veto-caster'.

92 (VIII. 7)

CAELIUS RUFUS TO CICERO

Rome, the day after the preceding

From Caelius to Cicero greetings.

How soon you want to leave your present whereabouts I don't know, but for my part, the more successful you have been so far the more I want it. As long as you remain out there, I shall be on thorns about the risk of a Parthian war, for fear some alarm may wipe the grin off my face. This letter will be rather brief – I am giving it without notice to one of the tax-farmers' couriers, who is in a hurry. I gave a longer one to your freedman yesterday.

Nothing new has happened really, unless you want to be told such items as the following – which, of course, you do. Young Cornificius has got himself engaged to Orestilla's daughter. Paula Valeria, Triarius' sister, has divorced her husband for no reason the day he was due to get back from his province. She is to marry D. Brutus. There have been a good many extraordinary incidents of this sort during your absence which I have not yet reported. Servius Ocella would never have got anyone to believe he went in for adultery, if he had not been caught twice in three days. Where? Why, just the last place I should have wished – I leave something for you to find out from other informants! Indeed I rather fancy the idea of a Commander-in-Chief enquiring of this person and that the name of the lady with whom such-and-such a gentleman has been caught napping.

93 (II. 13)

CICERO TO CAELIUS RUFUS

Laodicea, early May 50

From M. Cicero, Imperator, to M. Caelius, Curule Aedile, greetings.

Your letters, as they reach me, are few and far between – perhaps they are not getting through – but delightful. The last one[364] for instance, how wise, how full of friendship and counsel! I had in point of fact determined to act in every way on the lines you recommend, but my resolutions are strengthened when I find that wise and loyal advisers are of the same opinion.

I have a real regard for Appius, as I have often told you, and as soon as we buried our hatchet I perceived the beginning of a corresponding feeling on his side. As Consul he showed me consideration and became a pleasant friend, not without an interest in my literary pursuits. That friendliness on my side was not wanting *you* can testify. And now, I suppose, Phanias corroborates, like a witness in a comedy.[365] And I do assure you that I valued him the more because I saw he had an affection for you. Further, that I am devoted to Pompey you know, and you are aware of my affection for Brutus.[366] Why on earth should I *not* be gratified to welcome the friendship of such a man – in the prime of life, wealthy, successful, able, surrounded by children, by connections of blood and marriage, and by

364. Letter 88 (VIII.6).
365. The Witness (e.g. to the long-lost heroine's identity) was a stock role in Attic New Comedy and 'Phanias' a common dramatic name.
366. One of Appius' daughters was married to Pompey's elder son, another to M. Brutus.

friends – a colleague too, who has put his learned work to the glory of our College in the form of a compliment to me? I have written at some length on this topic because your letter suggested the shadow of a doubt in your mind about my feelings towards him. I suppose you have heard some story. If so, believe me, it is untrue. There is some dissimilarity, generally speaking, between his administration of the province and my own ordinances and principles. Hence perhaps some have suspected that I differ from him out of personal animus, not from theoretical disagreement. But I have never said or done anything with a wish to injure his reputation, and after this recent trouble and our friend Dolabella's precipitate behaviour, I am ready with my intercession in his hour of danger.

In the same letter you speak of a 'community coma'. Well, I was glad of it. It was good news that inactivity had cooled our friend to freezing point. The last little page in your own hand gave me quite a jolt. You don't say so! Curio now standing up for Caesar? Who would have thought it? – except me! For upon my soul, I *did* think it. Powers above, how I should enjoy a laugh with you!

I have completed the assizes, put money into the communal treasuries, assured the tax-farmers of their arrears even for the previous quinquennium without a word of complaint from the provincials, and made myself pleasant to private individuals from the highest to the lowest. So I propose to set out for Cilicia on the Nones of May. Then, as soon as I have touched the fringe of a summer campaign and settled the troops in their stations, I shall vacate the province in conformity with the Senate's decree. I am anxious to see you in office and feel a marvellous longing for Rome and for all my folk, you especially.

94 (VIII. 13)

CAELIUS RUFUS TO CICERO

Rome, early June 50

From Caelius to Cicero greetings.

I congratulate you on the connection you are forming with a very fine fellow,[367] for that, upon my word, is what I think him. In some respects he has done himself poor service in the past, but he has already shaken off these failings with the years and, if any traces remain, I feel sure that your association and influence and Tullia's modest ways will soon remove them. He is not recalcitrant in bad courses or lacking in the intelligence to perceive a better way. And the capital point is that I am very fond of him.

You will like to know that our friend Curio has done very nicely with his veto on the provinces. When the question about the veto was put (this was done in accordance with the Senate's decree) and M. Marcellus' proposal to the effect that representations should be made[368] to the Tribunes was the first pronounced, the House voted it down in large numbers. Pompey the Great's digestion is now in such a poor way that he has trouble finding anything to suit him![369] They have come round to accept that a person should be allowed to stand for office without handing over his army and provinces. How Pompey is going to take this I'll tell you when I know. As for what is to happen if he either resists in arms or just lets it go, you rich

367. Dolabella.
368. The stock phrase for putting pressure upon a Tribune to withdraw his veto, backed by the threat of suspension from office or other coercive action by the Senate.
369. Pompey was actually in poor health and soon afterwards fell seriously ill.

old gentlemen can worry! As I write, Q. Hortensius is at death's door.

95 (II. 12)

CICERO TO CAELIUS RUFUS

Camp on the River Pyramus, 20 (?) June 50

From M. Cicero, Imperator, to M. Caelius, Curule Aedile, greetings.

I am worried about affairs in Rome, with reports of rowdy meetings and a very disagreeable Feast of Minerva[370] – I have no more recent news. But the most worrying thing of all is that, whatever there may be to laugh at in all this unpleasantness, I cannot laugh at it with you – there is in fact a good deal, but I dare not put such things on paper. I do take it hard that I have not yet had a line from you about these matters. When you read this, I shall already have completed my year's assignment, but I hope that a letter from you will meet me on the road to tell me about the whole political situation, so that I don't come to Rome as a complete foreigner. Nobody can do this better than yourself.

Your Diogenes, whose manners I can commend, left me along with Philo for Pessinus. They were going to Adiatorix, despite reports which held out no hope of a kind or affluent reception there.

Rome! Stick to Rome, my dear fellow, and live in the limelight! Sojourn abroad of any kind, as I have thought from my youth upwards, is squalid obscurity for those whose efforts can win lustre in the capital. I knew this well enough, and I only wish I had stayed true to my conviction. I do assure you that

---

370. 19–23 March. The disturbances were probably due to Curio's activities as Tribune.

in my eyes all I get from the province is not worth a single stroll, a single talk with you. I hope I have won some credit for integrity, but I should have gained as much of that by despising the province as I have by saving it from ruin. You suggest the hope of a Triumph. My Triumph would have been glorious enough; at any rate I should not have been so long cut off from all that is dearest to me. However, I hope to see you soon. Send me letters worthy of yourself to meet me on my way.

96 (II. 15)

CICERO TO CAELIUS RUFUS

Side, 3 or 4 August 50

From M. Cicero, Imperator, to M. Caelius, Curule Aedile, greetings.

Your negotiation with Curio on the matter of the Supplication was a model of thoughtfulness and discretion. The result is indeed to my satisfaction. I am pleased that the thing has been settled so quickly, and also that your and my angry rival[371] gave his assent to the fervid encomiast of my official record.[372] You may take it therefore that I am hoping for the sequel.[373] Be ready to play your part.

I am glad you speak so well of Dolabella, glad too that you are fond of him. As for the features which you hope may be toned down by my dear Tullia's good sense, I know which of your letters[374] to turn up. For that matter you ought to read the letter *I* sent to Appius at the time on receipt of yours! But

371. Hirrus.
372. Cato.
373. A Triumph, which would no doubt have been forthcoming but for the Civil War.
374. It has not survived.

what is one to do? Such is life. The Gods bless what is done! I hope to find him an agreeable son-in-law, and there your kindly tact will help us much.

The political situation is very much on my mind. I wish Curio well, I want to see Caesar respected, I can lay down my life for Pompey; but nothing is closer to my heart than the commonwealth itself. You do not make very much of your own political role. I fancy you find yourself torn between loyalties, as a good citizen and as a good friend.

On vacating the province I left my Quaestor Coelius in charge. A boy,[375] you may say! Well, but he is Quaestor, he is a young man of noble family, and I am following an almost universal precedent. Nor had I anyone available for the appointment who had held a higher office. Pomptinus had left long before. My brother Quintus could not be prevailed upon – but even if I *had* left him, unfriendly tongues would be saying that I had not really vacated my province after a year, as the Senate had determined, since I had left an *alter ego* behind me. They might perhaps have added that the Senate had designated as provincial governors persons who had not previously held such office, whereas my brother had been governor of Asia for three years. And then, as things are, I have no need to worry; if I had left my brother in charge, I should have had all manner of apprehensions.[376] Lastly, I did not so much act of my own volition as follow the example of the two most powerful men of our day, who have made friends of every Cassius and Antonius[377] who comes their way. I did not so much want to attract the friendship of a young man as not to alienate him. You have no choice but to approve my decision, because it cannot be changed.

375. In fact, Coelius must have been about thirty.

376. Cf. *Letters to Atticus* 121 (VI.6).4.

377. Q. Cassius Longinus and M. Antonius (Mark Antony) had been chosen as their Quaestors by Pompey and Caesar respectively. Normally Quaestors were assigned by lot.

What you wrote to me about Ocella was none too clear, and there was nothing in the Gazette![378] Your official actions are so well known that Matrinius is news even this side of Mt Taurus.[379] As for me, unless the Etesians hold me back, I hope I shall see you all in the near future.

97 (VIII. 14)

CAELIUS RUFUS TO CICERO

Rome, c. 8 August 50

From Caelius to Cicero greetings.

What a spectacle you have missed here! If you've made Arsaces[380] prisoner and stormed Seleucia, it wasn't worth the sacrifice. Your eyes would never have been sore again if you'd seen Domitius' face when he heard of his defeat.[381] The polling was heavy, and support for the candidates quite on party lines. Only a tiny minority gave their backing in conformity with personal loyalties. Accordingly Domitius is my bitter enemy. He has not a friend in the world whom he hates more than me![382] – all the more so because he regards himself as having been robbed of the Pontificate[383] and me as the author of the outrage. Now he is furious at the general rejoicing over his

378. This seems to be a joke; cf. p. 194.
379. Nothing is known of this incident.
380. i.e. the King of Parthia. The Parthian kings bore the name of the founder of their line in addition to their individual names, like the Ptolemies of Egypt.
381. As a candidate for the vacancy in the Augural College created by the death of Hortensius. He was beaten by Mark Antony.
382. Cf. Letter 20 (I.9).2.
383. The reading is conjectural. If right, it refers to a previous failure of Domitius to gain a place in the College of Pontiffs, of which he later became a member.

discomfiture and at the fact that Antony had only one more ardent supporter (Curio) than myself. As for young Cn. Saturninus, he has been charged by none other than Cn. Domitius.[384] To be sure his past makes him far from popular. We are now waiting for the trial. Actually there is good hope for him after Sex. Peduceaus'[385] acquittal.

On high politics, I have often told you that I do not see peace lasting another year; and the nearer the inevitable struggle approaches, the plainer the danger appears. The question on which the dynasts will join issue is this: Cn. Pompeius is determined not to allow C. Caesar to be elected Consul unless he surrenders his army and provinces; whereas Caesar is persuaded that he cannot survive if he leaves his army. He makes the proposition, however, that both surrender their military forces. So this is what their love-affair, their scandalous union, has come to – not covert backbiting, but outright war! As for my own position, I don't know what course to take; and I don't doubt that the same question is going to trouble you. I have ties of obligation and friendship with these people. On the other side, I love the cause but hate the men.

I expect you are alive to the point that, when parties clash in a community, it behoves a man to take the more respectable side so long as the struggle is political and not by force of arms; but when it comes to actual fighting he should choose the stronger, and reckon the safer course the better. In the present quarrel Cn. Pompeius will evidently have with him the Senate and the people who sit on juries,[386] whereas all who live in present fear and small hope for the future will rally to Caesar. His army is incomparably superior. To be sure there is time

384. L. Domitius' son. Cn. (Sentius) Saturninus had no doubt supported Antony.

385. Not Cicero's former Praetor or his son (see Glossary of Persons), but perhaps a supporter of Caesar who became governor of Sardinia in 48. The circumstances of his trial are unknown.

386. i.e. the rich and respectable.

enough to consider their respective resources and choose one's side.

I almost forgot the most interesting item of all. Did you know that Appius is performing prodigies of censorial vigour – works of art, size of estates, debt are all grist to his mill. He is convinced that the Censorship is face cream or washing soda, but I fancy he is making a mistake; in trying to scrub out the stains he is laying open all his veins and vitals.[387] Make haste in God's name and man's and get here as soon as you can to laugh at our frolics – at Drusus trying offences under the lex Scantinia,[388] at Appius taking official action about works of art.[389] Believe me, you must hurry. Our friend Curio is considered to have shown good sense in not pressing his point about pay for Pompey's troops.

Well, to sum up: what do I think will happen? If neither of the two goes off to the Parthian war, I see great quarrels ahead in which strength and steel will be the arbiters. Both are well prepared, morally and materially. If it were not for the personal risk involved, Fate is preparing a mighty and fascinating show for your benefit.

98 (VIII. 12)

CAELIUS RUFUS TO CICERO

Rome, c. 20 November 50

From Caelius to Cicero greetings.

I am mortified to have to admit and complain to you about

387. Or 'flesh'.

388. See Glossary of Terms. Drusus was apparently a notorious offender.

389. Appius had allegedly plundered Greece to assemble his own art-collection.

the scurvy treatment I have received from Appius. The man is a monster of ingratitude. Just because he is indebted to me for important favours,[390] he turned against me; and being too much of a skinflint to bring himself to repay them, he declared covert war on me – not so covert though but that I heard tell of it from many quarters and saw his malevolence plainly enough for myself. But when I found that he had been sounding his colleague[391] and that he had talked openly to certain persons and was colloguing with L. Domitius (a bitter enemy of mine these days) with the idea of presenting this little *douceur* to Cn. Pompeius – well, I could not bring myself to tax him personally and ask a man who I thought owed me his life not to do me harm. So what did I do? Notwithstanding my reluctance, I spoke to a number of Appius' friends who had personal knowledge of what I had done for him, as though enquiring as to the true facts. Finding that he did not even consider me worth the trouble of an explanation, I chose to put myself under an obligation to his colleague (an almost total stranger to me and none too well disposed, because I am a friend of yours) rather than subject myself to the sight of that supercilious monkey. When he heard of that, he flew into a rage and went on bawling that I was trying to pick a quarrel so as to use a show of enmity as a pretext for victimizing him if he failed to meet my wishes in a matter of money. Since then he has been continually sending for Servius Pola, the professional prosecutor, and talking with Domitius. They were looking for a charge on which they could put him up to prosecute me, but were puzzled to find one. So they thought they would have me put in court on a charge which they could not decently name (?).[392] They are having the effrontery to get me summoned under the lex

390. Probably with reference to efforts on Appius' behalf when he was under prosecution; see p. 189.

391. L. Calpurnius Piso Caesoninus, Consul in 58, elected Censor along with Appius in 51.

392. Text and sense doubtful.

Scantinia at the end of my Circus Games.[393] The words were hardly out of Pola's mouth when I charged Censor Appius under the same statute! It's the greatest success I ever saw. All Rome (and not just the lower orders) approves; so that Appius is more upset by the scandal than by the prosecution. Furthermore, I have instituted a claim against him for a chapel[394] that is in his house.

I[395] am much put out by the delay of this slave who is bringing you my letter. After receiving my earlier letter,[396] he took more than forty days before setting out. I don't know what else I can write to you. You know that they are marking time at home (?). You are holding things up (?).[397] I am much looking forward to your return, and am eager to see you, as soon as possible. I ask you to take my injuries to heart, as you judge that I am in the habit of taking yours and of avenging them.

99 (XV. 7)

CICERO TO C. MARCELLUS

Between Iconium and Cybistra, early September 51

From M. Cicero, Proconsul, to C. Marcellus, Consul-Elect, greetings.

The news of your election as Consul gave me great happiness. I wish the Gods may prosper you in that high office, and that you may discharge it in a manner worthy of yourself and your father. You have always had my affection and regard, and in all

393. i.e. the Roman Games, which ended on 19 September.
394. Claimed as public property.
395. This postscript seems to have been added a day or two later.
396. Letter 97 (VIII.14).
397. Apparently a reference to Tullia's wedding. But the text is very doubtful.

the vicissitudes of my career I have had evidence of your warm affection for me. From your father also I have received a great many kindnesses – defence in bad times, furtherance in good. So I am, and ought to be, devoted to your family – the more so as that venerable and excellent lady, your mother, has shown an active concern for my welfare and standing beyond what could be expected from her sex. Accordingly I would earnestly solicit your regard and protection during my absence.

100 (XV. 8)

CICERO TO C. MARCELLUS (SENIOR)

Between Iconium and Cybistra, early September 51

From M. Cicero, Proconsul, to his Colleague C. Marcellus, greetings.

I am marvellously pleased to hear that your son Marcellus has been elected Consul and that the joy you most longed for is indeed yours. My happiness is both for his own sake and because I consider you deserving of every possible good fortune. In my trials as in my successes you have always shown me conspicuous good-will; indeed I have found your whole family most active and ardent for my welfare and my standing. I shall accordingly be grateful if you will convey my congratulations to that highly respected and excellent lady, your wife Junia. As for yourself, let me request you to continue to favour me in my absence with your regard and protection.

101 (XV. 9)

CICERO TO M. MARCELLUS

Between Iconium and Cybistra, September (early or middle) 51

From M. Cicero, Proconsul, to M. Marcellus, Consul, greetings.

I am thoroughly delighted that with C. Marcellus' election to the Consulship you have reaped the reward of your family affection, patriotism, and your own most distinguished and meritorious record in that office. Of sentiment in Rome I have no doubt; as for me, far away as I am, dispatched by none other than yourself to the ends of the earth, I assure you I exalt it to the skies in praises most sincere and well grounded. I have had a very particular regard for you from your childhood. On your side, you have ever desired and believed me to stand high in all respects. And what has now happened, whether we call it your achievement or an expression of the sentiments of the Roman people concerning you, very sensibly augments and enhances my affection for you, and it gives me the keenest pleasure when I hear from persons of the highest perspicacity and probity that in all our words, acts, pursuits, and habits I resemble you – or you resemble me. If only you add one more thing to the splendid achievements of your Consulship, I shall feel that you have left me nothing further to wish for – I mean the early appointment of a successor to my post, or at any rate no extension of the term which you fixed for me by decree of the Senate and by law.

Take care of your health and favour me in my absence with your regard and protection.

I still do not think I should write officially on the reports reaching me about the Parthians, and for that reason I prefer not to write to you on the subject either, even as a close personal friend, for fear that a letter to the Consul might be interpreted as an official communication.

102 (XV. 12)

CICERO TO L. PAULUS

Between Iconium and Cybistra, September (early or middle) 51

From M. Cicero, Proconsul, to L. Paulus, Consul-Elect, greetings.

I never had a doubt but that the Roman People would enthusiastically and unanimously elect you Consul in recognition of your great services to the state and the exalted position of your family. All the same, my happiness when I heard the news was more than you can well conceive. I wish the Gods may prosper you in your high office and that you may discharge it in a manner worthy of yourself and your forbears. I only wish I could have been on the spot to see the day for which I have always longed, and to do you yeoman service in return for your signal acts of good-will and kindness towards me. That opportunity was snatched away from me by the sudden, unforeseen chance which sent me on service abroad; but I trust I may still see you as Consul administering the commonwealth in a manner worthy of your standing. To that end I earnestly beg of you to use your best efforts and prevent any unfairness to me or any extension of my year's term. If you do that, you will generously crown your past tokens of good-will.

103 (XV. 3)

CICERO TO CATO

Camp near Iconium, 3 September (or shortly after) 51

From M. Cicero to M. Cato greetings.

In view of the close relations between us I feel I should write to inform you that a mission from Antiochus of Commagene has arrived in my camp near Iconium on 3 September with the news that the Crown-Prince of Parthia, who is married to a sister of the King of Armenia, has arrived on the banks of the Euphrates with a massive Parthian army and a large force in addition, drawn from many different nationalities; that he has already begun the passage of the river; and that there is talk of the King of Armenia invading Cappadocia.

I have not written an official dispatch for two reasons. The envoys says that the King of Commagene himself sent messengers and a letter to the Senate immediately; and I expect that Proconsul M. Bibulus, who left by sea from Ephesus for Syria about the Ides of August, has already arrived in his province, since he had favourable winds. I presume that everything will be more reliably reported to the Senate in a dispatch from him. In such a situation, with a war on so large a scale, my own principal preoccupation is to hold by gentleness and moderation, through the loyalty of our subjects, what I can hardly hold by the troops and resources at my disposal. I hope that, as in the past, I shall have your regard and protection in my absence.

104 (XV. 1)

CICERO TO THE MAGISTRATES AND SENATE

Near Cybistra, 18 September 51

From M. Tullius Cicero, son of Marcus, Proconsul, to the Consuls, Praetors, Tribunes of the Plebs, and Senate, greetings.

I trust you are well. I and the army are well.

Although receiving clear reports that the Parthians had crossed the Euphrates with virtually their entire force, I supposed that M. Bibulus, Proconsul, would be able to give you more reliable information on these matters, and therefore decided that it was unnecessary for me to send an official account of reports which concerned a province other than my own. Subsequently, however, the information reached me on unimpeachable authority, by emissaries, verbal reports, and letters. Bearing in mind the importance of the matter, as also that I have no news as yet of Bibulus' arrival in Syria and that I may almost be said to carry joint responsibility with him in the conduct of this war, I thought it my duty to write apprising you of my intelligence.

Envoys from King Antiochus of Commagene were the first to announce to me that large forces of Parthians had begun to cross the Euphrates. On receiving this report, I decided that it would be best to wait for something more reliable, since there were those who thought the king was not entirely to be trusted. On 18 September, as I was leading my army into Cilicia, I received a letter on the borders of Lycaonia and Cappadocia from Tarcondimotus, who is considered to be our most faithful ally beyond Taurus and a true friend to Rome. This told me that Pacorus, son of King Orodes of Parthia, had crossed the Euphrates with a very large force of Parthian cavalry and pitched camp at Tyba, creating great turmoil in the province of Syria. On the same day I had a letter on these same matters from Iamblichus, Phylarch of the Arabs, who is generally thought to be loyal and friendly to our country.

After receiving this intelligence, I determined to march to the Taurus, for several reasons. I realized that our subjects were in a wavering mood, poised in expectation of change; but I trusted that those with whom I had already been in contact and who had perceived the gentleness and integrity of my government had become more friendly to Rome, and that the loyalty of Cilicia would be strengthened if that area shared in the benefits of my equitable administration. I also wanted to crush the rebellious elements in the Cilician nation and to let the enemy in Syria know that on receipt of the aforesaid intelligence a Roman army was not merely not retreating but actually approaching closer.

If, however, my advice carries any weight with you, especially in circumstances which you have heard by report but which I have almost before my eyes, I would emphatically urge and warn you to take thought for these provinces even at this all too late hour. You are not ignorant of the resources and defensive forces with which you sent me out to face the prospect of a major war. It was not blind folly but a sense of shame that prevented me from declining the task; for I have never thought any danger grave enough to care to evade it by failing in obedience to your authority.

The present situation is this: Unless you send to these provinces without loss of time an army as large as you usually send to cope with war on a grand scale, there is the gravest risk that all the provinces on which the revenues of Rome depend may have to be given up. You should rest no hopes whatever on the local levies. Their numbers are small, and those there are scatter at sight of danger. My gallant colleague, M. Bibulus, gave his verdict on this description of troops in Asia, when he declined to hold a levy, although you had given him permission. As for the auxiliaries supplied by our allies, the harshness and injustices of our rule have rendered them either so weak as to be of little use or so disaffected that it would appear imprudent to expect anything from them or entrust anything to them. I think we can fully depend on the loyalty of King Deiotarus and such forces as he commands. Cappadocia is a vacuum; the remaining kings and rulers are undependable in point both of resources and of loyalty. Few as our numbers are, I shall assuredly not be found wanting in courage, nor yet, I trust, in judgement. What will happen no man can tell. I pray that I may be able to provide for our safety, as I certainly shall for our honour.

105 (XV. 2)

CICERO TO THE MAGISTRATES AND SENATE

Camp near Cybistra, 21 or 22 September 51

From M. Tullius Cicero, son of Marcus, Proconsul, to the Consuls, Praetors, Tribunes of the Plebs, and Senate, greetings.

I trust that you are well. I and the army are well.

On arriving in my province on 31 July, no earlier date being practicable by reason of the difficulties of travel both by land and sea, I considered that I should best conform to my duty and the public interest by making appropriate provisions for the army and for military security. Having made my dispositions with care and diligence rather than plenitude of means, I received reports and letters almost daily concerning a Parthian invasion of the province of Syria. I therefore thought it proper to march through Lycaonia, Isauria, and Cappadocia, since it was strongly suspected that, if the Parthians attempted to leave Syria and break into my province, they would come by way of Cappadocia, where there was least to stop them.

Accordingly I and my army marched through that part of

Cappadocia which adjoins Cilicia and pitched camp near Cybistra, a town lying close to the Taurus mountains, in order that Artavasdes, King of Armenia, whatever his disposition might be, should know that a Roman army was not far from his frontiers, and that I should have King Deiotarus close at hand, a most faithful and friendly ally to our country, whose advice and material support might be of service to the commonwealth.

While stationed in that spot, having previously sent a force of cavalry on to Cilicia so that the news of my arrival might strengthen morale generally in the communes situated in that region and at the same time I might get early intelligence of events in Syria, I thought it proper to devote the three days of my halt in this camp to an important and necessary duty. I had your resolution charging me to take good care of King Ariobarzanes Eusebes and Philorhomaeus, to defend his welfare, security, and throne, and to protect king and kingdom; to which you added that the welfare of this monarch was a matter of great concern to the People and Senate – something that had never before been decreed by our House with respect to any monarch. I therefore considered it incumbent upon me to convey your mandate to the king, and to promise him my faithful protection and care, adding that, since his personal welfare and the security of his realm had been commended to me by yourselves, I should be glad to learn his wishes, if any.

When I had addressed the king to this effect in the presence of my Council, he began his reply with a proper expression of profound gratitude to yourselves, and then proceeded to thank me also. He felt it as a most important favour and a very high compliment that his welfare should be of so much concern to the Senate and People of Rome, and that I should be at such pains to demonstrate my sense of obligation and the weight attaching to your recommendation. At first he gave me to understand, to my great satisfaction, that he had no knowledge or even suspicion of any plots against his life or throne. I congratulated him, and said I was delighted to hear it, at the same time urging the young man to remember the sad end that had overtaken his father;[398] he should guard himself vigilantly and take good heed for his safety, conformably to the Senate's admonition. He then took his leave, and returned to the town of Cybistra.

On the day following, however, he arrived in my camp along with his brother Ariarathes and some older persons, friends of his father's. In a state of tearful agitation, as were also his brother and their friends, he appealed to me in the name of my pledged word and your commendation. When I asked in some surprise what had happened, he said that he had received information of a manifest conspiracy, which had been kept secret prior to my arrival because those who might have revealed it were afraid to speak. But now, in the hope of my protection, a number had plucked up courage to come to him with what they knew. Among them was his brother, who loved him dearly and who had a strong sense of family loyalty. He was alleging (and Ariarathes confirmed the king's words in my presence) that he had been invited to aspire to the throne. This could not have come to anything while his brother was alive; but until now he had been too much afraid to bring the facts into the open. Having heard this speech, I admonished the king to take every precaution for his own safety and exhorted the tried friends of his father and grandfather to take warning by the tragic fate of the former and defend the life of their sovereign with every care and safeguard.

The king then asked me for some cavalry and cohorts from my army. I was aware that under your decree I had not only a right but a duty to agree. But in view of the reports coming in daily from Syria, the public interest demanded that I should conduct the army to the borders of Cilicia as soon as possible. Moreover, now that the plot had been exposed, the king did not appear to me to need a Roman army; his own resources seemed adequate for his protection. I therefore urged him to

398. Ariobarzanes II, murdered by conspirators.

make the preservation of his own life his first lesson in the art of ruling. He should exercise his royal prerogative against the persons whom he had found organizing the conspiracy against him, punishing where punishment was necessary and relieving the rest of apprehension. He should use the sanction of my army to intimidate the guilty rather than for actual combat. But all would understand, knowing the terms of the Senate's decree, that if need arose, I should come to the king's defence on your authority.

So I leave him in good heart. I am breaking camp and setting out on my way to Cilicia, leaving Cappadocia amid a general persuasion that by your policy and an amazing, if not providential, accident my advent has rescued the king from the immediate danger of a conspiracy – one upon whom unsolicited you conferred the royal title in the most honourable terms, whom you recommended to my protection, and whose welfare you decreed to be of great concern to you. I have deemed it appropriate to send you an account of the incident to enable you to appreciate from what nearly happened your own foresight in providing long in advance against that very contingency. And I have been all the more studious to inform you because I believe I have seen in King Ariabarzanes such evidences of character, intelligence, loyalty, and good-will towards your House as appear to justify the care and concern you have lavished upon his welfare.

106 (XV. 14)

CICERO TO CASSIUS

Cilicia, late October (?) 51

From M. Cicero, Imperator, to C. Cassius, Proquaestor,[399] greetings.

399. In Syria.

Your recommendation gives me a friend in the person of M. Fabius; but I am none the richer on his account. These many years past he has been mine absolutely, highly regarded by me for his good nature and attentive courtesy. However, I have become much the more his friend for having perceived what an exceptional regard he has for you. So his own disposition towards you, now that I am thoroughly aware of it, has been in some degree a better passport to my favour than your letter, though that too has had its effect. Anyhow, as to Fabius I shall spare no effort to comply with your request.

For many reasons I am sorry you were unable to meet me. Fond of you as I have long been, I should have liked to see you after so considerable an interval; I should have liked to congratulate[400] you in person as I did by letter; I should have liked to exchange views on such of our several concerns as either of us cared to raise; lastly, I should have liked to see a further strengthening of our friendship, which has been fostered on both sides by substantial services but interrupted, as to daily contact, by lengthy periods of separation.

Since that was not to be, we shall make the best of correspondence and get pretty well the same results apart as if we were together. Of course the satisfaction of seeing you cannot be enjoyed by letter; and the satisfaction of congratulating you would be more full-bodied if I were looking you in the eye as I did it. However, I have done so once, and I do so again. Yes, I congratulate you upon the magnitude of your success, and no less upon its timeliness, for you are leaving for Rome with the thanks and plaudits of your province ringing in your ears.

Then there is the third point – the exchange of views about our concerns which would have taken place had we met must be managed by correspondence. On all grounds but one I am strongly of the opinion that you should make haste back to Rome. When I left, all was quiet so far as you were concerned, and your recent brilliant victory will clearly shed lustre on your

400. On his successful action against the Parthian invaders.

advent. But if those near to you[401] are under fire, we must pause. Should it be such as you can cope with, then make haste – it will be the brightest feather in your cap. But if it's too powerful for that, you must consider. It would be a pity to arrive just at the least favourable moment. The matter is entirely for you to judge. You know your own strength. If you *can*, there is credit and popular approval to be had. But if you really cannot, you will find the talk less annoying elsewhere.

As for me, my plea in this letter is the same as in my last. Strain every nerve to prevent any prolongation of my present office, which both Senate and People fixed for one year. I press you on this point feeling that my worldly welfare depends on it. You can look to our friend Paulus, a thorough well-wisher of mine. There is Curio, there is Furnius. Do try your hardest, in the persuasion that it means everything to me.

The last of the points I mentioned was the strengthening of our friendship. On that little need be said. As a boy you drew towards me, and on my side I always believed that I should be proud of you. You also defended me in my darkest days. After you went abroad, I formed a very close friendship with your connection[402] Brutus. In your joint talents and energy I think I have a rich prospect of pleasure and prestige; and I earnestly ask you to confirm that opinion by your zeal. Send me a letter at once, and when you are back in Rome write as often as you can.

401. As often the plural probably refers to an individual, Cassius' cousin Q. Cassius Longinus. He seems to have been threatened with prosecution in respect of his ill-treatment of provincials in Spain, where he had served as Pompey's Quaestor.

402. Cassius had married Brutus' half-sister Junia, sometimes called Tertulla.

107 (II. 7)

CICERO TO CURIO

In camp at Pindenissum, soon after 17 December 51

From M. Cicero, Imperator, to C. Curio, Tribune of the Plebs, greetings.

Belated congratulations usually pass unrebuked, especially if the omission is not due to negligence – I am far away and news reaches me late. At all events I do congratulate you, and pray that your Tribunate will earn you everlasting credit. And I urge you to guide and govern all your actions by your own good sense, not to be carried away by the counsels of others. No one can advise you more wisely than yourself; if you listen to yourself, you will never go wrong. I do not write this in-advisedly. I am aware whom I am addressing, I know your spirit and intelligence. I have no fear of your acting timidly or foolishly, if you defend what you yourself feel to be right.

You see, I am sure, the political situation which you have chosen (not happened) to enter – for by your own decision, not by chance, you have brought your term of office to coincide with the very crisis-point.[403] I do not doubt that you are bearing in mind the power of circumstances in politics, the shifting nature of affairs, the uncertainty of events, the instability of men's sentiments, the snares and falsehoods of which life is full. But do, I beg you, give care and consideration to – nothing new, only what I wrote to start with: be your own confidant and counsellor. Listen to yourself, defer to yourself. It would not be easy to find one better able to advise others than you, and assuredly no one will better advise yourself. Ah, why am I not there as a spectator of your laurels, as sharer, partner, agent in your plans? Not that you stand in any need of such; but the

403. See p. 168.

measure and strength of my affection would lend me power to help you with advice.

I shall be writing more later on. In a few days' time I shall be sending couriers of my own household, since I wish to present in a single letter a full report to the Senate of the entire summer's operations, which I have conducted with considerable success and to my own satisfaction. As for your Priesthood,[404] you will learn from the letter I have given to your freedman Thraso how much attention I have given to this delicate and difficult matter.

My dear Curio, I have a solemn plea to make to you in the name of the unbounded kindness you bear me and I no less bear you, not to allow my tenure of this tiresome provincial post to be extended for any additional period. I took this up with you in person when I had no idea that you would be Tribune of the Plebs for the year in question, and have often mentioned it in my letters. But at that time I asked you as a member of the Senate, though to be sure a young man of the highest birth and personal influence; now I ask you as Tribune, and what is more as Tribune Curio. I do not want anything new decreed, which is apt to be difficult, but just the opposite. I want you to defend the Senate's decree and the laws of the land, and I want the terms on which I came here to stand intact. Allow me once more to make this pressing request of you.

108 (XV. 10)

CICERO TO C. MARCELLUS

Tarsus, 51 (end) or 50 (beginning)

From M. Cicero, Imperator, to C. Marcellus, son of Gaius, Consul, greetings.

404. This must refer to Curio's election to the College of Pontiffs, of which his father had been a member.

Since my dearest wish has come to pass, namely that the good-will of all the Marcelli, and the Marcellini[405] too – for the friendly disposition of your house and name towards me has always been extraordinary – since, I repeat, it has come to pass that the good-will of your entire family can find its fulfilment through your consular office, with which my own military achievements and the credit and honour thereto appertaining have so opportunely coincided, allow me to request you to ensure that, when my dispatch has been read to the Senate, a decree[406] follows in terms as handsome as possible. That will be very easily done, for the House, as I confidently anticipate, will receive such a proposal without disfavour.

If my relations with yourself were any less close than with the rest of your family, I should make the latter my advocates with you – you know that they have a special regard for me. From your father I have received the most signal favours; no better friend either to my survival or to my advancement can be named. As for your cousin,[407] I suppose nobody is ignorant of his attachment to me, now and always. In fact your whole family circle has always showered favours of the greatest consequence upon me. And yet *you* have yielded to none of your relatives in your regard for me. May I therefore specially request you to desire me to gain all possible distinction through your agency, and both in the matter of a decree of Supplication and in all others to consider my reputation as sufficiently commended to your care?

405. A branch of the Marcellus family which had passed by adoption into the Cornelii Lentuli. The best known of its members is Cn. Cornelius Lentulus Marcellinus, Consul in 56.

406. For a Supplication.

407. M. Marcellus, Consul in 51.

109 (XV. 13)

CICERO TO L. PAULUS

Tarsus, 51 (end) or 50 (beginning)

From M. Cicero, Imperator, to L. Paulus, Consul, greetings.

I should have wished above all things to be with you in Rome for many reasons, but especially to give you clear token of the good-will I owe you both in your candidature for the Consulship and in your conduct of the office. Of your prospects of election I was always well assured, but still I wished to put my shoulder to the wheel. In office I certainly hope that you are having a comparatively easy time; but it irks me that when I was Consul and you were a young man I saw proof of your good-will, while at my present time of life I am unable to show you corresponding proof of mine.

However, I think it must be fated somehow that you are always given opportunity to do me honour, whereas I find nothing but the will with which to requite you. You added lustre to my Consulship and to my return from exile; my time for military achievement has just coincided with *your* Consulship. So it is that, although your exalted position and dignity on the one hand and on the other the great honour I have in view, in which my public reputation is so largely involved, seem alike to require me to press a request upon you in as many words as I can muster – a request, namely, that you ensure the passage of a decree concerning my successes in the most complimentary terms – yet in fact I dare not press you strongly for fear of seeming either to forget your consistent behaviour towards me through the years or to suppose that *you* have forgotten it.

Accordingly, I shall do as I imagine you would have me do, and be brief in addressing a request to one whose past kindnesses towards me are known to all mankind. If the Consuls in office were not who they actually are, you, my dear Paulus, would be the man to whom I should be sending to secure their most friendly dispositions towards me. As it is, the highest power and the highest influence are yours, and the relations between us are universal knowledge. Therefore I earnestly beg you to ensure that a decree in the most complimentary terms goes through concerning my successes, and as rapidly as possible. That they are worthy of recognition and congratulation you will find from the dispatch which I have addressed officially to you and your Colleague and the Senate. And I hope you will regard yourself as having undertaken to look after all other concerns of mine, my reputation above all. In particular I trust you will take care that my tenure is not extended, as I requested in my previous letter. I want to *see* you Consul, and while you are in that capacity to attain all my hopes, not only in my absence, but also on the spot.

110 (XV. 4)

CICERO TO CATO

Tarsus (?), late December 51

From M. Cicero, Imperator, to M. Cato, greetings.

Your exalted prestige and the respect which I have always held for your outstanding personal qualities make me feel it to be highly important to me that you should know of my achievements and not be unaware of the equity and moderation which has characterized my care for our subjects and my administration of my province. For I believe that when you are acquainted with those things I shall find it easier to win your approval for what I have at heart.

Arriving in my province on 31 July, I saw that in view of the advanced season I ought to join my army with all speed. I spent two days at Laodicea, then four at Apamea, three at Synnada, and as many at Philomelium.[408] There were large gatherings in these towns, and I relieved many communes of oppressive imposts, harsh interest dues, and wrongful debt. Before my arrival the army had been scattered by a mutiny or something of the kind. Five cohorts had taken up a position near Philomelium without a Legate or Military Tribune, without even a Centurion, in command. The remainder of the army was in Lycaonia. I ordered my Legate, M. Anneius, to take these five cohorts to join the main body, and having concentrated the entire force to encamp near Iconium in Lycaonia.

Anneius faithfully carried out his orders, and on 24 August I reached the camp, having in the interval (in accordance with the Senate's decree) raised a strong force of reservists and a quite serviceable body of cavalry along with auxiliaries voluntarily supplied by free peoples and allied kings. Meanwhile, after I had reviewed the army and begun the march to Cilicia on the Kalends of September, a mission sent to me by the King of Commagene announced in a great state of excitement (but correctly enough) that the Parthians had crossed over into Syria. I was much alarmed by the news both for Syria and for my own province, and indeed for the rest of Asia. I therefore thought it best to take my army through that district of Cappadocia which adjoins Cilicia. Had I descended into Cilicia, I should have had no difficulty in holding Cilicia itself because of the natural features of Mt Amanus (there are two entries into Cilicia from Syria, both so narrow as to need only small forces to block them – there is no more defensible a position than Cilicia against an attack from Syria); but I was concerned about Cappadocia, which lies open from the Syrian side and is bordered by kings who, even if they are friendly to us, dare not be openly

408. The dates ran: Laodicea 31 July – 3 August; Apamea 5–9 August; Synnada 10–14 August; Philomelium 16–20 August. Cicero seems here to give one day too many to Apamea.

hostile to the Parthians. Accordingly I pitched camp in a corner of Cappadocia not far from the Taurus near the town of Cybistra, where I could at once protect Cilicia and hold Cappadocia, thus applying a brake to any changes of policy on the part of the neighbouring potentates.

In the midst of this agitation, with war on a grand scale in imminent prospect, King Deiotarus sent a mission to tell me that he proposed to march to my camp with his entire forces. It is not without good warrant that you and I and the Senate have always held him in the highest esteem, for he is both notably well-disposed and loyal to Rome and remarkable for his lofty spirit and sound judgement. Impressed by this gesture of friendly zeal, I wrote to thank him and to urge him to make haste.

Having made a stay of five days at Cybistra for military reasons, I unexpectedly came to the rescue of King Ariobarzanes, whose welfare had been commended to me by the Senate at your instance, from the immediate threat of a conspiracy, not only saving his life, but consolidating his authority as ruler. Metras and Athenaeus (the latter the subject of your special recommendation to me), both sentenced to exile by the cruelty of Athenais,[409] were established by me in high favour and influence at court. There was the prospect of a major war flaring up in Cappadocia, should the High Priest[410] defend himself by force of arms, as was generally thought likely; for the young man had horse, foot, and money in readiness, and was supported by those who wanted a change of régime. I so managed that he withdrew from the kingdom. The full authority of the Palace was safeguarded without turmoil or violence, and the king settled in his royal estate and dignity.

409. The Queen-Mother.
410. Of Ma-Bellona at Comana, whose power in Cappadocia was second only to the king's. We do not know his name. Archelaus, with whom he is commonly confused, was High Priest of a similar establishment at Comana in Pontus.

Meanwhile, I learned from many letters and reports that a large Parthian and Arab force had approached the town of Antioch, and that a large body of their cavalry, which had penetrated Cilicia, had been cut to pieces by squadrons of my horse and the Praetorian Cohort, which had been left in garrison at Epiphanea. Seeing that the Parthians had turned away from Cappadocia and were not far from the borders of Cilicia, I led my army to the Amanus by the longest marches I could achieve. On arrival there I learned that the enemy had withdrawn from Antioch, and that Bibulus was in the town. I informed Deiotarus, who was already hastening to join me with a large and reliable body of horse and foot along with his entire forces, that there appeared to be no reason for him to absent himself from his kingdom; if there was any new development I should send him a letter and messengers immediately.

I had come with the intention of lending aid to either province, if occasion arose. Moreover, I had already decided that the pacification of the Amanus and the removal of the traditional enemy from those mountains was of great importance to both. I therefore proceeded with this objective. Pretending to withdraw from the mountains and make for other parts of Cilicia, I pitched camp near Epiphanea, one day's march from the Amanus. On 12 October, as evening drew on, I marched the army in light equipment so rapidly during the night that by daybreak on 13 October I was moving up the mountain. The cohorts and auxiliary formations were divided into three forces, one commanded by my brother Quintus (Legate) along with myself, another by Legate C. Pomptinus, the third by Legates M. Anneius and L. Tullius. We took many of the enemy by surprise, cutting off their escape and killing or taking them prisoner. Erana, the capital of the Amanus region, which was more like a city than a village, together with Sepyra and Commoris, fell to us after a strenuous and lengthy resistance (Pomptinus was in that part of the mountains) lasting from early twilight till four in the afternoon; a large number of the enemy were slaughtered. We also took a number of strongholds by storm, and burned them. After these operations we pitched camp for four days near Alexander's Altars[411] in the foothills of the Amanus, employing the whole period in destroying whatever was left in the mountains and devastating the countryside – that part of the mountains which falls within my province.

These operations concluded, I led the army against Pindenissum, a town of the Free Cilicians. It was in a situation of great strength, perched high up, and inhabited by a race who have never yielded obedience even to the native kings. They were harbouring deserters and eagerly looking forward to the arrival of the Parthians, so that I considered it a matter of imperial prestige to curb their presumption, whereby others not well affected to the rule of Rome would be more easily discouraged. I surrounded the place with a rampart and moat, protecting these with six blockhouses and a very large camp, then pressed the assault with an earthwork, penthouses, and towers, using artillery and archers in large numbers. By dint of much personal effort and without putting our subjects to any trouble or expense, I finished the operation in fifty-seven days. Every part of the city was demolished or burned and the population driven to surrender to me. They had neighbours no less guilty and presumptuous than themselves, the inhabitants of Tebara, from whom I received hostages after the capture of Pindenissum. I then dismissed the army to winter quarters, putting my brother Quintus in charge of stationing the troops in villages which had either been captured or were still in a state of unrest.

Now I should like you to realize that, if a motion concerning these performances is put to the Senate, I shall take it as a signal compliment if, when your turn comes, you will support the honour proposed for me. And although I am aware that personages of the highest dignity often address and receive requests in

411. Set up by Alexander the Great on the bank of the river Pyramus to commemorate his victory over the Persians at Issus.

such cases, I conceive that from me to you a hint is more appropriate than a request. After all, I am writing to one whose motions in the House have again and again done me honour, and who both there and at public meetings has praised me to the skies in language of unstinted panegyric. I have always attached so much weight to your words that a single one of them tinctured with eulogy of myself has represented to my mind the summit of attainment. Finally, I recall that in opposing the grant of a Supplication to a most worthy and illustrious gentleman[412] you said you would have supported it had the motion been based on his achievements as Consul in Rome; and you likewise voted a Supplication[413] to me as a civilian in unprecedented terms – not as having served the commonwealth well (that has been said of many others), but as having saved it. I pass over the fact that you took upon yourself my unpopularity and danger and all the various turns of fortune that have befallen me, and that you were very ready to go a long way further in that direction had I permitted it; that finally, you looked upon my enemy[414] as yours, and gave your approval to his destruction (yes, I fully appreciated how much you were doing for my sake), when you defended Milo's action in the Senate. On my side there has been forthcoming this much (and I do not regard it as a favour but as testimony of a sincerely held opinion), that I have not confined myself to tacit admiration of your extraordinary qualities (that, after all, is universal), but have publicly exalted you beyond any man we have seen or of whom history tells us. This I have done in all my speeches, whether addressing the Senate or pleading in court, in all my writings, Greek or Latin, in fact throughout the entire range of my literary output.

Perhaps you will wonder why it is that I should set so much store by this bauble of congratulation and honour from the

412. Probably Lentulus Spinther.
413. In 63.
414. P. Clodius.

Senate. I will be candid with you – our philosophical pursuits, our mutual good offices, our close friendship, the ties too between our parents, make that only fitting. If there was ever a man indifferent by nature, and still more (so at least *I* fancy) by understanding and instruction, to empty plaudits and the talk of the crowd, I may surely claim to be such a man. My Consulship stands witness. In that office, as in the rest of my career, I confess that I sought eagerly after the sources from which true glory might arise; but glory in and for itself never seemed to me worth the pursuing. I waived a well-appointed province and the clear prospect of a Triumph. Finally, I did not reach out my hand for a priestly dignity when in your opinion, I believe, it could have been mine without any great difficulty.[415] But after the wrong I suffered (*you* always call it a calamity for the state, but for myself no calamity, even an honour) it has been otherwise. I have been ambitious to receive tokens of esteem, the more flattering the better, from the Senate and People of Rome. Accordingly in this later period I was desirous of becoming Augur, something I had formerly disregarded; and I now think the honour customarily conferred by the Senate for military successes worth my seeking, although I waived it aside in days gone by.

I wrote just now that I would not make a request. For all that, I *do* request you earnestly for your benevolent assistance in this wish of mine, which is not without an element of an injured man's craving for balm to heal his wound. I do so, however, always supposing that you find my modest exploits not altogether paltry and contemptible – of such a kind and measure, on the contrary, that many have won the highest distinctions from the Senate for achievements by no means comparable. Furthermore, I think I have observed (you know how attentively I listen to you) that in conceding or withholding such distinctions it is your practice to pay greater regard to a commander's conduct, his principles and way of life, than to

415. Cf. *Letters to Atticus* 25 (11.5).2.

his operations in the field. If you apply such considerations in my case, you will find that with a weak army I made fair and clean administration my strongest bulwark against the threat of a major war. Thus aided, I obtained results which no legions could have secured. I found our subjects thoroughly alienated and disloyal; I have made them thoroughly well-affected and reliable, winning over their minds, poised as they were in expectation of change, to a sentiment of good-will towards the old régime.

But I have written too much about myself, especially to you, the one man to whose ears all our subjects bring their grievances. You will learn of it all from those who feel that my system of government has brought them back to life. All, virtually with one accord, will describe my administration to you in such terms as I should most like to hear. In particular, two communities who call you their patron, the island of Cyprus and the kingdom of Cappadocia, will tell you about me. So, I believe, will King Deiotarus, with whom you have the most intimate of connections. Are not these things of greater moment? Is it not true that in all ages fewer have been found capable of conquering their own passions than of defeating hostile armies? If so, when you have added to military achievements these rarer and more difficult kinds of merit, it will surely be in your character to rate those very achievements of higher account and desert than they would otherwise have appeared.

In conclusion, as though lacking confidence in the efficacy of my plea, let me make Philosophy my advocate with you – than which nothing in my life has been more precious to me, nor have the Gods bestowed any greater gift upon mankind. Think then of the pursuits and acquirements we have in common and to which we have been devoted heart and soul since we were boys. We two almost alone have brought the old authentic philosophy, which some regard as an amusement of leisure and idleness, down into the market-place, into public life, one might almost say into the battlefield. This companionship of ours pleads with you on behalf of my renown. I do not think Cato can in conscience say no.

Take it then, if you please, that, should the honour for which I ask in my dispatch be accorded to me by your voice in the House, I shall regard myself as having attained my dearest wish through the weight of your prestige and through your good-will towards me.

III (XV. 5)

CATO TO CICERO

Rome, latter April 50

From M. Cato to M. Cicero, Imperator, greetings.

Patriotism and friendship alike urge me to rejoice, as I heartily do, that your ability, integrity, and conscientiousness, already proved in great events at home when you wore the gown of peace, are no less actively at work in arms abroad. Accordingly, I did what my judgement allowed me to do: that is to say, I paid you tribute with my voice and vote for defending your province by your integrity and wisdom, for saving Ariobarzanes' throne and person, and for winning back the hearts of our subjects to a loyal support of Roman rule.

As for the decree of a Supplication, if *you* prefer us to render thanks to the Immortal Gods in respect of provision taken for the public good by your own admirable policy and administrative rectitude, not at all the result of chance, rather than to put it down to your own credit – why, I am very glad of it. If, however, you regard a Supplication as an earnest of a Triumph, and on that account prefer the praise to go to accident[416] rather than to yourself, the fact is that a Triumph does not always follow a Supplication. On the other hand, the Senate's judgement that a province has been held and preserved by its governor's mild and upright administration rather than by the swords of an army or the favour of the Gods is a far greater distinction than a Triumph; and that is what I proposed in the House.

I have written to you at some length on this subject (contrary to my normal habit) so that you may realize, as I most earnestly hope you will, my anxiety to convince you of two things: firstly, as touching your prestige, I desired what I conceived to be most complimentary to yourself; secondly, I am very glad that what you preferred has come to pass.

Goodbye, remember me kindly, and follow your chosen course, rendering to our subjects and to the state their due of a strict and conscientious administration.

112 (XV. 6)

CICERO TO CATO

Tarsus, late July 50

From M. Cicero to M. Cato greetings.

I think it is Hector in Naevius who says 'Glad thy praise doth make me, father, praise from one that praisèd is.'[417] Praise is pleasant, you will agree, when it comes from those who have themselves led honoured lives. Yes, I assure you that the congratulatory terms of your letter and the testimonial you gave

416. Cato as a Stoic believed in a Providence, but in ordinary language and thought the ideas of fate, providence, gods, and fortune were much confused at this period.

417. See p. 76.

me in the House represent to my mind the sum of attainment. I am particularly flattered and gratified to feel that you were glad to accord to friendship what you would have had no hesitation in according to truth. And if many (not to say all) members of our society were Catos (the marvel being that it has produced *one*), how could I think of comparing the triumphal car and crown with an encomium from you? To my way of thinking, and by the unbiased and delicate standards of a philosopher, nothing can be more complimentary than that speech of yours of which my friends have sent me a copy.

But I have explained the reason for my inclination (I will not say 'desire') in my previous letter. Perhaps you did not find it altogether convincing; at any rate it means that I do not regard the honour[418] as something to be unduly coveted, but at the same time that, if proffered by the Senate, I feel I ought by no means to spurn it. I trust, furthermore, that in view of the labours I have undertaken for the public good the House will deem me not unworthy of an honour, especially one so commonly bestowed. If it so turns out, all I ask of you is that (to use your own very kind expressions), having accorded to me what in your judgement is most complimentary to myself, you should be glad if what I prefer comes about. Your actions, your views as expressed in the Senate, your letter, and the very fact that you were present at the drafting of the decree are clear evidence to me that the grant of the Supplication in my honour was agreeable to you. For I am well aware that such decrees are usually drafted by the closest friends of the persons honoured.

I shall see you soon, as I hope, and only pray we meet in a better political atmosphere than I fear we shall.

418. A Triumph.

113 (VII. 32)

CICERO TO VOLUMNIUS EUTRAPELUS

Laodicea (?), February or March 50 (?)

M. Cicero to Volumnius greetings.

As you headed your letter in familiar style (and quite right) without first name, I was at first inclined to wonder whether it might not be from Senator Volumnius, with whom I have much acquaintance. But its *eutrapelous* quality[419] gave me to understand that it was yours. The contents all made most agreeable reading, with one exception: as my agent-in-charge you are not careful enough in protecting my property – my *salt mines*![420] You say that since my departure every witticism, whosoever it be, not excluding even Sestius' efforts,[421] is fathered upon me. Well, do you allow this? No opposition, no resistance?

I *had* hoped to have left my various categories of *bons mots* so clearly branded as to be recognizable at sight. But since Rome is so full of scum that the most banausic[422] of jests will find someone to relish its elegance, in friendship's name bestir yourself! If there be no pungent *double entendre*, no tasteful hyperbole, no pretty pun,[423] no comical surprise; if the other

419. 'Eutrapelia', defined by Aristotle as 'cultured insolence'. The *cognomen* 'Eutrapelus' was personal and descriptive, Volumnius being a well-known wit.

420. 'Salt' (*sal*) = 'wit'.

421. P. Sestius notoriously lacked *sal* (cf. *Letters to Atticus* 141 (VII. 17).2).

422. The Greek word used means 'charmless'.

423. Strictly, a joke depending on letter-substitution, as in Manutius' example from Terence *inceptio est amentium, haud amantium*.

varieties which I discussed through Antonius'[424] mouth in the second volume of my treatise *On the Orator* shall not appear neatly pointed and *secundum artem*: why you may go bail that the thing is not mine.

As to your grumbles about the trials, I am much less concerned. Every defendant may go to the devil for aught I care. Selius[425] may wax eloquent enough to prove himself freeborn – it doesn't worry me. But my property in wit is another matter. Let us protect that for pity's sake! Get any court order you like. The only rival I fear in this field is yourself, the rest I despise. You think I'm poking fun at you? Very good, I perceive *now* that you are a man of sense.

But really, joking apart, your letter struck me as most entertaining and elegant reading. One part though, however amusing (and it was certainly that), did not make me smile. I am anxious for that friend of ours[426] to carry all possible weight in his career as Tribune, both for his own sake (as you know, I am very fond of him) and also, I may add, for the sake of the commonwealth, which, however poor my return, I shall never cease to love.

Well, my dear Volumnius, now that you have made a start and see that I appreciate it, write to me as often as you can about affairs in Rome and the political situation. I enjoy the way your letters talk. Furthermore, do encourage and confirm Dolabella in his sentiments towards me, which I perceive and judge to be those of sincerely affectionate good-will. Make him mine entirely – not, to be sure, that anything is lacking. But keenly desirous as I am, I don't think I am labouring the point unduly.

424. Apparently a slip on Cicero's part. The section on jokes in the *de Oratore* is in fact given to C. Julius Caesar Strabo.
425. Unknown.
426. Curio.

114 (IX. 25)

CICERO TO PAPIRIUS PAETUS

Laodicea, mid March (?) 50

From Cicero, Imperator, to Paetus.

Your letter has made a first-rate general out of me. I had no idea you were such a military expert – evidently you have thumbed the treatises of Pyrrhus and Cineas.[427] So I intend to follow your precepts, with one addition – I mean to keep a few boats handy on the coast. They say there's no better weapon against Parthian cavalry! But why this frivolity? You don't know what sort of Commander-in-Chief you have to deal with. In my command here I have put into practice the whole *Education of Cyrus*,[428] a work which I read so often that I wore out the book. But we'll joke another time when we meet, as soon I hope we shall.

Now stand by for orders (or rather to obey them), to use the ancient expression.

I have a great deal to do with M. Fabius, as I think you know, and a great regard for him as a man of the highest integrity and unusual modesty, also because he helps me very effectively in my controversies[429] with your Epicurean boozing-partners. After he joined me at Laodicea and I asked him to stay with me, he received a quite appalling letter, a bolt from the blue, informing him that a farm near Herculaneum, which he owns jointly with his brother, Q. Fabius, had been put up for sale by

427. King Pyrrhus of Epirus wrote a treatise on tactics, and his minister Cineas epitomized a work on strategy by one Aelian.

428. Xenophon's work on the Ideal Ruler (cf. *Letters to Atticus* 23 (11.3).2), much of which is concerned with the Ruler as General.

429. Perhaps with reference to the *de Republica*. M. Fabius Gallus was an Epicurean and a *littérateur*.

the latter. M. Fabius has taken this very much to heart. He believed that his brother, who is not remarkable for good sense, had been instigated by his (Marcus') enemies to take this extraordinary step.

Now, my dear Paetus, be a friend and take the whole affair upon yourself, and relieve Fabius of the worry. We need your name and sound judgement, and your personal influence too. Don't let the brothers get into litigation and become embroiled in discreditable lawsuits. Mato and Pollio[430] are Fabius' enemies. Briefly, I assure you that I cannot write down in full how much you will oblige me if you put Fabius' mind at ease. He thinks, and persuades me, that it all depends on you.

115 (II. 18)

CICERO TO Q. THERMUS

Laodicea, early May 50

From M. Cicero, Imperator, to Q. Thermus, Propraetor, greetings.

I am very happy to find you appreciative of the service I rendered Rhodo and of my other acts of good-will towards you and yours – gratitude is a great point with you. Please rest assured that my solicitude for your credit increases every day, though your own integrity and clemency have so enhanced it that any addition seems impossible. But constantly thinking of your interests as I do, I grow more and more convinced of the soundness of the view I originally intimated to our friend Aristo when he came to see me, that you would make formidable enemies if you put a slight upon a powerful young nobleman.[431] And it *will* be a slight, make no mistake. You have

430. Unknowns, unless Pollio is the famous Asinius Pollio.

431. L. Antonius, Thermus' Quaestor. Cicero advises that he be left in charge of the province of Asia after Thermus' departure.

nobody of superior official rank available, and the young man in question has a better claim than your excellent and irreproachable Legates from the very fact (to say nothing of family) that he is Quaestor and *your* Quaestor. I am well aware that nobody's grudge can hurt you, but I should none the less be sorry to see you an object of resentment to three brothers of the highest birth and no mean qualities of enterprise and eloquence, especially if their resentment was justified. It is apparent that they will become Tribunes of the Plebs in three successive years.[432] Who can tell what sort of political conditions lie ahead? To me they seem likely to be disturbed. So why should I want you to fall in the way of tribunician menaces, especially when you can give a Quaestor preference to quaestorian Legates without a word of criticism from anybody? If he proves himself worthy of his forbears, as I expect and hope he will, some part of the credit will go to you. If he stumbles, the damage will be entirely his, not yours at all.

I feel it right to let you know such thoughts as cross my mind and seem to concern you, because I am leaving for Cilicia. Whatever you do, the Gods be with it! But if you listen to me, you will keep clear of feuds and take thought for a quiet future.

116 (II. 19)

CICERO TO COELIUS CALDUS

Camp on the Pyramus, c. 22 June 50

From M. Tullius, son of Marcus, grandson of Marcus, Imperator, to C. Coelius Caldus, son of Lucius, grandson of Gaius, Quaestor, greetings.

432. Apparently an inference from the fact (not otherwise established) that L. Antonius' two elder brothers, Marcus (Mark Antony) and Gaius, had been Quaestors in 52 and 51 (or, more probably, both in 51). Marcus stood successfully for the Tribunate in 50.

After I received the most welcome news of your appointment by lot as my Quaestor, it was my expectation that the more time you spent with me in the province the more pleasure I should derive from that event. I felt it very important that the close tie which chance had established between us should be supplemented by personal intercourse. But time passed, and no word of your arrival reached me either from yourself or any other person; so I began to fear, as I still do, lest it might turn out that I left the province before you entered it. I have received a letter from you while in camp in Cilicia on 21 June. It is most kindly expressed, clear evidence of a conscientious and talented writer; but it contains no indication of the place and date of dispatch or of when I may expect you; neither could the bearer, who did not receive it from your own hand, enlighten me as to where and when you sent it.

Despite my uncertainty on these points, I judge it proper to send you orderlies and lictors of mine with a letter. If you receive it in good enough time, you will greatly oblige me by joining me in Cilicia as soon as possible. Your cousin Curius,[433] who, as you know, is a close friend of mine, and your relative C. Vergilius, also one of my nearest intimates, have written to me at length about you. Their words carry great weight with me, as a particular recommendation from such friends ought to do; but most of all I am impressed by your letter, especially by what you say of your own standing and our association. No Quaestor more welcome could have fallen to me. Therefore whatever I can do by way of compliment to you shall be done, and my sense of your personal and family status[434] shall be made plain to all. But this will be easier for me if you join me in Cilicia, which I believe will be in my and the public interest and most of all in your own.

433. Usually but not very plausibly identified with M'. Curius of Patrae.

434. In fact Coelius' nobility was of recent vintage, starting with his grandfather, Consul in 94.

117 (II. 17)

CICERO TO CN. (?) SALLUSTIUS[435]

Tarsus, c. 18 July 50

From M. Cicero, Imperator, to Cn. (?) Sallustius, Pro-quaestor,[436] greetings.

Your orderly delivered your letter to me at Tarsus on 17 July. I shall reply point by point, as that seems to be what you wish.

I have heard nothing about my successor, and I am not expecting any appointment. There is no reason why I should not leave on the day fixed, especially now the Parthian danger is out of the way. I hardly expect to make any considerable halts. I think I shall touch at Rhodes for the sake of our two boys, but that is not certain. I want to get back to Rome as soon as possible. However, the ordering of my journey will depend upon the political situation and the state of affairs in the capital. Your successor cannot possibly make such good time as to enable you to meet me in Asia.

As regards the rendering of accounts, there would have been some convenience in making no return, for which you say you have Bibulus' licence. But I hardly think you can take that course in view of the lex Julia. Bibulus has his own reasons for not observing that law,[437] but I think you should be very careful to observe it.

You say that the garrison ought not to have been withdrawn

435. Almost certainly not Cicero's friend of that name nor yet the historian C. Sallustius Crispus. The manuscripts have 'CANINI SALUSTIO'.

436. In Syria.

437. Bibulus denied the validity of Caesar's legislation as Consul, since it had been passed in defiance of his own religious veto.

from Apamea.[438] I find that your opinion is generally shared, and I am sorry that this step has caused some untoward talk among the ill-disposed. But nobody except yourself seems to be in any doubt as to whether or not the Parthians have crossed the river. Accordingly, under the impression of the general, unambiguous report, I have dismissed all the defensive forces which I had prepared in great strength.

It would not have been correct for me to send you my Quaestor's accounts, and in any case they are not ready. I intend to deposit them at Apamea. Not a penny of my booty has been or will be touched by any person except the City Quaestors, which is to say the Roman People. I propose to take sureties at Laodicea for all public moneys, so that both the state and I myself may be insured against transport risks. As for the 100,000 drachmae you mention, I am unable to oblige anyone in such a matter. All moneys are handled by the Prefects or the Quaestor; booty by the former, funds assigned to me by the latter.

You ask my opinion about the legions which have been decreed for Syria. I was previously doubtful whether they would be coming. Now I have no doubt that they will *not* be coming, if the news that all is quiet in Syria arrives beforehand. I suppose your successor Marius will be delayed because the Senate instructed him to accompany the legions.

Having replied to one letter, I come to the other. You request me to recommend you to Bibulus as warmly as possible. The will on my side is not lacking, but I think I have a bone to pick with you in this connection. Of all Bibulus' entourage you are the only one who had never told me how causelessly unfriendly his disposition towards me is. Any number of people have let me know that, when Antioch was in great danger and great hope rested on me and my army, he used to say that he would

438. Not the Phrygian city mentioned in the next paragraph, nor, as usually supposed, Apamea on the Orontes, but another place of the same name on the east side of the Euphrates.

sooner anything than appear to have stood in need of help from me. I was not annoyed with you for keeping silent from a sense of your duty as Quaestor towards your official superior, although I heard of the treatment to which you were subjected. As for Bibulus, although he wrote to Thermus about the Parthian war, he never sent a line to me, whom he knew to be directly involved in the danger of that war. He only wrote to *me* about an Augurate for his son. Out of pity,[439] and because I was always very friendly to him, I was at pains to write to him in the kindest possible way. If he has a spite against the whole world, which I never supposed to be the case, I do not so much resent his behaviour to me. But if he is unfriendly to me in particular, a letter of mine will not do you any good: I may add that in the dispatch which Bibulus sent to the Senate (a) he took sole credit for a thing we did jointly – he says that *he* took steps to see that moneys were exchanged at a profit to the state; (b) with reference to an action entirely mine, my declining to make use of Transpadane auxiliaries, he writes that *he* has relieved the state of that obligation also; (c) on the other hand he makes me share in something for which he was solely responsible: 'When we asked for an additional issue of grain for the auxiliary cavalry,' says he. His pettiness of spirit, the paltry, piddling character of his very malice, comes out when he calls Ario-barzanes in his dispatch not 'King' but 'son of King Ariobar-zanes', because the Senate had granted him the royal title through me and had recommended him to my care. Persons of this mentality are not improved by being asked favours. However, I have complied with your wish and written a letter addressed to him. When you get it, you will do what you please.

439. Bibulus had just lost two sons, murdered in Egypt.

118 (XV. 11)

CICERO TO C. MARCELLUS

Tarsus, late July 50

From M. Cicero, Imperator, to C. Marcellus, Consul, greetings.

All my friends have told me in their letters (though the facts speak loudly enough for themselves) of the interest you have taken in the honour[440] conferred upon me. As Consul you have shown the same concern for my distinction and advancement in dignity as you always showed in the past, together with your parents and your whole family circle. Accordingly no service on my part can exceed your deserts, and there is none which I shall not zealously and gladly render. When one owes a favour, personalities make a great difference, and there is no man in respect to whom I have been more content to be in that position. Our common pursuits and the kindness I have received from your father and yourself had already attached me to you, but to this has now to be added what is in my eyes the greatest bond of all – your past and present administration of the commonwealth, which is as precious to me as anything in the world. I have no reluctance to owe you in my single person just as much as the whole body of honest citizens. Accordingly let me wish you such results as you deserve and as I believe will be yours.

As for me, I look forward to seeing you shortly, if I am not delayed on the voyage, which is just coinciding with the Etesians.

440. The Supplication.

119 (XIV. 5)

CICERO TO TERENTIA

Athens, 16 October 50

From Tullius to his dear Terentia greetings.

If you and our beloved Tullia are well, darling Marcus and I are well too.

We arrived in Athens on 14 October, having experienced pretty unfavourable weather at sea – it has been a slow, disagreeable voyage. Acastus met us with letters as we came ashore. He had been three weeks on the way, which is pretty good going. I got your letter, in which you appear to be afraid that your earlier letters have not been delivered. All of them were in fact delivered. You covered all items most carefully, and I was most grateful. Nor was I surprised at the shortness of the letter which Acastus brought. After all, you are now expecting me in person, or rather *us* in person, and very impatient we are to see you both – though I well see what sort of situation we are coming home to. Letters brought by Acastus from many friends tell me that war is on the horizon, so that, once I arrive, I shall not be able to disguise my sentiments. But we must take what fortune sends, and I shall try to come all the faster so that we can consult together about the whole position. I shall be glad if you will come to meet us as far as you can without detriment to your health.

About the Precius[441] bequest (I am really sorry to get it – I was very fond of him), would you please see that, if the auction takes place before my arrival, Pomponius or, if he can't manage it, Camillus looks after my interest? When I am safely back I shall see to the rest myself. If you have already left Rome, please arrange this all the same. If the Gods are

441. Cf. *Letters to Atticus* 123 (VI.9).2.

kind, we hope to be in Italy about the Ides of November.

Now my darling and most longed-for Terentia, if you both love us, take care of yourselves. Goodbye.

Athens, 16 October.

120 (XVI. 1)

CICERO TO TIRO

Between Patrae and Alyzia, 3 November 50

From Tullius to his dear Tiro best greetings, also from my son Marcus, and my brother and nephew.

I thought I could bear the want of you not too hardly,[442] but frankly I find it unendurable; and though in view of the honour I have in prospect it is important for me to get back to Rome as soon as possible, I feel I did wrong to leave you. However, since it seemed to be your definite inclination not to sail until your health was recovered, I approved your plan; nor am I changing now, if you are still of the same mind. But if, after you are able to take nourishment, you think you can overtake me, the decision is in your hands. I am sending Mario to you with the intention that he should either join me in your company as soon as possible or return to me at once, if you stay on.

Now do understand that, provided it can be managed without detriment to your health, there is nothing I want more than to have you with me; but that if you find you need to stay a little longer at Patrae to convalesce, there is nothing I want more than for you to be well again. If you take ship straight away, you will catch us up at Leucas. If you want to get back your strength, however, you must take good care

442. Tiro had been left behind sick at Patrae.

that you have suitable companions, good weather, and the right sort of boat. Only, if you love me, my dear Tiro, do be sure not to let Mario's arrival and this letter affect your judgement. If you do what is best for your health, you will best comply with my wishes. So think it over in that clever head of yours. I miss you, but I love you. Loving you, I want to see you fit and well; missing you, I want to see you as soon as possible. The former, therefore, must come first. So make it your chief concern to get well. Of your countless services to me this will be the one I shall most appreciate.

3 November.

121 (XVI. 2)

CICERO TO TIRO

Alyzia, 5 November 50

From Tullius to his dear Tiro greetings.

I can't and don't want to write to you how I feel. I will only say that it will be to our very great pleasure, both yours and mine, if I see you in good health as soon as possible. Two days after leaving you we put in at Alyzia, within 120 stades[443] distance of Leucas. At Leucas I expect I shall see you in person or get a letter from you by Mario. As you care for me, so be sure to look after your health – or as you know I care for you.

Nones of November, from Alyzia.

443. About fourteen English miles.

122 (XVI. 3)

CICERO TO TIRO

Alyzia, 6 November 50

From Tullius and Marcus to their dear Tiro greetings, also from Quintus senior and junior.

We stayed at Alyzia (from where I sent you a letter yesterday) for one day, because Quintus had not come up with us. That was the Nones of November. From there I am dispatching this letter as we leave before daybreak on the 6th.

If you love us all, and especially me, your schoolmaster, get back your strength. I am looking forward in great suspense, first of course to seeing you, but, if not that, to seeing Mario with a letter from you. We all, and I especially, are anxious to see you as soon as possible, but fit and well, my dear Tiro. So no hurry. I shall see you soon enough if you are in good health. I can do without your manifold usefulness, but I want you to be well again, first for your sake and then for my own.

My dear Tiro, goodbye.

123 (XVI. 4)

CICERO TO TIRO

Leucas, 7 November 50

From Tullius to his dear Tiro best greetings, also from Marcus and my brother Quintus and Quintus junior.

I read your letter with varying feelings. The first page upset me badly, the second brought me round a little. So now, if not before, I am clear that until your health is quite restored you should not venture upon travel either by land or water. I shall see you soon enough if I see you thoroughly strong again.

You say the doctor has a good reputation, and so I hear myself; but frankly, I don't think much of his treatments. You ought not to have been given soup[444] with a weak stomach. However, I have written to him at some length, and also to Lyso.[445] To Curius, who is a most agreeable fellow, very obliging and good-natured, I have written a great deal, including the suggestion that, if you agree, he should move you over to his house. I am afraid our friend Lyso is a little casual. All Greeks are; also, he has not replied to a letter he received from me. However, you commend him; so you must judge for yourself what is best. One thing, my dear Tiro, I do beg of you: don't consider money at all where the needs of your health are concerned. I have told Curius to advance whatever you say. I imagine the doctor ought to be given something to make him more interested in your case.[446]

Your services to me are beyond count – in my home and out of it, in Rome and abroad, in private affairs and public, in my studies and literary work. You will cap them all if I see you your own man again, as I hope I shall. I think it would be very nice, if all goes well, for you to sail home with Quaestor Mescinius. He is not uncultivated, and he seemed to me to have a regard for you. But when you have given every possible attention to your health, *then* my dear Tiro, attend to sailing arrangements. I don't now want you to hurry in any way. My only concern is for you to get well.

Take my word for it, dear Tiro, that nobody cares for me who does not care for you. Your recovery is most important

444. Or 'gravy' or 'sauce'.

445. Cicero's host at Patrae in whose house Tiro was staying.

446. Apparently the doctor (whose name was Asclapo; cf. Letter 286 (XIII.20)) was not charging a special fee. He may have looked after Lyso's household for a regular payment.

to you and me, but many others are concerned about it. In the past you have never been able to recruit yourself properly, because you wanted to give me of your best at every turn. Now there is nothing to stand in your way. Put everything else aside, think only of your bodily well-being. I shall believe you care for me in proportion to the care you devote to your health.

Goodbye, my dear Tiro, goodbye and fondest good wishes. Lepta sends you his, so do we all. Goodbye.

7 November, from Leucas.

124 (XVI. 5)

CICERO TO TIRO

Leucas, 7 November 50

From Tullius and Marcus and the Quinti to their nicest and best of Tiros best greetings.

Look what a charmer you are! We spent two hours at Thyrreum,[447] and our host Xenomenes is as fond of you as though he had been your bosom companion. He has promised you everything you need, and I believe he will be as good as his word. I think it would be a good plan for him to take you to Leucas when you are stronger, to finish your convalescence there. You must see what Curius and Lyso and the doctor think. I wanted to send Mario back to you for you to send him to me with a letter when you were a little better, but I reflected that Mario could bring me only one letter, and I expect them one after another.

So do what you can, and, if you care for me, see that Acastus goes down to the harbour every day. There will be plenty of folk to whom you can safely give a letter and who will be glad

447. On the outward journey in 51.

to carry it to me. For my part I shall take advantage of every traveller to Patrae.

I pin all my hope of your getting proper treatment and attention on Curius. He has the kindest of hearts and the truest affection for me. Put yourself entirely in his hands. I had rather see you fit and well a little later on than weak straight away. So attend to nothing except getting well – I shall attend to the rest.

Goodbye once again.

Leaving Leucas, 7 November.

125 (XVI. 6)

CICERO TO TIRO

Actium, 7 November 50

From Tullius and Marcus and the Quinti to Tiro best greetings.

This is my third letter to you in one day. I am writing it more to keep up my established practice, having happened on a bearer, than because I have anything to say. Well then, yet again: as you care for me, so take care of yourself. Add this to your countless services to me; it will be the most agreeable to me of them all. When you have done (I hope) thinking about your health, think about arrangements for sailing too. Please give all travellers to Italy letters to me, just as I never fail to take advantage of anyone going to Patrae. Look after yourself, my dear Tiro, do. Seeing that bad luck has prevented you sailing with me, you have no reason to hurry or to bother about anything except getting well.

Goodbye once more.

7 November, from Actium, in the evening.

126 (XVI. 7)

CICERO AND HIS SON TO TIRO

Corcyra, 16 November 50

From Tullius and Marcus to their dear Tiro greetings.

We have been held up at Corcyra for a week. Quintus senior and junior are at Buthrotum. We are dreadfully anxious about your health, but not surprised that there has been no letter from you; for the sailing winds from your present whereabouts are the same winds but for the want of which *we* should not be stuck at Corcyra. So look after yourself and get strong, and when your health and the time of year enable you to make the voyage conveniently, rejoin us who love you dearly. Nobody loves us who is not fond of you. Everybody will be glad to see you and looking forward to your return. Take care of your health.

Goodbye again, dear Tiro.

16 November, from Corcyra.

127 (XVI. 9)

CICERO TO TIRO

Brundisium, 26 November 50

From Tullius and Marcus to their dear Tiro best greetings.

As you know, we left you on 2 November. We reached Leucas on 6 November and Actium on the 7th, where we stayed over the 8th on account of the weather. Thence on the 9th we had a beautiful voyage to Corcyra. At Corcyra we stayed until the 15th, held up by weather. On the 16th we moved on 120 stades to Corcyra Harbour near Cassiope. Contrary winds held us there until the 22nd. Meanwhile many travellers who were too impatient to wait were shipwrecked. That day we weighed anchor after dinner. A gentle southerly breeze was blowing, the skies were clear. Sailing at our ease through the night and the next day, we reached Italy at Hydrus, and on the day following (24 November) under the same wind arrived at Brundisium at 10 a.m. Terentia, who thinks a great deal of you, entered the town at the same time as ourselves.

At Brundisium on 26 November a slave of Cn. Plancius gave me at long last the letter from you that I had been waiting for so impatiently, dispatched on the Ides of November. It greatly relieved my anxiety – if only the relief had been total! However, Doctor Asclapo definitely assures us that you will soon be well.

Now I do not think I need urge you to apply all possible care to the business of convalescing. I know your good sense, your temperate habits, and your affection for me. I know you will do everything in your power to be with us at the earliest possible moment. But at the same time I should not want you to be in any sort of hurry. I wish you had stayed away from Lyso's concert – you might have had a fourth weekly crisis.[448] However, since you chose to put good manners before your health, be careful in future. I am sending word to Curius to do something for the doctor and advance you what you need, with a promise that I shall repay to anyone he designates. I am leaving a horse and mule for you at Brundisium. I am afraid there will be great alarms and excursions in Rome after the Kalends of January. I shall take a moderate line in all things.

The only other thing is to ask and beg you not to take ship without proper care. Sailors with their money to make are apt to be in a hurry. Take no chances, my dear Tiro. You have a long, difficult voyage ahead. If possible, go with Mescinius –

448. Illnesses were supposed to reach a crisis every seventh day.

he is not one to take chances with the sea. If not, then with some man of position whom the skipper will respect. If you take every care about this and render yourself up to me safe and sound, I shall have all I ever want of you.

Again, dear Tiro, goodbye. I have written to the doctor, to Curius, and to Lyso most particularly about you. Goodbye and good wishes.

128 (v. 20)

CICERO TO MESCINIUS RUFUS

Outside Rome, c. 5 January 49

From Cicero to Rufus.

One way or another I should have met you if you had chosen to go to the place arranged. Regardful of my convenience, you did not want to put me about; but I should like you to believe that, if you had sent me word, I should have set your wish above my convenience.

It would be easier for me to reply to your letter in detail if my Secretary,[449] M. Tullius, were here. As to him, I am fully assured that so far as the rendering of accounts goes (on other matters I cannot speak for certain) he has not intentionally done anything contrary to your financial interest or reputation. Further, I can assure you that, if the old law and ancient custom were still in force, I should not have rendered my accounts without previously comparing and making them up with you, suitably to the intimate connection between us. Now that the lex Julia makes it necessary to leave accounts in the province and present an identical copy to the Treasury, I did in the province what I should have done at Rome if the previous practice had still held good. Nor did I do it in such a way as to oblige you to

449. See Glossary of Terms.

conform to my pattern, but on the contrary gave you a latitude which I shall never regret having given. I put my Secretary, of whom I see you now entertain suspicions, entirely in your hands. You associated with him your brother,[450] M. Mindius. The accounts were made up in my absence with your co-opera-tion. All I did was to read them, and I regarded the book I received from my Secretary as coming from your brother also. If this was a compliment, I could not have made you a greater; if an act of trust, I placed almost more trust in you than in myself; if the object was to ensure that nothing should be presented other than to your credit and advantage, I had nobody more proper to the business than the person to whom I gave it. At any rate what the law required was done; I deposited accounts, made up and compared, with the two communes which appeared to me most suitable since it had to be done in this way, namely Laodicea and Apamea. So on this point my first answer is that, although for good reasons I was in a hurry to present my accounts, I should have waited for you, if I had not looked upon the accounts left behind in the province as already rendered. Therefore ✶✶✶.

As for what you write about Volusius, this does not concern the accounts. I was advised by experts, including the greatest expert of them all and my very good friend, C. Camillus,[451] that the debt could not be transferred from Valerius[452] to

450. i.e. brother (or cousin) by adoption, or brother (or cousin) adopted into another family, or half-brother.

451. He seems to have acted as Cicero's agent-in-charge (*procurator*) in Rome during the Proconsulate.

452. Probably the P. Valerius mentioned in *Letters to Atticus* 114 (v.21).13 as a penniless dependent of King Deiotarus. He seems to have acted as an agent of Q. Volusius, one of Cicero's following (cf. ibid. 6), in a speculation on a public (revenue?) contract and to have given as sureties certain of the principal members of Cicero's staff. When Valerius failed to pay the Treasury, the sureties became liable. The manoeuvre by which Cicero extricated them is not clearly stated. Accord-ing to an interpretation first advanced in 1961 he reckoned money paid by Valerius in respect of an earlier contract as discharging the debt.

Volusius, and that Valerius' sureties were liable (the amount was not HS3,000,000, as stated in your letter, but HS2,000,000). For the money was paid to me in the name of Valerius as purchaser. That part of it which was arrears I entered in the accounts. But writing as you do, you rob me of the satisfaction of liberality, conscientiousness, and a measure of business sense (though I set little enough store by *that*). (a) Liberality: you prefer to suppose that it was thanks to my Secretary, and not to me, that my Legate, M. Anneius, and my Prefect, Q. Lepta, were relieved of a very heavy liability, which moreover they should not in fairness have incurred. (b) Conscientiousness: you suppose that I neither knew nor thought about a matter so gravely involving my duty, and with such dangerous potentialities, but presented whatever my Secretary thought fit without even having him read it over to me. (c) Business sense: you imagine that the procedure which I rather intelligently thought out was not so much as thought about. Actually the plan of freeing Volusius was mine, and it was I who devised the expedient whereby Valerius' sureties and T. Marius[453] himself escaped so severe a penalty. That expedient has been universally approved, applauded in fact; and, if you want the truth, my Secretary was the only one who, as I could see, was not too happy about it. But I took the view that an honourable man should have regard to the financial welfare of so many friends or fellow-countrymen, seeing that the public kept its due.

As regards Lucceius (?), what happened was that the money was deposited in a temple at the instance of Cn. Pompeius. I acknowledged that this was done on my instructions. Pompey has used the money, just as Sestius[454] has used the sum you

453. Unknown.
454. We know no details about these two deposits. P. Sestius was appointed governor of Cilicia in the second week of January, but was still in Italy.

deposited. But so far as I can see, all this has nothing to do with you. I should be very sorry, however, that I inadvertently omitted to add that you deposited the money in the temple on my instructions, were it not that there is the most weighty and unimpeachable documentary evidence showing to whom that money was given as well as the senatorial decrees and the written authorities, yours and mine, on which it was handed over to P. Sestius. Seeing that all this was unmistakably attested in a number of places, I did not put in a supplement which would have been of no advantage to you. But I wish I had, since you evidently regard it as an omission. You say that *you* had better enter it so, and I quite agree; there will not be the least discrepancy on this point between your accounts and mine. You will add that it was on my instructions; and I, though I did not so add, have no reason to deny it; nor, if I *had* such a reason, should I deny it against your wish.

The entry concerning the HS900,000 was certainly made in the form in which you, or your cousin, wanted it made. However, if there is any point which even at this stage I might be able to correct in presenting the accounts, since you thought the entry about the contribution rather maladroit(?), I shall have to consider what is legally permissible, as I have not taken advantage of the senatorial decree. At all events I don't think you should have entered these items from my rendered accounts under the heading of 'money levied', unless I am in error – I am not the world's greatest expert. One thing you must never doubt, that I will do anything I think your interests or even your wishes require, if I possibly can.

With reference to what you say about bounties,[455] I must tell you that I have given in the names of the Military Tribunes, Prefects, and my personal staff only. Here I was under a mis-

---

455. Gratuities or other benefits given or promised to military and other personnel by a governor during his term of office. A list had to be presented to the Treasury. Apparently this could be done either by the Governor himself or by his Quaestor.

apprehension. I thought I had time at my disposal in which to present the list. But I was later informed that it had to be sent in within thirty days after I rendered the accounts. I was extremely sorry that those bounties should not have stood to your credit rather than mine, having myself no axe to grind. However, on the Centurions and the staffs of the Military Tribunes we are still uncommitted, bounties in this category not being specified in the statute.

That leaves the matter of the HS100,000.[456] I remember getting a letter from you on this point written from Myrina, and the mistake was not mine but yours. The persons to blame, if blame there was, appeared to be your brother and Tullius. Correction being impossible, because I deposited my accounts before leaving the province, I believe I did reply in as accommodating a fashion as I could, in accordance with my personal feelings and my financial expectations at that time. But I do not consider myself as bound by the accommodating terms of my letter then, nor today, having received your letter about the HS100,000, do I feel myself in the position of persons to whom letters these days spell trouble![457] You should also bear in mind that I deposited the whole of the sum which had legally accrued to me with the tax-farmers at Ephesus, that it amounted to HS2,200,000, and that Pompey has taken the lot.[458] Whether I like that or whether I lump it, you ought to take a matter of HS100,000 coolly enough. You should set it off against your allowances or my liberality. Suppose you had made me a loan of that HS100,000, you have too amiable a disposition and

456. This sum would seem to have been entered in the accounts by error as due from Mescinius to the Treasury.

457. Debtors. With war about to break out creditors were trying to call in their loans.

458. This was not so. A year later the money was still in Ephesus (*Letters to Atticus* 211 (XI.1).2); shortly afterwards Cicero withdrew half of it and lent it to Pompey. But he may have told Pompey that it was at his disposal.

too much affection for me to wish to take my property at valuation at this time – as for cash, I couldn't raise it if I wanted. But don't think I mean all this seriously; no more do I suppose you were serious either. All the same, if you think it would be of any use, I'll send Tullius over to you, when he gets back from the country.

There is no reason why I should want this letter torn up.

129 (XIII. 55)

CICERO TO MINUCIUS THERMUS

Tarsus (?), 51 (end) or 50 (early)

From Cicero to Thermus, Propraetor, greetings.

When I spoke to you in Ephesus about the affair of my Legate, M. Anneius, I formed the impression that you were very anxious to oblige him for his own sake. But I think so much of him that I feel I must leave nothing undone which might be to his benefit, and I have sufficient confidence in your regard for me to feel sure that my recommendation will serve to enhance your friendly sentiments towards him in no small measure. I have long had a regard for M. Anneius. My opinion of him is evident from the fact that I offered him his present post of my own accord after refusing many applications for it. And now that he has been with me on active service in the recent operations, I have so highly approved his courage, skill, loyalty, and personal good-will towards me that nobody stands higher in my esteem.

You know that he has a dispute with the people of Sardis. I explained the case to you in Ephesus, but you will acquaint yourself more easily and accurately face to face. For the rest, I give you my word that for some time I could not make up my mind just what to write to you. Your manner of administering justice is well-known, and redounds to your great credit; and in this case all we need is for you to follow your usual judicial practice. However, I am not unaware of the weight of a governor's influence, especially of one so upright, responsible, and merciful as you are universally acknowledged to be. May I therefore request you in virtue of the very close connection between us and our many equal and mutual good offices to exert your benevolent influence on M. Anneius' behalf, so as to make it clear to him that you are his friend (which he does not doubt – he has often talked to me) and have become much more so as a result of this letter of mine. In the whole sphere of your authority you could do nothing to oblige me more. As for Anneius himself, he is an excellent fellow and does not forget a kindness. I imagine you make no doubt that your friendly efforts will be well placed.

130 (XIII. 53)

CICERO TO MINUCIUS THERMUS

Province of Cilicia, 51 or 50

From Cicero to Thermus, Propraetor, greetings.

I have long been on very familiar terms with L. Genucilius Curvus, a very worthy gentleman who never forgets a service. I thoroughly recommend him to you, and put him in your hands. In the first place, I hope you will accommodate him in all respects so far as your conscience and dignity will allow – and allow they always will, for he will never ask you for anything unbecoming to your character, or for that matter his own. In particular, however, I would recommend to your notice his affairs in the area of the Hellespont with the request that he enjoy rights over certain lands as decreed and granted him by the township of Parium, rights which in the past have always been undisputedly his; further, that if he has any dispute with a native of the Hellespont, you remit it for settlement to that district. But since I am most warmly recommending to you all that he is and has, I do not think I need write in detail of his various concerns. Let this be the long and the short of it: whatever service, kindness, or compliment Genucilius receives at your hands, I shall regard it as rendered to myself and my personal interests.

131 (XIII. 56)

CICERO TO MINUCIUS THERMUS

Province of Cilicia, 51 or 50

From Cicero to Thermus, Propraetor, greetings.

Cluvius of Puteoli pays me much attention, and we are on a very familiar footing. He is convinced that unless he settles some business which he has in your province during your period of office through my recommendations, he may as well give it up for lost. Now since a friend of mine, one who never grudges a service, places such a burden on my shoulders, I for my part shall place it on yours in consideration of the very good turns you have done me in the past – but with the proviso that I don't want to put you to any serious trouble.

The towns of Mylasa and Alabanda owe Cluvius money. Euthydemus told me when I was in Ephesus that he would see that Mylasian counsel were sent to Rome. This has not been done. I hear that *envoys* have been dispatched, but prefer counsel so that something can be settled. Accordingly, may I request you to direct both Mylasa and Alabanda to send counsel to Rome? Furthermore, Philocles of Alabanda has given Cluvius a mortgage, which has now expired. I should be grateful if you would see that he either gives up the property and hands it over to Cluvius' agents or else pays the money; also that the towns of Heraclea and Bargylia, which likewise owe money, either pay up or secure the debts on their revenues. The town of Caunus also owes money, but they say they have been keeping it on deposit. Would you please make enquiries, and if you find that they have not been authorized to keep it on deposit by edict or decree, please see that Cluvius does not lose the interest, according to your rule?

I am all the more concerned about these matters because our friend Pompey's interests are also involved and because he seems to me to be even more exercised than Cluvius himself.[459] I very much want him to feel content with us. Let me again earnestly beg your assistance in these matters.

132 (XIII. 54)

CICERO TO MINUCIUS THERMUS

Laodicea, February–April 50

From Cicero to Thermus, Propraetor, greetings.

Among the many things you have done as a result of my recommendations I am particularly obliged for your most handsome treatment of M. Marcilius, son of my friend and interpreter. He has come to Laodicea and told me how very grateful he is to you, and to me because of you. For the future, let me request you, since your kindness is not falling on stony ground, to be all the readier to accommodate its recipients, and, so far as your conscience will allow, to see that the young man's mother-in-law is not prosecuted. My recommendation of Marcilius is now much more enthusiastic even than before, because I have found Marcilius senior in the course of a long

459. It has been plausibly supposed that Cluvius was merely Pompey's agent.

term of service quite remarkably (I might almost say unbelievably) loyal, honest, and well-conducted.

133 (XIII. 57)

CICERO TO MINUCIUS THERMUS

Laodicea, early April (?) 50

From Cicero to Thermus, Propraetor, greetings.

Every day I learn from letters and reports that a major war is in progress in Syria. That makes me all the more insistent in asking you as a friend to send me back my Legate, M. Anneius, as soon as possible. His services, advice, and military experience may clearly be invaluable to me and to the state. If he had not had so much at stake, nothing would have induced him to leave me or me to let him go. I propose to set out for Cilicia about the Kalends of May. M. Anneius should return to me before that date.

I have already both spoken and written to you very particularly about his business with the people of Sardis, and I would again beg you to see that he settles it in a manner befitting the justice of his case and his personal dignity. From what you said when I talked to you in Ephesus I understood that you were very anxious to oblige M. Anneius for his own sake. But please take it that you can do nothing more agreeable to me than if I understand that thanks to you he has personally settled the business to his satisfaction, and I beg you once again to bring that about as soon as possible.

134 (XIII. 65)

CICERO TO P. SILIUS

Province of Cilicia, 51 or 50

From M. Cicero to P. Silius, Propraetor, greetings.

With P. Terentius Hispo, who works for the Grazing Rents Company[460] as their local manager, I have a great deal of familiar contact, and each of us is indebted to the other for important services, equal and mutual. His reputation very largely depends on his concluding tax agreements with the communes still outstanding. I do not forget that I tried my own hand at the business in Ephesus and was quite unable to get the Ephesians to oblige. However, according to the universal persuasion and my own observation, your complete integrity combined with your remarkable civility and gentleness have earned you the heartiest compliance of the natives with your every nod. I would therefore particularly request you as a compliment to me to make it your wish that Hispo should get this credit.

Furthermore I am closely connected with the members of the Company, not only because it is under my patronage as a whole but because I am on very close terms with many of them individually. So you will both do my friend Hispo a good turn at my instance and strengthen my relations with the Company. You yourself will reap a rich reward from Hispo's attentiveness (he is very appreciative of a service) and from the influence of the Company members, persons of the highest consequence. You will also do me a great kindness. For you may take it that within the whole sphere of your provincial authority you could do nothing that would oblige me more.

460. i.e. a Roman company which bought the right to collect these rents from the provincials.

135 (XIII. 61)

CICERO TO P. SILIUS

Province of Cilicia, 51 or 50

From M. Cicero to P. Silius, Propraetor, greetings.

I think you know that I was on very familiar terms with T. Pinnius, as he himself has testified in his will, under which I am appointed both guardian and second heir. His son, a remarkably studious, erudite, and modest young man, is owed a large sum by the people of Nicaea, about eight million sesterces, and, so I hear, they are particularly desirous to pay him. Not only the other guardians, who know how much you care for me, but the boy himself is convinced that you will do anything for my sake. You will therefore deeply oblige me if you see to it (so far as your conscience and dignity will allow) that as much of the amount as possible is paid to Pinnius as soon as possible on behalf of the people of Nicaea.

136 (XIII. 62)

CICERO TO P. SILIUS

Province of Cilicia, 51 or 50

M. Cicero to P. Silius, Propraetor, greetings.

I was truly beholden to you in the matter of Atilius[461] — thanks to you I saved a respectable Roman Knight from ruin, though I came late upon the scene. And, to be frank, I have

461. Possibly this had to do with the business mentioned in *Letters to Atticus* 94 (V.I).2.

always considered you as quite at my command because of your exceptionally close and friendly relations with our good Lamia. So you see that, having thanked you for relieving me of all anxiety, I go on to offer a piece of impertinence! But I shall make amends by ever cultivating your friendship and protecting your interests with all the devotion in the world.

If you care for me, be sure to think of my brother Quintus as you do of myself. In that way you will pile one great favour on top of another.

137 (XIII. 63)

CICERO TO P. SILIUS

Laodicea, 4 April (?) 50

From M. Cicero to P. Silius, Propraetor, greetings.

I never thought to find words failing me, but in recommending M. Laenius[462] fail me they do. So I shall explain the case to you briefly, but in terms which will make my sentiments quite clear. You would hardly believe how much I and my dearest brother think of M. Laenius. That arises from his many services, but also from his sterling character and exceptional modesty. I was most reluctant to let him go, both because of the charm of his familiar companionship and because I was glad to avail myself of his sound and loyal advice.

But I am afraid you may be thinking that the words I said would fail me are now all too abundant! I recommend him as you will understand that I am bound to recommend a person of whom I have written the foregoing. And I most earnestly request you to expedite the business he has in your province, and to tell him in person what you consider to be proper. You will find him the soul of good nature and generosity. So I beg

462. A friend of Atticus, in Cilicia on business.

you to send him back to me as soon as you can, free and unencumbered, with his affairs settled thanks to you. My brother and I will be very much beholden.

138 (XIII. 64)

CICERO TO P. SILIUS[463]

Laodicea, April (?) 50

From M. Cicero to P. Silius, Propraetor, greetings.

My friend Nero has told me of his gratitude to you in quite extraordinarily glowing terms. No compliment, he says, which you could possibly have offered him was overlooked. Nero himself will richly repay you, for nobody has a better memory for a service than this young man. But I do assure you that you have greatly obliged me as well. In the whole range of our aristocracy there is no man I value more. And so you will oblige me greatly if you will do certain things which he has asked me to raise with you.

First, will you please hold over the matter of Pausanias of Alabanda until Nero arrives – I know he is very anxious to help him and so I beg this favour of you earnestly. Next, will you kindly regard the people of Nysa as specially recommended to your favour? Nero has the closest ties with them and is most active in championing their interests. So please let the commune understand that in Nero's patronage they have a most powerful protection. I have often recommended Servilius Strabo to you, and do so now the more emphatically because Nero has taken up his case. All we ask is that you handle the matter, lest otherwise you leave an innocent man to the rapacity

463. For several reasons I have suggested that this letter is mistakenly addressed, and that it was really written to the governor of Asia, Minucius Thermus.

of a successor who may not be like yourself. That will oblige me, and I shall feel that your good nature has had its way.

The sum and substance of this letter is to ask you to continue to confer all possible favours upon Nero, as you have made it your practice to do already. Your province, unlike mine, offers a wide scope to a talented and disinterested young nobleman to recommend himself and advance his reputation. With your backing, which I am sure will be and has already been forthcoming, he will be able to confirm the loyalty of the distinguished body of clients inherited from his ancestors and attach them by favours personal to himself. If you help him in this respect as actively as you have promised, your kindness will be excellently placed with Nero; but I too shall be very greatly beholden.

139 (XIII. 9)

CICERO TO CRASSIPES

Rome (?), 54 (?)[464]

From Cicero to Crassipes greetings.

I have already recommended the Company of Bithynia[465] to you in person as strongly as I could, and it was evident to me that of your own volition as well as in consequence of my recommendation you were anxious to accommodate the Company in any way in your power. However, since those concerned consider it very much to their advantage that I

464. The letter is usually assigned to the end of 51 or the beginning of 50. Although I believe this to be erroneous, I have kept it among the correspondence of the Proconsulate because its date is most conveniently considered (in my commentary) in that context.

465. Apparently a consortium of companies operating in Bithynia, where Crassipes was serving as Quaestor.

should also declare to you by letter my friendly disposition in their regard, I have not hesitated to write these lines.

I have always been very ready to study the interests of the tax-farmers as a class, which is only right in view of the important services they have rendered me. But I should like it to be clear to you that I have a special regard for this Company of Bithynia. The quality of the membership in itself makes the Company an important section of the community (it is a consortium of all the other companies) and, as it happens, it contains a great many very good friends of mine. I would mention one of them in particular who has a special responsibility at the present time, namely the Chairman, P. Rupilius, son of Publius, of the Tribe Menenia.

In view of the above, let me particularly request you to give your most generous support to the Company's agent, Cn. Pupius, assisting him in every way you can. I hope you will ensure, as you easily can, that his employers are thoroughly satisfied with his services, and will be good enough to protect and further their business interests as far as possible – and I am not unaware how much a Quaestor can do in that direction. I shall be greatly beholden. I can also promise and guarantee from experience that if you oblige the Company of Bithynia you will find that its members have good and grateful memories.

140 (XIII. 58)

CICERO TO C. TITIUS RUFUS

Laodicea, February 50

From M. Cicero to C. Titius Rufus, son of Lucius, Praetor Urbanus, greetings.

L. Custidius is a member of my Tribe, a native of my town, and my good friend. He has a case, which he will be submitting to your judgement. Allow me to recommend him to you within the limits imposed by conscience on your side and propriety on mine, merely asking that he find access to you easy and obtain his fair demands with your good-will; and that he have reason to feel that my friendship, even at so great a distance, is advantageous to him, especially where you are concerned.

141 (XIII. 59)

CICERO TO CURTIUS PEDUCAEANUS

Laodicea, February 50

M. Cicero to M. Curtius Peducaeanus, Praetor, greetings.

I have a unique regard for M. Fabius.[466] My personal intercourse with him is of the closest, and our friendship goes back a very long way. I do not make any request as to your verdict on the matters he has at issue (you will follow your edict and rule, as your conscience and dignity require), but only ask that he find access to you as easy as possible and obtain such points as shall appear just with your good-will, so that he may feel that my friendship, even at a long distance, is of advantage to him, particularly where you are concerned. This I beg of you as a special favour.

142 (XIII. 48)

CICERO TO C. SEXTILIUS RUFUS

Italy, beginning of 49

From Cicero to C. Sextilius Rufus, Quaestor, greetings.

466. Gallus; cf. p. 235.

I recommend all the inhabitants of Cyprus to your favour, but more especially those of Paphos. Anything you do for them I shall greatly appreciate. I am all the more ready to recommend them to you because I think it is to the advantage of your own reputation (which I have much at heart) that on your first arrival in the island as Quaestor you should set a pattern for others to follow. This I think you will the more easily achieve if you see fit to follow the enactment of your friend P. Lentulus and my own ordinances. I am confident that this will tend much to your credit.

143 (XVI. 11)

CICERO TO TIRO

Outside Rome, 12 January 49

From Tullius and Marcus, Terentia, Tullia, and the Quinti to Tiro best greetings.

Although I miss your timely service at every turn, your continued ill-health distresses me for your sake more than for my own. But seeing that the violence of the disease has turned into a quartan [467] fever (so Curius writes), I trust that with care you will soon be stronger. Only be considerate of others as you always are, and think of nothing at the present time except how best to get well. I know well enough how painfully you are missing us. But all will be easy if you regain your health. I don't want you to hurry for fear of your exposing yourself to the miseries of sea-sickness while you are still an invalid, and of your having a dangerous winter voyage.

I arrived outside Rome on 4 January. They streamed out to meet me on the road – a most flattering welcome. But I have fallen right into the flames of civil conflict, or rather war. I

467. It had previously been a tertian.

should dearly have liked to heal the mischief, and I believe I could, had not the personal desires of certain people (there are warmongers on both sides) stood in my way. To be sure, our friend Caesar has sent a threatening, harsh letter to the Senate, and persists in his shameless determination to hold his army and province in defiance of the Senate, and my friend Curio is egging him on. Our friend Antony and Q. Cassius[468] have gone to join Caesar along with Curio. They were not expelled by violence of any kind but left after the Senate had charged the Consuls, Praetors, Tribunes, and us Proconsuls to see that the state took no harm.[469] Never was the community in greater peril, never did bad citizens have a leader more ready to strike. Not but what preparations are going forward actively on our side too. This is taking place by the authority and zeal of our friend Pompey, who late in the day has begun to be afraid of Caesar.

Despite these commotions the Senate in large numbers has demanded a Triumph for me. But Consul Lentulus, to make it a bigger favour on *his* part, said he would put the matter before the House as soon as he had cleared up necessary state business. I am showing no undue eagerness, which makes my public influence the greater. Italy has been divided into districts, each under an appointed supervisor. I am taking Capua.[470]

I wanted you to know these facts. On your side, once again, see that you get well, and send me a letter as often as you have anybody to bring one. Again, goodbye.

Dispatched 12 January.

468. Both Tribunes.
469. The so-called 'Ultimate Decree of the Senate', amounting to a declaration of martial law.
470. The controversial matter of Cicero's command in Campania is discussed in my C.U.P. edition of the *Letters to Atticus*, Vol. IV, Appendix II.

144 (XIV. 18)

CICERO TO TERENTIA AND TULLIA

Formiae, 22 January 49

From Tullius to his dear Terentia, and her father to his darling daughter, and Marcus to his mother and sister best greetings.

My dear hearts, I think you should yet again carefully consider what you are to do – whether you should stay in Rome or with me or in some place of safety. The decision is yours as well as mine.

The points that occur to me are these: Thanks to Dolabella[471] you can stay in Rome safely, and your doing so might help us if there is any outbreak of violence or looting. But on the other hand I am concerned when I observe that all honest men have left Rome and have their womenfolk with them. Moreover, this district where I am is full of towns friendly to me and also of properties of mine, so that you could be with me a good deal, and when we are separated could live comfortably in places of our own. Frankly I have not yet made up my mind which is the better course. You must observe what other ladies of your rank are doing, and take care that when and if you do want to leave you don't find the way barred. Do please consider the matter again together and with our friends. Tell Philotimus to see that the house is barricaded and guarded and please arrange reliable couriers, so that I get some sort of a letter from you every day. But your chief care must be for your health, if you want us[472] to keep ours.

22nd, from Formiae.

471. Now one of Caesar's supporters.
472. Cicero and his son.

145 (XIV. 14)

CICERO TO TERENTIA AND TULLIA

Minturnae, 23 January 49

From Tullius to Terentia, and from her father to Tullia, his two dear hearts, and from Marcus to his best of mothers and darling sister best greetings.

If you are well, we are well.

The decision as to what you should do is now yours, not mine only. If Caesar is going to come back to Rome in civilized fashion, you can safely stay at home for the present. But if in his madness he is going to give the city over to plunder, I am afraid that even Dolabella's protection may not be enough for us. I also have the fear that we may soon be cut off, so that when and if you want to leave you may not be able. There remains the question, on which you yourselves will be the best judges, whether other ladies in your position are staying in Rome. If they are not, you should consider whether *you* can do so without discredit. As things now stand, provided that we can hold this area, you can stay very nicely with me or at my properties in the country. There is also the danger of a food shortage in Rome in the near future. I should like you to discuss these points with Pomponius and Camillus and any others you think proper, and, in fine, to keep stout hearts. Labienus[473] has improved the situation, and Piso [474] too helps by leaving Rome and branding his son-in-law as a criminal.

My dearest hearts, write to me as often as you can to tell me

473. Caesar's principal lieutenant, who went over to Pompey on the outbreak of war.

474. L. Piso Caesoninus, Consul in 58, whose daughter Calpurnia was married to Caesar.

how you are and what is going on in Rome. Quintus senior and junior and Rufus send you their greetings.

Goodbye.

23 January, from Minturnae.

146 (XVI. 12)

CICERO TO TIRO

Capua, 27 January 49

From Tullius to his dear Tiro greetings.

My existence and that of all honest men and the entire commonwealth hangs in the balance, as you may tell from the fact that we have left our homes and the mother-city herself to plunder or burning. We have reached the point when we cannot survive unless some God or accident comes to our rescue.

From the day I arrived outside Rome all my views, words, and actions were unceasingly directed towards peace. But a strange madness was abroad. Not only the rascals but even those who pass for honest men were possessed with the lust of battle, while I cried aloud that civil war is the worst of calamities. Swept along by some spirit of folly, forgetting the name he bears and the honours he has won, Caesar seized Ariminum, Pisaurum, Ancona, and Arretium. So we abandoned Rome – whether wisely or courageously it is idle to argue.

You see our predicament. To be sure, he is offering terms: that Pompey go to Spain, that the levies already raised and the forces at our disposal be dismissed. On his side he will hand over Further Gaul to Domitius and Hither Gaul to Considius Nonianus, their appointed governors; he will come to Rome to stand for the Consulship, and no longer desires his candidature to be accepted *in absentia*; he will canvass for the period of three market days in person. We have accepted the terms, on condition that he withdraws his forces from the places he has occupied so that a meeting of the Senate may be called in Rome, free of duress, to discuss these same terms. If he complies, there is hope of peace, though not peace with honour, since the conditions are dictated; but anything is better than to be as we are. On the other hand, if he refuses to abide by his own terms, war is ready to hand. Caesar, however, will not be able to bear the brunt of it, especially having run away from his own terms. Only we must cut him off so that he cannot get to Rome, which we trust can be done. For we are raising levies on a large scale, and think he is afraid that if he advances on the capital he will lose the Gallic provinces. Both,[475] except for the Transpadanes, are thoroughly disaffected towards him, and he has six legions and large auxiliary forces to his rear in Spain, commanded by Afranius and Petreius.[476] If he does not come to his senses, it looks as though he can be crushed – let us only hope without harm to the capital. He has had a body-blow in the defection of T. Labienus, the most distinguished of his officers, who has refused to be party to his criminal enterprise and joined us. Many are said to be about to follow Labienus' example.

I am still in command of the coast, which I exercise from Formiae. I did not wish to take a more important charge, in order that my letters and exhortations to peace may carry the greater weight with Caesar. But if war is to be, I envisage myself as commanding an army and specified legions. To add to my vexations, my son-in-law Dolabella is with Caesar.

I wanted you to be aware of these facts. Mind you don't let them upset you and hinder your recovery. I have very

475. i.e. Cisalpine and Transalpine Gaul.
476. Pompey's Legates.

particularly recommended you to A. Varro, whom I know to be very fond of me and anxious to assist you, asking him to interest himself in your health and sailing arrangements and in general to take you under his wing. I am sure he will do everything. He gave his word, and spoke to me very nicely.

Since you could not be with me when I most needed your services and loyalty, mind you do not hurry or be so foolish as make the voyage either as an invalid or in winter. I shall never think you have been too long in coming if you come safe and sound. I have not yet met anyone who had seen you later than M. Volusius, from whom I received your letter. That does not surprise me. I don't suppose that my letters either are getting through to you in the depth of winter. But do your best to get well, and once you *are* well and the voyage can be made safely, make it then. My son Marcus is at Formiae, Terentia and Tullia are in Rome. Take care of your health.

27 January, from Capua.

147 (XVI. 8)

Q. CICERO TO TIRO

Rome or Campania, January 49

From Q. Cicero to Tiro greetings.

Your health makes us terribly anxious. Travellers report 'no danger, but it will take time', which is a great consolation. Still it's a huge anxiety, if you are going to be away from us for long. Missing you brings home to us how useful and pleasant it is to have you. But though I long to see you with my every thought, I do ask you in all sincerity not to venture upon so long a journey by water and land in winter unless you are thoroughly strong, and not to take ship without careful preliminary enquiries. Cold is hard enough for an invalid to avoid in town houses; how much more difficult to escape the inclemency of the weather at sea or on the road! As Euripides says, 'Cold is a tender skin's worst enemy.'[477] How much trust you put in him I don't know, but *I* look upon every verse he wrote as an affidavit. Mind you get well, if you love me, and come back to us as soon as possible hale and hearty.

Love us and goodbye. Young Quintus sends you his love.

148 (VII. 27)

CICERO TO T. FADIUS

Early 49

From M. Cicero to T. Fadius greetings.

I am surprised that you should reproach me, when you have no right to do so; but even, if you *had* the right, it would ill become you. You say you paid me many attentions when I was Consul, and that Caesar will restore you.[478] You say a great deal, but nobody gives you credit.[479] You say you stood for the Tribunate on my account. A pity you are not Tribune all the time, then you would not be looking for an intercessor![480] You say I don't dare to speak my mind – as though my answer to your impudent request smacked of timidity!

The above is just to let you see that even in the style in which

477. From one of the lost plays.
478. From exile; cf. Letter 51 (V.18).
479. Latin *credit* = (a) 'believes', and (b) 'lends money to'. Fadius had apparently asked Cicero to stand surety and, on receiving a negative answer, written again in terms which put Cicero in a rage. The harsh, offensive tone of this letter is unique in his correspondence.
480. *intercessor* = (a) 'one who (as Tribune) casts a veto', and (b) 'surety'.

you aspire to shine you are a total failure. If you had expostu-
lated with me in civil fashion, I should willingly and easily
have cleared myself. I am not ungrateful for what you did, but
I *am* vexed at what you wrote. And I am much surprised that
you take me, to whom my fellows owe their freedom, for no
better than a slave. If the information [481] you say you gave me
was false, what do I owe you? If it was true, you are in an excellent position to testify what the Roman People owes *me*.

149 (VIII. 15)

CAELIUS RUFUS TO CICERO

Central or north Italy, c. 9 March 49

From Caelius to Cicero greetings.

Have you ever seen a more egregious ass than your Cn.
Pompeius? What a commotion he has created, and he such a
fraud! And have you ever read or heard tell of a leader more
energetic in action or more moderate in victory than our
Caesar? And what about these troops of ours who have finished
a war by the use of their legs, in the roughest and coldest country
and the filthiest winter weather – do you think they feed on
sugar-plums?[482] 'What's all this brag?' you may say. If you
only knew how I am beset with anxieties, you would find this
bragging of mine, which has nothing to do with *me*, quite
funny. I cannot explain to you what I mean otherwise than in
person, and I hope this will shortly be possible – he has decided
to recall me to Rome when he has driven Pompey out of Italy.

481. Evidently in connection with Catiline's conspiracy.
482. Literally 'rounded apples', a variety mentioned by Varro,
Columella, and others. Such things were served at dessert, not the kind
of fare to interest tough soldiers (like Agesilaus of Sparta; see Plutarch's
Life of him, 36).

That business, I imagine, is already done, unless Pompey has preferred to stand siege in Brundisium. Hang me if my mortal impatience to see you and exchange all our most intimate thoughts is the least important reason for my hurry to be back! I have a great many such thoughts, but I'm terribly afraid that when I see you the usual thing will happen – I'll forget the lot!

Be that as it may, what have I ever done to deserve the bad luck of this compulsory journey back to the Alps? The Intimilii[483] are up in arms, for no very momentous reason: Demetrius, Bellienus' slave-boy,[484] being stationed there with a detachment of troops, was bribed by the opposite party to seize and strangle one Domitius, a notable of the district and a host of Caesar's. The people rushed to arms. Now I have to trudge there through the snow with *[485] cohorts. You'll remark that the Domitii[486] are coming to grief all along the line. Well, I could wish our scion of Venus had shown as much spirit in dealing with *your* Domitius as Psecas'[487] offspring showed with this one!

Please give my regards to your son.

150 (IV. 1)

CICERO TO SERVIUS SULPICIUS RUFUS

Cumae, c. 21 April 49

M. Cicero to Ser. Sulpicius greetings.

My friend C. Trebatius has written informing me that you

483. A people in Liguria.

484. The man was no doubt a freedman.

485. A number is missing.

486. An allusion to the capture of L. Domitius Ahenobarbus and his army at Corfinium. Caesar ('our scion of Venus', the supposed ancestress of the Julian clan) let him go free.

487. Typical name for a woman slave (cf. Juvenal, VI.491).

enquired of him as to my present whereabouts. He says you are sorry your health did not permit you to see me when I came to the neighbourhood of Rome, [488] and that you would like to take counsel with me at the present time, if I come nearer, on what both of us ought to do.

My dear Servius, if only we could have conferred together before the disaster (one has to use such words)! Surely we should have lent some succour to the foundering commonwealth. Even before my return I knew you to be a champion of peace both during and after your Consulship, foreseeing these calamities, as you did, long in advance. As for me, though I approved your policy and shared your views, it was no use. I arrived on the scene too late and stood alone, regarded as a newcomer to the situation, finding myself surrounded by an atmosphere of insensate bellicosity. Now that it no longer seems in our power to be of any assistance to the commonwealth, if there is any step we can take for our personal benefit (not with the object of retaining any part of our former status, but so as to mourn with what dignity we may), there is no man in the world with whom I should think it more appropriate to take counsel than yourself. You do not need to be reminded of the examples of famous men, whom we should resemble, or of the precepts of learned men, to whom you have always been devoted. Indeed I should myself have written to you earlier expressing the opinion that your attendance in the Senate, or rather the meeting of Senators,[489] would serve no useful purpose, but that I was afraid of offending one who desired me to follow your example. When the person to whom

488. Cicero had stayed outside the old city boundary so as not to lose his *imperium* and so forfeit the hoped-for Triumph.

489. Convened at the beginning of April 49, when Caesar returned to Rome. The Consuls and many other magistrates having left Italy with Pompey, Cicero considered the meetings to be irregular, even though the Senate could constitutionally be summoned by a Praetor in default of Consuls.

I refer asked me to come to the Senate, I made it plain that I should say exactly what you have said on the subject of peace and the Spanish Provinces.[490]

You see the situation. The whole world is ablaze with war, distributed into military commands. Rome lies abandoned to fire and plunder; statutes, courts, law, credit have ceased to exist. I cannot imagine anything to hope for, I can scarcely any longer imagine anything I dare to pray for. But if you in the fullness of your wisdom think it useful for us to confer, I will come nearer Rome, though I have it in mind to go still further away and hate to hear the very name of the city. I have asked Trebatius to be good enough to forward any communication you may wish to send me, and would request you to do this, or else, if you prefer, to send me some trustworthy person from your entourage. That way it may not be necessary for you to leave Rome or for me to go there. I feel well assured (in saying which I allow you no less than, perhaps presumptuously, I claim for myself) that whatever we decide by mutual consent will be universally approved.

Goodbye.

151 (IV. 2)

CICERO TO SERVIUS SULPICIUS RUFUS

Cumae, 28 or 29 April 49

M. Cicero to Ser. Sulpicius greetings.

On 28 April I received your letter at my house near Cumae. Having read it, I apprehend that Philotimus has not acted very sensibly in forwarding the letter to me instead of coming in

490. Cicero's interview with Caesar on 28 March is described in *Letters to Atticus* 187 (IX.18).

person, when he had, as you say, a message from you covering all points. I realize that your letter would have been longer if you had not expected him to carry it to its destination. However, after I read it, your lady wife Postumia and our dear Servius[491] met me. They thought you should come to Cumae, and urged me to write to you to that effect.

You ask my advice. It is such as I can more easily take myself than offer to another. What course could I venture to recommend to one so respected and wise as yourself? If we ask which is the most clearly right, the answer is obvious. If we ask which is the most expedient, it is doubtful. But if we are the men we surely should be and judge nothing to be expedient except what is right and honourable, there can be no question how we ought to act.

You judge that your situation and mine are allied, and it is assuredly true that with the best intentions we both went astray in much the same way. Both of us made concord the sole object of our policy; and as nothing could have been more to Caesar's own advantage, we expected actually to earn his gratitude by defending peace. You see the extent of our miscalculation, and the point to which the situation has deteriorated. And you perceive not only the steps which are being, and have already been, taken but the future course and issue of affairs. So one must either approve current proceedings or live amongst them, even though one disapproves. The first plan seems to me dishonourable, the second dangerous as well. I am left to conclude that the right course is to go abroad. That would seem to leave two questions, what plan of departure to adopt and what part of the world to head for. To be sure there was never a sadder business, or a more difficult problem either. Every possible decision runs into some major difficulty.

As for yourself, the advice which I venture to offer is this: if you have already settled what you think you ought to do and your plan is not of a nature to fit in with mine, you should

491. Sulpicius' son.

spare yourself this troublesome journey. If, on the other hand, you have something on which you wish to confer with me, I shall wait for you. I beg you will come as soon as you conveniently can; I gathered that both Servius and Postumia would like you to do so.[492]

Goodbye.

152 (V. 19)

CICERO TO MESCINIUS RUFUS

Cumae, c. 28 April 49

Cicero to Rufus.

Although I never doubted your warm regard for me, I see it every day more plainly. This is the fulfilment of the promise you made in one of your letters, that you would be more zealous in your attentions to me than you had been in Cilicia (not that in my judgement the solicitude you showed out there admits of any addition) in proportion as your choice in friendship could be more freely exercised. Your earlier letter gave me great pleasure. I found that you had waited for my coming, which was friendly of you, and that, when the matter turned out otherwise than you had expected, you were heartily glad of my advice. And from this last letter of yours I appreciate with satisfaction your sound principles and your sense of friendly obligation. As for the first, I perceive that you hold, as all brave and good men ought to hold, nothing expedient but what is right and honourable. As for the second, you promise that you will be my companion in whatever I decide to do; nothing can be more agreeable to me, nor, I fancy, more creditable to you.

492. The interview took place, but led to nothing; cf. *Letters to Atticus* 206 (x.14) and 207 (x.15).2.

My resolution[493] was taken long ago. If I did not write to you about it earlier, it was not that it seemed best to keep you in the dark, but because its communication at such a time has somewhat the air of a reminder of obligation, or rather of an urgent demand of the recipient to take a share in hazard and toil. But since your friendly disposition, kindness, and good-will towards me are what they are, I gladly welcome such a spirit – but with one qualification (for I am not going to put aside my feeling of delicacy in making a request): if you carry out your promise, I shall be deeply grateful, and if you do not, I shall understand. I shall take it that you could not bring yourself to deny me (hence the promise), nor yet to deny your fears (hence the withdrawal). To be sure the matter is of great moment. The right course is plain, the expedient doubtful; and yet, if we are the men we ought to be, worthy of our studies and our books, we cannot doubt that whatever is most right is also most advantageous.

So, if it is to be you and I together, you will join me immediately. If, however, you concur in my plan and destination, but cannot manage it straight away, I shall keep you fully informed. I shall count you as my friend, whatever you decide; but if you decide the way I would fain hope, as a friend indeed.

153 (VIII. 16)[494]

CAELIUS RUFUS TO CICERO

Liguria (?), c. 16 April 49

From Caelius to Cicero greetings.

Much agitated as I am by your letter,[495] in which you make it

493. To join the republicans overseas.

494. This letter is also included in the correspondence with Atticus (200 A (X.9A)), to whom Cicero sent a copy.

495. Not extant.

plain that you have none but gloomy ideas in mind but do not say in detail what they are, and yet do not conceal the general nature of your intentions, I am writing this letter to you straight away.

I beg and implore you, Cicero, in the name of your fortunes and your children, to take no step which will jeopardize your well-being and safety. I call Gods and men and our friendship to witness that I have told you how it will be, and that it is no casual warning I give; having met Caesar and found what his disposition is likely to be once victory is won, I am telling you what I know. If you suppose that Caesar will continue his policy of letting opponents go free and offering terms, you are making a mistake. He thinks and even talks of nothing but ruthless severity. He left Rome angry with the Senate, he is thoroughly incensed by these vetoes.[496] Believe me, the time for intercession will be past.

Accordingly, if you care for yourself, for your only son, for your household, for your remaining hopes, if I and your excellent son-in-law have any influence with you, whose careers you surely do not wish to ruin by forcing us to hate or abandon the cause with which our welfare is bound up or else to harbour an undutiful wish contrary to *your* welfare ★★★. Finally, consider that any odium which may attach to your hesitancy has already been incurred. When Caesar's prospects were doubtful, you were unwilling to harm him; to go against him now, in his hour of victory, and to join a routed party which you did not choose to follow when they were fighting back, is the acme of folly. Don't be so much afraid of failing the 'right' side as to think too little about making the right choice. But if I cannot persuade you altogether, do at least wait until it is known how things go with us in Spain. You may take my word for it that these provinces will be ours as soon as Caesar arrives. What hope your friends will have with Spain lost I do not know,

496. The Tribune L. Metellus had been obstructing Caesar in the Senate.

and what sense it makes for you to join a hopeless party on my honour I cannot imagine.

What you conveyed to me without putting it into words Caesar had heard already. He scarcely said good day to me before he told me what he had heard about you. I professed ignorance, but asked him all the same to write to you in terms best adapted to induce you not to leave. He is taking me with him to Spain. Otherwise, before returning to Rome, I should have hurried to you wherever you were, and urged my plea in person, and held you back with all my might.

Think, Cicero, again and yet again before you bring utter ruin on yourself and your family, before you plunge with your eyes wide open into a situation from which you see there is no escape. If, however, you are worried by what the optimates may be saying, or if you find the arrogance and bounce of certain people too much for you, my advice is to choose some town well away from the war while these issues are deciding. It will not be long before they are settled. If you do that, I shall judge you to have acted wisely and you will not offend Caesar.

154 (II. 16)

CICERO TO CAELIUS RUFUS

Cumae, 2 or 3 May 49

From M. Cicero, Imperator, to M. Caelius, greetings.

Your letter would have given me great distress, were it not that by now the power of reason has dispelled all vexations and inveterate despair of the world has hardened my mind against new sorrows. All the same, I do not know how you came to form the suspicion of which you write from my last letter. What did that contain apart from complaint against the times we live in? And that surely weighed no less upon your mind than upon mine. I have not formed so poor an opinion of your intellectual acumen as to suppose you blind to what I see myself. But I *am* surprised that you, who ought to know me thoroughly, could have been led to believe me so improvident as to desert the rising sun for the setting and almost set, or so unstable as to throw away the hard-won favour of an eminently successful personage, to turn false to myself, and to take part in civil war, a course which I have always shunned from the very first.

Well then, what is this 'melancholy' project of mine? To withdraw, it may be, to some place of solitude. You must know how the unseemly behaviour of insolent upstarts irritates my spleen (you used to have a similar organ), even my eyes. Then there is this tiresome parade of lictors and the military title[497] by which I am addressed. If I could shed this load, I should be content with a hiding-place in Italy, however exiguous. But these laurels[498] of mine obtrude themselves upon the eyes of my ill-wishers, even on their petty little tongues. And yet I never entertained a thought of leaving without your and your associates' approval. But you know my little properties. I must stay on them, so as not to be a nuisance to my friends. The fact that I find it most convenient to stay on those which are near the coast makes some people suspect that I want to take ship. After all, perhaps I should not mind doing that if I could sail to peace. As for war, the idea is incongruous – especially to fight against one who I trust is satisfied with my conduct, on the side of one who cannot now be satisfied whatever I do.

Furthermore, you have been in a particularly good position to see into my mind ever since you visited me at Cumae. I did not conceal from you what T. Ampius had said. You saw how much I disliked the idea of abandoning the capital after I heard of it. Did I not assure you that I would put up with anything rather than leave Italy to join in civil war? Well then, what has

497. Imperator.
498. On the lictors' *fasces*, in token of victory.

occurred to change my decision? Has not everything rather tended to confirm me in my views? I hope you will believe my assurance, which I think conforms to your own opinion, that I seek nothing from this unhappy situation except to convince the world at last that peace was my chief desire and that, since all hope of peace disappeared, civil war has been my chief aversion. I do not think I shall ever wish to change this resolution. I remember how our old friend Q. Hortensius used to plume himself in this connection, because he had never taken part in a civil war. Mine will be the brighter glory in that *his* conduct was put down to lack of spirit, whereas I do not think the same can be thought of me.

Nor am I alarmed by the bogies which you, in all loyalty and affection, bring out to frighten me. In this world-wide commotion every sort of distress can be seen hanging over every head. For my part, I should have been only too glad to have saved the country from this fate at the cost of private and domestic misfortunes of my own, even those of which you warn me to beware. I am glad you care for my son. If a free constitution survives in any form, I shall leave him a sufficient inheritance in the memory of my name. If there is to be none, nothing will happen to him outside the general lot of his countrymen. You also ask me to think of my son-in-law. He is a fine young man and very dear to me. Knowing as you do my affection for him, and still more for my Tullia, can you doubt that I am most keenly concerned on his behalf? – all the more so because I was flattering myself with one ray of hope amidst the general misery, that my dear Dolabella (*our* dear Dolabella, I should say) would free himself from the difficulties in which his open-handed ways had involved him. You should inform yourself what sort of days he went through while he was in Rome, how painful to himself and how embarrassing even for me as his father-in-law.

Accordingly, I am not waiting for the outcome of this Spanish affair, which I am sure is going exactly as you say, and

I am making no shrewd calculations. If there is to be a civic community one day, there will presumably be a place in it for me. If not, I expect you yourself will come and join me in the lonely retreat in which you will hear that I have settled down. But perhaps I am just a prophet of woe and all this will have a happier ending. I remember how despairingly old men talked when I was young. Perhaps I am doing as they did and indulging the weakness of my age. I wish it may be so; but I doubt it.

I expect you have heard that Oppius' purple-bordered gown is a-weaving. Our friend Curtius has a double-dyed one in mind, but the dyer is keeping him waiting.[499] There's a pinch of seasoning, just to show that I like to laugh even when I am exasperated. I recommend you to pay attention to what I have written about Dolabella as though it were your own affair.

Now this is my final word: I shall do nothing wildly or hastily. All the same, I beg you to stand by me and my children, in whatever part of the world we may be, as our friendship and your honour shall require.

155 (XIV. 7)

CICERO TO TERENTIA

Aboard ship, Caieta, 7 June 49

From Tullius to his dear Terentia best greetings.

All the miseries and cares with which I plagued you to des-

499. The purple-bordered gown (*toga praetexta*) was worn by, among others, members of the four principal priestly colleges. One of these, the Augurs, also wore a distinctive gown, the *trabea*, of purple and yellow. Oppius and Curtius Postumus were friends of Caesar ('the dyer'), and apparently expecting priestly office as indicated.

peration (and very sorry I am for it) and Tulliola too, who is sweeter to me than my life, are dismissed and ejected. I understood what lay behind them the day after our parting. I threw up pure bile during the night, and felt an instantaneous relief as though a God had cured me. To that God you will make due acknowledgement in piety and purity after your custom.

I trust we have a very good ship – I am writing this directly after coming aboard. I shall next write many letters to our friends, commending you and our Tulliola most earnestly to their care. I should give you words of encouragement to make you both braver if I had not found you braver than any man. And after all, I trust things are now in better train. You, I hope, will be as well off as possible where you are, and I shall at last be fighting for the commonwealth alongside my peers. First and foremost, I want you to take care of your health. Second, if you agree, please use the country houses which will be farthest away from army units. The farm at Arpinum with the servants we have in town will be a good place for you if food prices go up.

Darling Marcus sends you his best love. Once again take care of yourself and goodbye.

Dispatched 7 June.

156 (VIII. 17)

CAELIUS RUFUS TO CICERO

Rome, January (?) 48

From Caelius to Cicero greetings.

To think then that I was in Spain instead of at Formiae when you left to join Pompey! If only Appius Claudius had been on our side or C. Curio on yours! It was my friendship with him that little by little landed me in this god-forsaken camp. I realize now that pique and affection robbed me of my good sense. And then, you, when I visited you that night as I was leaving for Ariminum[500] and you gave me a peace-message for Caesar, and played your fine patriotic role – you neglected the duty of a friend, you did not think of *me*! I don't say all this because I doubt our party's success. But, believe me, death is better than the spectacle of these people.

But for the fear of your party's ferocity we should have been thrown out of here long ago, for apart from a few capitalists there's not a man or a class here that is not for Pompey. Thanks to *me*, the lower classes especially, and the general public, which used to be on our side, are now on yours.[501] You ask why. No, you and your friends must wait and see. I'll make you win in spite of yourselves. Cato and company will be smiling on me yet! You folk are fast asleep. You don't seem to me to understand conditions over here as yet – where we are vulnerable, how weak we are. And I shall not be doing this in the hope of any reward, but from what is apt to be the most powerful motive with me – indignation and outrage.

What are you and your friends doing over there? Waiting for a battle? There lies Caesar's *forte*. I don't know about your army, but our fellows are desperate fighters and accustomed to take cold and hunger in their day's work.

500. On 7 January, along with Curio and the Tribunes Mark Antony and Q. Cassius. This is the only record of Caelius' interview with Cicero.
501. As Praetor Caelius had started an agitation for the relief of debtors.

157 (IX. 9)

DOLABELLA TO CICERO

Caesar's camp near Dyrrachium, May 48

From Dolabella to Cicero greetings.

If you are well I am glad. I myself am well and so is our Tullia. Terentia has been rather out of sorts, but I know for certain that she has now recovered. Otherwise all your domestic affairs are in excellent shape.

You did me an injustice if at any time you suspected that in advising you to throw in your lot with Caesar and with me, or at least to retire into private life, I was thinking of party interests rather than of yours. But now, when the scales are coming down on our side, I imagine that only one thing can possibly be thought of me, namely, that I am proffering advice to you which it would be contrary to my duty as your son-in-law to withhold. On your side, my dear Cicero, you must take what follows, whether it meets with your approval or not, in the persuasion that I have thought and written it out of the most sincere loyalty and devotion to yourself.

You see Cn. Pompeius' situation. Neither the glory of his name and past nor yet the kings and nations of whose dependence he used so often to boast can protect him. Even the door of an honourable retreat, which humble folk find open, is closed to him. Driven out of Italy, Spain lost, his veteran army taken prisoner, he is now to crown all blockaded in his camp, a humiliation which I fancy has never previously befallen a Roman general. Do therefore, as a man of sense, consider what he can have to hope or we to fear; so you will find it easiest to take the decision most expedient for you. One thing I beg of you; if he does manage to escape from his present dangerous position and takes refuge with his fleet, consult your own best interests and at long last be your own friend rather than anybody else's. You have done enough for obligation and friendship; you have done enough for your party too and the form of commonwealth of which you approved. It is time now to take our stand where the commonwealth is actually in being rather than, in following after its old image, to find ourselves in a political vacuum.

Therefore, dearest Cicero, if it turns out that Pompey is driven from this area too and forced to seek yet other regions of the earth, I hope you will retire to Athens or to any peaceful community you please. If you decide to do that, please write and tell me, so that if I possibly can I may hasten to your side. Any concessions that you need from the Commander-in-Chief to safeguard your dignity you will yourself obtain with the greatest ease from so kindly a man as Caesar; but I believe that *my* petitions will carry more than negligible weight with him.

I trust to *your* honour and kindness to see that the courier I am sending you is able to return to me and brings a letter from you.

158 (XIV. 6)

CICERO TO TERENTIA

Pompey's camp, 15 July 48

To my family, greetings.

It is not often that I have anyone to take a letter, nor have I anything I want to write about. From the last letter I received from you I learned that it was impossible to sell any property. So I shall be grateful if you and the others will consider how to meet the claims of the person[502] whose claims you know I

502. Dolabella, to whom money was due in respect of Tullia's dowry; cf. *Letters to Atticus* 212 (XI.2).2.

want met. As to what you say about our girl thanking you, I am not surprised that you should give her good reason to do that. If Pollex has not yet left, please pack him off as soon as possible. Take care of your health.

Ides of July.

159 (XIV. 12)

CICERO TO TERENTIA

Brundisium, 4 November 48

From Tullius to his dear Terentia greetings.

I hope your joy at our safe arrival in Italy may be a lasting one. But distracted as I was by my unhappiness and the cruel ill-treatment of my family, I am afraid I may have taken a road with no easy outcome. So help me as far as you can – though what you can do I cannot imagine. There is no reason for you to leave home at present. It is a long, unsafe journey, and I do not see what good you can do if you come.

Goodbye.

Dispatched 4 November from Brundisium.

160 (XIV. 19)

CICERO TO TERENTIA

Brundisium, 27 November 48

From Tullius to his dear Terentia greetings.

In my own deep distresses Tullia's illness is an agony to me. There is no need for me to write any more to you on the subject, for I am sure that you are no less gravely concerned. As for your joint wish that I should come nearer Rome, I see that I ought to do so; and I should have done so already, but have been held up by various obstacles which even now have not been cleared. However, I am expecting a letter from Pomponius, and shall be grateful if you will see that it is forwarded as quickly as possible.

Take care of your health.

161 (XIV. 9)

CICERO TO TERENTIA

Brundisium, 17 (?) December 48

Tullius to his dear Terentia best greetings.

In addition to my other distresses I am now worried about Dolabella's and Tullia's illnesses. In general, I just don't know what plans to make or what to do about anything. I hope you will take care of your own health and Tullia's.

Goodbye.

162 (XIV. 17)

CICERO TO TERENTIA

Brundisium, 23 (?) December 48

From Tullius to his dear Terentia greetings.

I hope you are well, as I am.

I should write to you at greater length and more often if I had anything to say. As it is, you see how matters stand. Of my own sorry state Lepta and Trebatius will tell you. Be sure to take care of your health and Tullia's.

Goodbye.

163 (XIV. 16)

CICERO TO TERENTIA

Brundisium (?), 4 January 47 (?)

From Tullius to his dear Terentia greetings.

I hope you are well, as I am.

In my present circumstances I have no reason to expect anything in the way of a letter from you or to write to you myself. And yet somehow I do expect letters from home and write when I have a bearer.

Volumnia[503] ought to have been more ready to oblige you than she was; and what she did do might have been done with more care and circumspection. However, we have more important matters to occupy and vex us. They are overwhelming me, as was the purpose of those who forced me away from my original intention.

Take care of yourself.

4 January.

164 (XIV. 8)

CICERO TO TERENTIA

2 June 47

From Tullius to his dear Terentia greetings.

I hope you are well, as I am.

I want you to take the greatest care of your health, for I have been told both by letter and word of mouth that you had a sudden attack of fever. Thank you for informing me so

503. Probably Volumnia Cytheris (see Glossary of Persons).

promptly about Caesar's letter.[504] In future too, please let me know if there is anything needful or any new development. Take care of yourself.

Goodbye.

Dispatched 2 June.

165 (XIV. 21)

CICERO TO TERENTIA

Brundisium, June (early) 47

From Tullius to his dear Terentia greetings.

I hope you are well, as I am.

Do your best to regain your health. Please make all necessary provisions and arrangements as circumstances require and write to me as often as possible on all points.

Goodbye.

166 (XIV. 11)

CICERO TO TERENTIA

Brundisium, 14 June 47

From Tullius to his dear Terentia greetings.

I hope you are well, as I am.

Tullia joined me on 12 June. She is so wonderfully brave and kind that it gives me even greater pain to think that through my carelessness she is placed far otherwise than befitted a girl of her station and so good a daughter.

504. Cf. *Letters to Atticus* 227 (XI.16).I.

I am thinking of sending Marcus to Caesar, and Cn. Sallustius with him. I shall send you word when he leaves. Take good care of your health.

Goodbye.

14 June.

167 (XIV. 15)

CICERO TO TERENTIA

Brundisium, 19 June 47

Tullius to Terentia greetings.

I hope you are well.

As I wrote to you earlier, I had decided to send Marcus to Caesar, but changed my mind because there are no reports of his coming home. On other matters there is nothing new, but Sicca will tell you what I wish and think expedient at this time. I still have Tullia with me. Take good care of your health.

Goodbye.

19 June.

168 (XIV. 10)

CICERO TO TERENTIA

Brundisium, 9 July 47

From Tullius to his dear Terentia greetings.

I wrote to Pomponius, later than I ought, telling him what I thought should be done.[505] When you have had a talk with

505. Concerning Tullia's divorce from Dolabella.

him, you will understand my wishes. There is no need to write more explicitly, since I have written to him. Please send me a letter as soon as possible on this and other matters. Take good care of your health.

Goodbye.

9 July.

169 (XIV. 13)

CICERO TO TERENTIA

Brundisium, 10 July 47

From Tullius to his dear Terentia greetings.

As regards what I wrote in my last letter about sending notice of divorce, I don't know how powerful he is at the present time[506] nor how excited the state of popular feeling. If he is likely to be a formidable enemy, don't do anything – perhaps he will take the initiative even so. You must judge of the whole position and choose whatever you think the least of evils in this wretched situation.

Goodbye.

10 July.

170 (XIV. 24)

CICERO TO TERENTIA

Brundisium, 11 August 47

From Tullius to his dear Terentia greetings.

I hope you are well, as I am.

506. Dolabella was Tribune in 47.

I have nothing definite yet either about Caesar's arrival or the letter which Philotimus is said to have.[507] If anything definite comes along, I shall let you know at once. Take good care of your health.

Goodbye.

11 August.

171 (XIV. 23)

CICERO TO TERENTIA

Brundisium, 12 August 47

From Tullius to his dear Terentia greetings.

I hope you are well, as I am.

I have at last received a letter from Caesar, quite a handsome one. He is said to be arriving in person sooner than was expected. I shall let you know when I have decided whether to go to meet him or to wait for him here. Please send the couriers back as soon as possible. Take good care of your health.

Goodbye.

Dispatched 12 August.

172 (XIV. 22)

CICERO TO TERENTIA

Brundisium, 1 September 47

From Tullius to his dear Terentia greetings.

I hope you are well, as I am.

507. Cf. *Letters to Atticus* 232 (XI.23).2.

I am expecting our couriers any day. When they arrive, perhaps I shall know better what to do, and I shall at once inform you. Take good care of your health.

Goodbye.

Kalends of September.

173 (XIV. 20)

CICERO TO TERENTIA

Near Venusia, 1 October 47

From Tullius to his dear Terentia greetings.

I think I shall get to Tusculum either on the Nones or on the following day. Kindly see that everything there is ready. I may have a number of people with me, and shall probably make a fairly long stay there. If there is no tub in the bathroom, get one put in; likewise whatever else is necessary for health and subsistence.

Goodbye.

Kalends of October, from the district of Venusia.

174 (XV. 15)

CICERO TO CASSIUS

Brundisium, August 47

M. Cicero to C. Cassius greetings.

Both of us, hoping for peace and hating civil bloodshed, decided to hold aloof from persistence in an unnecessary war.

But as I am regarded as having taken the lead in that course, perhaps my feeling towards you in this context should hold more of responsibility than of expectation. And yet I often recall how in talking familiarly to each other, you to me no less than I to you, we were both led to the persuasion that our verdict, if not the entire issue, might properly be decided by the result of a single battle. Nor has anyone ever fairly blamed us for taking this view, excepting those who think the commonwealth had better be wiped out altogether than survive in an enfeebled and attenuated form. For my part I saw no hope (obviously) from its destruction, but great hope from its remnants.

The sequel, however, was unexpected – the wonder is that such events could happen rather than that we did not see them coming and, being but human, could not divine them. For my part, I confess my forecast was that, once the fated and fatal battle, so to speak, had been fought, the victors would turn their attention to the general survival and the vanquished to their own. At the same time I thought that both the one and the other depended upon swift action by the victorious leader. Had that been forthcoming, Africa would have experienced the clemency which Asia came to know, as did Achaia also, whose ambassador and intercessor was, I believe, none other than yourself. But the crucial moments were lost, the moments which matter most, especially in civil warfare. A year intervened, leading some to hope for victory and others to care nothing even for defeat. The blame for all these calamities lies at fortune's door. Who could have expected that the main hostilities would have been so long held up by the fighting at Alexandria, or that this what's-his-name, Pharnaces, would menace Asia so formidably?

We thought alike, but we fared differently. *You* made for a quarter[508] where you would be present at the making of decisions and able to foresee events to come, the best comfort for

508. Cassius had joined Caesar in the East.

an anxious mind. *I* made haste to meet Caesar in Italy (so we thought), on his way home after sparing many valuable lives, and to urge him to peace – spurring a willing horse, as they say. The consequence was that I have been, and still am, at a vast distance away from him. I am living amidst the groans of Italy and the pitiful plaints of Rome. Perhaps I and you and every man, each according to his powers, might have done something to help, if authoritative backing had been available.

So I would ask you, in virtue of your unfailing kindliness toward me, to write to me and tell me what you see and feel, what you think I have to expect and ought to do. A letter from you will mean a great deal to me. I only wish I had followed the advice in that first letter of yours from Luceria.[509] I should have kept my standing and avoided all unpleasantness.

175 (IX. 1)

CICERO TO VARRO

Rome, 47 (late) or 46 (early)

From Cicero to M. Varro greetings.

The letter which you sent to Atticus and which he read to me informed me of your doings and whereabouts, but as to when we are to see you, I could not so much as make a guess from that letter. However, I am coming to hope that your advent is not far away.[510] I wish I may find some comfort in it, though our afflictions are so many and so grievous that nobody but an arrant fool ought to hope for any relief. And yet either you may

509. The letter here referred to must have advised Cicero to stay out of the war. It was probably written in February 49, just before the fall of Corfinium. Pompey set up his headquarters at Luceria about 25 January.

510. Varro may not yet have returned to Italy.

be able to help me or perhaps I may in some way be able to help you. For I should tell you that since my return I have restored my relations with my old friends, that is to say my books. Not that I had renounced their companionship because I was annoyed with them – it was because they gave me a sense of shame. I felt that in casting myself into a turmoil of events with altogether untrustworthy associates I had failed in obedience to their precepts. They forgive me. They call me back to the old intercourse and tell me that you in staying faithful to it were wiser than I. And so I have made my peace with them and we are together again. That is why I think I may properly hope that once I see you I shall find both present and impending troubles easy to bear.

So whatever rendezvous you favour, be it Tusculum or Cumae,[511] or my house or yours, or (what would be my last choice) Rome, you may be sure I shall make it appear the most convenient for both of us, only provided we are together.

176 (IX. 3)

CICERO TO VARRO

Rome, c. 18 April 46

From Cicero to Varro.

Although I have nothing to write about, I could not let Caninius[512] go to you without giving him something. So what *should* I write? What I think you want to read, that I shall be coming to visit you soon. But pray ask yourself whether it is quite proper for us to be down there[513] at such a time of national convulsion. We shall be giving a chance for gossip to those who

511. Both Cicero and Varro had villas in both areas.
512. No doubt L. Caninius Gallus.
513. On the coast of Campania.

don't know that, wherever we are, our style and way of living remain the same. And yet, what does it matter? They will gossip about us anyway. When all mankind is wallowing in every sort of crime and outrage, I hardly suppose we need concern ourselves overmuch about possible aspersions on our idleness, whether by ourselves or in one another's company. Yes, I shall follow you[514] and take no notice of these ignorant barbarians. However melancholy the times, and melancholy indeed they are, our pursuits seem somehow to yield more generous rewards now than they did in days gone by. Perhaps it is because we have no other means of relief; or perhaps the severity of the disease puts us in need of the medicine, and its strength, which we did not perceive when we were well, is now manifest.

But why am I now sending such reflections to *you*, who have them home-grown – an owl to Athens?[515] No reason, to be sure, except for you to write a line in return, and to expect me. So please do.

177 (IX. 2)

CICERO TO VARRO

Rome, c. 22 April 46

From Cicero to Varro.

Your (and our) friend Caninius called upon me late one evening and told me that he would be leaving betimes next day to join you; so I said I would give him something to carry, and asked him if he would kindly call for it in the morning. I wrote a letter[516] that night; but he did not come back after all

514. Down to Cumae.
515. Like 'coals to Newcastle'.
516. Letter 176 (IX.3).

and I assumed he had forgotten. I should have sent you the letter all the same by messengers of my own, had I not heard from Caninius that you would be leaving Tusculum[517] early the following day. Well, a few days later who should arrive at my house early in the morning out of the blue, when I was least expecting him, but Caninius? He said he was just off to join you. My letter was by now *passée*, particularly as such important news had come in since I wrote it; but still I did not want my midnight oil to be wasted, and so I gave it to Caninius as it stood. But I also said certain things to him, knowing him to be a man of culture and a very warm friend of yours, which I expect he has passed on to you.

To you I have the same advice to offer as to myself. Let us avoid men's eyes, even if we cannot easily escape their tongues. The jubilant victors[518] regard us as among the defeated, whereas those who are sorry for the defeat of our friends feel aggrieved that we are still among the living. Perhaps you will wonder why, with this going on in Rome, I am not elsewhere like you. Well, and have you yourself, a shrewder man than I or any other, foreseen everything, has *nothing* turned out contrary to your expectations? I can hardly believe that. Whose eyes are so preternaturally sharp[519] as to avoid every obstacle, every pitfall, in darkness such as this? In point of fact it did cross my mind long ago that it would be nice to get away somewhere, so as not to see or hear what was being done and said in Rome. But I made difficulties for myself. I thought that whoever came my way would suspect or, even if he did not suspect, would say, as might suit his individual purpose, 'Aha! He took fright, that's why he ran away; or else he's up to something, has a boat all ready.' Even the most charitable (and per-

517. For Cumae. In fact, Varro's departure was postponed.

518. The news of Caesar's victory over the republicans at Thapsus reached Rome about 20 April.

519. Literally 'who is such a Lynceus?' The Argonaut Lynceus could see in the dark.

haps best acquainted with the kind of man I am) would have thought that I was leaving because I could not stand the sight of certain persons. With all this in mind I stay on in Rome. And after all, long custom has imperceptibly anaesthetized my spleen.

So my conduct is explained. Now my counsel to *you* is to lie low for the present where you are,[520] while these rejoicings are at boiling-point and also until we hear just how the affair has been settled – for settled I believe it is. A great deal will depend on the victor's disposition and the way things turned out. I have my own guess to be sure, but am waiting for news.

No, I don't think you ought to go to Baiae,[521] unless rumour itself grows hoarse. Even when we go away from here, it will be more seemly to appear to have chosen that part of the world for weeping rather than for bathing. But you will judge better than I. Only let us be firm on one point – to live together in our literary studies. We used to go to them only for pleasure, now we go for salvation. If anybody cares to call us in as architects or even as workmen to help build a commonwealth, we shall not say no, rather we shall hasten cheerfully to the task. If our services are not required, we must still read and write 'Republics'. Like the learned men of old, we must serve the state in our libraries, if we cannot in Senate-House and Forum, and pursue our researches into custom and law.[522]

Such are my sentiments. You will oblige me greatly if you will write and tell me what *you* are going to do and what you think best.

520. At Tusculum.

521. The fashionable resort (as distinct from Varro's own villa at Cumae).

522. Cicero may have resumed work on his unfinished treatise *On Laws*.

178 (IX. 7)

CICERO TO VARRO

Rome, May (late) 46

Cicero to Varro.

I was at dinner with Seius when a letter from you was delivered to each of us. Yes, I think it's seasonable now.[523] As for the difficulties I put up previously, I'll confess my craftiness. I wanted to have you near by in case some chance of good turned up. 'Two heads',[524] you know. Now, since all is settled, we must hesitate no longer – full speed ahead.[525] When I heard about L. Caesar junior,[526] I said to myself 'What can I, his father, look for?'[527] So I go dining every night with our present rulers. What am I to do? One must go with the times.

But joking aside (especially as we have nothing to laugh about), 'Africa, grim land's a-tremble in terrific tumult tossed.'[528] There is nothing 'negative'[529] that I don't apprehend.

523. To go to Campania.
524. *Iliad* x.224: 'When two go together, one notices before the other.'
525. Literally 'with horse and foot', i.e. without any holding back. 'We must make friends with the winning party' is implied.
526. i.e. about his death in Africa. Cicero, perhaps mistakenly, implies that this took place by Caesar's orders.
527. i.e. 'what have *I* got to expect?' Cicero recalls this scrap of Terence's *Girl from Andros* (112) (probably without remembering its dramatic context, which is foreign to his point) because 'father' suggests an old man as compared to a young one.
528. From Ennius' *Annals*.
529. A Greek term from Stoic philosophy, which recognized virtue as the only good but allowed that other things (e.g. health, wealth, and their opposites) were on one side or other of complete indifference. Varro was an expert on Greek philosophy.

In answer to your questions as to date, route, and destination, we know nothing yet. Even as to Baiae,[530] some think he may come by way of Sardinia. That is one of his properties that he has not yet inspected. It's the worst he owns, but he doesn't despise it. I myself, to be sure, think he's more likely to travel by way of Sicily. But we shall soon know. Dolabella is coming, and I expect he will be our schoolmaster. 'The teacher's oft inferior to the taught.'[531] However, if I know what you have decided, I shall try to accommodate my plans to yours. So I expect to hear from you.

179 (IX. 5)

CICERO TO VARRO

Rome, May (late) 46

From Cicero to Varro.

The Nones? Yes, that will be very seasonable, I think, literally as well as politically speaking.[532] So I approve your date and shall keep it in view myself. As for our line of conduct,[533] we ought not in my opinion to regret it, even if those who took a different line were not regretting *that*. It was not

530. There seems to have been a rumour that Caesar would land at Baiae. He did in fact come by way of Sardinia and landed at Ostia.

531. A Greek line from an unknown dramatic source. Cicero had given Dolabella lessons in rhetoric (cf. Letter 192 (VII.33)).

532. Literally 'not only because of the circumstances (*tempus*) of the commonwealth but because of the time (*tempus*) of year'. 5 June by the calendar in 46 represented 7 April, a pleasant time for a visit to the Bay of Naples. The reference to politics means, I think, that it would be wise to take the proposed holiday before Caesar's return.

533. In supporting Pompey in the first place and in withdrawing from the war after Pharsalia.

hope, but duty, whose call we followed; and it was not duty, but despair, that we abandoned. We had a tenderer conscience than those who never stirred from home and a sounder sense of reality than those who, after the loss of our resources, did not return there. But what I find hardest to stomach is the censure of do-nothings. However things stand, I have more respect for the men who perished in the war than time for persons who cannot forgive us for being alive.

If I have leisure for a visit to Tusculum before the Nones, I shall see you there. If not, I shall follow you to Cumae, and let you know in advance, so that the bath be ready.

180 (IX. 4)

CICERO TO VARRO

Tusculum, end of May or beginning of June 46

From Cicero to Varro.

'Concerning things possible', let me tell you that I pronounce with Diodorus.[534] So if you are coming, you may be sure that it is necessary for you to come; if you are not coming, it is impossible for you to come. Now ask yourself which pronouncement you prefer, Chrysippus' or this – which our friend Diodotus used to be unable to stomach. But we will talk of these matters as well as others when we have time to spare. This too is possible according to Chrysippus.

Thank you for what you have done about ★[535] – I had asked

534. Fourth-century philosopher. His so-called 'Master Argument' sought to prove that what is or will be actual is possible, and that what is not going to be actual is not possible. It was contraverted by the great third-century Stoic Chrysippus, who defined the possible as that which was capable of being actual (if circumstances did not prevent it).

535. 'Coctius' in the manuscripts is not attested as a Roman name. Perhaps it should be 'Cottius'.

Atticus too to attend to that matter. If you don't come to me I shall run over to you. If you have a kitchen garden in your library we shall lack for nothing.[536]

181 (IX. 6)

CICERO TO VARRO

Rome, June (latter half) 46

From Cicero to Varro.

Our friend Caninius told me from you to write if there should be anything which I thought you ought to know. Well, the arrival is awaited – that is no news to you. But when he wrote, as I suppose, that he would be coming to his place at Alsium,[537] his friends wrote to dissuade him, telling him that there were many people thereabouts whose presence would be annoying to him, and many whom *his* presence would annoy; Ostia, in their opinion, would make a more convenient landing-place. I do not myself see what odds it makes, but Hirtius told me that both he and Balbus and Oppius wrote advising him in this sense – persons whom I know to be fond of you.

I wanted you to hear of this so you should know where to arrange to stay, or rather so you should make arrangements in both localities, since what *he* will do is uncertain. At the same time I have shown off to you the familiar footing on which I stand with these gentry, and how I am taken into their counsels. I see no reason why I should object to that. It is one thing to put up with what has to be put up with, another to approve what ought to be disapproved – though for my part I don't any

536. Having food for both mind and body. Even so a rather obscure remark.

537. Or 'the district of Alsium'.

longer know what to disapprove of, except the beginnings of it all, which were a matter of volition. I saw (you were away) that our friends were desirous of war, whereas the person we are expecting was not so much desirous as unafraid of it. That then came within the scope of design, all else followed inevitably. And victory had to fall to one side or the other.

I know that your heart was always as heavy as mine. Not only did we foresee the destruction of one of the two armies and its leader, a vast disaster, but we realized that victory in civil war is the worst of all calamities. I dreaded the prospect, even if victory should fall to those we had joined. They were making savage threats against the do-nothings, and your sentiments and my words were alike abhorrent to them. As for the present time, if our friends had gained the mastery, they would have used it very immoderately. They were infuriated with us. One might have supposed that we had taken some resolution for our own safety which we had not advised them to take for theirs, or that it was to the advantage of the state that they should go to brute beasts[538] for help rather than die outright or live in hope – admittedly no very bright hope, but still hope.

We live, it may be said, in a state that has been turned upside down. Undeniably true. But that bears hard on persons who have not prepared resources for themselves against all life's contingencies. Here is the point to which the flow of these remarks, more prolix than I wished, has been tending. I have always thought you a great man and I think you so now, because in this stormy weather you almost alone are safe in harbour. You reap the most precious fruits of learning, devoting your thoughts and energies to pursuits which yield a profit and a delight far transcending the exploits and pleasures of these worldlings. These days you are now spending down at Tusculum are worth a lifetime by my reckoning. Gladly would I leave all earthly wealth and power to others, and take in

538. The elephants of King Juba of Numidia, an ally of the republicans.

exchange a licence to live thus, free from interruption by any outside force. I am following your example as best I can, and most gladly find repose in literary studies. Surely nobody would begrudge us this. Our country will not or cannot use our services, so we return to a mode of life which many philosophers (mistakenly perhaps, but many) have considered actually to be preferred to the political. The state now grants its permission. Are we not then at liberty to give full rein to pursuits which in the judgement of great thinkers carry a sort of exemption from public employment?

However, I am going beyond Caninius' commission. *He* asked me to write if anything came to my knowledge of which you were unaware; and here am I telling you what you know better than I, your informant. So I shall do what I was asked, and see that you are not left in ignorance of any items relevant to the present situation that may come my way.

182 (v. 21)

CICERO TO MESCINIUS RUFUS

Rome, mid April 46

From M. Cicero to L. Mescinius greetings.

Many thanks for your letter. It told me what I thought even before I read it, that you have a great desire to see me. That I welcome, but at the same time I don't allow you any priority in such a feeling. To be with you is my ardent wish, by all my hopes I swear it. Even when there was a greater plenty of good men and good citizens and of pleasant and friendly company, I liked nobody's society better than yours and few people's so well. But now, when some are dead, others away, others changed towards me, upon my soul I would rather spend a day with you than this whole period with most of those whose company I keep perforce. Don't imagine that solitude is not more agreeable to me (though I am not allowed it) than the talk of my usual visitors, one or two at most excepted.

And so I take refuge, as I would advise you to do, in my literary dabbling, and also in my political conscience. I am one, as you are in an excellent position to judge, that never put his own interest before his countrymen's. Had a personage[539] for whom you never much cared (you cared for *me*) not been jealous of me, it would be well with him and with all honest men today. I am one that wished no man's violence to prevail over public tranquillity and honour; but when I found the armed might which I had always dreaded more potent than the union of honest men of which I had myself been the architect, I was for peace, however unfair the terms, rather than a trial of force against a stronger adversary. But of this and much besides we shall soon be able to talk together.

The only thing that keeps me in Rome, however, is the expectation of events in Africa, where a crisis seems to be imminent. I feel it is of some moment to me (though what actual difference it makes I hardly see, but even so) not to be far away from my friends' advice, whatever news comes in from that quarter. The situation is now such that, although there may be a good deal to choose between the causes of the combatants, I think the victory of either will amount to pretty much the same.

But the fact is that my spirit, which was perhaps inclined to frailty when the issue was in doubt, has been much stronger in despair. Your earlier letter strengthened it still further, for it showed how bravely you bore your ill-usage;[540] and it did me good to see how your fine culture, and especially your literary work, stood you in good stead. For, to tell the truth, I thought you a trifle too easily hurt, like nearly all of us who have lived

539. Pompey.
540. Though back in Italy, Mescinius had been in some way penalized by Caesar, perhaps forbidden to return to Rome.

an independent life in a happy community under a free constitution. But as we observed moderation in the good days gone by, so we ought to take our present adversity, or rather utter ruin, with fortitude. In the midst of disaster we gain one advantage at least: death, which even in the days of our happiness it was incumbent on us to despise on the ground that it would be devoid of consciousness, we ought in our present plight not merely to despise but positively to pray for.

If you care for me, enjoy your present leisure, and persuade yourself that no matter for fear or trembling can befall a man apart from fault and wrongdoing; and of this you are free, and always will be. If I feel I can safely do so, I shall join you shortly, and if anything occurs to alter my intention, I shall let you know immediately. Eager to see me as I should like you to be, in your poor state of health you must not stir from where you are without first writing to me and asking what I wish you to do. I hope you will continue to care for me, and pay proper regard to your health and peace of mind.

183 (VII. 3)

CICERO TO M. MARIUS

Rome, mid April 46

From M. Cicero to M. Marius greetings.

Considering, as I very often do, the general miseries in which we have been living for so many years and, as I see it, shall continue to live, I am apt to call to mind the last time we were together. I remember the very day – 12 May in the Consulship of Lentulus and Marcellus.[541] I had come down to my place near Pompeii that evening, and found you there to meet me in

541. i.e. 49; see *Letters to Atticus* 208 (x.16).4.

a troubled state of mind – troubled by the thought of my duty, and my danger too. You were afraid that if I stayed in Italy I should be failing in my duty, whereas if I set off for the war you were disturbed by the risk I should run. No doubt you saw on that occasion that I too was in such a state of mental turmoil that I could not work out what was best to do. However, I preferred to yield to the claims of honour and reputation than to calculate for my own safety.

I came to regret my action, not so much on account of my personal hazard as of the many deplorable aspects of the situation which confronted me on arrival. To begin with, the forces fell short both in numbers and in fighting spirit. Secondly, apart from the Commander-in-Chief and a few besides, all (I am referring to the principal figures) showed their greed for plunder in the war itself, and talked in so bloodthirsty a style that I shuddered at the prospect of *victory*. Moreover, those of the highest rank were up to their ears in debt. In a phrase, nothing good except the cause. With these things before my eyes, I started by recommending peace, of which I had always been an advocate. When Pompey showed himself strongly averse to that policy, I set myself to recommend delaying tactics. At times he tended to favour this course and seemed likely to make it his policy. Perhaps he would have done so, had not the result of a particular engagement[542] given him confidence in his troops. From then on that great man ceased to be a general. With his raw medley of an army he fought a pitched battle against the hardiest soldiers in the world, and was defeated. Even his camp was lost. He fled shamefully, alone.

For me that was the end of the war. Our full strength had proved no match for the enemy. I saw no prospect of getting the upper hand after a shattering reverse. I withdrew from the conflict. What were the choices? To die on the battlefield, or to fall into some trap, or to come into the hands of the victor, or

542. At Dyrrachium in July 48.

to take refuge with Juba, or to select a place of virtual exile, or suicide. Nothing else surely, if one would not, or dared not, trust oneself to the victor. Of all the aforesaid evils exile is as tolerable as any – especially an innocent exile, with no stain of discredit, and (let me add) exile from a country that holds nothing one can look upon without distress.

For my part, I preferred to be with my own people, and my own belongings too – if anything belongs to anybody nowadays. All that has happened I foretold. I came home, not that the life there offered was particularly attractive, but still, if there was to be some shape or form of free constitution, I wanted to feel as though I was living in my country; and if not, it would serve as a place of exile. I saw no reason to take my life, though many reasons to pray for its ending. It's an old saying that when a man is no longer what he was he has nothing to live for. However, there's a great comfort in having nothing with which to reproach oneself; and I have two further supports, conversance with noble arts and the glory of great achievements. Of the first I shall never be deprived in life, of the second not even in death.

In writing all this I have not spared words. I have thus imposed upon you because I know how deeply you care for me and for the commonwealth. I wanted you to be acquainted with my whole mind and purpose, to know in the first place that I never wished any man to have more power than the state entire; but when by the fault of somebody or other a single person became too strong to resist, I was for peace. With the loss of the army and of the leader upon whom all our hopes were pinned I wanted an end to the war for all concerned; unable to bring that to pass, I made an end for myself individually. At present, if this is a body politic, I am a citizen; if it is not, I am an exile in no worse a place than if I had betaken myself to Rhodes or Mytilene.

I would rather have discussed all this with you in person; but since time was dragging on, I thought it desirable to do so by letter, in order to give you something to say if you should happen to fall in with people who speak ill of me. There are those who hold it an offence in me to be alive, even though my destruction would have brought no advantage to the commonwealth. I am well aware that they think the death-roll not long enough. Had those upon it listened to me, they would at least be living honourably, however harsh the terms of peace, proved weaker in military strength but not in the justice of their cause.

So here you have a wordier letter, it may be, than you would have wished. I shall believe you think so, unless you send me a longer one in return. I have certain matters I want to clear up; that done, I hope I shall see you shortly.

184 (XVI. 19)

CICERO TO TIRO

Tusculum, July (?) 46

From Tullius to his dear Tiro greetings.

I am looking forward to a letter from you on many topics, but to you in person even more. Make Demetrius my friend, and do any other good work you can. I won't urge you about Aufidius' debt, for I know you have it in mind. But get a settlement. If you are taking time on that account, I accept your excuse; but if that is not detaining you, hurry. I am impatiently looking forward to a letter.

Goodbye.

185 (XVI. 22)

CICERO TO TIRO

Tusculum, July (?) 46

From Tullius to his dear Tiro greetings.

From your letter I trust that you are better, certainly I very much hope so. Mind you consider that in every way, and don't take it into your head that you are acting against my wishes in not being with me. You *are* with me if you are looking after yourself. So I want you to care for your health rather than for my eyes and ears. Of course I enjoy hearing and seeing you, but that will be a much greater pleasure if you are fit and well.

I am idling here because I don't write anything myself, though I am reading with great gusto. If the copyists up there can't make out my handwriting, you will put them right. There *is* a rather difficult inset which I don't find easy to read myself, the story about Cato as a four-year-old.[543] See about the dining-room, as you are doing. Tertia will be there, provided that Publilius[544] is not invited.

That fellow Demetrius was never a Phalereus[545] but now he is an absolute Bellienus![546] So I appoint you my deputy – you show him the courtesies. 'Though to be sure . . .,' 'All the same

---

543. Cicero had recently written a 'Eulogy of Cato' (now lost). The story of the four-year-old Cato's defiance of Poppaedius the Marsian is told by Valerius Maximus (III.1.2) and Plutarch in his Life (2).

544. The manuscripts have 'Publius' (a common mistake). Why (Junia) Tertia objected to Publilius is unknown.

545. i.e. a man of polish and wit, qualities for which Demetrius of Phalerum was celebrated.

546. i.e. an assassin; cf. Letter 149 (VIII.15). He could bore his company to death.

. . .,' 'As to that . . .' – you know how it goes on. Still, if you have any talk with him, please write and tell me, so that I get a theme for a letter and as long as possible a letter of yours to read.

Look after your health, my dear Tiro. You can do nothing to please me more.

Goodbye.

186 (XVI. 17)

CICERO TO TIRO

Tusculum, July (?) 46

From Tullius to Tiro greetings.

I see your game! You want your letters too put into rolls. But just a moment, you yardstick of my literary style, where did you come by so bizarre a phrase as 'faithfully[547] studying my health'? What is 'faithfully' doing in such a context? The home territory of the word is the performance of a duty, but it makes many excursions into other fields. For example, it can be applied to acquired knowledge or a house or a vocation or a piece of land within the bounds of decent metaphor as approved by Theophrastus.[548] But of this when we are together.

I have had a visit from Demetrius, from whose company on the road I disengaged myself rather neatly. Of course you could not have seen him. He will be in Rome tomorrow, so see him you will. For my part, I intend leaving here early the day after.

Your health makes me very anxious, but study it and leave

547. *fideliter*. Tiro no doubt meant 'conscientiously'. Cicero seems to have taken him to mean that he was giving his health *its* due.

548. He had discussed metaphor in his treatise *On Speech*.

nothing undone. *Then* you may feel that you are with me and that I am more than satisfied.

Thank you for helping Cuspius, whose hearty well-wisher I am.

Goodbye.

187 (v. 16)

CICERO TO TITIUS[549]

Rome (?), late summer or autumn 46 (?)

From M. Cicero to Titius greetings.

Of all men I am the least suited to console you, since I am so grieved by your distress that I stand in need of consolation myself. But seeing that my grief falls shorter than yours of the ultimate bitterness of sorrow, I have concluded that our friendship and my anxiety for your welfare make it wrong to be silent so long in your heavy affliction, and require me to proffer a measure of comfort, which may alleviate, if it cannot heal, your pain.

There is a very well-worn form of consolation which we should always have on our lips and in our minds. We must remember that we are but men, the law of whose birth requires that our lives be a target for all the darts of fortune. We must not rebel against the condition to which we are born. We must bear less hard those misfortunes which we cannot by any prudence avoid. We must recall the experiences of our fellows, and reflect that nothing new has befallen us. But more efficacious perhaps than these and other forms of consolation em-

---

549. Not certainly identifiable with any of the other Titii who crop up at this period. He had apparently lost two or more sons in an epidemic; cf. the reference in *Letters to Atticus* 247 (XII.10).

ployed by the wisest of mankind and consigned to memory in their writings should be the actual state of our community in these chaotic and desperate times. In the world of today those who have never raised children are most to be envied, and those who have lost them less to be commiserated than if they had been thus bereaved in a well-ordered commonwealth, or indeed in any commonwealth properly so called.

If it is the sense of your own loss that grieves you, if it is your own fate you lament, then I fear your pain cannot easily exhaust itself altogether. On the other hand, if the sting lies in your grief for the sad lot of the departed, a sentiment more closely in keeping with affection, it is another matter. I will not dwell on the arguments I have often heard and read in books to the effect that there is no evil in death, because if any conscious-ness remains thereafter, we should not think of it as death but as immortality, whereas if all consciousness disappears, misery unfelt should not be deemed misery at all; but this I can declare without hesitation, that to my mind at any rate whoever has left behind him the present political turmoil, and all that is in preparation, looming ahead of us, has been cheated of *nothing*. There is no place any more for honour, uprightness, manliness, honest pursuits and liberal accomplishments; none even for personal independence and existence as a citizen. I give you my word that whenever in this terrible year of pestilence I have heard of the death of a young man or a boy, I have con-sidered him as snatched by the Immortal Gods from these calamities and from a life of which all the terms were in his disfavour.

If only you can be divested of the idea that some evil has befallen those dear to you, that in itself will very sensibly diminish the sum of your sorrow. There will then remain the simple burden of your own grief, in which *they* will have no part; it will pertain to you individually. Now to bear the troubles chance has brought upon you more hardly than is fitting, when they involve no unhappiness or evil for those you loved, is really unworthy of the responsibility and sound sense which you have shown since your childhood days. The character you have always presented in public and in private requires you to maintain your dignity and faithfully to follow the pattern you have set. For it is our duty by reason and wisdom to anticipate the effects of time, which by its mere efflux cancels our deepest sorrows. After all, there was never a woman bereaved of children so frail of spirit that she did not in the end set a term to her mourning. Surely then *we* should apply in advance by using our reason what the passing of the days will bring; we ought not to wait for time to produce the medicine which our intelligence can supply to hand.

If this letter has done you good, I feel that I have achieved something worth praying for. But perhaps it has had but little effect, in which case I have at least discharged the duty of a sincere friend and well-wisher. That I have ever been such to you I hope you believe, and are confident that I shall so remain.

188 (IX. 21)

CICERO TO PAPIRIUS PAETUS

Date uncertain

From Cicero to Paetus greetings.

Really? You think you are out of your mind to be imitating my 'verbal thunderbolts'?[550] You would be if you could not make a success of it. Since in fact you actually go one better, you should make fun of me rather than yourself. So you don't

550. The context can only be guessed. Perhaps Paetus had been sent a copy of a Ciceronian speech and tried to produce something in the same vein. Cicero writes more than once of Demosthenes' 'thunderbolts' (*fulmina*).

need that quotation from Trabea.[551] The 'miss' was rather mine. But tell me now, how do you find me as a letter-writer? Don't I deal with you in colloquial style? The fact is that one's style has to vary. A letter is one thing, a court of law or a public meeting quite another. Even for the courts we don't have just one style. In pleading civil cases, unimportant ones, we put on no frills, whereas cases involving status or reputation naturally get something more elaborate. As for letters, we weave them out of the language of everyday.

Be that as it may, my dear Paetus, what possessed you to say that all the Papirii without exception were plebeians? They were in fact patricians, one of the Lesser Clans.[552] The roll begins with L. Papirius Mugillanus, who was Censor along with L. Sempronius Atratinus, having previously been his colleague in the Consulship in the year 312 after the foundation of Rome.[553] But in those days you used to be called Papisii. Thirteen held curule office between him and L. Papirius Crassus, the first of the race not to be called Papisius. He was appointed Dictator with L. Papirius Cursor as his Master of the Horse in the year 415 after the foundation,[554] and four years later became Consul with Kaeso Duilius. Cursor[555] followed him, a very distinguished official career. Then came L. Masso, of aedilician rank, and many Massos after him. All the foregoing were patricians, and I hope you will have their portraits in your hall.

Then follow the Carbos and the Turdi. These were plebeians, and I advise you to ignore them. For with the exception of the

551. Perhaps the quotation warned against reaching beyond one's grasp.

552. According to tradition King Tarquinius Priscus appointed a number of new Senators whose clans were called *gentes minores*.

553. = B.C. 443, by inclusive reckoning from a foundation date 754.

554. = B.C. 340.

555. Son of the Cursor just mentioned.

C. Carbo[556] who was killed by Damasippus, not one of the Carbos was an asset to his country. We knew Cn. Carbo[557] and his brother the wag – a pair of rascals if ever there was one. Of my friend who is still with us,[558] Rubria's son, I say nothing. There were the three famous brothers, C., Cn., and M. Carbo. Marcus, a great thief, was condemned after his career in Sicily on a charge brought by P. Flaccus. Gaius[559] is said to have swallowed Spanish Fly when prosecuted by Crassus. He was a seditious Tribune of the Plebs and was believed to have murdered P. Africanus. As for the man[560] who was put to death at Lilybaeum by our friend Pompey, he was in my opinion as arrant a rascal as ever breathed. His father before him was prosecuted by M. Antonius and is thought to have been acquitted by shoe-blacking.[561]

So I recommend you to 'revert to the *patres*'.[562] The plebeians were an unconscionable lot, as you see.

556. Surnamed Arvina. He was killed by the Marian leader L. Junius Brutus Damasippus in 82.

557. Probably not the Marian leader mentioned below, but a person otherwise unknown, perhaps son of the 'great thief', Marcus. His brother can be identified with a C. Carbo who seems to have been Tribune in 89 and a supporter of Sulla.

558. Another Gaius, perhaps son of the 'wag', who was condemned (probably in 58) for extortion in his province of Bithynia. Caesar may have brought him back from exile.

559. Father of Arvina.

560. Gnaeus, the Marian leader, son of the second of the three brothers. Pompey executed him in 81.

561. Generally supposed to mean that he poisoned himself like his brother Gaius, but such a coincidence could hardly have failed to attract notice in our sources. Probably the reference is to some sort of tampering with the voting tablets at the trial. The charge probably concerned his defeat by the Cimbri in 113.

562. Probably a facetious echo of a technical phrase. In default of patrician magistrates the auspices were said to 'revert to the Fathers' (i.e. the patrician members of the Senate); cf. *Letters to Marcus Brutus* 9 (XIII or I.5).3.

189 (IX. 22)[563]

CICERO TO PAPIRIUS PAETUS

46–44

From Cicero to Paetus.

I like your modesty! – or rather your freedom of language. But after all, this found favour with Zeno, a clever man, no getting away from it, though our Academy is mightily at loggerheads with him – but as I say, the Stoics hold it proper to call everything by its name. Their argument runs like this: There is no such thing as obscene or indecent language. For if there is anything shocking in obscenity, it lies either in the matter or in the word; there is no third possibility. Now it does not lie in the matter. Accordingly, there are accounts of the actual process, not only in Comedy (e.g. *The Demiurge*:[564] 'T'other day, as luck would have it . . .' – you know the solo,[565] you remember Roscius – 'so she left me bare': the whole speech is guarded as to the words, but pretty shameless as to the matter) but in Tragedy too.[566] What else is this bit: 'When one woman' (mark it now) 'sleeps in two beds'? Or

> His daughter's (?) bed
> This man did enter?

563. This exposition of the Stoic doctrine that 'the wise man will call a spade a spade' was provoked by the word *mentula* (cf. para. 2) in a letter from Paetus. That Cicero controverts or refutes the doctrine is a hallucination of certain annotators, though he does state (not very solemnly) a personal preference for 'Plato's modesty'. The whole thing is a *jeu d'esprit*.

564. By Sex. Turpilius, second-century writer of Latin comedies.

565. *canticum* (lyric monologue).

566. The sources of the following quotations are unknown.

Or 'Me, a virgin all unwilling, Jupiter did rudely force.' 'Force' is very well. And yet it means the same as the other word, which nobody would have tolerated. You see therefore that, although the matter is the same, there is not thought to be any indecency because the words are different. Therefore it does not lie in the matter.

Still less does it lie in the words. For if that which is signified by a word is not indecent, the word which signifies it cannot be indecent either. You say 'seat', using a transferred word: why not use the proper one? If it's indecent, you should not use the first even; if not, you should use the second. The ancients used to call a tail a penis – hence 'penicillus'[567] from the similarity. But nowadays 'penis' is an obscene word. And yet Piso Frugi in his *Annals* complains of young men being 'devoted to the penis'. What you call by its proper name[568] in your letter he more guardedly called 'penis'; but because many others did the same, it became no less obscene a word than the one you have employed. Again, 'When we[569] wanted to meet you' is an ordinary enough phrase. Is it obscene? I remember an eloquent Consular[570] once saying in the Senate 'Shall I call this or that[571] the more reprehensible?' Most obscene, was it not? no, you say, for he didn't intend it so. Very well then, obscenity does not lie in the word; and I have shown that it does not lie in the matter. Therefore it lies nowhere.

'Provide for the continuation of your family.' What a respectable phrase! Fathers even ask their sons to do it. But they dare not utter the word for this 'provision'. Socrates was taught the lute by a very celebrated player whose name was Connus. Do you think that obscene? When we say 'terni'[572]

---

567. = 'paintbrush'.
568. *mentula*.
569. *cum nos* pronounced like *cunnos*.
570. Possibly Cicero himself; cf. *Letters to Atticus* 44 (11.24).3.
571. *(il)lam dicam* pronounced like *landicam*.
572. 'Three each'.

there's nothing to shock; but when we say 'bini'[573] is it obscene? 'Yes,' you say, 'to a Greek.' Then there is nothing in the
word, since *I* know Greek, and I still say to you 'bini', and you
behave as though I spoke in Greek instead of in Latin. Take
'ruta' and 'menta'; both all right. But if I want a word for
'little mint' corresponding to 'rutula',[574] I can't have it.
'Tectoriola'[575] is a nice enough word. Try to make a diminutive from 'pavimentum' in the same way: you can't. Don't
you see that it's all nonsense, that indecency does not exist
either in word or matter, and therefore does not exist at all?

So we utter obscenities when we use respectable words. Take
'divisio'. A respectable word, wouldn't you say? But it contains an obscenity, just like 'intercapedo'. Are these words
obscene? Our practice is really comical. If we say 'he throttled
his father', we don't apologize; but if we say something about
Aurelia or Lollia,[576] an apology is due. Indeed even quite
innocent words have come to count as obscene. 'Battuit',
somebody says; shameless! 'Depsit': much more so! Yet
neither word is obscene. The world is full of fools. 'Testes' is a
perfectly respectable word in a court of law, elsewhere *not* too
respectable. Lanuvian bags are respectable, Cliternian not. Why
even an action is sometimes respectable, sometimes indecent,
is it not? It's shocking to break wind. Put the culprit naked in
the bath, and you won't blame him.

So there you have a Stoic lecture: 'The Sage will call a
Spade a Spade.' What a multitude of words out of one of
yours, to be sure! I like you to have no inhibitions when you
are addressing me. For myself, I adhere (and shall so continue,
since it is my habit) to the modesty of Plato. That is why I
have written to you in guarded language on a theme which the

573. 'Two each'. *bini* phonetically = Greek *binei*.
574. 'Little rue'. The corresponding diminutive from *menta* would
be *mentula*.
575. Diminutive of *tectorium*, 'wall-plaster'.
576. The notorious wives of Catiline and A. Gabinius.

Stoics handle with complete freedom. But they also say that we ought to break wind and belch with equal unconstraint. So let us respect the Kalends of March![577]

Remember me kindly and keep well.

190 (IX. 16)

CICERO TO PAPIRIUS PAETUS

Tusculum (?), mid July 46

Cicero to Paetus greetings.

Your letter gave me great pleasure. In the first place I was touched by the affection which prompted you to write, because you were afraid that Silius'[578] report had caused me some anxiety. You had written to me previously on the subject, sending two copies of your letter separately, so that I could well see how much it disturbed you; and I had replied in detail in such a way as to remove your concern, or at any rate to relieve it, so far as possible in such a case and at such a time.

But since your latest letter also shows how deeply you are taking this matter to heart, let me assure you, my dear Paetus, that whatever art could do (we cannot nowadays rely on the weapon of good judgement, a degree of artifice and ingenuity is called for) – anyhow, all that pains could effect towards gaining and gathering the good-will of these gentry[579] has been achieved by me, no effort spared; and I do not think I

577. The date of the *Matronalia* (festival of married women, on which husbands and lovers gave presents to their ladies).

578. Probably the ex-governor of Bithynia; possibly a former officer of Caesar, T. Sil(l)ius. His report seems to have concerned some sharp saying of Cicero which had been passed on to Caesar. Paetus was afraid it might give offence.

579. The leading Caesarians.

have wasted my endeavours. The courtesies and attentions I
receive from all who stand high with Caesar are such that I
believe they have an affection for me. Admittedly it is no easy
matter to distinguish the genuine article from the sham, unless
a situation happens to arise in which the gold of loyal attachment is discerned in the fire of danger – all other signs being
common to both. But one circumstance goes far to prove to
my own mind that their regard is sincere and genuine: my
position and theirs being what they respectively are, these
people have no motive to dissemble.

As for the All-Powerful, I see no reason why I should be
apprehensive, unless it be that all becomes uncertain when the
path of legality has been forsaken, and that there is no guaranteeing the future of what depends on someone else's wishes,
not to say whims. However, I have done nothing to offend
Caesar's personal sensibilities. In that very particular I have
been extremely careful to regulate my conduct. Time was when
I thought that free speech became me, for was not the existence
of freedom in the community due to my work? Now that
freedom is lost, I think it no less becomes me to say nothing
offensive to his sentiments or those of the people he likes. But
if I were to disclaim the authorship of certain pungent or amusing remarks, I should have to renounce my reputation as a wit.
Well, I should not object to the latter, if the former lay within
my power. But Caesar himself is a keenly discriminating
connoisseur. Your brother[580] Servius, in my judgement a man
of outstanding literary culture, could easily pronounce that
Plautus did not write one line or did write another, because his
taste has been refined by observation of the styles of poets and
by constantly reading their work. In the same way I hear that,
having in his day compiled volumes of *bons mots*,[581] Caesar will

580. Or 'cousin', Ser. Claudius; cf. *Letters to Atticus* 20 (1.20).7.
581. According to Suetonius' biography (56.7) Caesar made a collection of witticisms as a boy or young man; along with other of his
juvenilia Augustus forbade it to be published.

reject any specimen offered him as mine which is not authentic. He does this all the more now because his intimates are in my company almost every day. Talk of this and that produces many casual remarks which perhaps strike these people when I say them as not deficient in polish and point. They are conveyed to him with the rest of the day's news, according to his express instructions. Thus it is that if he hears anything about me from some other source he does not think it worth his attention.

So I don't need your Oenomaus;[582] not but what your Accian lines come à propos. But where is the envy? What is there about me nowadays to inspire such a sentiment? However, suppose there were all manner of things: I find that those philosophers who alone to my mind grasp the essence of virtue hold that the wise man is answerable for nothing save guilt. But of that I conceive myself doubly free, both in that my sentiments were thoroughly sound and because, when I saw that the strength to assert them was lacking, I did not think it right to struggle against superior force. Therefore I certainly cannot be said to have failed in the duty of a good citizen. All that remains is not to act or speak foolishly or rashly against the powers that be. That too I reckon part of wisdom. For the rest, what this or that person says I have said, how *he* takes such reports, how trustworthy are these associates of mine who pay me such assiduous attention and courtesy – for all this I cannot answer.

So I comfort myself with the consciousness of my motives in the past and the regulation of my conduct in the present, and I may apply that simile of Accius' to fortune instead of merely

582. Paetus had cited lines from Accius' tragedy *Oenomaus*, to the effect that *invidia* (envy, jealous ill-will) made no more impression on a strong mind than waves upon a rock (see next paragraph). Cicero remarks that he does not in fact have to fear *invidia*, and would rather apply the simile to fortune. The quotation was clearly intended to encourage Cicero, not to warn him. It should not be identified with the only surviving fragment of the play, in which there happens to be mention of a rock.

to envy; fickle and feeble as she is, I hold that she must break against a firm, constant mind like a wave against a rock. The records of Greece are full of instances of how men of the highest wisdom bore despotic régimes, whether at Athens or Syracuse,[583] and managed amidst the servitude of their communities to keep in some sort their personal liberty. Am I to suppose myself incapable of preserving my position while neither offending any man nor impairing my dignity?

Now I come to your jests, seeing that you have followed up Accius' *Oenomaus* with a mime *à la mode* instead of the old-fashioned Atellane farce.[584] What's this about Pompilius[585] and half-a-crown[586] and a plate of salt fish *au gratin*?[587] In days gone by I used to put up with that kind of thing, being an easy-going fellow, but times are changed. Hirtius and Dolabella are my pupils in oratory, but my masters in gastronomy. I expect you have heard, if all news travels to Naples, that they practise declaiming at my house, and I practise dining at theirs. As for making me an affidavit of insolvency, you'd be wasting your time. When you had money, a profitable little deal would make you all the closer. But now, when you are losing your pile so philosophically, why not take the view that when you entertain me you are being served with a valuation?[588] Such a

583. Socrates at Athens under the Thirty, Plato at Syracuse under the two Dionysii.

584. The former were both more witty and more indecent than the latter.

585. M. Demmel's correction *Pompilium* for *popillium* is most attractive. In his work on Grammarians (8) Suetonius tells us that M. Pompilius Andronicus was a devoted Epicurean, that he spent his later life at Cumae, and that he was poor and needy. Each of these three details helps to qualify him as a prospective guest at Paetus' dinner-table.

586. Literally 'a denarius'; Paetus would naturally mention price in telling Cicero what kind of meal he might expect.

587. A poor man's dish of which Paetus was particularly fond; cf. *Letters to Atticus* 370 (XIV.16).1.

588. By Caesar's legislation creditors were obliged to take their debtors' property in settlement at valuations based on pre-war prices.

knock actually hurts less coming from a friend than from a
debtor. Not that I am demanding the sort of banquet that
produces a great quantity of left-overs; but what there is must
be sumptuous and elegant. I remember your reciting Phamea's
dinner to me. Yours may start earlier,[589] but the rest should be
in the same style. However, if you insist on bringing me back
to your friend Matris'[590] bill of fare, all right, I'll put up with
that too. I should like to see anybody with the courage to dare
to serve me with the things you mention, or even with octopus
the colour of vermilioned Jupiter![591] No, no, you'll never dare!
The report of my stylish new ways will reach you before I
arrive, and make you shake in your shoes. And don't go building hopes on the *hors d'œuvres*. I have done away with that
entirely. I used to half-ruin my appetite with your olives and
sausages in the old days!

But what am I saying? I only wish I may be able to come
down! As for yourself, let me dispel your alarm; go back to
your old salt fish *au gratin*. My visit shall put you to no expense
except that you will have to heat a bath. All else shall be as
usual between you and me. I was only joking.

Thank you for taking so much trouble and writing so amus-
ingly about Selicius' country house. In view of what you say,
I think I'll pass it by. I have plenty of salt, but not enough
salt-cellars![592]

589. 'The grander the dinner party at Rome the earlier it began'
(Tyrrell and Purser).

590. Celebrated Athenian (or Theban) plain-liver of uncertain date,
who ate nothing but figs and drank nothing but water.

591. i.e., probably, in a red sauce. In ancient times the clay image
of Jupiter was given a new coat of vermilion paint on festal days.

592. i.e., if the conjecture *salinorum* is right, silver ('siller', money),
salt-cellars being normally made of that metal. 'Salt' here has a double
meaning, 'wit' (of which Paetus provided a sufficiency in his letter)
and (of a villa) 'elegance' (Paetus having presumably praised the villa
as having 'plenty of salt').

191 (IX. 18)

CICERO TO PAPIRIUS PAETUS

Tusculum, c. 23 July 46

Cicero to Paetus greetings.

While I was at a loose end at Tusculum, having sent my pupils to meet their friend[593] with the idea that they should at the same time put me in the best possible odour with him, I received your most charming letter. It appears then that my plan meets with your approbation: like Dionysius the tyrant,[594] who is said to have opened a school at Corinth after his expulsion from Syracuse, I have set up as a schoolmaster, as it were, now that the courts are abolished and my forensic kingdom lost. Well, I too am pleased with my plan, which brings me many advantages. To begin with, I gain some protection against the hazards of these times, which is what is most needed just now. What that amounts to I don't know; all I can see is that nobody else has yet produced a plan which I consider superior to mine – unless perhaps it would have been better to die. Better to die in one's bed, I admit it; but that did not happen. At the battle I was not present. The others – Pompey, your friend Lentulus,[595] Scipio, Afranius – came to miserable ends. But Cato's, you say, was splendid. Well, that will be open to me any time I choose. I have only to see that it does not become so much a matter of necessity for me as it was for him. I am doing just that. This then to begin with.

593. i.e. Hirtius and Dolabella to meet Caesar on his return from Africa. When he says he sent them Cicero is probably joking – they would naturally go anyway.

594. Dionysius II of Syracuse; cf. *Letters to Atticus* 176 (IX.9).1.

595. L. Lentulus Crus, Consul in 49.

Next, I benefit directly, first in health, which I lost when I gave up my exercises; and then my oratorical faculty, if I had any, would have dried up had I not gone back to these exercises. There is a final point, which *you* might perhaps put first: I have already polished off more peacocks than you young pigeons. While you enjoy Haterius' legal gravity[596] in Naples, I regale myself with Hirtius' gravy here. Be a man then, and come along! Let me teach you the principia you want to learn – though it will be a case of teaching my grandmother.[597] But, as I see the situation, if you can't sell your valuations[598] or fill a pot with sixpences,[599] you have got to move back to Rome. Better die of stomach-ache here than starvation down there. I see you have lost your money, and I expect it is just the same with your friends. So if you don't look ahead, it's all up with you. You can get up on that mule, which you say you still have left after spending your gelding on food, and ride to Rome. There will be a chair for you in school as assistant-master next to mine, and a cushion will follow.

192 (VII. 33)

CICERO TO VOLUMNIUS EUTRAPELUS

Rome, end of July (?) 46

From Cicero to Volumnius greetings.

In missing my declamations you lose nothing at all. As for

596. Literally 'Haterian law', Haterius being presumably a jurist. There is a play on two senses of *ius*, 'law' and 'sauce'.

597. Literally 'of the pig teaching Minerva' – a proverbial saying. The pig was regarded as the most stupid of animals.

598. i.e. properties compulsorily accepted in lieu of debts.

599. i.e. 'if you don't have enough money to fill a pot with silver coins (*denarii*)'.

your envying Hirtius if you were not so fond of him, you had no cause for such a feeling, unless perhaps you envied him his own oratorical gifts rather than the privilege of listening to me. As for myself, my charming friend, I am simply nothing; or if not that, I am disgusted with my own performance, now that I have lost my ol stable-mates who made me show my paces – to your applause. If ever I do strike out anything worthy of my reputation, I groan to think that

> On feathered, not on armoured forms I ply
> These shafts, my glory humbled,

as Philoctetes[600] says in Accius.

None the less, my whole horizon will brighten if you come. But, as you realize yourself, you are coming into a rush of pressing affairs. If I dispose of these satisfactorily, I shall bid a long farewell to Forum and Senate-House, and shall pass much of my time with you and our common admirers. Your friend Cassius and our friend Dolabella (I should rather say 'our' in both cases) are devoted to the same pursuits[601] and find in me a very well-disposed audience. We need your delicately filed and polished critical judgement and that recherché learning before which I often check my own exuberant tongue. For my part I am quite determined, if only Caesar either permits or welcomes my resolution, to lay aside the role in which he himself has often approved me and to bury myself in literary work, enjoying an honourable retirement in your company and that of other devotees of letters.

I wish you had not been afraid that I might read your letters like books,[602] if (as you say) they should happen to be on the lengthy side. In future do please depend upon it that the longer the letters you write the better I shall like them.

600. In a play of that name.
601. Apparently literary and philosophical rather than oratorical.
602. i.e. as too long to be read at one sitting. The reading is conjectural.

193 (IX. 20)

CICERO TO PAPIRIUS PAETUS

Rome, early August 46

From Cicero to Paetus.

I was doubly delighted with your letter – laughed myself, and saw that you are now capable of laughing. As a light-armed buffoon,[603] I did not object to your pelting me with insults.[604] What does vex me is that I have not been able to get down to your part of the world as I had arranged. You would have found me a comrade[605] in arms rather than a guest. And what a warrior! Not the man you used to lay low with your *hors d'œuvres*. I bring an appetite unimpaired to the eggs,[606] and so carrry on the good work down to the roast veal. 'What an accommodating fellow!' you used to say of me. 'What an easy man to entertain!' Not any more! I have dropped all my concern for public affairs, all preoccupation with what to say in the Senate, all study of briefs, and flung myself into the camp of my old enemy Epicurus. I don't aim at the excesses of Rome, however, but at *your* elegance – your former elegance, I mean, when you had money to spend (though, to be sure, you never owned more real estate[607] in your life).

603. Paetus had apparently called Cicero *scurra veles* ('skirmisher jester'), perhaps because he had begun the fight. The verb *velitari* is used elsewhere of verbal skirmishing.

604. Untranslatable pun on *malis* (with a short 'a') = 'abuse' and *malis* (with a long 'a') = 'apples' (which might be thrown at a buffoon).

605. Literally 'tent-mate'. The military metaphor continues, but the word may imply a longer stay than would be normal for a guest.

606. Here regarded as beginning the main meal, as opposed to the *hors d'œuvres*. The roast veal would be the last course, followed by dessert (*mensae secundae*).

607. Which Paetus had been forced to take from his debtors.

So be prepared! You are dealing with a hearty eater, no longer wholly ignorant of what's what; and you know how opsimaths assert themselves. You had best forget about your little baskets[608] and your scones. I have acquired enough of the the art by now to dare invite your friend Verrius and Camillus (the very acme of refinement and elegance!) on several occasions. More, I even had the audacity to give a dinner to Hirtius (think of it!) – no peacock, though. At that meal nothing proved beyond my cook's powers of imitation except the hot sauce.

So this is the way I live nowadays. In the morning I receive callers – both honest men (numerous, but depressed) and these jubilant victors, who, I must say, are most obliging and friendly in their attentions to me. When the stream has ceased to flow, I absorb myself in literary work, writing or reading. Some of my visitors listen to me as a man of learning, because I know a little more than themselves. All the rest of the time is given to the claims of the body. As for my country, I have already mourned her longer and more deeply than any mother ever mourned her only son.

But if you are my friend, take care of your health, or I shall be consuming your substance while you lie flat on your back. For I have made up my mind not to spare you, well or sick.

194 (IX. 19)

CICERO TO PAPIRIUS PAETUS

Rome, mid August 46

From Cicero to Paetus.

Still up to your tricks? You intimate that Balbus was satisfied

608. Containing dates, as at Trimalchio's feast (Petronius, 40.3), or something of the kind. The meaning of the word translated 'scones' is doubtful.

with a modest little spread. I suppose you imply that when kings[609] are so temperate, Consulars should be much more so. What you don't know is that I fished the whole story out of him – he came straight from the City gate, let me tell you, to my house (I'm not surprised that he didn't rather go to his own, but I *should* have expected him to go to his sweetheart).[610] My first four words were: 'What of old Paetus?' And *he* said he'd be hanged if he had ever had a better time. If you have achieved this by talk, you will find me no less discriminating a listener. But if the credit goes to your cuisine, I must ask you not to rate balbutients[611] above orators. Every day one thing after another holds me up. But if I get clear and can pay a visit to your part of the world, I shall take very good care not to let you think I have given you insufficient notice.[612]

195 (IX. 17)

CICERO TO PAPIRIUS PAETUS

Rome, late August or early September 46

Cicero to Paetus.

Aren't you a comedian? After a visit from our friend Balbus you ask *me* what I think is going to happen about these towns and lands![613] As though I know anything that he doesn't

609. *rex* is often applied to a rich and powerful personage, but has special reference here to Balbus' relations with the despot Caesar; cf. *Letters to Atticus* 259 (XII.12).1.

610. Play on *suam* (*domum*), 'to his house', and *ad suam*, 'to his mistress'.

611. *balbus* = 'stammerer'.

612. And so provide an excuse for meagre entertainment.

613. Paetus was afraid that land belonging to municipalities or private individuals might be confiscated by Caesar for distribution to his veterans.

know! Or as though, if ever I *do* know anything, I don't get my information from him! On the contrary, if you are a friend of mine, you tell me what is going to happen to us! After all, you had him in your power, you could have pumped him, drunk if not sober. But as for me, my dear Paetus, I am not inquisitive about such matters. For almost four years past the fact that we are still alive is a bonus to which we are not entitled – that is, if to survive freedom can be called a bonus or a life. Moreover, I fancy I know the answer too: what will happen will be whatever those who have the power want to happen. And power will always lie with armed force. So we ought to be content with whatever is allowed us. Anybody unable to put up with life on these terms should have taken leave of it.

They *are* surveying land at Veii and Capena. That is not so far from Tusculum. But I have no fears. I enjoy while I am able. I pray I may always be able. But if my prayer is not granted, well, as a man of courage and a philosopher, I thought life a very fine thing. Therefore I cannot but feel beholden to the man to whose favour I owe it. Even if he were to will that the state be such as he perhaps desires and as all of us ought to pray for, there is nothing he can do. He has too many associates to whom he has tied himself.

But I am going further than I meant – after all, I am writing to *you*. However, you may take my word for it that not only I, who am not in his counsels, but the great man himself does not know what will happen. We are his slaves, he is the slave of circumstances. So he cannot know what circumstances will demand, and we cannot know what he has in his mind.

If I have not replied sooner, it is not because I am habitually lazy, particularly where writing is concerned, but, having nothing solid to go on, I was reluctant to cause you anxiety by expressing a doubt or to raise your hopes by a positive statement. I will only add the bare truth, that so far I have heard nothing in recent times about the danger you fear. But you are a man of sense, and as such you should pray for the best, contemplate the worst, and bear whatever betide.

196 (IX. 15)

CICERO TO PAPIRIUS PAETUS

Rome, first (?) intercalary month 46

Cicero to Paetus greetings.

I am replying to two letters of yours. I received one of them four days ago by Zethus, the other was brought by your courier Phileros.

Your earlier letter had made it plain to me that my concern for your health was very welcome to you. I am glad you appreciated it, but, believe me, you could not appreciate it as it really is from a letter. I find myself the object of attention and regard from a fair number of persons (I cannot say otherwise), but none of them all is more agreeable to me than you. That you love me, and have done so steadily and long, is certainly important, perhaps the most important thing of all; but in this you are by no means alone. What is singular to yourself is that *you* are so lovable, such pleasant company, so agreeable in every way. And then there is the salt of your wit – not Attic, but genuine old Roman, saltier than the Athenian variety. For my part, make what you will of it, I am marvellously fond of pleasantries, our native brand most of all, especially in view of its present decline; for adulterated as it had already become after the influx of the foreign element into our city, it is now with the accession of the trousered tribes from over the Alps so overwhelmed (?) that no trace of the old gay charm is any more to be found. So when I see you, I imagine I have the wits of bygone days, Granius,[614] Lucilius, and their like – indeed, to say the truth, Crassus[615] and Laelius and *their* like – all before my eyes. Confound me if I have anyone but you in whom I can recognize the image of the good old home-bred humour! When these charms of wit are combined with so hearty an affection for myself, do you wonder that your serious illness threw me into such a panic?

In your second letter you excuse yourself. You say you were not dissuading me from buying a place in Naples, but encouraging me to spend my time in Rome. That was what I took you to mean; but I also understood (as I understand from this later letter) that you thought I do not have the right to abandon metropolitan life, as I conceive myself entitled to do, not altogether indeed, but to a great extent. You talk to me of Catulus and those days. Where is the resemblance? At that time I myself did not care to be absent too long from watching over the commonwealth. I was sitting in the poop, you see, with the helm in my hands. But now I have scarcely so much as a place in the hold. Do you suppose there will be any the fewer senatorial decrees if I am in Naples? When I am in Rome, up and down the Forum, decrees are drawn up at the residence of your admirer, my very good friend.[616] What is more, when it happens to occur to him, I am put down as present at drafting, and I hear of some decree, allegedly passed on my motion, reaching Armenia and Syria before I know that there has been so much as a mention of the matter concerned. You must not think I am joking. Let me tell you that letters have been brought to me before today from monarchs at the other end of the earth, thanking me for my motion to give them the royal title, when

614. The sharp-tongued auctioneer of Puteoli; cf. *Letters to Atticus* 28 (11.8).2.

615. L. Crassus, the orator. He and Laelius were men of high birth and official rank.

616. Doubtless Cornelius Balbus.

I for my part was unaware of their very existence, let alone of their elevation to royalty.

Very well then. Despite the foregoing, as long as our new Prefect of Morals[617] remains in Rome, I shall defer to your advice. But when he is gone, I'll betake myself to your mushrooms. If I have a house, I shall make the daily maximum under the sumptuary law[618] last ten days. But if I don't find anything to my taste, I've decided to make my home with you – I know I could do nothing that would please you more! I am now giving up hope of Sulla's house, as I said in my last letter, but still I have not quite abandoned it. Would you please inspect the place with the builders, as you say? If there is nothing wrong with the walls or roof, I shall find no fault with the rest.

197 (IX. 26)

CICERO TO PAPIRIUS PAETUS

Rome, shortly before 17 November (true calendar) 46

From Cicero to Paetus greetings.

I am scribbling the lines of which you are reading a copy on my tablets[619] after taking my place at dinner at two-thirty of the afternoon. If you wish to know where, my host is Volumnius Eutrapelus. Your friend Atticus and Verrius are on either side of me. Does it surprise you that we have become such a merry lot of slaves? Well, what am I to do? I ask *you*, since you are going to philosophy lectures. Am I to torture and torment myself? What should I gain? And how long should I keep it

617. Caesar was so appointed for three years by the Senate after his victory in Africa.

618. Caesar's.

619. See Glossary of Terms.

up? You may advise me to spend my life in literary work. Surely you realize that this *is* my only occupation, that if I did not spend my life in that way I could not live at all. But even literary work has, I won't say its saturation-point, but its due limit. When I leave it, little as I care about dinner (the one problem *you* put to philosopher Dio),[620] I really do not see anything better to do with the time before I go to bed.

Well, to the rest of my tale. Cytheris lay down next Eutrapelus. 'So?' I hear you say, '*Cicero* at such a party,

> 'He the admired, upon whose countenance
> The Greeks all turned their eyes?'[621]

I assure you I had no idea *she* would be there. But after all, even Aristippus the Socratic did not blush when someone twitted him with keeping Lais as his mistress. 'Lais is my mistress,' said he, 'but I'm my own master' (it's better in the Greek;[622] make your own rendering, if you care to). As for me, even when I was young I was never attracted by anything of that sort, much less now that I'm old. It's the party I enjoy. I talk about whatever comes uppermost, as they say, and transform sighs into shouts of laughter. Do you manage matters better, actually making mock of a philosopher? When he put his question whether anybody had anything to ask, you called out 'Who's going to ask me to dinner? Been wondering all day.'[623] The poor dunderhead[624] thought you would be enquiring whether there is one sky or an infinite number. What business is that of

620. Otherwise unknown; but see below.

621. Source unknown.

622. The Latin means literally 'I possess Lais but am not possessed by her'. In the Greek *ekhomai* has a double sense, 'I am possessed by' and 'I cling to'.

623. The lecturer asked '*numquid quis quaerit?*' ('any questions?'). Paetus replied '*cenam quaero*', 'I'm looking for a dinner'.

624. Cicero was fond of so referring to Epicurean philosophers because of their professed hostility to culture; cf. n. 230.

yours? But, confound it, is a dinner any business of yours, especially one in *this* house?[625]

Well, so life passes. Every day a bit of reading, or a bit of writing. Then, since something is due to my friends, I dine with them. We don't go beyond the law, if there is such a thing nowadays, we even stop short of it, and that by a considerable margin. So you don't have to dread my arrival. You'll receive a guest with a small appetite for food, but a large one for frolic.

198 (IX. 23)

CICERO TO PAPIRIUS PAETUS

Cumae, 22 November (true calendar) 46

From Cicero to Paetus.

I arrived at Cumae yesterday and shall perhaps be with you tomorrow. But when I know for certain, I shall send you word a little beforehand. To be sure, when M. Caeparius met me in Poultry Wood[626] and I asked after you, he told me you were in bed with the gout in your feet. I was properly sorry of course, but decided to come all the same – to see you, visit you, and even dine, for I don't suppose your cook is a fellow-sufferer. Expect a guest then – a small eater and a foe to sumptuous banquets.

625. The house of such a person as Eutrapelus.
626. Silva Gallinaria, a pine forest on the coast north of Cumae.

199 (VII. 4)

CICERO TO M. MARIUS

Cumae, 21 or 22 November (true calendar) 46

From M. Cicero to M. Marius greetings.

On 21 November I arrived at my place near Cumae with your, or rather our, friend Libo. I mean to go on to Pompeii straight away, but shall send you word in advance. I always wish you to keep well, but particularly during my visit; for you see what a long time it is since we were last in one another's company. So if you have an appointment with the gout, please put it off for another day. Take care of yourself then, and expect me in two or three days' time.

200 (VII. 28)

CICERO TO M. CURIUS

Rome, August (?) 46

From M. Cicero to Curius greetings.

I remember the time when I thought you were out of your mind to prefer life with your friends over there to life with us. When Rome was Rome, it would have been a much more suitable residence for a person of your culture and social gifts than the whole Peloponnesus, let alone Patrae. Today, on the contrary, I applaud your foresight then in betaking yourself to Greece when affairs here were in wellnigh hopeless case; and at the present time I think you not only sensible to be absent but happy too – though I don't know how a man of any sense *can* be happy at the present time.

However, what you have done, and were free to do, by locomotion, i.e. to live 'where nevermore of Pelops' line . . .' (you know how it goes on),[627] I am achieving more or less in a different way. After receiving my friends' morning calls, which are in even greater numbers than of yore because they seem to see a loyal citizen as a bird of good omen,[628] I bury myself in my library. And so I produce books – of their importance you will perhaps judge; for from a conversation you had with me at your house, when you were taking me to task for my gloom and despondency, I understood you to say that you wondered what had become of the spirit you saw in my writings.

But the truth is that I mourned in those days for the commonwealth, which for benefits conferred as well as received was dearer to me than my life, and that now, though solaced not only by reflection, which ought to be man's most efficacious comforter, but by time, which is wont to bring healing even to fools, I still grieve to see our common heritage so fallen to pieces that we are not even left the hope of better things in days to come. Nor does the fault now at any rate lie with our all-powerful governor (unless in the sense that there ought not to be any such person). No, events have so fallen out, part by chance but part also by our own fault, that recrimination is idle. I see no hope remaining. So, to go back to my starting-point, if calculation made you leave Rome, you are a sensible man; if chance, a lucky one.

627. Cf. *Letters to Atticus* 366 (XIV.12).2. The 'sons of Pelops' will represent the people now dominant in Rome.

628. Literally 'a white bird'. A white *crow* stood for something impossible or at any rate extremely rare, but the idea of rarity is not in Cicero's phrase, though implicit in the context.

201 (V. 13)

CICERO TO LUCCEIUS

Summer or autumn 46 (?)

From M. Cicero to L. Lucceius, son of Quintus, greetings.

The consolation you offer in your letter is in itself most welcome, showing, as it does, the most sincere good-will combined in equal measure with good sense. But the feature of your letter from which I have especially derived benefit was its revelation of your splendid disregard for human vicissitudes and your admirable readiness and equipment to meet the blows of fortune. This I hold to be the highest glory of wisdom, to depend upon oneself alone, and not to let externals govern one's ideas of the good life and the bad. This conception had not altogether fallen out of my mind, where indeed it had taken deep root, but the storm of calamities bursting all around had in some degree shaken its hold. I perceive that you aim to lend it support, and in your latest letter I am conscious that you have done so effectively and helped me a great deal. So I feel bound to say again and again, and not merely to intimate but to declare, that nothing could have been more welcome to me than your letter.

The arguments which you have so gracefully and copiously brought to bear have indeed their consolatory effect; but nothing is more effective than my perception of *your* steadfastness and imperturbability of spirit. I should be deeply ashamed if I did not imitate it. And I account myself even braver than you, my instructor in fortitude, in that *you* appear to cherish a hope that things will one day improve; the chances of gladiator fights and your other similitudes and the arguments you assemble in discussing the topic tell me not to despair

347

utterly of the commonwealth. No wonder then that you should be braver than I, since you have some hope; the wonder is that any hope remains to you. Can you say of any part that its decline does not amount to total annihilation? Survey all the members of the body politic with which you are well acquainted: I am sure you will find none that is not shattered or enfeebled. I should pursue the theme, if I saw all this more plainly than you see it, or could recall it without distress – though that is an emotion which according to your counsels and precepts must be utterly cast aside.

Therefore I shall bear domestic troubles[629] as you recommend, and public calamities a little more bravely, it may be, than my mentor himself. For you are comforted, so you say, by a measure of hope; whereas I shall be brave even in total despair, as, notwithstanding your hope, you enjoin and instruct me, offering me the agreeable recollections of a clear conscience and of those achievements which you were foremost to encourage. For I have done some service to my country; certainly no less than I owed her, and more, I suppose, than has ever before been demanded of a man's spirit and brain. You will forgive me for claiming something on my own behalf. You hope that the thought of these things will relieve my sore heart; in the mention of them also there is balm.

Therefore I shall follow your counsel. As far as I can, I shall withdraw myself from all that troubles and torments, transferring my mind to those pursuits by which prosperity is embellished and adversity aided. I shall be with you as much as the age and health of both of us allow. And if we cannot be together as much as we should wish, we shall so enjoy our unity of heart and our common studies that we shall never seem to be apart.

629. Terentia, Quintus, and Tullia (Dolabella) may all be in mind.

202 (IV. 3)

CICERO TO SERVIUS SULPICIUS RUFUS[630]

Rome (?), first half of September (?) 46

From M. Cicero to Ser. Sulpicius greetings.

Every day I hear reports from many informants that you are deeply troubled in mind, suffering a distress somehow over and above the general portion of afflictions. I am not at all surprised, and I might almost say that I recognize my own condition in yours. And yet I am sorry that a man so almost uniquely wise as you should not rather take satisfaction in the good things that are his than grieve over the ills of others. For myself, I will not allow that any man has been harder hit than I by the dire disaster that has overtaken the commonwealth. None the less, I now have much to console me, above all the knowledge of my past policies. Long before the storm broke, I saw it brewing as from a high tower – and that not simply by my own vision but far more by the aid of your admonitions and warnings. I was away, it is true, during a great part of your Consulship, but in my absence I was informed of the line you took, how you tried to guard against this disastrous war and foretold it; and I was myself on the spot in the early months of your term of office, when you gave the Senate the fullest warning. I remember how you rehearsed all the civil wars of former days, and told your audience both to fear the calamities they remembered and to be sure that, as the men of the past, with no such precedents in our history to follow, had perpetrated these atrocities, any subsequent armed oppressor of the commonwealth would be far worse to endure. People think they have a right to do what others have done, but they also

630. Now governor of Achaia by Caesar's appointment.

put in some contribution, say rather a large contribution, of their own.

So you must bear in mind that those who refused to follow your lead and listen to your advice have perished by their own folly when they might have been saved by your wisdom. You will ask what consolation that thought brings you in these dark days, when our country lies in ruins. Indeed it is a sorrow almost beyond comfort – the utter loss of all, and the despair of recovery. Yet in the judgement of Caesar himself and the estimation of all our countrymen your integrity, wisdom, and high standing shine like a lamp when all other lights are extinguished. These things should count much towards alleviating your troubles. As for absence from your family and friends, it should be the easier to bear because you are also away from many severe vexations. I should tell you about them all, if I were not reluctant to have you learn in absence what you do not see, and are on that account happier, I think, than we who do.

I judge my words of consolation well placed in so far as they tell you, from a true friend, of considerations which may serve to lighten your troubles. All other sources of comfort lie in yourself. I know them, and they are not small; or rather to my way of thinking, they are by far the greatest of all. I experience them every day and value them so highly as to see my salvation in them. I well remember how keen a student *you* have been from childhood in every branch of letters, how eagerly and attentively you learned all that the wisest of mankind have handed down to show us how to live. These studies could be useful and delightful in the height of prosperity; but in times like these we have nothing else to ease our hearts. I will not presume. I will not urge a man of your attainments and disposition to have recourse to the pursuits to which you have given your energies from your earliest years. I shall only say something I think you will approve: seeing that there is no further place in Senate-House or Forum for the craft which I have studied, *I* have devoted all my time and attention to philosophy. Little more scope is left for your branch of knowledge,[631] in which you have attained such outstanding distinction, than for mine.[632] So, not to offer you counsel, I feel sure that you are engaged in the same pursuits as myself. Even if they do little good, they distract the mind from its anxiety.

Your son Servius engages and excels in all the pursuits of a gentleman, especially in the one in which I have told you my heart finds ease. In my regard for him I yield to you and to nobody else; and he requites me. He thinks, as is plain to see, that in paying attention and respect to me he is doing what most pleases you.

203 (IV. 4)

CICERO TO SERVIUS SULPICIUS RUFUS

Rome, late September or early October 46

From M. Cicero to Ser. Sulpicius greetings.

I accept the excuse you make for often sending me identical[633] letters, but I accept that part of it only in which you say that letters are not always delivered to me because of the negligence or dishonesty of those who take charge of them. The other part, in which you write that you often send identically phrased letters because of your 'verbal poverty', I neither recognize nor approve. I myself, whom you jestingly (so I suppose) credit with verbal riches, acknowledge that I am not altogether unprovided with words (no need for false modesty!); but also, and with no false modesty, I readily yield the palm to the spareness and elegance of *your* compositions.

631. Jurisprudence.
632. Oratory.
633. i.e. virtually identical. The letters would not be actual duplicates.

I had all along approved the considerations which led you, as you say, not to refuse this job in Achaia, but my approval was notably confirmed after reading your most recent letter. All the reasons which you advance are thoroughly valid, eminently worthy of your reputation and wisdom. I do not at all agree with your judgement that the matter has turned out otherwise than you had supposed. But in the general perturbation and chaos, when all lies overthrown and prostrate in the wake of a hideous war, each man reckons his own whereabouts as the worst of places and himself as the most wretched of beings. That is why you regret your decision and why we at home seem happy to you; whereas to us *you* seem, not indeed trouble-free, but happy by comparison with ourselves. And your state is better than ours in this very respect, that you dare to put your discontents[634] on paper, whereas we cannot even do that without risk. It is the fault, not of the victor, who is as moderate as could be, but of the victory itself. In civil war victory is always insolent.

On one point we have had the advantage of you. We learned of your colleague Marcellus' restitution a little sooner than you, and I will add furthermore that we saw *how* the matter was handled. For I do assure you that since the start of these calamities, that is, since force of arms first came to be arbiter of constitutional right, no other piece of public business has been transacted with dignity. Caesar himself, after complaining of Marcellus' acerbity (that was the word he used) and lauding your fair-mindedness and wisdom in the most complimentary terms, suddenly and unexpectedly declared that, if only for the omen's sake, he would not say no to the Senate's petition on Marcellus' behalf. This was after the House had risen in a body and approached Caesar in supplication, which they did when L. Piso had made mention of Marcellus in his speech and C. Marcellus had fallen at Caesar's feet. All in all, it seemed to me a

634. These would concern private or provincial matters which might safely be put on paper.

fine day's work; I thought I saw some semblance of reviving constitutional freedom.

Accordingly, after all those called upon to speak ahead of me had expressed thanks to Caesar except Vulcatius (*he* said he would not have done it in Caesar's place), my name was called; and I changed my resolution. I had determined to hold my peace for ever, not, let me say, from sluggishness, but because I remembered the station that used to be mine and is mine no longer. This resolution of mine was overborne by Caesar's magnanimity and the Senate's solicitude. So I expressed gratitude to Caesar at considerable length,[635] and I am afraid I may have thus forfeited in other contexts the decent retirement which was my only consolation in adversity. However, now that I have escaped his displeasure (he might have thought I did not regard the present régime as constitutional if I never broke silence), I shall do this in moderation, or rather on the near side of moderation, so as to meet his wishes on the one hand and the claims of my literary pursuits on the other. From my childhood I have taken pleasure in every liberal art and branch of knowledge, most of all in philosophy; but my devotion to this study grows upon me every day. I suppose I have reached an age ripe for wisdom; and the evils of the times are such that nothing else can relieve one's mind of its burdens. I see from your letter that business is distracting you from this pursuit, but the lengthening nights will soon be some help.

Your boy, Servius, our boy rather, is most attentive to me. His sterling worth and high character, and more particularly his devotion to literary studies, are my delight. He often confers with me about the question of your staying on or coming home. So far I take the view that we should do nothing but what appears most in accord with Caesar's wishes. The state of affairs is such that, if you were in Rome, nothing could give you pleasure except your family and friends. That aside, the best feature in the scene is himself. Other persons and things are

635. The speech is extant (*pro Marcello*).

such as one would prefer to learn of by report than see, if it were necessary to do one or the other. This advice of mine is by no means agreeable to *me* – I am anxious to see you, but counsel for your good.

Goodbye.

204 (XII. 17)

CICERO TO CORNIFICIUS[636]

Rome, September (middle) 46

From Cicero to his Colleague Cornificius greetings.

I am truly gratified by your remembrance of me, which you signify in your letter. Let me ask you to keep it in being. I do so, not as doubting your constancy, but as a common form.

Reports of disturbances have reached us from Syria.[637] As you are nearer their source than we, I am more concerned on your account than on my own. Rome is profoundly quiet. One would prefer some action, of a wholesome and honourable sort. I hope there will be such – Caesar evidently has it in mind.

You may be interested to learn that, profiting by your absence, I have taken the opportunity and licence, so to speak, to write more adventurously. Most of the results, it is true, might pass muster even with you. But my latest work is a treatise 'On the Best Style of Oratory',[638] a subject on which I have often suspected that you are not altogether at one with my judgement – a case, naturally, of an expert differing from one not wholly without claim to that description. I hope you will befriend the book because you really like it; but if not that,

636. Now governing Cilicia.
637. First news of the soldiers' mutiny headed by Caecilius Bassus seems to have reached Rome shortly before Cicero wrote.
638. Known as *The Orator*; the title was decided later.

then for my sake. I shall ask your people to copy it if they please, and send it to you. For I fancy that, even if the contents do not quite meet with your approval, any product of my pen will be agreeable to you in your present isolation.

In commending your reputation and consequence to my care you follow the general form of courtesy; but I hope you will believe not only that I set great store by the mutual affection which I am conscious exists between us but also that in the brilliance of your talents, your devotion to culture, and the prospect of a splendid political future you stand second to none in my estimation and comparable to few.

205 (XII. 18)

CICERO TO CORNIFICIUS

Rome, September (end) or October (beginning) 46

From Cicero to his Colleague Cornificius greetings.

The latest point in the letter I most recently received from you is the one which I shall answer first (I have observed that you great orators do this now and then). You complain that you don't hear from me. The fact is that I have never failed to send a letter when notified by your people that someone was going.

I think I may gather from your letter that you will take no hasty step and make no definite decision until you know the upshot of this Caecilius Bassus fellow. That is what I had expected, counting upon your good sense, and your most welcome letter has confirmed it. I would particularly ask you to write as often as you can, so that I know what you are doing and what is going on, also your further intentions.

Although I was sorry indeed to say goodbye to you, I consoled myself at the time with the belief that all was completely quiet where you were going, and that on the other hand you were leaving the threat of serious trouble behind you. In both respects the opposite has happened. War has broken out there, peace has ensued here. But it is a peace in which many things would displease you if you were on the spot – things, however, which do not please Caesar either. This is what always happens at the end of a civil war. It is not just a matter of the victor's wishes coming into effect; he also has to humour the people with whose assistance the victory has been gained. For my part, I have grown so thick a skin that at our friend Caesar's show[639] I saw T. Plancus[640] and heard Laberius' and Publilius' verses with perfect composure.[641] Let me tell you that what I lack most is someone with whom to laugh at all this in an intimate, sophisticated way. You will fill the gap, if you come back as soon as possible. I think it is to your own interest that you should do so as well as to mine.

206 (XII. 19)

CICERO TO CORNIFICIUS

Rome, December 46

From Cicero to Cornificius greetings.

I was delighted to read your letter. What pleased me most was to know that mine had been delivered. I did not doubt that you would be glad to read it, but I was uneasy about its safe delivery.

Your letter tells me that the present war in Syria and the province itself have been entrusted to you by Caesar. I wish you good luck and success in that responsibility; and I feel

639. The *ludi Victoriae Caesaris*, instituted in honour of Caesar's victory at Thapsus.

640. Bursa, restored by Caesar from exile.

641. Cicero had to sit through the mimes lest his absence should offend the Dictator.

sure you will have it, counting as I do on your diligence and good sense. But what you say about the possibility of a war with Parthia has alarmed me not a little, for I could guess for myself the size of your forces, and now learn it from your letter. So I pray that nation makes no move for the time being, before the legions which I hear are being brought to your support actually reach you. If you do not have troops enough to engage on equal terms, I trust you won't fail to follow M. Bibulus' tactics, who shut himself inside an extremely well-fortified and well-provisioned town[642] so long as the Parthians remained in the province.

But you will be better able to decide this in the light of the situation at the time. I shall be wondering anxiously what you are doing, until I know what you have done. I have taken every opportunity of sending you a letter and request you to do the same. Above all please write to your people in such a way as to let them know that I am one of their number.

207 (XV. 21)

CICERO TO TREBONIUS[643]

Rome, beginning of December 46 (?)

From M. Cicero to C. Trebonius greetings.

It was a pleasure to read your letter, and a great pleasure to read your book. But there was a touch of pain too, for, having inflamed my eagerness to increase our intercourse (our *affection* admitted of no addition), you then go away. Missing you as sorely as I do, you leave me only one consolation – that long, frequent letters will mitigate the sense of loss we both feel in

642. Antioch.
643. On his way to Spain, where Caesar's last campaign against the resurgent republicans was about to begin.

each other's absence. I can vouch to you for my part, and to myself for yours too; for you have left me in no doubt how much you care for me. Suppose I put out of account what you did in full public view, when you made my enemy[644] yours, defended me in your speeches, as Quaestor took upon yourself the duty of the Consuls on my behalf and the public's, and as Quaestor refused to obey the orders of a Tribune, even though your colleague obeyed them. Suppose I forgot matters of recent date, which I shall always remember – your concern for me at the war, your gladness at my return, your anxiety and distress when you were told of *my* anxieties and distress, your intention to visit me at Brundisium had you not suddenly been ordered to Spain. Leaving all this aside (and I must needs value it as highly as I value my existence as a man and a citizen), this book[645] you have sent me, what a declaration of your affection! To begin with, you find wit in every saying of mine – another perhaps would not; and then, these things, whether witty or only so-so, become irresistible when you are their *raconteur*. In fact the laugh is nearly all over before *I* come on the scene. I should have a heart of stone not to love you simply for think-ing so long about me and me only, as in writing these pieces you necessarily did. But you could not have thought what you have put down on paper without the most sincere affection. So I cannot suppose that anybody loves himself more than you love me. I wish I could repay your affection in all other ways, but at least I shall repay it with my own; and, after all, I feel sure that this by itself will be all the return you desire.

I come now to your charming and communicative letter, to which there is no necessity for me to reply at great length. I sent that letter to Calvus[646] with no more idea that it would get

644. Clodius. We are not otherwise informed of Trebonius' activities as City Quaestor (apparently in 60, or perhaps 58).

645. A collection, as appears, of Ciceronian witticisms, each in its anecdotal setting.

646. The poet and orator, C. Licinius Macer Calvus, now dead.

into circulation than the one you are reading at this moment. Now our way of writing when we think we shall be read only by our addressee is not the same as when we write for a multitude of eyes. If I praised his talent more generously than in your opinion the truth could warrant, it was first and foremost because such was really my opinion. Calvus' intellect was keen and quick; he followed a style in which, though he failed in judgement (a strong point with him), he none the less succeeded in the manner of his choice; his reading was wide and recondite. But he lacked force, and I was urging him to make good the deficiency. Now in trying to rouse a man and spur him on, it works wonders if you mingle some praise with your admonitions. So that's what I think of Calvus, and why I wrote as I did. I praised in order to exhort; and I did think very highly of his talent.

It remains for me to let my affection follow you on your way, to look forward hopefully to your return, to remember you faithfully in your absence, and to mitigate all sense of loss by sending and receiving letters. I hope you will often think of all you have done for me and tried to do. *You* are at liberty to forget it, but for me to forget would be a sin. So you will not only rate me an honourable man but conclude that I have a deep affection for you.

Goodbye.

208 (XV. 20)

CICERO TO TREBONIUS

Rome, shortly after the foregoing

From M. Cicero to C. Trebonius greetings.

I have entrusted my *Orator*, as I have entitled it, to your friend Sabinus. His race gave me the notion that he would make a trustworthy messenger – unless he has taken a leaf out of the candidates' book, and laid hold of the name incontinent![647] But his modest face and his firm, even way of talking seemed to have something of Cures.[648] But that's enough of Sabinus.

My dear Trebonius, when you left Rome you poured some oil on the flame of my affection; and so, to make it easier for me to bear the smart of missing you, salute me with letters in plenty, on the understanding that the same shall be forthcoming on my side. To be sure, you ought to be more assiduous in this office than I for two reasons: firstly, because, whereas in the old days people in Rome used to write to their friends in the provinces about politics, it is now for you to write to me, for the body politic is over there with you; secondly, because I can give you your due by other services while you are away, but I do not see how you can give me mine except by writing letters.

You will be writing me the rest of your news later on, but now I want first of all to know what sort of a journey you are having, where you saw Brutus,[649] and how long you spent with him. Then, when you are further on your way, tell me about military matters and the whole situation, so that I can make an estimate of how we stand. I shall consider I know just as much as I learn from your letters.

Take care of your health and the affection which you so generously bestow on me.

647. The *cognomen* 'Sabinus' suggested Sabine origin, and Sabinum was traditionally the home of the old-time virtues. Or had Sabinus merely assumed his *cognomen*, like certain candidates for office (possibly an allusion to C. Calvisius Sabinus)? Perhaps, however, he was a slave.
648. Ancient chief town of the Sabines.
649. Now governing Cisalpine Gaul.

209 (VII. 23)

CICERO TO M. FABIUS GALLUS

Rome, December 46

From Cicero to M. Fabius Gallus greetings.

I had just got in from Arpinum when I was handed a letter from you. By the same bearer I received a letter from Avianius,[650] containing a very handsome offer to debit me after he arrives from any date I please. Now pray put yourself in my shoes. Can you reconcile it with your sense of decency or with mine to ask for credit in the first place, and in the second for more than a year's credit? But everything would be straightforward, my dear Gallus, if you had bought what I needed and within the price I had wished to pay. Not but what I stand by these purchases you say you have made, indeed I am grateful. I fully understand that you acted out of good-will, affection indeed, in buying the pieces which pleased you (I have always regarded you as a very fine judge in any matter of taste), and which you considered worthy of me. But I hope Damasippus doesn't change his mind, for, frankly, I don't need any of these purchases of yours. Not being acquainted with my regular practice you have taken these four or five pieces at a price I should consider excessive for all the statuary in creation. You compare these Bacchantes with Metellus'[651] Muses. Where's the likeness? To begin with, I should never have reckoned the Muses themselves worth such a sum – and all Nine would have approved my judgement! Still, that would have made a suitable acquisition for a library, and one appropriate to my interests. But where am I going to put Bacchantes? Pretty

650. Doubtless the sculptor, C. Avianius Evander; cf. Letter 314 (XIII.2). Gallus had bought some statues from him on Cicero's behalf.
651. Probably Metellus Scipio.

little things, you may say. I know them well, I've seen them often. I should have given you a specific commission about statues which I know, if I had cared for them. My habit is to buy pieces which I can use to decorate a place in my palaestra,[652] in imitation of lecture-halls. But a statue of Mars! What can I, as an advocate of peace, do with that? I'm glad there was none of Saturn – I should have thought those two between them had brought me debt! I had sooner have had one of Mercury[653] – we might fare better in our transactions with Avianius!

As for that table-rest which you had earmarked for yourself, if you like it, you shall have it; but if you have altered your mind, I'll keep it of course. For the sum you have spent I should really have much preferred to buy a lodge at Tarracina,[654] so as not to be continually imposing on hospitality. To be sure, I realize that my freedman is to blame (I had given him quite definite commissions), and Junius too – I think you know him, Avianius' friend. I am making some new alcoves in the little gallery of my house at Tusculum, and I wanted some pictures for their decoration – indeed, if anything in this way appeals to me, it is painting. However, if I have to keep these things of yours, please let me know where they are, and when they are sent for, and by what mode of transport. If Damasippus changes his mind, I shall find some Damasippus *manqué*, even if it means taking a loss.

You write again about the house. I had already given directions on this head to my girl Tullia as I was leaving – I got your letter that same hour. I had also taken it up with your friend

652. Probably in his house on the Palatine; cf. *Letters to Atticus* 24 (11.4).5.

653. The god of gain. In astrology Saturn and Mars generally bring the opposite.

654. Cicero had recently visited his Campanian villas and will have stayed at Tarracina *en route*; perhaps Gallus was his host.

Nicias, since he is on familiar terms with Cassius,[655]as you know. On my return, before I read this last letter of yours, I asked Tullia how she had got on. She said she had gone to work through Licinia (I have an impression, though, that Cassius does not have a great deal to do with his sister), and that Licinia in her turn said that while her husband was away (Dexius has left for Spain) she did not venture to move house in his absence and without his knowledge. I take it very kindly that you set so much store on our friendly day-to-day inter-course that you took a house so as to live not only in my neighbourhood but in my actual company, and that you are in such a hurry to move. But on my life I won't admit that you are any more eager for that arrangement than myself. So I shall try every way, conscious as I am of what it means to me and to both of us. If I have any success, I'll let you know. Write back on all points and inform me, if you will, when I am to expect you.

210 (VII. 26)

CICERO TO M. FABIUS GALLUS

Tusculum, late 46 or early 45

From Cicero to Gallus greetings.

For ten days my stomach had been seriously out of order, but as I did not have a fever I could not convince the folk who wanted my services that I was really sick. So I took refuge here at Tusculum, after two days of strict fasting – not so much as a drop of water! Famished and exhausted, I was craving your good offices rather than expecting you to demand mine. I

655. Probably not C. Cassius, but perhaps his younger brother Lucius.

am terrified of all forms of illness, but especially of dysentery – your master Epicurus gets a rough handling from the Stoics for complaining of trouble with his bladder and his bowels, the latter being according to them a consequence of over-eating and the former of an even more discreditable indulgence! Well, I was really afraid of dysentery. However, I think I am better for the change, or maybe the mental relaxation; or perhaps the malady is simply wearing itself into abatement.

But in case you wonder how this happened or what I did to deserve it, the Sumptuary Law, supposed to have brought plain living, has been my downfall. Our *bons vivants*, in their efforts to bring into fashion products of the soil exempted under the statute, make the most appetizing dishes out of fungi, potherbs, and grasses of all sorts. Happening on some of these at an augural dinner at Lentulus' house, I was seized with a violent diarrhoea, which has only today begun (I think) to check its flow. So: oysters and eels I used to resist well enough, but here I lie, caught in the toils of Mesdames Beet and Mallow! Well, I shall be more careful in future. As for you, you heard of it from Anicius (he saw me in the qualms), and that should have been reason enough for a visit, let alone a letter.

I intend to stay here until I have convalesced, having lost strength and weight. But I expect I shall recover both easily enough, once I have thrown off the attack.

211 (XIII. 68)

CICERO TO SERVILIUS ISAURICUS

Rome, October (?) 46

M. Tullius Cicero to P. Servilius Isauricus, Proconsul and Colleague, best greetings.

I am extremely grateful for your letter giving the stages of your voyaging;[656] it showed that you have not forgotten our friendly relations, and nothing could be more agreeable to me than that. For the future, I shall be even more grateful if you will write to me as friend to friend on public matters, that is to say the state of the province and the rules you institute. I shall hear all this from many informants (your light does not shine under a bushel), but I should like most of all to learn about it from your letters.

On my side, I shall not often be giving you my views on high politics because of the risk attached to such letters, but I shall write fairly often about what is going on. In spite of all, I think I see a hope that our colleague[657] Caesar will try, and is already trying, to get us some sort of a constitutional system. It would have been very desirable that you should have been present and party to his plans. But if it is more to your advantage, to your honour that is to say, to govern Asia and care for a part of our state interests that has suffered so severely, I too am bound to prefer what will benefit you and your reputation.

Whatever may seem to me to concern your public standing shall receive my most active care. In particular, I shall pay every respect and attention to your illustrious father, as is my duty in view of our old friendship, the kindness I have received from you both, and his own eminence.

212 (XIII. 77)

CICERO TO P. SULPICIUS RUFUS[658]

Rome, autumn 46

From M. Cicero to P. Sulpicius, Imperator, greetings.

Though I do not go to the Senate very often nowadays, I felt

656. To his province of Asia.
657. As Augur.
658. Now governor of Illyricum. His relationship to the jurist, Ser. Sulpicius Rufus, is uncertain.

after reading your letter that I should be failing in my obligations to our old friendship and the many good offices we have rendered one another if I was not present when the honour was conferred upon you. So present I was, and happy to vote for your Supplication. Nor shall a time ever come when I shall not play my part in furthering your interest or your reputation or your dignity. I should be glad if you would so inform your friends, so that they know of my disposition towards you and feel entitled to call upon me without hesitation if you should stand in need of any service.

M. Bolanus is an honourable, gallant, in every way respectable gentleman, and an old friend of mine. I recommend him to you warmly. You will oblige me very much if you let him realize that this recommendation has been of great assistance to him, and you will find himself an excellent, most appreciative person. I can promise you that his friendship will bring you no small gratification.

There is another matter in which I would earnestly request you to put yourself to some trouble, in virtue of our friendship and your unfailing readiness to serve me. My library, worth a considerable sum, was in the charge of a slave of mine called Dionysius.[659] Having pilfered a large number of books and anticipating a day of reckoning, he ran away. He's now in your province. Many people, including my friend M. Bolanus, saw him at Narona, but believed his story that I had given him his freedom. If you see to it that he is returned to me, I cannot tell you how much it will oblige me. In itself it is no great matter, but I am intensely vexed. Bolanus will tell you where he is and what can be done. If I recover the fellow thanks to you, I shall regard you as having done me a very great favour.

659. Cf. Letter 255 (v.9).

213 (XV. 18)

CICERO TO CASSIUS[660]

Rome, December 46

From M. Cicero to C. Cassius greetings.

This letter would have been longer, if I had not been asked for it just as your post was leaving – longer, anyhow, if I had had any bavardage to hand, since writing *au sérieux* is hardly possible without risk. Is joking possible then, you will ask. Well, it certainly isn't very easy, but we have no other means of diversion from our troubles. Where then is philosophy? Yours[661] is in the kitchen, mine is a scold – to be a slave makes me ashamed of myself. So I make believe to be otherwise occupied, so as not to have Plato's[662] reproaches in my ears.

Of Spain nothing certain yet, no news at all in fact. I am sorry for my own sake that you are away but glad for yours. But the courier is getting impatient. So keep well and fond of me, as you have been from a boy.

214 (XV. 17)

CICERO TO CASSIUS

Rome, January (beginning) 45

M. Cicero to C. Cassius greetings.

Your couriers are a queer set – not that *I* mind; but when they

660. Now in Brundisium.
661. Cassius had joined the Epicureans, whose master had written 'the beginning and root of all good is the pleasure of the belly'.
662. The founder of the Academic school to which Cicero belonged.

go away they demand a letter, while when they arrive they bring none. Even so, it would be more convenient if they gave me a little time to write, but they arrive with their travelling caps on and say their party is waiting for them at the city gate. So you must forgive me. You are going to get a second short letter. But you may look forward to full amends. Though I can't think why *I* am apologizing to *you*, when your people come to my house empty-handed and go back with letters.

Here in Rome (just to write you something after all) we have a death to talk about – P. Sulla senior. Some say it was bandits, others overeating. The public doesn't care which, as there's no doubt that he's ashes. You will bear the news like the philosopher you are. Still, the town has lost a *personnage*. They think Caesar will take it hard – he'll be afraid the public auctions[663] may go with less of a swing. Mindius Marcellus[664] and Attius the perfumer are delighted to have shed a competitor.

From Spain nothing new, but keen expectancy of news. Rumours tending to gloom, but nobody to vouch for them. Our friend Pansa left Rome[665] in uniform on 30 December, an unmistakable illustration of what you have latterly begun to question – that Right is to be chosen *per se*. He has given a helping hand to many persons in distress and behaved like a human being in these bad times; accordingly he went off in astonishingly good odour with honest men.

So you are still at Brundisium. I heartily approve and rejoice. Upon my word, I think you will do wisely to avoid worry to no purpose. We who care for you will be glad if you do. And in future, when you send a line home, be a good fellow and remember me. I shall never knowingly let anybody go to you without a letter from me.

Goodbye.

663. Sales of confiscated property.
664. Later a naval commander in the service of his friend and fellow-townsman, Octavian. Nothing is known of Attius.
665. We do not know where he was going.

215 (XV. 16)

CICERO TO CASSIUS

Rome, January (middle) 45

From M. Cicero to C. Cassius greetings.

I think you must be a trifle ashamed of yourself now. Here comes a third letter down upon you before you have produced so much as a sheet or a line! However, I am not pressing you. I shall expect a longer letter, or rather I shall require one. As for me, if I always had a bearer, I should dispatch them three an hour. I don't know how it is, but when I write something to you, I seem to see you here in front of me. I am not speaking according to the doctrine of appearances of images, to use the terminology of your new friends, who think that even mental appearances are aroused by Catius' *spectres*. For, in case you have not noticed it, what the Sage of Gargettus,[666] and Democritus before him, called 'images'[667] are termed 'spectres' by the late lamented Catius, Insubrian and Epicurean. Now even granting that those 'spectres' could strike the eyes, because they run upon the pupils of their own accord, I for one don't see how they can strike the mind – you will have to teach me when you are safely home again. Are we really to suppose that your 'spectre' is in my control, so that as soon as I take a fancy to think about you, up it comes? And not only you, who are in my heart all the time, but if I start thinking about the island of Britain, will its image fly into my brain?

But of all this later on. I am just testing your reactions. If

666. Epicurus belonged to the Attic district ('deme') of Gargettus.

667. Greek *eidôla*. *spectrum* in classical Latin occurs only in this letter and Cassius' reply. Perhaps Catius coined it (from *specio*, 'look at'). On the theory of visual perception through images see *Letters to Atticus* 23 (11.3).2.

you are nettled and upset, I shall continue and file a claim for your restitution to the philosophical persuasion[668] from which you have been ousted 'by violence, by force of arms'.[669] In this formula they don't usually add 'during the current year', so that if it is now two or three years since you were seduced by the wiles of Miss Pleasure into serving notice of divorce on Lady Virtue,[670] my action will still lie.

But to whom am I talking? Why, to the most gallant gentleman alive, whose every action since entering public life has been in the fullest accord with his splendid reputation. I am afraid that even this system of yours must have more spunk in it than I had supposed, that is if you are really an adherent.

'How on earth did he come to think of that?' you will be wondering. Why, because I have nothing else to write about. Of politics I can write nothing, for I do not care to write what I feel.

216 (XV. 19)

CASSIUS TO CICERO

Brundisium, January (last half) 45

From C. Cassius to M. Cicero greetings.

I trust you are well.

You may be sure that nothing I do in this sojourn of mine abroad is done more willingly than writing to you. It is as though I was chatting and joking with you in the flesh. That

668. What this was is uncertain. Perhaps, like Brutus, Cassius had been an adherent of Antiochus of Ascalon's 'Old Academy', which was close to Stoicism.

669. Cf. Letter 36 (VII.13). It seems to be implied that Cassius' conversion was in some way due to the Civil War.

670. See p. 73.

does not, however, come about because of Catius' 'spectres' – in return for him I'll throw so many clodhopping Stoics back at you in my next letter that you'll declare Catius Athenian born!

I am glad that our friend Pansa left Rome in uniform amid general good-will, both for his own sake and, let me add, for all our sakes. For I trust people will realize how intense and universal is hatred for cruelty and love for worth and clemency, so that they will see how the prizes most sought and coveted by the wicked come to the good. It is hard to persuade men that Right[671] is to be chosen *per se*; but that Pleasure and Peace of Mind are won by virtue, justice, and Right is both true and easily argued. Epicurus himself, from whom all these sorry translators of terms, Catius, Amafinius, etc., derive, says: 'To live pleasurably is not possible without living rightly and justly.' Thus it is that Pansa, whose goal is Pleasure, retains Virtue; and those whom you and your friends call Pleasure-lovers are Right-lovers and Justice-lovers, practising and re-taining all the virtues. And so Sulla[672] (whose judgement[673] we must respect) saw that the philosophers were at loggerheads: instead of trying to discover *what* was good, he went and bought up all the goods he could find! Indeed I have borne his death with fortitude. However, Caesar will not let us miss him long – he has other victims of justice to offer us in his place. Nor will *he* miss Sulla's activity in the auction rooms – he will only have to look at Sulla junior.

Now to get back to public affairs, let me know in your reply how things are going in Spain. I'm devilish worried, and I'd rather have the old easy-going master than try a cruel new one. You know what a fool Gnaeus[674] is, how he takes cruelty

671. *to kalon*; cf. *Letters to Atticus* 134 (VII.11).1. – Capitals indicate Greek terms.

672. Cf. Letter 214 (XV.17).

673. Perhaps in allusion to Sulla's conviction on charges of electoral malpractice in 66.

674. Pompey's elder son.

for courage, how he thinks we always made fun of him. I'm afraid he may answer our persiflage with his sword, hobblede-hoy-fashion. If you love me, tell me what is going on. Ah, how I should like to know your frame of mind as you read this! Anxious or easy? I should know by the same token what I ought to do.

Not to be too prolix, goodbye. Go on caring for me. If Casear has won, expect me quickly back.

217 (IX. 10)

CICERO TO DOLABELLA[675]

Rome, beginning of 45

From M. Cicero to P. Dolabella greetings.

I dare not let our friend Salvius[676] leave without giving him something in the way of a letter to you, though upon my word I have nothing to write except that I am marvellously fond of you; and of that I am sure you are convinced without my writing a word. In point of fact I have better cause to expect to hear from you than you from me. Nothing is afoot in Rome which I judge you would care to know, unless perhaps you wish to known that I am appointed arbiter between our friend Nicias and Vidius. The latter, I believe, is producing a couple of lines registering a payment to Nicias, who on his side Aristarchus-like obelizes these same. My job is to decide like a critic of old whether they are the poet's own or interpolated.

I expect you may ask now whether I have forgotten those mushrooms at Nicias' and the giant snails with ★ ★ ★.[677] Come now, do you suppose that my old austerity has been so

675. Now with Caesar in Spain.
676. Probably Caesar's freedman, not Atticus' slave.
677. Several words are corrupt in the manuscripts.

thoroughly shaken off that even in a court of law there isn't a remnant to be seen of my former grave demeanour? Never mind, I shall give our charming little *copain* back as good as new. I shan't be so foolish as to find against him only for you to rehabilitate him for fear Plancus Bursa be left without a school-master.[678]

But here I go rambling on and on, when I don't know whether your mind is at ease or whether you are anxiously employed on some substantial bit of military business. So when I am assured of finding you in a mood to laugh, I shall write more at length. However, I want you to know that there was much public concern about P. Sulla's death before it was known for certain. Now they have stopped wondering *how* he met his end. What they know is all they want to know. I bear the event philosophically, apart from one misgiving – I'm afraid Caesar's auctions may go with less of a swing.

218 (VI. 18)

CICERO TO Q. LEPTA

Rome, January 45

From Cicero to Lepta.

As soon as your letter came to hand by your man Seleucus, I at once sent a note to Balbus enquiring what the law [679] had to say. He replied that practising auctioneers [680] are debarred

678. Cicero playfully writes as though Nicias was facing a criminal charge and would go into exile if he lost the case. Nicias was a scholar, the obnoxious Bursa an ignoramus.

679. Evidently a new law of Caesar, drafted (presumably by Balbus) but not yet promulgated. The provision respecting auctioneers may have been taken over from earlier legislation.

680. Their trade was not highly regarded, perhaps because they made money out of the distress of others – debtors forced to sell their property.

from membership of a town council, but that the bar does not apply to persons who have practised in the past. So your friends and mine can set their minds at rest. It would have been intolerable, after all, if persons who had once practised as auctioneers were not allowed to sit on their town councils, while currently practising inspectors of entrails[681] were appointed members of the Roman Senate.

No news of Spain. But it is generally accepted that Pompey has a large army, as Caesar himself sent his people a copy of a letter of Paciaecus' stating the number of legions as eleven. Messalla[682] too has written to Q. Salassus[683] that his brother, P. Curtius, has been executed in front of the army by Pompey's orders on a charge of conspiring with certain Spaniards to seize Pompey, when he entered some town or other to obtain supplies, and hand him over to Caesar.

As regards your own affair (your standing surety for Pompey), when your co-surety Galba (a gentleman who cannot be accused of carelessness where his finances are concerned) gets back, I shall be in constant touch with him to see if a solution can be found. He seemed confident that it could.

I am greatly pleased that you think so well of my *Orator*. I do flatter myself that I have put into that book whatever judgement I may possess on the subject of public speaking. If it is as you say you find it, then I too amount to something. If not, I am content that my reputation for sound judgement and the book shall suffer in exactly the same proportion. I hope our little boy[684] has already developed a taste for such compositions. Though he has still to grow up, there is something to be said for letting his ears buzz with utterances of this kind.

My Tullia's confinement has kept me in Rome. But even now

681. *haruspices* practised the Etruscan system of divination from the entrails of sacrificial animals.

682. M. Valerius Messalla Rufus, Consul in 53.

683. Q. Curtius Salassus was a Prefect under Antony in 41.

684. Lepta's son.

that she has, as I hope, fairly well regained her strength, I am still kept here waiting to extract the first instalment[685] out of Dolabella's agents. And in point of fact I am not the gadabout I used to be. My buildings and the freedom from distraction were what I used to enjoy. Well, I have a town house as pleasant as any of my country places, and greater freedom from distraction than anywhere in the wilds. So even my literary work is not hampered, and I employ myself in it without any interruptions. I fancy therefore that I shall see you here before you see me there.

Your charming boy should learn Hesiod by heart and never forget 'Sweat before virtue', etc.[686]

219 (XVI. 18)

CICERO TO TIRO

Rome (?), 46 or 45 (?)

From Tullius to Tiro greetings.

Well then! Isn't that as it should be? *I* think so, and should like to make it 'to his dear Tiro'.[687] However, let us beware of jealous malice, if you wish – the malice I have often despised.

I am glad your perspiration has done you good. If my place at Tusculum has done you good too, heavens, how much

685. Of Tullia's dowry. She and Dolabella were now divorced.
686. 'The Gods set sweat in front of excellence', from Hesiod's *Works and Days* (289).
687. Tiro seems to have suggested that the heading of Cicero's previous letter, 'Tullius to Tiro greetings', was too familiar. To all other correspondents except his wife and brother Cicero uses his *cognomen*. Yet earlier letters to Tiro were similarly headed, and most of those after his manumission add *suo* ('his dear'). Perhaps the letter to which Tiro referred had to be shown to a third party.

better I shall love it! But if you love me, and if you don't you make a very pretty pretence of it, which after all answers nicely – well, however that stands, humour your health. In your devotion to me you have not hitherto devoted yourself enough to that. You know what it requires – digestion, no fatigue, a short walk, massage, proper evacuation. Mind you come back in good shape. I should love not only you but my house at Tusculum the more.

Prod Parhedrus to hire the garden himself. That will give the gardener a jolt. That rascal Helico used to pay HS1,000 when there was no sun-trap, no drain, no wall, no shed. After all my expense is this fellow going to make fools of us? Give him a hot time, as I did Motho[688] and in consequence have more flowers than I can well use.

I should like to know what is happening about Crabra,[689] even though nowadays water is really too plentiful. I shall send the sundial and the books when the weather is clear. But have you no books with you? Or are you composing something Sophoclean? Mind you have results to show.

Caesar's familiar A. Ligurius is dead, a good fellow and a friend of mine. Let me know when we are to expect you. Look after yourself carefully.

Goodbye.

220 (XVI. 20)

CICERO TO TIRO

Rome (?), shortly after the foregoing

From Tullius to Tiro greetings.

On my life, my dear Tiro, I am anxious about your health.

688. Perhaps gardener at the house on the Palatine.
689. The Aqua Crabra, an aqueduct running into Rome, supplied water to the villa, for which Cicero paid.

But I am sure that, if you continue to exercise the same care, you will soon be strong again. Put the books[690] away. Do the catalogue when Metrodorus[691] likes, since you have to live under his ordinance. Deal with the gardener as you think best. You can see the gladiators on the Kalends and return the following day. That is my advice – but as you please. Look after yourself carefully if you care for me.

Goodbye.

221 (VI. 22)

CICERO TO CN. DOMITIUS AHENOBARBUS

Rome (?), May (?) 46

From Cicero to Domitius.

I was not deterred from sending you a letter after your return to Italy by the fact that you had sent none to me. But I knew neither how to make you any promise, being myself in need of everything, nor how to advise you, when I was short of advice myself, nor how to comfort you in the midst of such afflictions. The present situation in these respects is no better, it is far more hopeless even. However, I prefer to write an empty letter than not to write at all.

Even if I saw that you had tried to take upon yourself for the sake of the commonwealth a greater burden of duty than you would have been able to sustain,[692] I should still urge you in every way I could to accept life as it is on the conditions on

690. Not Cicero's library at Tusculum but those mentioned in the previous letter.

691. Tiro's doctor.

692. i.e. 'had gone to Africa in 48 to carry on the fight against Caesar'. Cicero's convoluted way of putting this shows that he felt himself on dangerous ground.

which it is offered you. But you set a term to the course you so well and gallantly undertook, the same that Fortune herself decreed as the final limit to our struggles.[693] Therefore I implore and conjure you in the name of our old association and friendship, and of the abundant good-will I bear you and you equally bear me; preserve yourself for me, for your mother,[694] your wife, and all your family, to whom you are and have ever been most dear. Think of your own safety and that of those near to you, who depend on you. Make use now of what you have learned, those admirable teachings handed down by the wisest of mankind which from youth up you have absorbed into your memory and knowledge. Bear the loss of persons bound to you by good-will and good offices, signal in measure and number, if not with equanimity, then at any rate with fortitude.

What *I* can do I do not know, or rather I am conscious that it is all too little. But I promise you to do whatever in my judgement conduces to your safety and dignity with the same devotion that *you* have always shown to practical effect in *my* affairs. This disposition of mine I have freely conveyed to that excellent lady your mother, who bears you so deep an affection. If you write to me, I shall execute your wishes as I understand them. But if you do not write, I shall none the less pay most zealous and particular heed to everything that seems to me for your advantage.

Goodbye.

693. The defeat at Pharsalia.
694. Cato's sister Porcia.

222 (VI. IO. 4–6)

CICERO TO TREBIANUS[695]

Rome, August (?) 46

From M. Cicero to Trebianus greetings.

I should have written sooner, if I had seen what type of letter to write. In circumstances like these the part of friends is either to offer comfort or to make promises. I have not been doing the former, because I heard from many quarters of the courage and good sense with which you bear the times' ill-usage, and how efficacious a consolation you find in the consciousness of your past actions and motives. If you do this, you reap the reward of the noble studies in which I know you have always been engaged, and I earnestly urge you so to do.

Moreover you are very well versed in affairs and in all the lessons that history teaches, nor am I myself a novice in these matters, having engaged both in study, though less perhaps than I could wish, and in practical experience of affairs even more than I could wish. And I give you this pledge: the harsh ill-usage you now suffer will not long continue. The personage whose power is greatest seems to me to be inclining ever more and more towards justice and his own natural disposition; and the cause itself is such that it must soon revive and be constituted once more, along with freedom, which cannot lie for ever in the dust. Each day brings some act of unexpected lenity or liberality. All this depends on shifts of circumstances which are often slight, and so I shall keep my eyes open for every movement and let no opportunity slip of helping and alleviating your condition.

So I hope the other type of letter which I mentioned will

695. This Pompeian exile is otherwise unknown.

become easier for me every day, and that I shall also be in a position to make promises. That I shall do more gladly in deeds than in words. I would ask you to believe that (at least so far as I have been able to judge) you have more friends than most people who are, and have formerly been, in the same case as yourself; and that I yield to none of them. Keep a brave and lofty spirit – that depends on you alone. What depends on fortune will be governed by circumstances, and our calculations will provide for it.

223 (VI. 10. 1–3)

CICERO TO TREBIANUS

Rome, September (?) 46

From M. Cicero to Trebianus greetings.

How highly I regard you and always have, and how highly I have come to realize you regard me, I am my own witness. Your decision to continue fighting in the civil war, or rather the chance which led you to do so, was always a great distress to me; and the result, that the recovery of your position and status is taking longer than is right and than I should have wished, is a matter of no less concern to me than my misfortunes always were to you. Therefore I have freely opened my mind to Postumulenus, to Sestius, very often to our friend Atticus, and most recently to your freedman Theudas. I have told each one of them more than once that I am anxious to do my duty by you and your children in every way I can. I should like you to write to your people and tell them to regard my time, advice, money, and loyalty (these at least are under my own control) as at their disposal for all purposes. If my public and private influence counted for what it should in a commonwealth to which I have done such service, you too would be what you were – most worthy of any rank, however exalted, and assuredly by far the most distinguished member of your own order. But both of us have come down in the world at the same time and for the same reason. So I promise you the commodities I have just mentioned, which still belong to me, as well as those others which I fancy I retain in some degree as relics of my former status. Caesar himself, as I have had numerous opportunities to recognize, is not unfriendly to me; and almost all his most intimate associates happen to be bound to me by considerable services rendered in the past, and pay me assiduous attention and regard. If an opening occurs for me to make representations concerning your circumstances, I mean your status as a citizen, in which all else is included (and the way they talk makes me every day more hopeful of this), I shall make them personally and work hard.

There is no need to enter into details. My zeal and good-will are yours in entirety. But it is very important that all your people should know (your letters can make it clear to them) that everything that is Cicero's is at Trebianus' disposal. The point is that they must think nothing too difficult for me to undertake with pleasure on your behalf.

224 (VI. 11)

CICERO TO TREBIANUS

Tusculum (?), June (first half) 45 (?)

From M. Cicero to Trebianus greetings.

My feelings towards Dolabella used to be merely of regard. I *owed* him nothing, for it had never so happened that I had need of his services, and he was indebted to me for standing by him in his ordeals.[696] But now, by his superlative response

696. Cf. p. 151.

both previously in the matter of your estate and at the present time in that of your restoration, his kindness has placed me under so powerful an obligation that there is no man to whom I am more beholden. On this my hearty congratulations – and I would rather *you* congratulated me than thanked me. Thanks I do not at all crave, and congratulations you can offer in all sincerity.

For the rest, now that your high character and standing have cleared the way for your return to your family and friends, as a wise and high-minded man you must forget what you have lost and think of what you have recovered. You will live with your people and with me. You have gained more in respect than you have lost in possessions. And possessions themselves would be more enjoyable if there were a commonwealth.

Our friend Vestorius has written to me that you express the utmost gratitude to myself. Such acknowledgement on your part is very agreeable to me, and I am particularly willing that you make it among others to our friend Siro. One likes what one does to win approbation, and the approbation of a very wise man is especially welcome.

I am looking forward to seeing you as soon as possible.

225 (IV. 13)

CICERO TO NIGIDIUS FIGULUS

Rome, August (?) 46

From M. Cicero to P. Figulus greetings.

I have been asking myself this long while past just what to write to you, but nothing comes to mind – not any particular thing to say, not even a *manner* of writing normally used in correspondence. Circumstances have taken away one element[697] customary in the letters we used to write in happier

697. Jokes.

days. Fortune has made it impossible for me to write or even think in that vein. There remains a gloomy, doleful sort of letter-writing, suited to the times we live in. That too fails me. It should include either the pledge of some assistance or comfort for your distress. Now as for promises, I can make none, for I myself am in like case and support my misfortunes by others' means. I am more often inclined to complain of the life I lead than to be thankful for living at all.

True, I personally have suffered no conspicuous private injury, and I can think of nothing to wish for at such a time which Caesar has not spontaneously granted me. But my troubles are such that I feel guilty in continuing to live. I lack not only many personal intimates, snatched from me by death or scattered in exile, but all the friends whose good-will I won when I defended the state with you at my side. I live among the wreckage of their fortunes, the plundering of their possessions. To hear of it would be sad enough, but I have actually before my eyes the heartrending spectacle of the dissipation of their estates – the men who were my helpers when I put out that fire[698] in days gone by. In the city where not long ago I stood high in influence, respect, and fame, I now have none of these things. I do indeed enjoy the greatest consideration from Caesar himself, but that cannot counterbalance the violence, the total revolution of environment. Deprived, therefore, as I am of everything to which I had been accustomed by nature, inclination, and habit, I cut a sorry figure in other men's eyes, so at least I fancy, and in my own. Born as I was for action, incessant action worthy of a man, I now have no way to employ my energies or even my thoughts. I, who once had it in my power to help the obscure and even the guilty, now find myself unable even to make a kindly promise to P. Nigidius, the most accomplished and the most stainless man of our time, once so influential and assuredly so good a friend of mine.

698. Catiline's conspiracy. Cicero is said to have relied much on Nigidius' advice at that time.

This sort of letter-writing, therefore, is ruled out. It remains for me to offer you comfort and to try by reasoned argument to divert you from your troubles. But you have in the highest degree, if ever any man had, the faculty of consoling yourself or another. Therefore I shall not touch that side of the subject which starts from recondite philosophical theory. That I shall leave entirely to you. *You* will see what is worthy of a man of sense and courage, what is demanded of you by dignity, elevation of mind, your past, your studies, the pursuits in which you have distinguished yourself from childhood upwards. I merely assure you of what my understanding and intuition tell me, being in Rome and keeping a close eye on the course of events: that you will not have to bear your present troubles much longer, but that those that you share with us may be with you always.

To begin with the personage whose word is law, I think I see his mind and that it is favourable to your cause. These are not idle words. The less I have of his intimacy, the more curious I am to probe. It is only because he wants to make it easier for himself to give discouraging answers to people with whom he is more seriously annoyed that he has so far been slow to release you from your unpleasant predicament. But his friends, especially those he likes best, speak and feel about you with remarkable warmth. To that we can add the popular sentiment, or rather the universal consensus. Even the Republic, which counts for little enough at the moment but must count for something some day, will exert whatever power she may have to win your pardon from these very people in whose hands she lies, and, believe me, it will not be long.

So I will now go back on my tracks and make you a promise, which earlier in this letter I refrained from doing. I shall both cultivate his intimates, who have no small regard for me and are much in my company, and find a way into familiar intercourse with himself, from which a sense of shame on my part has deterred me hitherto. Assuredly I shall follow any path which I think likely to lead to our goal. In this whole sphere I shall do more than I venture to put on paper. Other kinds of service, I am sure, are at your disposal in many quarters; but from me they are most heartily at your command. Of my possessions there is none that I would not as soon were yours as mine. On this and all related points I say little only because I would rather have you expect to enjoy your own, as I am confident you will.

It only remains for me to beg and implore you to be of excellent courage and to remember not only the lessons you have learned from other great men but those of which you are yourself the author, the products of your intellect and study. If you put them all together, you will be in the best of hope; and, come what may, good or bad, you will bear it with philosophy. But all this you know better than I, or rather better than any man. For my part I shall attend with all zeal and diligence to whatever I find to concern you, and shall treasure the memory of your kindness to me in the darkest days of my life.

226 (VI. 12)

CICERO TO AMPIUS BALBUS

Rome, August or September (?) 46

From Cicero to Ampius best greetings.

I congratulate you, my dear Balbus, and in all sincerity. For I am not so foolish as to wish you temporary enjoyment of an illusory happiness, only to be dashed of a sudden and to fall so low that nothing later on could lift you into equanimity. I have pleaded your cause more openly than my present circumstances warranted, for I thought more of my fondness for you and the uninterrupted affection which you have been so sedulous to foster than of the debility which has overtaken my personal influence. All that concerns your return and restoration has been promised and confirmed, positively and definitely. I was present, observing and taking note.

The fact is, opportunely enough, that I have Caesar's intimates all linked to me in familiar intercourse and friendship, and stand with them second only to Caesar himself. Pansa, Hirtius, Balbus, Oppius, Matius, and Postumus carry their regard for me to really extraordinary lengths. If I had had to bring this about by my own exertions, I should not regret my trouble, considering the times we live in. But I have done nothing in the way of time-serving. With all of them I have friendships of long standing; and I have pleaded with them incessantly on your behalf. But my principal reliance has been on Pansa, who is most zealous for your welfare and anxious to please myself; for he has influence with Caesar founded on respect no less than personal liking. And I am very pleased with Tillius Cimber. When all is said, petitions founded on obligation carry more weight with Caesar than those of self-interest; and because Cimber had such an obligation, he carried more weight than he would have carried on behalf of any other person.

A passport was not granted straight away because of the unconscionable rascality of certain people, who would have resented the granting of a pardon to 'the Trumpet of the Civil War', as they call you, and who talk at large as though they were not glad enough that the war took place. It therefore seemed best to proceed discreetly and on no account to let it be generally known that your case had already been settled. But it will go through very soon; indeed I have no doubt that by the time you read these lines the thing will have been done. Pansa, a responsible and reliable person, assured me, in fact guaranteed, that he would procure the passport in no time. Nevertheless I thought I should tell you all this, for the way your dear Eppuleia spoke and Ampia's[699] tears make it evident that you are not in such stout heart as your letters suggest. Moreover, they think your trouble of mind will grow much worse now that they are no longer with you. So I considered it highly desirable to relieve your anxiety and distress by giving you the facts fully and definitely, since definite they are.

You know that in my earlier letters I have sought to console you as a brave, sensible man rather than hold out any assurance of restoration, apart from what I thought should be hoped for from the commonwealth itself, once this conflagration has been extinguished. Remember your own letters, in which you have always shown me a lofty spirit, steadfast and ready for whatever might betide. That gave me no surprise, recalling as I did that you have been engaged in public affairs from your youth upwards, that your periods of office have coincided with the very crises of our national fortunes and existence,[700] and that you embarked on this very war prepared for the role not only of happy winner but, should it so fall out, of philosophic loser. Since, furthermore, you devote your literary activity to recording the deeds of brave men for posterity, it behoves you to consider it your duty not to present yourself as in any way dissimilar to the objects of your eulogies.

Such words, however, would be more appropriate to a state of things which you have already left behind you. As matters now stand, you have only to prepare yourself to bear conditions here along with us. If I knew any remedy for them, I should pass it on to you. But the one refuge is learning and literary work, which we have always pursued. Merely a source of pleasure in good times, it now appears as our life-line.

But to return to my starting-point: have no doubt that all is settled for your restoration and return.

699. Ampius' wife and (probably) daughter. Apparently they had been with him but had recently returned to Italy.

700. Ampius was Tribune in Cicero's Consulship (63) and Praetor in Caesar's (59).

227 (VI. 13)

CICERO TO Q. LIGARIUS

Rome, August or September (?) 46

From Cicero to Ligarius.

In your present circumstances I owed it to our friendship to write to you something that might bring comfort or help, but hitherto I have not done so, because I did not see how my words could assuage or alleviate your distress. But now that I have begun to entertain high hopes that we shall soon have you back in your rightful place, I feel I must make clear to you both my opinion and my disposition.

First then, let me say that, as my understanding and perception tell me, Caesar will not be over-hard on you. Circumstances, time, public opinion, and, I think, his own nature make him more lenient every day. This I feel where others are concerned, and as regards yourself I also hear it from his most intimate friends. Ever since the news[701] arrived from Africa, I have never stopped pleading with them in conjunction with your brothers. *Their* high character, family feeling, conspicuous affection for you, and assiduous, unflagging concern for your rehabilitation are producing an effect; so much so that I believe there is nothing which Caesar himself will not concede. But if it goes more slowly than we wish, the heavy pressure of business upon him as the recipient of all petitions has made access to him more difficult, and at the same time he was especially irritated by the resistance in Africa, and seems inclined to prolong the anxieties of those who he feels caused himself protracted difficulty and annoyance. But in this too I understand that every day makes him more tolerant and forgiving. So

701. Of the battle of Thapsus (6 April); or possibly of Ligarius' subsequent capture at Hadrumetum.

trust me, and make a mental note of my assurance that you will not long remain in your present disagreeable position.

Having told you what I think, I shall make plain my friendly disposition towards you by deed rather than word, though if I had as much say as I ought to have in a state which I have served as you rate my services, you too would not be in this unpleasant situation. The same cause that has brought your civic existence into peril has dissolved the power I used to have. Nevertheless, whatever the shadow of my old prestige and the residue of my influence may count for, my zeal, advice, time, influence, money, and loyalty shall be at the disposal of your excellent brothers in all things.

You have always had a stout heart. Keep it now, partly for the reasons I have given and partly because of the political aims and sentiments you have always held. In view of these, not only ought you to hope for a favourable outcome now but, even if everything were against you, the consciousness of your past acts and motives should strengthen you to bear whatever may betide with fortitude and magnanimity.

228 (VI. 14)

CICERO TO Q. LIGARIUS

Rome, end of November 46

From Cicero to Ligarius.

Be assured that I am devoting all my effort, all my time, attention, and energy to your restitution. I have always had the greatest regard for you, and the conspicuous family loyalty and fraternal affection shown by your brothers, whose friendship I have embraced no less warmly than your own, do not permit me to omit any act or occasion of service and good-will towards you. But what I am doing, and have done, on your behalf I prefer you to learn from their letters rather than from mine. My hope, or rather, my confident assurance, of your restoration is what I want personally to make clear to you.

If any man tends to be apprehensive in affairs of moment and danger, always fearing the worst rather than hoping for the best, I am that man. If this is a failing, I confess that I am not immune from it. But I tell you this: on 26 November, at your brothers' request, I paid Caesar a morning visit. I had to put up with all the humiliating and wearisome preliminaries of obtaining admission and interview. Your brothers and relations knelt at his feet, while I spoke in terms appropriate to your case and circumstances. When I took my leave, it was with the persuasion, not only from Caesar's words, gentle and gracious as these were, but from the look in his eyes and many other indications more easily perceived than described, that there was no doubt about your reinstatement.

So keep a brave and lofty spirit. If you have been taking the foulest weather with philosophy, take the fairer with good cheer. Despite what I have told you, I shall lend my support to your cause as though it was one of the utmost difficulty, and shall continue to plead for you most gladly, not only with Caesar himself but with all his friends, whom I have found very friendly to me.

Goodbye.

229 (IV. 8)

CICERO TO M. MARCELLUS

Rome, August 46

From M. Cicero to M. Marcellus greetings.

I do not venture to offer advice to a man of your exemplary sagacity, or encouragement to the noblest and bravest of souls; and certainly I must not attempt consolation. If you are bearing all that has befallen as I am told you are, I ought rather to congratulate you on your manly spirit than to comfort your distress. If, on the other hand, you are bowed by the weight of the public calamities, I cannot boast such ingenuity as to find comfort for you when I can find none for myself. All that remains then is for me to proffer and render my services to you in all things and to be at the disposal of your family in any way they may desire, holding myself bound to do on your behalf not only whatever I can but what I cannot as well.

One thing though I will say, and you may take it as a piece of advice or as an expression of opinion, or you may suppose that the good-will I have for you made it impossible for me to keep silence: I hope you will come round to the view I take in my own case, that if there is to be some form of commonwealth, you ought to be in it, as one of its leaders in virtue of public opinion and reality, but of necessity yielding to the conditions of the time; whereas if there is no commonwealth, Rome is still a better place than any other, even for passing one's exile. After all, if liberty is our object, where does this ruler's writ not run? But if we are merely looking for a place to live, what is more pleasant than hearth and home? But believe me, even he in whom all power resides is well disposed towards talent; and as for birth and rank, he cherishes them so far as circumstances and his own political position allow.

But I am saying more than I had intended. Let me return then to the single point, that I am at your service. I shall stand with those near to you, if near they really are. Otherwise, I shall at any rate do no less in all things than is due to our friendship and mutual affection.

Goodbye.

230 (IV. 7)

CICERO TO M. MARCELLUS

Rome, September (?) 46

From M. Cicero to M. Marcellus greetings.

Your policy hitherto, as I understand it, is one with which I do not venture to find fault – not that I do not disagree with it, but because I think too highly of your wisdom to prefer my opinion to yours. However, the length of our friendship and your notable kindness towards me, of which I have had evidence ever since you were a boy, urge me to write to you in terms which I believe to be conducive to your welfare and judge not incompatible with your honour.

I very well remember that I am addressing a man who saw the seeds of these calamities long before they ripened; nor do I forget your fine and splendid record as Consul. But this is not all. I also saw your dissatisfaction, the utter lack of confidence you always felt in the way the civil war was conducted, in Cn. Pompeius' forces, in the type of army he led. I think you remember that I held the same views. Accordingly, you took little part in the conduct of operations, and I was always careful to take none. We were not fighting with the weapons with which we might have prevailed – policy, prestige, cause. In these lay our superiority, but we fought with brute force, in which we were outmatched. So we were vanquished, or, if moral standing cannot be vanquished, at any rate broken and cast down. Your reaction to that outcome cannot fail of high and universal acclaim. With the hope of victory you discarded the desire of combat, and showed that a wise man and a patriot will join with reluctance in the opening stages of a civil war, but willingly decline to pursue it to the end. Those who followed a different plan from yours manifestly split into two categories. Some, those who betook themselves to Africa, tried to resuscitate the war; others, like myself, committed themselves to the victor. You chose a middle way; you thought the former course savoured of obstinacy, the latter perhaps of pusillanimity.

I allow that your plan is generally, or shall I say universally, judged wise, and that many think it high-minded and courageous as well. But there is a limit, so at least it seems to me, to your present line of conduct; especially as I believe there is nothing except lack of will to hinder you from the enjoyment of all that is yours. For it is my understanding that the personage in whose hands power lies would not be hesitating but for one reason, a fear that you might not regard it as a favour at all.

My own opinion on this subject it is needless to state, since my action is manifest. None the less, even suppose you had determined to prefer perpetual absence to the sight of what you did not wish to see, you ought still to have reflected that, wherever you were, you would be in the power of the very man whose presence you avoided. Assume it were the case that he would be content to let you live a quiet, independent life far from your country and all that is yours, you would still have to ask yourself whether you would rather live in Rome, in your own house, under whatever conditions, than in Mytilene or Rhodes. But the power of him we fear is world-wide. Do you not prefer safety at your own hearth to danger at a stranger's? For my part, I would rather face death, if need were, at home in my country than as a stranger in a foreign land.

This view is shared by all who care for you – a mighty throng, to match your great and splendid qualities. We are also thinking of your private fortune, which we do not want to see dissipated. True, you can suffer no damage of a permanent sort, because neither the ruler of the commonwealth nor the commonwealth itself will tolerate that. All the same, I do not wish to see the pirates make an onslaught on your estate. I should not baulk at naming them if I were not confident that you know whom I mean.[702]

Here your best of cousins, C. Marcellus, intercedes for you as none other, with anxious thought, yes, and constant flow of tears. I stand next in solicitude and distress, but in supplication I am less forward because, having needed intercession myself, I do not have the right of approach, and my influence is that of a member of a vanquished party. But my counsel and zeal are at Marcellus' disposal. Your other relatives do not call me in. I am ready to do anything.

231 (IV. 9)

CICERO TO M. MARCELLUS

Rome, shortly after the foregoing

From M. Cicero to M. Marcellus greetings.

It is only a very few days since I gave Q. Mucius a letter for you of considerable length in which I made clear how I thought you ought to feel and what I thought you ought to do. But since your freedman Theophilus is setting out, whose loyalty and good-will towards you I have plainly seen, I did not wish him to go to you without a letter from me.

So once again, I urge you on the same points as in my previous letter, to choose without delay to live in whatever commonwealth we have. You will perhaps see much that you do not like, but no more than you *hear* every day. And it is not worthy of you to be affected by one sense only, that of sight, and to be less troubled when you perceive the very same thing

---

702. We do not know. M. Marcellus himself complains of the disloyalty of his family and friends, apart from his cousin (Letter 232 (IV.11)).

with your ears, although what is so perceived is apt to seem even bigger than it really is.

Perhaps you are afraid of having yourself to say things you do not mean, or do things you disapprove. Well, in the first place, to yield to the pressures of the time, that is, to obey necessity, has always been considered a wise man's part. In the second, this particular evil, at present anyway, is not in the case. One is not free, it may be, to say what one thinks, but one is quite free to keep silence. All power has been handed over to one man; and he follows no counsel, not even that of his friends, except his own. It would not have been very different if *our* leader[703] ruled the commonwealth. In the war, when all of us were united in danger, he followed his own judgement and that of certain persons by no means conspicuous for their good sense. Are we to suppose that he would have been more democratically minded in victory than he was when the issue hung in the balance? When you were Consul he did not follow your admirable advice; and when your cousin administered the office under your guidance, he would not make you his counsellors. If he were now supreme, do you suppose he would feel any need of our opinions?

In civil war, never once experienced by our forbears but often by our own generation, all things are sad, but none sadder than victory. Even if it goes to the better party, it makes them more fierce and violent; though they may not be so by nature, they are forced to it willy-nilly. For the victor has often to act even against his inclination at the behest of those to whom he owes his victory. Did you not see as I did how cruel that other victory would have proved? Would you *then* have kept away from your country for fear of seeing what you would not have liked? 'No,' you will say, 'for I myself should have retained my wealth and status.' Surely to a man of your moral stature his own affairs count as trifles, his deeper concern is for the commonwealth.

703. Pompey.

And then, where does this policy of yours end? So far your conduct is approved, and even your fortune is held to be good in the circumstances: the first, because you joined in the opening of the civil war of necessity and wisely declined to persevere to the end; the second, because you have retained your high standing and reputation in honourable retirement. But now no place should have more charms for you than your country, and you must not love her the less because her beauty is marred. You ought rather to pity her, and not deprive her of the sight of you also, bereft as she is of so many illustrious children.

Furthermore, if refusal to supplicate the victor was nobility of spirit, are you sure it is not pride to spurn his generosity? If it is wisdom to keep away from your country, is it not insensibility not to miss her? If you may not be able to enjoy public life, is it not foolish to refuse to enjoy your private fortune?

The capital point is this: if you feel the life you are leading suits you better, you must still consider whether it is equally secure. Swords are loose in their scabbards nowadays; but abroad there are fewer scruples to check a deed of violence.

In my concern for your safety I can claim to rival, or at any rate to approach, your cousin Marcellus. It is for you to take thought for your present circumstances, your status as a citizen, your life, and your estate.

232 (IV. 11)

M. MARCELLUS TO CICERO

Mytilene, October 46

From Marcellus to Cicero greetings.

That your advice has always weighed heavily with me you can judge from all previous experience, but the matter in hand is a notable example. My cousin C. Marcellus, who is dearly fond of me, not only advised, but begged and implored me; yet he could not persuade me until your letter determined me to follow your joint judgement rather than any other.

The letters I have had from you both tell me how the affair went through. I cordially accept your congratulations because of the friendly spirit in which they are offered; but I am far more pleased and grateful to find that, when so very few of my friends and relatives and connections sincerely wished for my restoration, you have shown such conspicuous affection and good-will towards me. As for the rest, it is such that, given the times, I was quite well content to do without it. But *this* is another matter; without the good-will of such men and such friends as you, nobody, in my judgement, can truly live, whether in good fortune or bad. So herein I do congratulate myself; and I shall not fail to give you substantial proof that the man to whom you have rendered your service is your very sincere friend.

Goodbye.

233 (IV. 10)

CICERO TO M. MARCELLUS

Rome, December 46 (?)

From Cicero to Marcellus greetings.

I have no news to give you, and was in fact beginning to expect a letter from you, or rather you yourself in person; but since Theophilus is leaving, I could not let him go without something in the way of a letter. Be sure then to come as soon as you can. Your coming, believe me, is eagerly awaited, not only by us your friends but by every man in Rome. I am sometimes visited by a sneaking apprehension that you are disposed to take your time about your homecoming. If your

eyes were your only organ of perception, I should quite forgive you for preferring to avoid the sight of certain individuals.
But things heard are not much less vexatious than things seen,
and I suspect that your early arrival will be much to the advantage of your private estate; and the same applies from all other
points of view. So I have thought it right to say a word in
season. But having made my opinion plain, I leave the rest to
your wise consideration. I should, however, be grateful if you
would let me know when we may expect you.

234 (VI. 6)

CICERO TO A. CAECINA[704]

Rome, October (?) 46

From M. Cicero to A. Caecina greetings.

I fear you may think me negligent, which I have no business
to be towards a friend to whom I am bound by many obligations and by pursuits in common; still, I fear you find me a
neglectful correspondent. I should have written long ago and
often but that, as my hopes rose higher day by day, I wanted to
send you a letter of congratulation rather than one of moral
encouragement. As matters stand, I hope to congratulate you
soon, and so I defer that theme to another occasion.

In *this* letter I think I should use yet again the influence I
command with you, not indeed as one much wiser than the
ordinary but as a most sincere friend, to fortify your spirit;
though, from what I hear and hope, it is very far from feeble. I
shall not console you as a man undone beyond all hope of
recovery, but as one of whose rehabilitation I feel no more
doubt than I remember you used to feel of mine. For I recall

704. Now in Sicily, awaiting Caesar's permission to return to Italy.

that, after my expulsion from the commonwealth by those who believed it could not fall so long as I stood upright, many travellers coming to me from Asia, where you were at the time, told me how confidently you predicted my speedy and glorious return. Now if *you* had a system which did not mislead you, based on the marvellous lore of Etruria as imparted to you by your noble and excellent father, no more shall I be led astray by my prophetic skill. I gained it not only from the admonitions and precepts of sages and by assiduous theoretical study, as you know, but also by my long experience as a statesman and the remarkable vicissitudes of my career. My reliance upon it is the more secure because in all these dark and perplexed transactions it has never once deceived me. I would give you examples of my predictions, were I not afraid of being thought to have manufactured them *ex post facto*. However, there are witnesses in abundance to attest that I originally advised Pompey against allying himself with Caesar, and later against dissolving the alliance. I saw that the alliance broke the power of the Senate, whereas its dissolution spelt civil war. I was on the closest terms with Caesar, and held Pompey in the greatest regard; but my advice was loyal to Pompey and salutary to both.

Of my other previsions I say nothing, because I would not have our present ruler, who has been very good to me, think that I gave counsels to Pompey which, had Pompey heeded them, would have meant that he himself would indeed be enjoying a position of distinction and leadership in civil life, but would not be holding so much power as is now his. I recommended that Pompey should go to Spain.[705] Had he done so, there would have been no civil war. I did not so much contend that Caesar should be granted permission to stand for office in his absence as that his candidature should in fact be admitted, seeing that at Pompey's own urging during his Consulship the

705. Perhaps in January 49, immediately before war broke out. Earlier Cicero had been against Pompey going to Spain (cf. *Letters to Atticus* 104 (V.11).4).

People had so ordered.[706] A pretext[707] for war arose. Did I leave anything undone in the way of warning or protest in advocating the most inequitable peace as preferable to the most righteous of wars? My advice was overborne, not so much by Pompey, on whom it made an impression, as by persons who in reliance on Pompey's generalship conceived that victory in such a war would be highly opportune for their personal affairs and ambitions. When hostilities were joined I remained passive, and I stayed in Italy as long as I was able after they had been shifted elsewhere. But sensibility prevailed with me over fear. I was ashamed to fail Pompey in his hour of need, when he in time gone by had not failed me. Duty then, or my reputation with the honest men, or sensibility carried the day. Like Amphiaraus[708] in the plays I set out

> witting full well,
> To bane right plain to see.

And no reverse befell us in that war which I did not predict.

Well then, since after the manner of augurs and astrologers I have established with you, as a public Augur, the credit of my augural and divinatory claims on the basis of my past predictions, my prophecy will be entitled to respect. I do not make it from the flight of one kind of ominous bird or the left-hand cry of another, as our system prescribes, nor yet from *tripudia solistima* or *sonivia*;[709] I have other signs to watch – no

706. In 52 the ten Tribunes had carried a law allowing Caesar to stand for the Consulship *in absentia*. Pompey backed it and Cicero assisted (*Letters to Atticus* 124 (VII.1).3).

707. The flight of the two Tribunes, Antony and Q. Cassius, to Caesar's camp on 7 January 49.

708. In the legend of the Seven against Thebes the seer Amphiaraus was persuaded by his wife Eriphyle to join the Argive expedition though he knew it would end in disaster. The quotation that follows may be from Accius' tragedy *Eriphyle*.

709. Omens taken from food dropping from the mouths of the sacred chickens.

surer, perhaps, but less difficult to perceive and less readily mistaken. For the purpose of my divining the signs are observed in two categories, one deriving from Caesar's personality, the other from the general nature of political conditions. In Caesar we find a mild and merciful disposition, as portrayed in your excellent volume of *Remonstrances*.[710] Moreover, he is remarkably partial to outstanding talents like your own. He also defers to a widespread sentiment, when it is just and inspired by principle, not frivolous or self-interested; and in that connection he will be powerfully impressed by the united voice of Etruria. Why then have these factors hitherto failed of their due effect? Because he reckons he will be unable to resist a multitude of claims if once he gives way to you, with whom he is supposed to have more right to be angry. You will ask what in that case we have to hope for from an angry arbiter. This: he will realize that he is going to draw his praises from the fountain that sprinkled him with cold water. Finally, he is a very clever, far-sighted man. He realizes that a man like you, of birth easily the highest in your part of Italy, which is a very far from contemptible part, and in our common body politic equal to any of the best of your generation in talent, influence, and public reputation, cannot be barred from the commonwealth in the long run. He will not wish you to owe your eventual restoration to time rather than to himself straight away.

Having spoken of Caesar, I pass to the nature of things and circumstances. Nobody is so unfriendly to the cause which Pompey espoused with more spirit than forethought as to dare to call us bad citizens or scoundrels. In this connection I often admire Caesar's responsibility, fairness, and good sense. He never mentions Pompey's name except in the most respectful

710. Caecina had written a 'very libellous' (so Suetonius, *Iul.* 75) book against Caesar during the war. Later he tried to make amends by a book of 'Remonstrances' (*querelarum*), extolling Caesar's merciful disposition.

terms. It may be said that he has committed many acts of harshness towards Pompey, but these were the work of war and victory, not of Caesar personally. And think how he has taken us into his favour: Cassius made his Legate, Brutus appointed to Cisalpine Gaul, Sulpicius to Greece, Marcellus, against whom he was especially incensed, restored in a fashion most honourable to Marcellus himself. All this I mention to show that it would be intolerable to the nature of things and political circumstances and incompatible with existing policy or any change of policy (a) that all men engaged in the same cause should not receive the same treatment and lot, and (b) that honest men and good citizens, to whom no stigma of disgrace has been attached, should not return to a community which has readmitted so many found guilty of heinous crimes.

There then is my augury. If I felt any uncertainty about it, I should not employ it in preference to a different consolation, which I might easily offer a brave man to sustain his spirits. If you took up arms for the state (as you then thought) in a full assurance of victory, your conduct would not be particularly praiseworthy; but if you recognized the possibility of defeat, the issues and events of warfare being uncertain, you ought not to have been fully prepared for good fortune but quite unable to bear bad. I should also speak of the comfort you should find in your conscience, and the pleasure in adversity which literary work should provide. I should recall the melancholy fates not only of men long dead but of your own late leaders and comrades. I should cite many celebrated names from the history of foreign peoples; for a reminder of the common law, so to speak, and the condition of humanity makes sorrow weigh less heavily. I should also set forth our mode of life here, where all is turmoil and confusion. After all, one cannot but miss a ruined commonwealth less keenly than a sound one. But nothing in this style is called for. As I hope, or rather as I perceive, we shall shortly see you restored to your rights.

Meanwhile, I long ago promised you in your absence and

that present mental and physical image of you, your steadfast and excellent son, my support and friendly offices, my time and trouble; and they have been at your disposal. I do so now in larger measure, because Caesar's attitude towards me is every day more expressive of the warmest friendship, while his intimates pay me a quite unparalleled regard. Whatever influence I come to have with him, whether public or private, it shall be for your behoof. Do you keep up your spirits, not only in fortitude of mind but in the brightest of hope.

235 (VI. 8)

CICERO TO A. CAECINA

Rome, December 46

From Cicero to Caecina.

Largus, who is much concerned for your welfare, told me when we met that the Kalends of January had been fixed as the limit of your stay. Having observed in all sorts of contexts that Caesar is in the habit of confirming arrangements made by Balbus and Oppius in his absence, I made strong representations to them that as a favour to myself you should be allowed to stay in Sicily as long as we wished. Usually I find they readily agree to anything that does not fall foul of their own ideas, or else they say no and give their reason. But to this request of mine, or rather urgent demand, they made no immediate reply. However, later the same day they came back, and gave me their assurance that you shall stay in Sicily as long as you like, personally guaranteeing that you will incur no disfavour thereby.

Now that you know what you *may* do, I think I ought to tell you what in my view you ought to do. After the aforesaid transactions I received a letter from you in which you ask my advice; do I think you should stay where you are in Sicily or set off to see to what remains of your business in Asia? This deliberation on your part did not seem to me consistent with what Largus had said. He had spoken to me as though it was not open to you to stay in Sicily indefinitely, whereas you pose your question as though you had permission. But whichever is right, for my part I think you should remain in Sicily. Its proximity allows frequent interchange of letters and messengers, and is thus an advantage in the process of gaining your pardon. It will also enable you to come back quickly when that goes through, as I hope it will, or the business is settled in some other way. Therefore I strongly advise you to remain.

I shall particularly recommend you to my friend T. Furfanus Postumus and to his Legates, who are also friends of mine, when they return – they are all at Mutina. They are excellent people, with a regard for men like yourself and closely attached to me. Anything that occurs to me in furtherance of your interests I shall do without prompting. Certain points may lie outside my knowledge; once my attention is drawn to such, I shall press harder than anybody. I shall speak of you personally to Furfanus in a way which will make it needless for you to have a letter addressed to him from myself; but since your people thought it desirable that you should have a letter of mine to present to him, I have complied with their wish. I append a copy of the letter.

236 (VI. 9)

CICERO TO FURFANUS POSTUMUS

Rome, December 46

From M. Cicero to Furfanus, Proconsul, greetings.

My familiar friendship with A. Caecina has always been of

the most intimate. I had a great deal to do with his father, a gallant and distinguished gentleman, and have entertained a warm regard for Caecina himself ever since he was a boy, both for the high promise I saw in him of exceptional character and oratorical ability and from the closest association in common pursuits as well as the usual offices of friendship. There is no man with whom I have lived on closer terms.

There can be no need for me to write at greater length. You see how compelling an obligation I have to make every effort on behalf of his welfare in person and estate. It remains to say that, aware as I am from many indications of your sentiments concerning the plight of honest men and the misfortunes of the commonwealth, I shall only ask you to let my recommendation go to increase in a measure proportionate to the regard I know you have for me the good-will which you will bear Caecina spontaneously. You can render me no greater service.

Goodbye.

237 (VI. 7)

A. CAECINA TO CICERO

Sicily, December or early January 46

From Caecina to Cicero greetings.

As regards the delay in forwarding the book[711] to you, do please forgive our nervousness and sympathize with our situation. I hear that my son was afraid, and not unreasonably so,

711. Not the book of 'Remonstrances', which Cicero had already seen and praised, but a new production. From what follows it appears to have contained praise of Cicero, though less lavish than its author would have wished, and criticism of others. Since Caecina was a noted orator, it may have been on the subject of eloquence.

CICERO'S LETTERS TO HIS FRIENDS

that if the book got out, this might do me a stupid damage, seeing that it is the reader's attitude rather than the writer's that counts. And after all, I am still suffering for my pen.[712] Mine is a strange fate. A *lapsus calami* is removed by an erasure, folly is punished by talk; whereas my mistake is corrected by exile! And the sum total of my offence is that as a fighting soldier I said nasty things about the enemy! None of us, I dare say, but made his vows to Victory – *his* victory – and, even when offering a sacrifice to the Gods in some other connection, used at the same time to pray for Caesar's speedy defeat. If he does not think of this, he's a happy man all round! If he knows and is persuaded of it, why is he angry with somebody for writing something to his displeasure, when he has pardoned all the folk who often prayed heaven for his destruction?

But to resume, the reason for our nervousness was this: I have written about yourself, sparingly and gingerly enough upon my word,[713] not only keeping myself in check but almost running the other way. Now we all know that this type of composition[714] calls for freedom, indeed for excitement and enthusiasm. Restraint is thought out of place in an *attack* upon another person; all the same one has to be on one's guard against degenerating into bullying. Praise of *self* is held to be fraught with embarrassment – the vice of arrogance is at its heels. Only praise of others is regarded as completely uninhibited, for any stinting is ascribed to fickleness or jealousy. But perhaps it was more agreeable and convenient to you so. What I could not do supremely well it would have been best to leave alone, but the second-best kindness was to do it very sparingly. Anyhow, restrain myself I did. Much I toned down, deleted much else, and there was a good deal that never got on paper. Think of a ladder. If you take away some of the rungs, and hack into others, and leave others loose, you will be setting a booby-

712. i.e. the attack on Caesar written during the war.
713. Inhibited presumably by fear of offending Caesar.
714. Eulogy of another person.

406

trap, not constructing a means of ascent. So with my literary endeavour. Clogged and fractured by so many adversities, how can it produce anything fit to hear or worthy of approval?

Coming to the name of Caesar himself, I tremble from head to foot for fear, not of punishment, but of his critical opinion. Of Caesar I know personally nothing at all. Imagine my feelings when I take counsel with myself: 'He'll like *that*. But *this* word might be misconstrued. Well then, suppose I change it – but I'm afraid I may make matters worse.' Now then, I praise so-and-so: am I giving offence? Again, when I criticize, suppose he doesn't like it. He persecutes a fighting man for his pen; what will he do to a beaten enemy, still under sentence of banishment? You yourself add to my apprehension, when I see you in your *Orator* making Brutus your shield and casting about apologetically for a partner.[715] When every man's advocate behaves so, what am *I* to feel, your old client[716] and now every man's? Armed against all contingencies by superlative genius, you may not know by experience how difficult it is to make a tolerable showing in such a torment of self-induced anxiety and groping surmise, writing for most of the time not as one's judgement directs but with a view to the probable effect on another person's mind. I *feel* it. However, I did tell my son to read the volume to you and then take it away, or else to give it to you on condition that you undertook to correct it, that is, to make a totally different book of it.

Concerning the trip to Asia, despite the urgent and compelling character of my business, I have done as you commanded.

I do not need to urge you on my own behalf. You see that the time has arrived when a decision on my case must be made. There is no call, my dear Cicero, for you to wait for my son. He is a young man. Eagerness, youth, and anxiety make it

715. In allusion to Cicero's statement in the *Orator* (35) that his eulogy of Cato was written at Brutus' instigation.

716. Probably a reference to Cicero's (extant) speech on behalf of the writer's father.

impossible for him to think everything out. *You* must carry the whole affair. My entire hope lies in you. In your sagacity you know the kind of thing that gives Caesar pleasure and wins him over. The whole campaign must start with you and be conducted by you to the finish. You have much influence with himself, and more with his whole circle. If only you make up your mind that it is not only your business to do what is asked of you (though that is a great deal in all conscience), but that the whole load is yours to bear, you will succeed. Or do I act like a fool in my present sorry state, or presume too far upon friendship, when I saddle you so? But your habit of conduct offers an excuse for both. You are so indefatigable on your friends' behalf that they have come not merely to hope for your help as I do, but to demand it as I am doing.

As for the book which my son will give you, let me beg of you not to let it get into circulation, or else to revise it in such a way that it can do me no damage.

238 (XIII. 66)

CICERO TO SERVILIUS ISAURICUS

Rome, December 46 (?)

From M. Cicero to P. Servilius greetings.

Since A. Caecina is a particularly attached client of your family, and since I know how loyal you are to those connected with you and how merciful to the unfortunate, I should not be recommending him to you, were it not that the memory of his father, who was on very close terms with me, and his own adversity affects me as it ought in the case of a person with whom I have the most intimate and comprehensive ties of common pursuits and good offices. May I request you with all urgency – I could ask nothing with more earnestness and concern of mind – to let my letter add a little extra to what you would have done of your own accord, without anybody's recommendation, for so eminent and worthy a person in distress, hoping that on this account you will assist him all the more actively in any way you can?

If you had been in Rome, my opinion is that we should actually have obtained A. Caecina's pardon through your intercession. However, I have high hopes of this, founded on the merciful disposition of your colleague.[717] As matters stand, since in his reliance on your sense of justice he has chosen your province as his securest haven, I would entreat you once again to assist him in gathering together the remnants of his old business, and to give him in other ways the benefit of your shield and support. You can do nothing to oblige me more.

239 (VI. 5)

CICERO TO A. CAECINA

Rome, January 45 (?)

From M. Cicero to A. Caecina greetings.

Whenever I see your son, and I see him practically every day, I promise him my zeal and service, without reservation as to work or pressure of business or time; my personal and public influence I promise with the reservation 'so far as it extends, so far as I can'.

I have read, and am reading, your book carefully, and am keeping it most carefully in custody. Your affairs and fortunes are the object of my closest solicitude. They look to me to be in daily process of easement and amelioration; and I notice that many people have them much at heart. I am sure your son has

717. Caesar, as Consul in 48.

written to you in detail of the support given by these persons and of his own hopes.

As for what lies in the sphere of conjecture, I do not pretend myself to see more ahead than I take to be apparent to your vision and understanding. But since it may be that you consider the prospects under a greater mental stress, I think I ought to set out my impressions. The nature of things and the trend of events make it impossible that this plight in which you and others find yourselves should be of long duration. So cruel an injustice to good citizens in a good cause cannot last. The hope we entertain in all such cases is reinforced by that which applies peculiarly to yourself: not only on account of your standing and wealth, distinctions you possess in common with others, but what is additional and special to yourself, your outstanding talents and qualities, attributes of much importance, I do assure you, in the eyes of the personage in whose power we lie. You would not have been a moment in your present predicament if he had not thought himself injured by the very gift[718] of yours that pleases him. But his resentment grows milder every day, and his associates intimate to me that your literary reputation will in fact count with him heavily in your favour.

First, then, you must keep a stout heart and a lofty spirit. One born, educated, taught, and I may add, proved, as you have been can do no less. Second, you must be confidently hopeful, for the reasons I have given. Please rest assured that I am most ready to assist you and your children in every way. I owe it to our long-standing affection, and my habits of behaviour to my friends, and your many services to me.

718. Skill as a writer.

240 (IV. 14)

CICERO TO CN. PLANCIUS

Rome, winter of 46–45 (?)

From M. Cicero to Cn. Plancius greetings.

I have received two letters from you, dispatched at Corcyra. In one you felicitate me on hearing that I maintain my former standing. In the other you wish me good fortune and prosperity in the step I have taken.[719]

Well, if 'standing' means to feel as a loyal citizen and to have one's sentiments approved by honest men, then I do maintain my standing. But if it consists in the power to implement one's feelings, or even to speak freely in their defence, not a vestige of standing is left us. We have good cause for satisfaction if we can discipline our own selves to bear calmly evils both present and imminent. That is no easy matter in a war which threatens to end in massacre from one side or in slavery from the other.[720] In this peril I take some comfort in recollecting that I foresaw these consequences in the days when I feared our party's success as well as its disaster, and perceived the deadly danger involved in settling a constitutional issue by force of arms. If such force brought victory to those with whom I had associated myself, not desiring war but hoping for peace, I saw none the less the cruelty with which angry, greedy, and unbridled men would exploit it. On the other hand, I realized what their defeat would cost in the lives of our countrymen, some of the highest and some of the best too, men who, when I declared these views and advised in their own best interests, preferred

719. Cicero had divorced Terentia and married his young ward Publilia, only to divorce her a few months later.

720. Caesar was now fighting his last campaign against the republicans in Spain. Their victory would mean massacre, Caesar's slavery.

to have me considered unduly timid than reasonably far-sighted.

As for your felicitations on the step I have taken, I am sure your good wishes are sincere. But I should not have taken any new decision at so sad a time, if on my return I had not found my household affairs in as sorry a state as the country's. In my own house I knew no security, had no refuge from intrigue, because of the villainy of those to whom my welfare and estate should have been most precious in view of the signal kindnesses I had showered upon them. Therefore I thought it advisable to fortify myself by the loyalty of new connections against the treachery of old ones.

But there's enough or perhaps too much about *my* affairs. As for yours, I would have you think as you should, that is, you must not suppose that you have anything specially to fear. If there is to be a settlement of the community, of whatever nature, you will clearly be free of all hazards. One party is now appeased, as I gather, and the other you have never offended. As for my own disposition towards you, I should like you to feel assured of my support for your estate, reputation, and civil rights in all matters where it seems required. I am well aware of my present position and capabilities, but I can promise my service and advice, and certainly my zeal. I hope you will keep me informed as fully as possible of your activities and plans.

Goodbye.

241 (IV. 15)

CICERO TO CN. PLANCIUS

Rome, winter of 46–45

From M. Cicero to Cn. Plancius greetings.

A very brief letter from you has come to hand. I was unable to learn from it what I wanted to know; I did learn what I have never doubted. That is to say, it does not tell me with what courage you are facing the common lot of affliction, but your affection for me is plain to see. The latter, however, I knew. If I knew the former, I should frame my letter accordingly.

Nevertheless, although I have previously written what I thought proper to write, I feel I should now briefly advise you that you ought not to regard yourself as in any peculiar danger. All of us are in great danger, but we share it in common. So you must not demand a special, privileged lot, or reject the common one. Therefore let us feel towards one another as we have always felt. I hope you do, and can answer for myself.

242 (VI. 1)

CICERO TO TORQUATUS[721]

Rome, early January 45

From M. Cicero to A. Torquatus greetings.

In the present state of universal upheaval each one of us thinks his own lot the hardest and would rather be anywhere but where he is. Even so, I have no doubt that residence in Rome is

721. In Athens.

the worst of all for an honest man at the present time. True, wherever a man may be, his feelings are the same; public and private ruin fills him with the same bitterness. But the eyes add to the pain, forcing us to look at what others only hear and forbidding us to turn our thoughts away from our sorrows. So although you must be suffering from the absence of much that you miss, do free your spirit from the distress which I hear weighs upon you most heavily – that you are not in Rome. Painfully as you miss your people and possessions, the objects of your regret continue in their usual state, and would be in no better if you were here. They are in no special danger, and in thinking of what is yours you ought not to claim a privileged lot or reject the common one.

As for yourself, dear sir, when you revolve the situation, it would ill become you to take despair or fear into your mental council-chamber. The individual[722] who has been less fair to you hitherto than your personal eminence made incumbent has given no small indications of a softening in his attitude towards you. Yet he himself, from whom men beg their lives, has no plain assurance for his own. Bearing in mind that no war has a certain issue, I perceive that you have nothing to fear from the victory of the one side, apart that is from involvement in a universal destruction; from that of the other[723] I am sure that you yourself have never apprehended any danger.

There remains the possibility that what I am placing almost in the light of a consolation may constitute your chief torment – the general danger to the commonwealth. For so vast an evil I fear that, much as philosophers have to say on the subject, no true consolation is to be discovered, excepting one; and the efficacy of that one is in proportion to each individual's spiritual strength and energy. If an honest heart and rectitude of conduct suffice for the good and happy life, I ask myself whether it be not blasphemy to speak of a man who can rest upon an ex-

722. Caesar.
723. The republicans, whose cause had revived in Spain.

cellent political conscience as unfortunate. After all, I do not suppose it was for the prizes of victory that we left country, children, and estate years ago. We thought we were fulfilling a valid and sacred duty to the commonwealth and to our own public characters, and in thus acting we were not so deluded as to take victory for granted. So if what we knew *might* happen when we first embarked upon the struggle has come to pass, we ought not to let it deject us, as though a thing had come about which we never reckoned within the bounds of possibility. Let us then follow the dictates of truth and reason, not holding ourselves answerable for anything for which we are not to blame, and, so long as we are blameless, bearing all the chances of mortality with sober composure. The purport of what I am saying is that, when all is lost, virtue must still be thought capable of resting upon its own support. But if there is some hope for our communal affairs, you must have your share in it, whatever the nature of the settlement is to be.

As I write, it crosses my mind that it was you who used to challenge *my* despair, and whose bracing words raised me from hesitation and despondency. It was not our cause with which I found fault in those days, but the conduct of it. I saw that it was too late for us to oppose the military power which we ourselves had long ago made strong, and I was sorry that constitutional questions should be decided by spears and swords rather than by our counsels and characters. When I foretold what has come about, I had no prophetic vision; perceiving what *could* happen, and would be disastrous if it did, I feared it, especially since, if I had been obliged to predict the final outcome one way or the other, I could have predicted that which actually occurred with greater confidence. For while we were superior in matters extraneous to the battlefield, we were weaker in military experience and in the calibre of our troops. Well, pray now yourself take the courage which you used then to think I ought to display.

I write in this strain because your man Philargyrus told me

(in reply to my searching enquiries about you and, as it seemed to me, in a spirit of thorough loyalty) that you were subject to fits of rather severe depression. This ought not to happen. You ought not to doubt that either you will take your proper place in the commonwealth, if there is one, or, if that is lost, your state will be no more unhappy than anyone else's. You have two special reasons for self-control just now, when all of us are holding our breath in suspense: the city where you are residing is the mother and nurse of reason and restraint applied to the conduct of life; and you have Ser. Sulpicius, for whom you have always had a unique regard, at your side. I am sure his good-will and wisdom are a comfort to you. If we had followed his weighty advice, we should have succumbed to the power of a citizen[724] rather than to the sword of a conqueror.

But perhaps all this has been more prolix than was necessary. Let me put what is of greater moment more succinctly. I have nobody to whom I owe more than to yourself. There were others [725] to whom I owed much, you know how much; but the chances of this war have swept them away. Of my position at this time I am well aware. But nobody is in so sorry a case but that he can do yeoman service, if he applies himself whole-heartedly to the matter in hand. I hope you will believe that anything I can give in advice, time, and devotion at least is yours and your children's by right.

724. More strictly, 'a civilian'.
725. Pompey, Lentulus Spinther, Milo.

243 (VI. 3)

CICERO TO A. TORQUATUS

Rome, January 45

From M. Cicero to A. Torquatus greetings.

In my earlier letter I wrote at considerable length, more out of friendly feeling than because the case required it. Your manly spirit needed no fortifying by me; and in my present forlorn and unhappy predicament I am poorly qualified to fortify another. Now too I should be brief. If many words were unnecessary then, they are no more necessary today; if they were needed then, what I wrote is sufficient, particularly as no new development has supervened. Every day, to be sure, we hear some part of the events which I imagine are reaching your ears, but the sum total remains the same, as does the final outcome. I see it in my mind as plain as what we see with our eyes, but I am sure I see nothing which is not equally visible to you. The outcome of the battle nobody can divine, but I see the outcome of the war; or if not that, at any rate I see what the victory of either side will mean – and, after all, one or the other must win. Perceiving this very plainly, I find the picture such that, if what is presented as the ultimate terror[726] comes to pass even sooner, it will be no misfortune. For to live what would then be life is misery indeed; whereas no wise man ever counted it misery to die, even for the happy. But you are in a city where one fancies the very walls can say these things, only more, and more eloquently.

One thing I can tell you confidently, though it is a poor comfort that is founded on the miseries of others: you are in no greater danger now than any one of those who fought on or of those who gave up. The former are fighting, the latter fear

726. Death.

the victor. But that is a poor comfort. There is a better, of which I hope you avail yourself, as I certainly do. While I exist, nothing will give me pain, since I have nothing with which to reproach myself; and if I cease to exist, I shall feel nothing at all. But here I go again, sending an owl to Athens![727]

You and your family and your possessions are all the objects of my closest care, and shall be while I live.

Goodbye.

244 (VI. 4)

CICERO TO A. TORQUATUS

Rome, January 45

From M. Cicero to A. Torquatus greetings.

I have no news to tell you and anyhow, if there were any, I know your own people keep you informed. Of things to come it is always difficult to speak, but sometimes a guess can land near the mark, when the nature of the matter makes it possible to foresee the outcome. Now so much only seems clear, that the war will not last long – though even that is not everybody's opinion. At the time of writing I think something decisive has already taken place, but *what* – that is hard to guess. In every war the God of Battles fights in both ranks, and the outcome of a battle is always in doubt. But at the present time the forces on both sides are said to be so large and so ready to fight to the death that whichever of the two wins it will be no matter for surprise. One general conviction gains ground with every passing day: that even though there may be a certain amount to choose between the causes for which they are in arms, the victory of either side will amount to much about the same. One

727. See n. 515. Here the saying has additional point, in that Torquatus *was* in Athens.

set[728] we have by now pretty well experienced. As for the rival leader,[729] the formidable figure of an angry conqueror sword in hand is in everybody's mind.

Here I may seem to be adding to your distress, which I ought to console and alleviate. I must admit that I find no consolation for our common calamities, save one; but that one, if we can make it ours, is sovereign, and I myself have recourse to it more and more every day. I mean that the consciousness of honest intentions is a sovereign consolation in adversity, and that there is no great calamity apart from guilt. We are free of that. On the contrary our hearts have always been in the right place, and the issue of our course of action is deplored rather than the course itself. Having done our duty, let us bear the event without too much repining. However, I do not take it upon myself to console you for the common afflictions. They are such that consolation demands a greater intellect than mine, endurance an exceptional courage. But anyone may easily show why you ought not specially to distress yourself. A certain personage[730] has been slower to come to your relief than we might have expected, but I have no doubts about his purpose concerning your rehabilitation. As for the others,[731] I do not suppose you are waiting for me to express my opinon.

There remains the pain you feel at so long an absence from your friends and family – a loss indeed, especially those quite delightful boys. But as I wrote to you earlier, the times are such that every man thinks his own lot the hardest and would least wish to be where he actually is. For my part I rate us who are in Rome as most to be pitied, not merely because in all calamities it is more bitter to see than to hear but also because we are more exposed to every sudden, dangerous accident than if we were elsewhere.

728. The Caesarians.
729. Cn. Pompeius the younger.
730. Caesar.
731. The republicans.

Yet I, your comforter, have felt my grief assuaged not so much by the books to which I have always been devoted as by the passing of time. You remember how sorely distressed I was. My first consolation is that I saw further than others in desiring peace, on terms however unfavourable. That was chance, not any prophetic gift of mine; and yet the credit I get for foresight gratifies my vanity. And then, a comforting reflection which you and I have in common, if I were to be called upon to meet life's end, I should not be torn away from a commonwealth which I should grieve to lose, especially as the condition will be entirely unconscious. My age helps too, and all the years behind me. There is satisfaction in the thought of a race well run; I must not be afraid of violence at a juncture which I have now almost reached in the course of nature. Finally, when I think of the great man,[732] I might even say men, who perished in this war, I should feel shameless if I rebelled against a like fate, should it be forced upon me. To be sure I set all manner of contingencies before my mind; no catastrophe so terrible that I do not envisage it as imminent. But since fearing hurts us more than the actuality of what we fear, I desist. Besides, the impending doom will be painless, indeed it will be the end of pain.

However, I have written enough in this strain, or rather more than was necessary. But it is my friendly concern, not loquacity, that make my letters long.

I was sorry to hear of Servius' departure from Athens, for I don't doubt that you found daily meetings and talks with so close a friend and so excellent and wise a man a great solace. Let me hope that you fall back upon your own strength of mind, as is your duty and your wont. I shall give zealous and sedulous attention to anything I think to be your wish, or of concern to you and yours. In so doing I shall emulate your good-will towards me, but shall not equal your deserts.

Goodbye.

732. Pompey.

245 (VI. 2)

CICERO TO A. TORQUATUS

Atticus' villa near Nomentum, April 45

From M. Cicero to A. Torquatus greetings.

I beg you not to suppose that, if my letters come less frequently than of yore, it is because I have forgotten you. The cause lies in my poor health, though now I think it has a little improved, and my absence from Rome, which prevents me hearing of travellers to your whereabouts. So I want you to be sure once for all that I keep you in mind with the most friendly feelings and pay as much attention to all your affairs as to my own.

Considering the bad times we live in, you ought not, believe me, to take it hard that your case has hitherto gone through more ups and downs than was generally hoped or expected. There are three possible futures for the commonwealth: oppression in endless armed conflict, eventual revival when arms are laid aside, and complete annihilation. If arms are to prevail, you should not fear the side which is pardoning you, nor yet that which you assisted. If arms are laid aside on terms, and the state breathes once more, you will be free to enjoy your rank and fortune. If, however, the sum of things goes down to destruction, the end feared long ago by a very wise man, M. Antonius,[733] when he surmised the vast calamities to come, well then, you have the consolation (a sad one indeed, especially for a man and a Roman like yourself, but necessary) that in what happens to all the individual has no special reason for distress.

If you will carefully consider the significance implicit in

733. The orator (see Glossary of Persons).

these few words (more it would not have been wise to commit to a letter), you will realize, as I am sure you do without any letter of mine, that you have something to hope and nothing, in this or any other state of the commonwealth, to be afraid of; and that if all goes to ruin, you must bear what fortune sends, especially as your conscience is clear. For you would not wish to survive the commonwealth, even if that were possible. But I have written enough on this topic.

Please write and tell me of your doings and your future whereabouts, so that I may know where to write to or where to go.

246 (VI. 21)

CICERO TO TORANIUS[734]

Rome, January 45

From Cicero to Toranius.

As I write these lines to you, it looks as though the final issue of this most disastrous of wars is approaching; or it may be that a decisive action has already taken place. But every day I recall how you and I alone in that great army shared each other's views, and saw, as no one else did, with what an infinity of evil that war was charged. All hope of peace being excluded, even victory was bound to prove a most bitter experience, fraught with destruction to the vanquished and slavery to the victors. In those days such paragons of courage and wisdom as Domitius and Lentulus[735] used to call me timid – and so indeed I was; I was afraid that what has happened

734. C. Toranius had probably been Quaestor in 73 and Plebeian Aedile in 64, the latter as colleague of C. Octavius, who left him guardian to his son, the future Augustus. He was now in Corcyra.

735. Lentulus Crus, Consul in 49.

would come to pass. But today I have no fears, and am ready for any outcome. When it still seemed possible to make some provisions against the future, I was sorry to see the chance neglected. But now that all is topsyturvy and nothing can be achieved by policy, resignation to whatever may betide appears the only rational course; especially as death is the end of all, and my conscience tells me that I took thought for the dignity of the commonwealth so long as I could and, when that was lost, was fain to save its existence.

I have written thus, not in order to talk about myself, but to put the same thoughts into your mind, since your view and aims were very close to mine. It is a great consolation to remember that one has meant well and honestly, even though things have fallen out awry. I only hope we may one day enjoy some form of settled constitution and talk over our anxieties, as we did in the days when we were thought timid because we said that what has come would come.

As for your affairs, I assure you that you have nothing to fear apart from the destruction of the whole commonwealth. As for me, I hope you will determine that, so far as I can, I shall ever stand by you, and by the cause of your restoration, and by your children.

Goodbye.

247 (VI. 20)

CICERO TO TORANIUS

Summer of 45

From Cicero to Toranius.

Three days ago I gave a letter for you to Cn. Plancius' boys so I shall now write more briefly; and whereas in my earlier letter I offered you comfort, I am now going to offer advice.

I think you have no better course than to wait where you are until you can decide what to do. Besides the risk in a long, stormy voyage along a coast very poorly provided with harbours, which you will thus avoid, there is the infinitely important consideration that, when you do hear something definite, you can set out straight away from your present place of residence. Also there is no reason why you should be all agog to put yourself in their way as they[736] approach. And I have many other apprehensions, of which I have told our friend Cilo. In short, you could have found no more convenient place to stay in these distressing circumstances; for it is one you can leave and go wherever may be advisable with the maximum of ease and expedition. If *he* returns on time, you will be close at hand; whereas if something hampers or delays him (many things can happen), you will be where you can get all the news. This really does seem to me best.

For the rest, as I have often borne in upon you in my letters, I hope you will make up your mind that you have nothing to fear in your present situation over and above the general fate of the community. That, no doubt, is a very hard one, but considering the character of our lives and the age we have now reached, we ought to bear with fortitude anything that happens to us for which we are not responsible. All your family here are well. They miss you and love you and cherish you with the fondest affection. See you keep fit and do not move from where you are without good reason.

736. Caesar and his party returning from Spain.

APPENDIX I

(i) Roman Dates

UNTIL Julius Caesar reformed the calendar the Roman year consisted of 355 days divided into twelve months, all of which bore the Latin forms of their present names except Quintilis (= July) and Sextilis (= August). Each month had 29 days, except February with 28 and March, May, July, and October with 31. The first, fifth and thirteenth days of each month were called the Kalends (*Kalendae*), Nones (*Nonae*), and Ides (*Idus*) respectively, except that in March, May, July, and October the Nones fell on the seventh and the Ides on the fifteenth. I have kept these names in translation.

The calendar was adjusted by means of 'intercalation'. At the discretion of the College of Pontiffs, usually every other year, an 'intercalary' month of 23 or 22 days was inserted after 24 or 23 February. But in the years immediately before the Civil War the College neglected this procedure, so that by 46 the calendar was well over two months in advance of the sun. Julius Caesar rectified the situation by inserting two 'intercalary' months totalling 67 days between November and December of that year in addition to the traditional one in February. He also gave the months their present numbers of days, thus almost obviating the need for future intercalations, though in 1582 a further discrepancy had to be met by the institution of a Leap-Year.

(ii) Roman Money

The normal unit of reckoning was the sesterce (HS), though the denarius, equal to 4 sesterces, was the silver coin most generally in use. Differences of price structure make any transposition into modern currency misleading, but very roughly HS25 may be taken as equivalent to the debased pound sterling of 1974. Sometimes sums are expressed in Athenian currency. The drachma was about equal to the denarius, the mina (100 drachmae) to HS400, and the talent (60 minae) to HS2,400. The Asiatic cistophorus was worth about 4 drachmae.

(iii) Roman Names

A Roman bore the name of his clan (*gens*), the *nomen* or *nomen gentilicium*, usually ending in -*ius*, preceded by a personal name (*praenomen*) and often followed by a *cognomen*, which might distinguish different families in the same *gens*: e.g., Marcus Tullius Cicero. The *nomen* was always, and the *cognomen* usually, hereditary. Sometimes, as when a family split into branches, an additional *cognomen* was taken: e.g., Publius Licinius Crassus Dives. Other additional *cognomina* were honorific, sometimes taken from a conquered country as Africanus or Numidicus, or adoptive (see below). Women generally had only the one clan-name (e.g., Tullia), which they retained after marriage.

Only a few personal names were in use and they are generally abbreviated as follows: A. = Aulus; Ap(p). = Appius; C. = Gaius; Cn. = Gnaeus; D. = Decimus; L. = Lucius; M. = Marcus; M'. = Manius; N. = Numerius; P. = Publius; Q. = Quintus; Ser. = Servius; Sex. = Sextus; Sp. = Spurius; T. = Titus; Ti. = Tiberius (I omit one or two which do not occur in our text). The use of a *praenomen* by itself in address or reference is generally a sign of close intimacy, whether real or affected, but in the case of a rare or distinctive praenomen, as Appius and Servius, this is not so.

The practice of adoption, of males at any rate, was very common in Rome. According to traditional practice the adopted son took his new father's full name and added his old *nomen gentilicium* with the adjectival termination -*ianus* instead of -*ius*: e.g., C. Octavius, adopted by C. Julius Caesar, became C. Julius Caesar Octavianus. But in Cicero's time the practice had become variable. Sometimes the original name remained in use.

A slave had only one name, and since many slaves came from the East, this was often Greek. If freed, he took his master's *praenomen* and *nomen*, adding his slave-name as a *cognomen*: e.g., Tiro, when freed by M. Tullius Cicero, became M. Tullius Tiro. Occasionally the *praenomen* might be somebody else's. Atticus' slave Dionysius became M. Pomponius Dionysius in compliment to Cicero (instead of Titus).

Much the same applied to Greek or other provincials on gaining Roman citizenship. Such a man retained his former name as a *cognomen* and acquired the *praenomen* and *nomen* of the person to whom he owed the grant: e.g., the philosopher Cratippus became M. Tullius Cratippus after Cicero had got Caesar to give him the citizenship.

APPENDIX II

Consuls, 68–43 B.C.

68 L. Caecilius Metellus
Q. Marcius Rex

67 C. Calpurnius Piso
M'. Acilius Glabrio

66 M'. Aemilius Lepidus
L. Vulcatius Tullus

65 L. Aurelius Cotta
L. Manlius Torquatus

64 L. Julius Caesar
C. Marcius Figulus

63 M. Tullius Cicero
C. Antonius

62 D. Junius Silanus
L. Licinius Murena

61 M. Pupius Piso Frugi
M. Valerius Messalla Niger

60 Q. Caecilius Metellus Celer
L. Afranius

59 C. Julius Caesar
M. Calpurnius Bibulus

58 L. Calpurnius Piso Caesoninus
A. Gabinius

57 P. Cornelius Lentulus Spinther
Q. Caecilius Metellus Nepos

56 Cn. Cornelius Lentulus
Marcellinus
L. Marcius Philippus

55 Cn. Pompeius Magnus
M. Licinius Crassus

54 L. Domitius Ahenobarbus
Ap. Claudius Pulcher

53 Cn. Domitius Calvinus
M. Valerius Messalla

52 Cn. Pompeius Magnus
(Sole Consul)
. . . .
Q. Caecilius Metellus Pius
Scipio

51 Ser. Sulpicius Rufus
M. Claudius Marcellus

50 L. Aemilius Paulus
C. Claudius Marcellus

49 C. Claudius Marcellus
L. Cornelius Lentulus Crus

48 C. Julius Caesar
P. Servilius Isauricus

47 Q. Fufius Calenus
P. Vatinius

46 C. Julius Caesar
M. Aemilius Lepidus

45 C. Julius Caesar (Sole Consul)
. . . .
Q. Fabius Maximus (suffect)
C. Trebonius (suffect)
C. Caninius Rebilus (suffect)

44 C. Julius Caesar
M. Antonius
. . . .
P. Cornelius Dolabella (suffect)

43 C. Vibius Pansa Caetronianus
A. Hirtius

GLOSSARY OF PERSONS

The glossaries cover the whole correspondence, but references are to the *Letters to his Friends*, unless otherwise stated. A number of unimportant names are omitted. 'Nobles' are marked with an asterisk.

ACASTUS: Slave of Cicero's.

ACCIUS: Late second-century writer of Latin tragedies.

ACIDINUS: See MANLIUS.

ACILIUS (M. Acilius Caninus?): Caesarian officer, Proconsul in Sicily 46–45.

M'. ACILIUS Glabrio: Consul in 67.

ADIATORIX: Son of a Galatian Tetrarch under Deiotarus' suzerainty.

AEGYPTA: Freedman, apparently of Cicero's.

*L. AELIUS Lamia: Hereditary friend of Cicero's. As a prominent Knight, was banished from Rome by Gabinius in 58 for championing Cicero's cause. Later entered the Senate, becoming Aedile in 45 and probably Praetor in 43.

L. AELIUS Tubero: Friend and marriage connection of Cicero's and one of Q. Cicero's Legates in Asia. His son prosecuted Q. Ligarius in 45, Cicero defending.

M. AEMILIUS Avianianus: Friend of Cicero's known only from letters of recommendation.

*M'. AEMILIUS Lepidus: Consul in 66. Seems to have died in Italy during the Civil War.

*M. AEMILIUS Lepidus: Consul in 46 and one of Caesar's leading followers. After Caesar's death succeeded him as Chief Pontiff and became governor of Narbonese Gaul and Hither Spain in 44–43. Joined Antony and became Triumvir, Consul again in 42, and governor of Africa in 40–36. Forced by Octavian to retire from public life.

*L. AEMILIUS Paulus: Elder brother of the above and Consul in 50. Allegedly bought by Caesar. Probably neutral in the Civil War, he was proscribed by the Triumvirs but escaped to end his days in Miletus.

*M. AEMILIUS Scaurus: (1) Consul in 115 and Leader of the Senate.

*(2) His son, Praetor in 56. As candidate for the Consulship in 54 was successfully defended by Cicero on a charge of extortion in his province (Sardinia), but found guilty in a second trial for bribery (Cicero still defending) and disappeared into exile.

AESOPUS: See CLODIUS.

L. AFRANIUS (nicknamed 'Aulus' son'): Lieutenant of Pompey, who 'bought' him the Consulship of 60. Later governed Further Spain as Pompey's Legate and fought on his side in the Civil War. Perished in Africa after Caesar's victory in 46.

AFRICANUS: See CORNELIUS Scipio.

AGESILAUS: King of Sparta c. 401–360.

AHALA: See SERVILIUS.

C. ALBANIUS: Father-in-law of P. Sestius (manuscripts sometimes, and editors usually, call him Albinius).

ALEDIUS: Friend of Cicero's brother(?)-in-law Publilius in 46–45 and a strong Caesarian.

ALEXANDER: Of Ephesus, called Lychnus ('The Lamp'), perhaps contemporary with Cicero. Among other activities wrote poems on astronomy and geography, the latter named after the three continents.

ALEXIO: (1) Atticus' bailiff (?) in Epirus. (2) Cicero's doctor, who died in 45.

ALEXIS: Favourite slave or freedman of Atticus.

C. ALFIUS Flavus: Praetor (?) in 54.

A. ALLIENUS: Friend of the Ciceros. Praetor in 49 and a supporter of Caesar.

C. AMAFINIUS: Probably the first writer on Epicureanism in Latin, usually thought to have 'flourished' early in the first century.

AMMONIUS (Hammonius): Minister of Ptolemy the Piper and later (if the two are one) of Cleopatra.

T. AMPIUS Balbus: Praetor in 59 and governor of Asia the following year, then transferred to Cilicia. Henchman of Pompey and friend of Cicero, who probably obtained permission for him to return to Italy in 46.

C. ANICIUS: Senator and friend of Cicero.

T. ANICIUS: Agent of Q. Cicero.

M. ANNEIUS: Legate of Cicero in Cilicia.

T. ANNIUS Milo: As Tribune in 57 stoutly championed Cicero's recall and raised armed bands against Clodius. Candidate for the Consulship in 53, was condemned after Clodius' murder in January 52 and retired to Massilia. In 48 returned to Italy to take part in Caelius Rufus' rising and was killed.

ANTEROS: Name of one or more slaves in the Cicero family.

ANTIOCHUS: (1) Of Ascalon, contemporary Greek philosopher. Succeeded Philo as head of the Academy. (2) Literary clerk of Atticus. (3) King of Commagene.

ANTISTHENES: Disciple of Socrates and founder of the Cynic school.

Pacuvius 'ANTISTIUS' Labeo: One of Caesar's assassins, later Legate of M. Brutus, he ordered his slave to kill him after Philippi. His name was probably Pacuvius Labeo (praenomen unknown).

C. ANTISTIUS Reginus: Legate of Caesar in Gaul, apparently in charge of the western coast of Italy in 49 along with the younger Hortensius.

C. ANTISTIUS Vetus: Caesarian officer, in charge of Syria in 44. In 43 an Antistius Vetus figures as a friend of Brutus with republican sympathies. A C. Antistius Vetus was Consul-Suffect in 30 and became owner of Cicero's villa at Puteoli. Whether these are two or one is doubtful.

*C. ANTONIUS: (1) Caesar's colleague in the Consulship of 63, having previously been expelled from the Senate for rapacity and insolvency. Governor of Macedonia in 62–60. Condemned after his return to Rome, went into exile but lived to become Censor (!) in 42. Mark Antony was his nephew. *(2) Brother of Mark Antony. A Caesarian officer in the Civil War, became Praetor in 44. Captured in 42 by Brutus in Greece and later executed.

*L. ANTONIUS: Youngest brother of Mark Antony. Quaestor in 50 to Q. Minucius Thermus in Asia, Tribune in 44, and Consul in 41, when he and Antony's wife Fulvia started an unsuccessful war against Octavian in Italy. His life was spared but probably ended soon afterwards.

M. ANTONIUS: (1) Grandfather of Mark Antony, Consul in 99, and a celebrated orator. *(2) Mark Antony. Caesar's Quaestor in 51 and one of his principal lieutenants in the Civil War. Tribune in 49. Consul with Caesar in 44 and would-be successor to his power, he eventually formed the Triumvirate of 43 along with Octavian and Lepidus. Later quarrelled with Octavian and committed suicide after defeat at Actium (31).

APELLA: Freedman of M. Fabius Gallus (several other persons of this name crop up).

APELLES: The most famous painter of antiquity (late-fourth-century).

APOLLODORUS: Of Athens. Second-century writer of a historical chronicle in verse.

APPIUS: See CLAUDIUS.

M. APULEIUS: One of Gabinius' would-be prosecutors in 54, Augur and Quaestor in 45, Consul in 20.

AQUILA: See PONTIUS.

C. AQUILIUS Gallus: Praetor in 66 and an eminent jurist.

ARCHIAS: See LICINIUS.

ARCHILOCHUS: Seventh-century poet, famous for the virulence of his lampoons.

ARCHIMEDES: Third-century mathematician.

ARIARATHES: Brother of the following, whom in 42 he succeeded as Ariarathes X. Later deposed and probably killed by Antony.

ARIOBARZANES III: Succeeded his murdered father as King of Cappadocia in 52. Killed by Cassius' orders in 42.

ARISTARCHUS: Homeric critic and keeper of the Alexandrian library in the earlier second century.

ARISTIPPUS: Of Cyrene. Pupil of Socrates and author of a hedonistic system of philosophy.

ARISTOPHANES: (1) Fifth–fourth-century Athenian comic dramatist. (2) Grammarian, Aristarchus' predecessor as head of the Alexandrian library.

ARISTOTLE: The great fourth-century philosopher and polymath.

ARISTOXENUS: Pupil of Aristotle, especially noted for his works on music.

ARISTUS: Brother of Antiochus of Ascalon, whom he succeeded as head of the Academy.

C. ARRIUS: Cicero's neighbour at Formiae.

Q. ARRIUS: Henchman of M. Crassus. He seems to have been exiled in 52 and dead by 46.

ARTAVASDES: King of Armenia. Dethroned by Antony in 34 and subsequently executed.

ARTAXERXES I: King of Persia with whom Themistocles took refuge.

ASCLAPO: Doctor who treated Tiro at Patrae in 50–49.

C. ASINIUS Pollio: Born about 76, Praetor in 45, Consul in 40. Soldier, orator, tragic dramatist, and historian. Governor of Further Spain at the time of Caesar's death, he joined Antony in 43 and remained his supporter, but lived on under Augustus until A.D. 5.

C. ATEIUS Capito: As Tribune in 55 an ally of Cato, but after expulsion from the Senate in 50 supported Caesar. A close friend of Cicero.

L. ATEIUS Capito: Senator in 51.

ATHENODORUS: (1) The Bald. Stoic philosopher of Tarsus, brought to Rome by Cato. (2) Son of Sandon. Also a Stoic philosopher, tutor to the future Emperor Augustus.

ATILIUS: Early writer of Latin comedy.

C. ATIUS Paelignus: Pompeian officer.

ATTICA: See CAECILIA.

ATTIUS Dionysius: Friend of Cicero and Cornificius.

P. ATTIUS Varus: Pompeian officer. In 49 irregularly took over the province of Africa, which he had previously governed. Defeated and killed Curio. Probably fell at Munda.

Aulus' son: See AFRANIUS.

*AURELIA Orestilla: Wife of Catiline, 'in whom no respectable person ever found anything to praise except her good looks' (Sallust).

AURELIUS: Apparently acting as agent for M. Tullius Montanus in 44. Perhaps one of the brothers for whom Cicero wrote a recommendatory letter (Letter 59 (XIII. 40)).

*L. AURELIUS Cotta: Consul in 65. A relative of Caesar's mother, he took no part in the Civil War and later seems to have been at Caesar's disposition. After Caesar's murder retired from public life.

*M. AURELIUS Cotta: Governor of Sardinia in 49.

P. AUTRONIUS Paetus: Elected Consul in 66 but deprived of office by a conviction for bribery. Condemned in 62 for complicity with Catiline, he went into exile in Greece.

C. AVIANIUS Evander: Freedman of Aemilius Avianianus and distinguished sculptor.

C. Avianius Flaccus: Corn-merchant of Puteoli, well known to Cicero.

Q. Axius: Wealthy Senator. A collection of Cicero's letters to him was extant in antiquity.

Balbus: See Cornelius.

Basilus: See Minucius.

Bassus: See Caecilius.

Bibulus: See Calpurnius.

Brogitarus: Galatian, son-in-law of Deiotarus. In return for a bribe Clodius as Tribune had him made Priest of the Great Mother at Pessinus with the title of king.

Brutus: See Junius.

Bursa: See Munatius.

Caecilia Attica: Atticus' daughter, born probably in 51.

*Caecilia Metella: Wife of the younger P. Lentulus Spinther and perhaps daughter of Clodia ('Ox-Eyes').

Q. Caecilius: Atticus' maternal uncle, a Roman Knight. Died in 58 leaving Atticus his heir.

Statius Caecilius: Early writer of Latin comedy.

Q. Caecilius Bassus: Former Pompeian who raised a mutiny in 46 against Caesar's governor of Syria and took command of his troops.

C. Caecilius Cornutus: (1) Tribune in 61 and Praetor in 57, when he supported Cicero's recall. (2) Perhaps son of the foregoing, City Praetor in 43. Committed suicide when Octavian seized Rome.

*L. Caecilius Metellus: Tribune in 49.

*Q. Caecilius Metellus Celer: As Praetor in 63 co-operated with Cicero against Catiline. Governor of Cisalpine Gaul in 62, Consul in 60. Died in 59. His wife was the notorious Clodia ('Ox-Eyes').

*Q. Caecilius Metellus Creticus: Consul in 69. Gained his honorific cognomen by conquering and annexing Crete (68–65).

*Q. Caecilius Metellus Nepos: Younger brother of Celer. Served with Pompey in the East. As Tribune in 62 agitated against Cicero and was suspended from office. Consul in 57 and then governor of Hither Spain. Celer and Nepos were P. Clodius' half-brothers.

*Q. CAECILIUS Metellus Numidicus: Consul in 109. In 100 he went into voluntary exile rather than swear an oath to uphold legislation by the demagogue Saturninus, and was brought back the following year.

*Q. CAECILIUS Metellus Pius Scipio: A Scipio Nasica adopted by a Metellus (Numidicus' son), 'vaunting an unmatched pedigree, yet ignorant as well as unworthy of his ancestors, corrupt and debauched in the way of his life' (R. Syme). Became Pompey's father-in-law and colleague in the Consulship of 52. After Pompey's death led the Republican forces in Africa and committed suicide after Thapsus.

A. CAECINA: Friend of Cicero, of noble Etruscan family; noted orator and author among other things of a treatise on divination by lightning.

CAELIUS: A debtor of Faberius.

M. CAELIUS Rufus: Born c. 88. Placed by his father under Cicero's patronage and successfully defended by him on a criminal charge in 56. Tribune in 52, Curule Aedile in 50. One of the leading speakers of his time. Previously an opponent of Caesar, he changed sides just before the outbreak of the Civil War and was made Praetor in 48. As such started an agitation in favour of debtors ending in an attempted rising against Caesar in which he and his partner Milo lost their lives.

CAEPIO: See M. JUNIUS Brutus.

CAERELLIA: A friend of Cicero's later years, considerably his senior, with philosophical interests. His letters to her, allegedly of a *risqué* character, were extant in antiquity.

CAESAR: See JULIUS.

L. CAESIUS: Member of Q. Cicero's entourage in Asia, later employed on his building operations near Arpinum.

M. CAESIUS: Aedile of Arpinum in 46.

CALDUS: See COELIUS.

CALENUS: See FUFIUS.

M. CALIDIUS: Distinguished orator. As Praetor in 57 supported Cicero's recall. A Caesarian in the Civil War, he died as governor of Cisalpine Gaul in 47.

CALLISTHENES: Latter-fourth-century historian.

*L. CALPURNIUS Bestia: (1) Tribune in 62 and enemy of Cicero. (2) Friend of Cicero, defended by him in 56. Some identify the two.

*L. CALPURNIUS Bibulus: Son of the following. Joined his step-father Brutus in 43 but after Philippi served Antony, dying as governor of Syria in 32.

*M. CALPURNIUS Bibulus: As Consul in 59 opposed Caesar's legislation, shutting himself in his house and 'watching the skies'. Governor of Syria in 51–50. Died of overstrain while commanding Pompey's fleet in 48. Married Cato's daughter Porcia, later wife of Brutus.

*C. CALPURNIUS Piso: Consul in 67, then governor of Transalpine and Cisalpine Gaul. Defended by Cicero on a charge brought in this connection in 63.

*L. CALPURNIUS Piso Caesoninus: Consul in 58, when he took a line unfriendly to Cicero. Hence a bitter attack (extant) in 55. As Censor in 50 tried to moderate his colleague Appius Pulcher's harsh measures. Neutral in the Civil War (Caesar was his son-in-law), he opposed Antony in 44 but in 43 tried to promote an understanding.

*C. CALPURNIUS Piso Frugi: Tullia's first husband. Quaestor in 58, he died before Cicero's return from exile.

CALVINUS: See DOMITIUS.

CALVUS: See LICINIUS Macer.

C. CAMILLUS: An expert on business law, friend of Atticus and Cicero.

P. CANIDIUS Crassus: Consul-Suffect in 40. Commanded Antony's land forces at Actium and was executed by Octavian.

L. CANINIUS Gallus: Friend of Cicero, who defended him in 55. As Tribune in 56 he worked for Pompey's appointment to replace Ptolemy the Piper on his throne. Died in 44.

C. CANINIUS Rebilus: Caesarian officer and one-day Consul in 45.

Ti. CANNUTIUS: As Tribune in 43 bitterly hostile to Antony. Escaped proscription, but was later executed by Octavian.

CANUS: See GELLIUS.

CARBO: See PAPIRIUS.

D. CARFULENUS: Able Caesarian officer who, after Caesar's death, opposed Antony as Tribune in 44. Commanded Martian Legion at the battle of Forum Gallorum, in which he was reported killed.

CARNEADES: Second-century philosopher and head of the 'New' Academy.

T. CARRINAS: Caesarian acquaintance of Cicero's in 45. Perhaps the praenomen should be Gaius (C.) to identify him with a Consul-Suffect of 43 who played a considerable role in the Triumviral period.

CASSIUS Barba: Caesarian officer, later supporter of Antony.

*C. CASSIUS Longinus: As Quaestor took charge of Syria after Crassus' death at Carrhae in 53. Gained a success against invading Parthians in 51. As Tribune in 49 joined Pompey. Pardoned and favoured by Caesar, he became Praetor in 44 and one of the leading conspirators against Caesar's life. Subsequently organized forces against the Triumvirs in the East and perished with Brutus at Philippi in 42. Married to Brutus' half-sister, Junia Tertulla.

*L. CASSIUS Longinus: Brother of the above but a Caesarian. Tribune in 44.

*Q. CASSIUS Longinus: Cousin of the foregoing. Formerly a favourite with Pompey, as Tribune in 49 he supported Caesar. His misgovernment of Hither Spain (49–47) provoked mutiny and his attempted assassination. Recalled by Caesar, he died at sea.

C. CASSIUS Parmensis: Quaestor in 43. According to the historian Velleius (who may, however, have confused him with someone else) he was one of Caesar's assassins and the last of them to die (killed at Athens after Actium). Probably the author of elegies mentioned by Horace (*Epistles*, 1. 4.3).

M. CASSIUS Scaeva: As a Centurion in 48 his epic courage is recorded by Caesar. It seems to have been matched by his rapacity.

CASTRICIUS: A person with whom Q. Cicero had financial dealings.

CATILINE: See SERGIUS

CATIUS: Native of Cisalpine Gaul and author of a treatise or treatises on Epicureanism.

CATO: See PORCIUS.

CATULUS: See LUTATIUS.

CELER: See CAECILIUS Metellus and PILIUS.

CENSORINUS: See MARCIUS.

CEPHALIO: Letter-carrier in 49–47.

CHAERIPPUS: Friend, or perhaps freedman or client, of Q. Cicero, probably to be distinguished from a friend of Cornificius mentioned in letters addressed to the latter.

CHRYSIPPUS: (1) Third-century Stoic philosopher. (2) Freedman in charge of Cicero's library. (3) See VETTIUS.

CICERO: See TULLIUS.

L. CINCIUS: Man of business and confidential agent of Atticus.

CINEAS: Minister of King Pyrrhus and author (or rather epitomizer) of a work on strategy.

CINNA: See CORNELIUS.

L. (?) CISPIUS Laevus: Officer (not necessarily Legate) of Plancus in 43.

Ser. CLAUDIUS: Roman knight and scholar, half-brother or cousin to Papirius Paetus. Drew up a list of Plautus' authentic plays.

*C. CLAUDIUS Marcellus: (1) Praetor in 80. *(2) Son of the foregoing. As Consul in 50 in opposition to Caesar, but neutral in the Civil War. Married Caesar's great-niece Octavia. *(3) Cousin of the foregoing and Consul in 49. A naval commander under Pompey in 48, he seems to have died before Pharsalia.

*M. CLAUDIUS Marcellus: Brother of Gaius (no. 3), Consul in 51. A steady though not fanatical opponent of Caesar, he joined Pompey in the war but retired to Mytilene after Pharsalia. Publicly pardoned by Caesar in 46 (hence Cicero's extant speech of gratitude), he was murdered by a friend on his way home.

*Ti. CLAUDIUS Nero: One of Tullia's suitors in 50, he served and held office under Caesar. Praetor in 42, died after various vicissitudes about 35. His wife Livia married Octavian; his son became Octavian's (Augustus') successor, the Emperor Tiberius.

*Ap. CLAUDIUS Pulcher: As Praetor in 57 at enmity with Cicero but later reconciled. Consul in 54, he became Cicero's predecessor as governor of Cilicia. Censor in 50. Supported Pompey in the Civil War, but died before Pharsalia. One of his daughters married Pompey's elder son, another M. Brutus.

GLOSSARY OF PERSONS

*Ap. CLAUDIUS Pulcher (major): Son of Gaius. Probably served under Caesar in Gaul. After Caesar's death joined Antony, but temporarily regretted it. Later a Triumviral partisan and Consul in 38.

*Ap. CLAUDIUS Pulcher (minor): Younger brother of the above, adopted by his uncle Appius. In 51 figured in the proceedings following C. Pulcher's conviction (this distribution of the two young Appii, due to Mommsen, is generally accepted but not certain).

*C. CLAUDIUS (CLODIUS) Pulcher: Brother of Appius. Legate of Caesar in Gaul, Praetor in 56, then governor of Asia. Condemned for extortion after his return, he may have remained in exile until 43.

CLITARCHUS: Third-century author of a history of Alexander the Great.

*CLODIA (CLAUDIA, 'Ox-Eyes'): Sister to C. Claudius Pulcher (Clodius; above) and wife of Metellus Celer; probably the 'Lesbia' to whom Catullus wrote his love-poems. Perhaps owner of a suburban property which Cicero wanted to buy in 45. The Clodia mentioned in Letters to Atticus 172 (IX.6).3 may have been her sister.

L. CLODIUS: 'Prefect of Engineers' to Ap. Pulcher in 51.

CLODIUS Aesopus: Great tragic actor, well known to Cicero personally. His son (mentioned also by Horace) was a notorious reprobate.

*P. CLODIUS Pulcher: Younger brother of Appius and Gaius. As Tribune in 58 drove Cicero into exile and remained his arch-enemy. From then until his death in an affray with Milo in 52 he was a power in politics through his popularity with the Roman mob and organized street-rowdyism. Often called Publius or Pulchellus ('Little Beauty', 'Pretty-boy') in Cicero's letters.

Sex. CLOELIUS: P. Clodius' chief lieutenant and gang-organizer. Traditionally known as Sex. Clodius after an error in some inferior manuscripts.

CLUATIUS: An architect.

M. CLUVIUS: Wealthy banker of Puteoli from whom Cicero inherited an estate there.

COCCEIUS: Perhaps an agent or surety of Dolabella's, possibly one of the brothers L. and M. Cocceius Nerva, prominent in the Triumviral period (see NERVA).

*C. COELIUS Caldus: Quaestor to Cicero in 50 and left by him in charge of Cilicia.

Q. CONSIDIUS: Wealthy old Senator in 59. Q. Considius Gallus of Letter 431 (XII. 26) may have been a relative, as also the following.

M. CONSIDIUS Nonianus: Praetor perhaps in 52; named by the Senate in 49 as Caesar's successor in Cisalpine Gaul.

C. COPONIUS: Praetor in 49 and Pompeian naval commander in 48.

Q. CORNELIUS: Jurist, teacher of Trebatius Testa.

L. CORNELIUS Balbus: (1) Native of Gades (Cadiz), received Roman citizenship in 72 through L. Cornelius Lentulus Crus. Attached himself to Caesar, becoming his confidential agent and financial adviser, and later to Octavian. Appointed Consul-Suffect in 40, not having held (at least until Caesar's death) any previous magistracy. Present at Atticus' death-bed in 32. (2) Nephew of the foregoing. In Caesar's entourage during the Civil War, he became Quaestor in 44, serving under Pollio in Spain. Rose to Consular rank under Augustus and triumphed in 19.

*L. CORNELIUS Cinna: Consul in 87. Expelled from Rome he re-established himself by military force and after Marius' death remained at the head of affairs until his own death in 84.

*P. CORNELIUS Dolabella (after adoption Cn. Cornelius Lentulus Dolabella?): Defended by Cicero on two capital charges, he married Tullia in 50, but was divorced in 46. A favoured follower of Caesar (despite demagogic activities as Tribune in 47), whom he succeeded as Consul in 44. After some wavering joined Antony and left for his province of Syria late in the year. On the way killed C. Trebonius, governor of Asia and one of Caesar's assassins. Soon afterwards committed suicide to avoid capture by Cassius.

C. CORNELIUS Gallus: Distinguished poet, friend of Pollio and Virgil. After high promotion from Augustus his career ended in disgrace and suicide.

*CORNELIUS Lentulus: Son of Dolabella and Tullia, born in January 45; lived only a few months.

*L. CORNELIUS Lentulus: Son of the Flamen, L. Lentulus Niger. Unsuccessfully prosecuted Gabinius in 54.

*L. CORNELIUS Lentulus Crus: Praetor in 58 (friendly to Cicero). Consul in 49. After Pharsalia fled to Egypt, where he was murdered in prison.

*Cn. CORNELIUS Lentulus Marcellinus: Consul in 56. Not heard of thereafter.

*L. CORNELIUS Lentulus Niger: Flamen of Mars. Died in 55.

*P. CORNELIUS Lentulus Spinther: (1) As Consul in 57 took a leading part in Cicero's restoration. Governor of Cilicia 56–54. Supported Pompey in the Civil War. Taken prisoner by Caesar at Corfinium and released, he joined Pompey in Greece. Put to death in Africa in 46, perhaps by Caesar's orders. The name Spinther, derived from an actor who resembled him, is used by Cicero only for his son. *(2) Son of the foregoing. Falsely claimed to have taken part in Caesar's murder. Went to Asia in 43 as Trebonius' Quaestor, after whose death he was active in support of Brutus and Cassius. Probably put to death after Philippi.

CORNELIUS Nepos: Friend of Atticus and Cicero. Author of a short biography of the former in his book *On Famous Men*.

*P. CORNELIUS Scipio Aemilianus Africanus: Destroyer of Carthage in 146 and leading Roman statesman, idealized by Cicero, who gave him the chief role in his dialogue *On the Republic*.

*Faustus CORNELIUS Sulla: Son of the Dictator. Served with distinction in the East under Pompey, whose daughter he married. Active republican in the Civil War, killed in Africa.

*P. CORNELIUS Sulla: (1) Nephew of the Dictator. Elected to the Consulship in 66 along with P. Autronius and deprived of office for the same reason, he retired to Naples. Defended in 62 by Cicero in an extant speech on a charge of complicity in Catiline's plot. Prominent after Caesar's victory, he enriched himself by buying confiscated property. Died in 46. *(2) Son of the foregoing. It was probably he rather than his father who held military commands in the Civil War, including that of Caesar's right at Pharsalia.

*L. CORNELIUS Sulla Felix: The Dictator. Held supreme power in Rome from 82 till his abdication in 79. Died in 78.

Q. CORNIFICIUS: (1) Praetor in 67 or 66 and a fellow-candidate with Cicero for the Consulship of 63. (2) Son of the above. Quaestor in 48, he served Caesar in and after the Civil War. Governor of Africa 44–42, until defeated and killed by the neighbouring governor, T. Sextius. A notable orator and poet, friend and correspondent of Cicero.

CORNUTUS: See CAECILIUS.

L. COSSINIUS: Like his friend Atticus a Roman Knight and landed proprietor in Epirus, with a role in Varro's dialogue *On Agriculture*.

COTTA: See AURELIUS.

CRASSIPES: See FURIUS.

CRASSUS: See LICINIUS.

CRATERUS: Attica's doctor, a celebrated physician mentioned by Horace and Galen.

CRATIPPUS: Eminent philosopher of the Peripatetic (Aristotelian) school, mentor of young M. Cicero at Athens. Cicero obtained him Roman citizenship from Caesar.

CRISPUS: See MARCIUS.

CULLEO: See TERENTIUS.

CURIO: See SCRIBONIUS.

M'. CURIUS: Roman businessman resident at Patrae, a close friend of Atticus and later of Cicero.

M. CURTIUS: Recommended by Cicero to Caesar for a military Tribunate in 54.

CURTIUS Nicias: A noted scholar. In 45–44 closely attached to Dolabella, who perhaps introduced him to Cicero. Sometimes identified with a despot of Cos, his native island, during Antony's régime.

C. CURTIUS Postumus: A vigorous Caesarian, almost certainly the C. Rabirius Postumus whom Cicero defended in an extant speech in 56.

CYRUS: (1) Founder of the Persian empire. Xenophon's *Education of Cyrus* is a highly idealized account of him. (2) See VETTIUS.

CYTHERIS: See VOLUMNIA.

DAMASIPPUS: Well-known art expert who, as we learn from Horace, went bankrupt and turned Stoic philosopher.

DECIMUS: See JUNIUS.

DEIOTARUS: Tetrarch of part of Galatia, made king by Pompey, whom he supported in the Civil War. Caesar let him keep his throne and acquitted him on a charge of attempted assassination (Cicero's defence is extant). Died about 40 in extreme old age. His son and namesake, also given the royal title by the Senate, probably predeceased him.

DEMETRIUS: (1) A freedman of Pompey (*Letters to Atticus* 86 (IV.11).1). (2) A freedman, probably of Atticus (*Letters to Atticus* 371 (XIV.17).1). (3) Of Magnesia, a contemporary littérateur, author of a book *On Concord*. (4) A tiresome personage, perhaps identical with No. 1, perhaps an influential freedman of Caesar's (Letters 184–6 (XVI.19, 22, 17)). (5) Caesarian officer in 49 (Letter 149 (VIII.15)). (6) Megas, a Sicilian recommended by Cicero in 46. (7) Of Phalerum, late fourth-century Athenian orator and statesman.

DEMOCRITUS: Fifth-century philosopher, developed the atomic theory of the universe.

DEMOSTHENES: Great fourth-century Athenian orator and patriot.

DICAEARCHUS: Pupil of Aristotle and like him a polymath, author of works on philosophy, history, literature, etc.

DIODOTUS: (1) Stoic philosopher and Cicero's teacher. Lived in Cicero's house for many years and died leaving him his money. (2) Freedman of Lucullus.

DIOGENES: Greek friend or agent of Caelius Rufus, sent out to Cilicia in 51.

DIONYSIUS: (1) Fourth-century despot of Syracuse. (2) His son and successor. (3) Freedman and librarian of Cicero, pilfered his books and ran away. (4) See ATTIUS, POMPONIUS.

DIPHILUS: (1) An actor. (2) An architect.

DOLABELLA: See CORNELIUS.

*Cn. DOMITIUS Ahenobarbus: Son of the following. Returned to Italy after Pharsalia. Later a partisan of Antony (Shakespeare's Enobarbus), whom he finally deserted. Consul in 32.

*L. DOMITIUS Ahenobarbus: Cato's brother-in-law and bitter opponent of Caesar. Captured at Corfinium in 49 and released, he stood siege in Massilia but fled before the town fell to Caesar's forces. Commanded Pompey's left at Pharsalia and was killed in flight.

*Cn. DOMITIUS Calvinus: Consul in 53. Probably condemned for bribery and restored from exile by Caesar. Held high commands in the war, and a second Consulship and Triumph after Caesar's death.

DRUSUS: See LIVIUS.

DURIS: Historian, 'flourished' c. 300.

L. EGNATIUS Rufus: Roman Knight with whom Cicero and his brother had financial dealings.

Q. ENNIUS: Third-second-century Latin poet.

EPAMINONDAS: Theban soldier and statesman, killed in the battle of Mantinea (362).

EPHORUS: Fourth-century historian.

EPICHARMUS: Sixth-century Sicilian writer of comedy.

EPICURUS: Fourth-century philosopher.

ERATOSTHENES: Third-century savant, head of the Alexandrian library and founder of scientific geography.

EROS: Slave (perhaps of Philotimus) or freedman who looked after Cicero's finances in 45–44.

EUPOLIS: Athenian writer of comedy, contemporary with Aristophanes.

EURIPIDES: Athenian writer of tragedy.

EUTRAPELUS: See VOLUMNIUS.

Q. FABERIUS: Caesar's Secretary, served Antony after Caesar's death.

FABIUS: A lover of Clodia's, perhaps identical with Q. Fabius Maximus.

C. FABIUS: Legate of Caesar and friend of Atticus. Seems to have died in 49.

M. FABIUS Gallus: Usually but wrongly called Fadius. Friend of Cicero, author, Epicurean, connoisseur of art.

*Q. FABIUS Maximus: Supporter of Caesar and Consul-Suffect in 45. Died in office.

Q. FABIUS Vergilianus: Legate to Ap. Pulcher in Cilicia. Perhaps the Q. Fabius who brought Pompey a message in 49 (*Letters to Atticus* 161A (VIII.11A)).

L. FADIUS: Aedile of Arpinum in 44.

T. FADIUS: Cicero's Quaestor in 63, Tribune in 57 (supported Cicero's recall), probably Praetor in a later year. Condemned for bribery in 52.

*C. FANNIUS: Anti-triumviral Tribune in 59, probably Praetor later, governor of Asia in 49. Proscribed in 43, he fled to Sex. Pompeius and later to Antony.

*FAUSTA: Sulla's daughter and wife of C. Memmius, later of Milo.

FAUSTUS: See CORNELIUS Sulla.

M. FAVONIUS: Follower of Cato. Fled from Pharsalia with Pompey. Later pardoned by Caesar, but proscribed in 43 and put to death at Philippi.

FIGULUS: See MARCIUS.

FLACCUS: See VALERIUS.

FLAMINIUS Flamma: Debtor mentioned in 45.

C. FLAVIUS: Friend and 'Prefect of Engineers' to M. Brutus. Fell at Philippi.

L. FLAVIUS: As Tribune in 60 acted in Pompey's interest. Praetor in 58. The Caesarian officer of *Letters to Atticus* 190 (x.1).2 may or may not be the same.

FUFIDIUS: The Fufidii were a prominent family in Arpinum.

Q. FUFIUS Calenus: Tribune in 61, Praetor in 59. Served under Caesar in Gaul and the Civil War. Governor of Greece in 48. Consul in 47. After Caesar's death supported Antony in Rome. Disliked by Cicero, who had known and respected his father.

*FULVIA: Wife of P. Crassus, Curio, and Antony.

C. FUNDANIUS: Friend and apparently ex-client of Cicero.

FUNISULANUS: Twice mentioned as carrying a letter from Atticus to Cicero.

T. FURFANUS Postumus: Friend of Cicero and governor of Sicily in 46–45.

*FURIUS Crassipes: Married Tullia about 55, soon afterwards divorced. Quaestor in Bithynia, perhaps in 54.

C. FURNIUS: Friend of Cicero, Tribune in 50. A Caesarian, he served as Munatius Plancus' Legate in 43 and later supported Mark Antony and his brother Lucius. Pardoned and dignified by Octavian, he lived to see his son Consul in 17.

A. GABINIUS: Military lieutenant and political supporter of Pompey. As Consul in 58 backed Clodius against Cicero. As governor of Syria restored Ptolemy the Piper to his throne in 55. Went into exile in 54 after conviction on charges of extortion. Reappears as Caesar's Legate in 48. Died in 47.

GALBA: See SULPICIUS.

M. GALLIUS: Along with his brother prosecuted Calidius in 51. Identifiable with an ex-Praetor and partisan of Antony in 43.

Q. GALLIUS: Brother of the foregoing, both being sons of a former client of Cicero's, Q. Gallius. Probably Praetor in 43, deposed from office by Octavian.

GALLUS: See FABIUS.

L. GAVIUS: Agent of Brutus in Cappadocia 50–49.

GELLIUS Poplicola: Brother of L. Gellius Poplicola, Consul in 72, and a follower of Clodius. F. Münzer wished to identify him with Q. Gellius Canus (or Kanus), a close friend of Atticus, saved by him from proscription in 43. The L. Gellius of Letter 398 (x.17).3 may be his nephew, Consul in 36.

GLABRIO: See ACILIUS.

GNAEUS: See POMPEIUS.

GRAECEIUS: Friend of Cassius and D. Brutus.

HAMMONIUS: See AMMONIUS.

HEGESIAS: Third-century rhetorician, regarded as the creator of the 'Asiatic' style of oratory, one feature of which was a fondness for short, staccato sentences.

HERACLIDES: Of Pontus. Pupil of Plato, author of works on a variety of subjects, mostly in dialogue form.

HERMIA(s): Apparently a slave of Cicero's or of his brother's.

HERODES: An Athenian, probably of high rank, acquainted with Atticus and Cicero.

HERODOTUS: Fifth-century historian.

HESIOD: Early Greek poet.

HILARUS: Four freedmen of this name occur in the Letters.

HIPPARCHUS: Second-century astronomer and geographer.

HIRRUS: See LUCILIUS.

A. HIRTIUS: Caesarian officer, Praetor in 46 and Consul in 43 until his death at Mutina. Man of letters and gourmet. Nine or more books of his correspondence with Cicero were extant in antiquity.

T. HORDEONIUS: Member of a Campanian merchant family and co-heir to the estate of M. Cluvius.

*Q. HORTENSIUS Hortalus: (1) Consul in 69 and before Cicero Rome's leading forensic orator. A devoted friend of Atticus, his relations with Cicero varied. Died in 50. *(2) Son of the foregoing and on bad terms with him. Joined Caesar in the Civil War, who made him Praetor and governor of Macedonia. Joined Brutus in 43. Put to death after Philippi by Antony in reprisal for the execution of his brother Gaius.

HOSTILIUS Saserna: Three brothers of this name, Gaius, Lucius, and Publius, served in Caesar's armies. One of them was with Antony at Mutina.

HYPSAEUS: See PLAUTIUS.

ISOCRATES: Fourth-century Athenian rhetorician.

JUBA: King of Numidia, allied with the Pompeians in the Civil War.

*C. JULIUS Caesar: The Dictator.

*L. JULIUS Caesar: (1) Distant relative of the above. Consul in 64 and Legate in Gaul, he stood neutral in the Civil War. Proscribed in 43, he was saved by his sister, Antony's mother Julia. *(2) Son of the above. After acting as messenger in abortive peace negotiations early in the Civil War he joined Pompey. Killed after Thapsus, perhaps at Caesar's orders.

*C. JULIUS Caesar Octavianus: Caesar's great-nephew and adopted son. Later Triumvir and Emperor Augustus.

*JUNIA: Half-sister of Brutus and wife of Lepidus.

*JUNIA Tertia (or Tertulla): Sister of the above and wife of C. Cassius. Her funeral in A.D.22 is described by Tacitus.

L. JUNIUS Brutus: Rome's first Consul, who drove out the last king, Tarquin the Proud.

*M. JUNIUS Brutus: Sometimes called (Q. Servilius) Caepio (Brutus) after adoption by his uncle Q. Servilius Caepio. On his career see the introductory note in Letters to Friends, Vol. II.

*D. JUNIUS Brutus Albinus: Not closely related to the above. Served under Caesar in Gaul and the Civil War, governor of Transalpine Gaul in 48–46. Regarded by Caesar with special favour and named as Consul for 42 along with L. Plancus, he became a leading conspirator against his life. Later besieged by Antony at Mutina in his province of Cisalpine Gaul, after Antony's defeat and escape he too crossed the Alps to join Plancus. When the latter went over to Antony he fled, but was killed by a Celtic chieftain on Antony's orders.

*D. JUNIUS Silanus: Consul in 62. Married Brutus' mother Servilia by whom he had three daughters (see JUNIA).

*M. JUNIUS Silanus: Officer of Lepidus in 43, who (probably) sent him to Antony at Mutina but later disavowed him. Consul in 25.

*M. JUVENTIUS Laterensis: Praetor in 51. As Lepidus' Legate killed himself when his chief joined Antony.

*JUVENTIUS Talna: Friend of Cicero's, whose son came into consideration as a future husband for Attica. The rascally juryman at Clodius' trial mentioned in *Letters to Atticus* 16 (1.16).6 is no doubt another man.

KANUS: See GELLIUS.

LABEO: See 'ANTISTIUS'.
D. LABERIUS: Roman Knight, author of mimes.
T. LABIENUS: Tribune in 63. Caesar's principal lieutenant in Gaul, but deserted him at the outbreak of the Civil War and fought against him to the end. Killed at Munda.
D. LAELIUS: Family friend and supporter of Pompey. Allowed to return to Italy after Pharsalia.
*C. LAELIUS Sapiens: Consul in 140 and life-long friend of the younger Scipio Africanus.
*LAENAS: Perhaps Popilius Laenas, Senator and friend of Caesar.
LAÏS: Famous Corinthian courtesan.
LAMIA: See AELIUS.
LATERENSIS: See JUVENTIUS.
LENTULUS: See CORNELIUS.
LEONIDES: Athenian, apparently of high position, who kept an eye on M. Cicero junior in 45–44.
LEPIDUS: See AEMILIUS.

LEPTA: See PACONIUS.

LIBO: See SCRIBONIUS.

A. LICINIUS Archias: Poet, author of some surviving epigrams. Cicero successfully defended his title to Roman citizenship in an extant speech (62).

*L. LICINIUS Crassus: Consul in 95 and one of the greatest Roman orators.

*M. LICINIUS Crassus: (1) Consul in 70 and 55. Joined Pompey and Caesar in 60 to form the so-called First Triumvirate. Left for Syria late in 55. Defeated and killed at Carrhae in 53 leading an invasion of Parthia. *(2) Son (probably younger) of the above.

*P. LICINIUS Crassus: Son (probably elder) of the 'Triumvir'. Much attached to Cicero in his early days, he served brilliantly under Caesar in Gaul. Went out to Syria with his father and was killed at Carrhae. In the *Brutus* Cicero seems to blame him for the disaster.

*P. LICINIUS Crassus Dives: See *Letters to Atticus*, p. 98, n.147. He was Praetor in 57.

*L. LICINIUS Lucullus Ponticus: Lieutenant of Sulla and Consul in 74. In 73–66 waged a brilliant series of campaigns against King Mithridates of Pontus, ending ingloriously through disaffection in his army. After supersession by Pompey returned to Rome to live in ease and luxury until his death in 56.

*M. LICINIUS Lucullus: (1) See TERENTIUS. *(2) Son of Ponticus. Died at Philippi, or soon afterwards.

C. LICINIUS Macer Calvus: Son of C. Licinius Macer (see *Letters to Atticus*, p. 39, n.15); a distinguished orator and poet.

Q. LIGARIUS: Pompeian, defended in 45 by Cicero before Caesar in an extant speech. Allowed to return to Rome he joined the conspiracy against Caesar.

T. LIGARIUS: Brother of the above. He and another brother perished in the proscriptions of 43.

A. LIGURIUS: Caesarian officer and friend of Cicero's.

L. LIVINEIUS Regulus: Friend of Cicero, at some time Praetor; later exiled.

L. LIVINEIUS Trypho: Freedman of the above.

*M. Livius Drusus Claudianus: Father of Augustus' wife Livia, originally a Claudius Pulcher. Successfully defended by Cicero in 54. Praetor or President of Court in 50. Owner of suburban estate coveted by Cicero in 45. Killed himself in his tent at Philippi.

M. Lollius Palicanus: Tribune in 71. Mob orator and agitator against the post-Sullan régime.

Cn. Lucceius: Member of a locally aristocratic family of Cumae, friend of Cicero and Brutus.

L. Lucceius (son of Quintus): Praetor in 67 and unsuccessful candidate for the Consulship in 60. On amicable terms with Cicero, he remained one of Pompey's most intimate friends until Pharsalia. Pardoned by Caesar, he may have died in the proscriptions of 43. Cicero admired his historical work, which was perhaps never published.

P. Luccius: Friend of Cornificius (wrongly called Lucceius).

C. Lucilius: Roman satirist late in the second century.

C. Lucilius Hirrus: Great-nephew (probably) of the above and cousin to Pompey. Tribune in 53, he annoyed Cicero by standing against him for the Augurate. Defeated in 51 in his candidature for the Aedileship. Followed Pompey in the Civil War but survived to lend Caesar 6,000 fish for his triumphal banquet in 45 and flee proscription in 43–42. A great landowner and in Cicero's opinion an egregious ass.

Lucius: See Saufeius.

Q. Lucretius: Whether certain Lucretii mentioned in the Letters are identical and whether they are to be identified with Q. Lucretius Vespillo, who commanded a Pompeian squadron in the Adriatic and lived to become Consul in 19, is doubtful.

T. Lucretius Carus: One of Rome's greatest poets. His work *On the Nature of Things* is an exposition of Epicurus' physical philosophy.

Lucullus: See Licinius.

Lupus: (1) Friend of D. Brutus. (2) See Rutilius.

*Q. Lutatius Catulus: (1) Colleague of Marius as Consul in 102, killed by his orders in 87. *(2) Son of the foregoing. Consul in 78 and leading conservative figure until his death in 61 or 60.

Lysippus: Fourth-century sculptor.

LYSO: Friend and host of Cicero at Patrae.

P. MAGIUS Cilo: Friend and murderer of M. Marcellus.

MAMURRA: 'Prefect of Engineers' to Caesar and a *nouveau riche*. Savagely lampooned by Catullus.

M'. MANILIUS: (1) Consul in 149, one of Rome's great jurists. *(2) Friend of Trebatius Testa, also a jurist and probably descended from the foregoing.

*MANLIUS Acidinus: Student at Athens in 45, perhaps identical with Horace's friend Torquatus.

*A. MANLIUS Torquatus: Praetor perhaps in 70 and friend of Cicero, who tried through Dolabella to get Caesar's permission for him, as an ex-Pompeian living in Athens, to return to Italy. After Caesar's death an active republican, he was befriended by his old friend Atticus after Philippi.

*L. MANLIUS Torquatus: Of a different branch of the family, Praetor in or before 49. Also friend of Cicero, who made him the Epicurean spokesman in his *De Finibus*, and of Atticus. Perished in Africa in 46. A writer of erotic verse, he is almost certainly the bridegroom in Catullus' Wedding Ode.

*T. (?) MANLIUS Torquatus: Apparently son of Aulus, mentioned in letters to Atticus of 45–44. Probably to be distinguished from Pansa's Quaestor in 43.

MARCELLINUS: See CORNELIUS Lentulus.

MARCELLUS: See CLAUDIUS.

MARCIANUS: See TULLIUS.

*L. MARCIUS Censorinus: Partisan of Caesar, then of Antony. Got possession of Cicero's house on the Palatine after its owner's murder.

C. MARCIUS Crispus: Caesarian officer. Proconsul in Bithynia in 45–44. Brought three legions to help Staius Murcus in Syria against Caecilius Bassus.

*L. MARCIUS (?) Figulus: Commanded Dolabella's fleet in 43.

*L. MARCIUS Philippus: (1) Consul in 91. Censor under Cinna's régime, but joined Sulla when he returned to Italy. *(2) Son of the foregoing. Consul in 56. Husband of Caesar's niece and Cato's father-in-law, he took no part in the Civil War. Counselled caution to his stepson Octavian in 44. A moderating influence in the struggle between the Senate and Antony.

C. MARIUS: Of Arpinum. Great general, seven times Consul, destroyer of invading northern tribes. Driven into exile by Sulla in 88, returned to Rome by force in 87 and killed off numbers of opponents before his own death early the following year.

'C. MARIUS': An impostor, who in 45 claimed to be grandson of the above. Executed by Antony in 44.

M. MARIUS: Friend, correspondent, and perhaps relative of Cicero, resident near Pompeii.

P. MATINIUS: Agent of Brutus in Cilicia in 51–50.

C. MATIUS: Old friend of Cicero's, closely attached to Caesar, whom he accompanied in Gaul without official rank. Cicero calls him by nicknames referring to his baldness.

MAXIMUS: See FABIUS.

MEGABOCCHUS: Friend and contemporary of P. Crassus, he committed suicide at Carrhae.

MEMMIUS: Stepson of P. Sulla, associated with him in a proposed prosecution of Gabinius in 54. Perhaps identical with the following.

C. MEMMIUS (son of Gaius): Tribune in 54.

C. MEMMIUS (son of Lucius): First husband of Sulla's daughter Fausta, who was a ward of L. Lucullus, hence perhaps an enemy of the two Luculli. An erratic political career ended in exile after conviction for bribery in 52. Noted orator and poet, generally supposed to be the friend to whom Lucretius dedicated his poem *On the Nature of Things*.

L. MESCINIUS Rufus: Cicero's Quaestor in Cilicia. Seems to have joined Pompey in the Civil War but was allowed to return to Italy in 46.

MESSALLA: See VALERIUS.

C. MESSIUS: Pro-Ciceronian Tribune in 57 and adherent of Pompey; but in 46 Legate to Caesar in Africa.

METELLUS: See CAECILIUS.

METRODORUS: A doctor, probably a freedman of Cicero's.

MILO: See ANNIUS.

M. MINDIUS: Brother (?) of L. Mescinius Rufus.

L. MINUCIUS Basilus: Legate of Caesar in Gaul and the Civil War and Praetor in 45, joined the conspiracy in 44. Murdered by his slaves the following year. A friend of Cicero, he may or may not be identical with a person or persons here and there referred to as 'Minucius'.

*Q. MINUCIUS Thermus: Governor of Asia in 51–50. A Pompeian in the Civil War and proscribed in 43, he escaped to join Sex. Pompeius and then Antony.

*MUCIA: Pompey's third wife and half-sister to the Metelli, Celer and Nepos.

*Q. MUCIUS Scaevola: (1) The Augur. Consul in 117, died in 87. Cicero knew him well. *(2) Pontifex Maximus. Consul in 95. A great jurist and a model governor of Asia, also well known to Cicero until his murder by the Marians in 82. *(3) Perhaps grandson of the Augur. After Tribunate in 54 served on Ap. Pulcher's staff in Cilicia, but a Caesarian in the Civil War. Author of erotic verse.

L. MUMMIUS Achaicus: Consul in 146 and destroyer of Corinth.

C. MUNATIUS Plancus: See PLOTIUS.

L. MUNATIUS Plancus: Family friend of Cicero. Served under Caesar in Gaul and the Civil War. City Prefect during Caesar's absence in 46–45. As governor of Transalpine Gaul (except the Narbonensis), he finally joined Antony in 43. Consul in 42. Changed sides again before Actium and became Censor in 22.

T. MUNATIUS Plancus Bursa: Brother of the above. Tribune in 52 and follower of Clodius, he was successfully prosecuted by Cicero as a ringleader in the riots following Clodius' death. In exile joined Caesar, who brought him back in 49. Later an active supporter of Antony.

MURCUS: See STAIUS.

MURENA: See TERENTIUS.

Cn. NAEVIUS: Early Roman epic and dramatic poet.

NASICA: See CAECILIUS Metellus Pius Scipio.

L. NASIDIUS: Republican naval commander in 47.

NATTA: See PINARIUS.

NEPOS: See CAECILIUS Metellus and CORNELIUS.

NERO: See CLAUDIUS.

NERVA: Officer under Lepidus, perhaps one of the brothers C. and

M. Cocceius Nerva prominent in the Triumviral period (see also COCCEIUS).

NICIAS: See CURTIUS.

P. NIGIDIUS Figulus: As a Senator assisted Cicero in 63. Praetor in 58. Joined Pompey in the Civil War and died in exile in 45. A prolific writer on various branches of learning, he was chiefly remembered as an astrologer and magician.

L. NINNIUS Quadratus: Member of a distinguished Campanian family. Opposed Clodius as Tribune in 58.

M. NONIUS (Struma?): Probably governor of Macedonia in 50.

M. NONIUS Sufenas: Tribune in 56. Sometimes identified with the above.

OCELLA (L. Livius Ocella?): Friend of Cicero and Atticus, sometime Praetor.

Servius OCELLA: Subject of a Roman scandal in 50.

OCTAVIANUS or OCTAVIUS: See JULIUS.

C. OCTAVIUS: Father of Augustus. Praetor in 61, succeeded C. Antonius as governor of Macedonia. Died in 58.

*M. OCTAVIUS: Caelius Rufus' colleague as Curule Aedile in 50. Active as a Pompeian admiral in the Civil War, he probably perished in Africa.

A. OFFILIUS: Jurist, pupil of Ser. Sulpicius. Probably one of Cluvius of Puteoli's heirs in 45.

OPPII: Probably bankers, from Velia in southern Italy.

C. OPPIUS: Roman Knight, friend and agent of Caesar, usually mentioned in conjunction with Cornelius Balbus and like him a friend of Atticus and Cicero.

L. OPPIUS: Subject of several letters of recommendation in 47–46. Was in business at Philomelium and agent of Egnatius Rufus.

ORESTILLA: See AURELIA.

ORODES: King of Parthia 57–37.

OTHO: (1) L. Roscius Otho, Tribune in 67. (2) Co-heir to the estate of one Scapula which included a suburban property coveted by Cicero in 45.

OVIA: In some sort of financial relationship with Cicero in 45 and later co-heir to Cluvius of Puteoli's estate.

PACIAECUS: See VIBIUS.

Q. PACONIUS(?) Lepta: Cicero's 'Prefect of Engineers' in Cilicia.

PACORUS: Son of and eventually co-ruler with Orodes, King of Parthia. Killed in battle in 38.

PAETUS: See PAPIRIUS.

PALICANUS: See LOLLIUS.

PANAETIUS: Eminent second-century Stoic philosopher, friend of the younger Scipio Africanus.

PANSA: See VIBIUS.

*Cn. PAPIRIUS Carbo: Leading Marian, killed by Pompey after surrender in 82.

L. PAPIRIUS Paetus: Wealthy resident of Naples and an old friend of Cicero.

Q. (?) PATISCUS: Apparently a Roman businessman in Asia, then a Caesarian officer, in 43 a Republican Proquaestor taking part in naval operations in the East (if these are identical).

PATRO: Successor of Phaedrus as head of the Epicurean school at Athens, old friend and protégé of Atticus and Cicero.

PAULUS: See AEMILIUS.

Q. PEDIUS: Caesar's nephew or great-nephew. Died in office as Octavian's colleague in the Consulship of 43.

Sex. PEDUCAEUS: (1) Praetor in 77, then governor of Sicily. Cicero served under him as Quaestor. (2) Son of the foregoing and intimate friend of Atticus. References in the Letters, except when explicitly to the father, are probably to the son, whom Cicero sometimes calls simply 'Sextus'.

M. PETREIUS: Sometime Praetor, Legate of C. Antonius in 62, when he commanded the government forces in the final battle against Catiline. Legate to Pompey in Spain 55–49. After the collapse of the Pompeian armies there continued to fight against Caesar and committed suicide in Africa.

PHAEDRUS: Patro's predecessor as head of the Epicurean school. Cicero as a boy heard him lecture in Rome.

PHALARIS: Sixth-century tyrant of Agrigentum in Sicily, notorious for his cruelty.

PHAMEA: Uncle or grandfather of Tigellius. Nothing proves that he was a freedman, as often supposed.

PHANIA(s): Freedman of Ap. Pulcher.

GLOSSARY OF PERSONS

Pharnaces: (1) Son of Mithridates the Great of Pontus and King of Bosporus. Recovered his father's kingdom in 48 and defeated Caesar's lieutenant, Domitius Calvinus. Caesar 'came, saw, and conquered' him the following year. (2) Clerk of Atticus.

Philippus: See Marcius.

Philistus: Fourth-century historian of Sicily.

Philo: (1) Of Larissa. Antiochus' predecessor as head of the Academic school of philosophy. (2) Freedman of Caelius Rufus, sent out to Cilicia in 51.

Philogenes: Freedman of Atticus, employed in financial transactions with Cicero.

Philotimus: (1) Freedman of Terentia, up till 50 much employed by Cicero in financial business. (2) Clerk of Cicero (it is not always possible to be sure which of the two is meant).

Philoxenus: Slave or freedman of Q. Cicero.

Phocylides: Sixth-century author of versified maxims, which he prefaced: 'This also says Phocylides.'

Pilia: Atticus' wife, married in 56. May have died in 44.

Q. Pilus Celer: Relative, probably brother, of the above. Supported Caesar in the Civil War and brought letters from M. Brutus and C. Antonius to the Senate in 43. Cicero thought well of him as a speaker.

*L. Pinarius Natta: Brother-in-law of Clodius, to whom as Pontifex in 58 he gave his services in connection with Cicero's house. The family was immemorially old. Several other Pinarii, probably not of aristocratic origin, crop up in the Letters, not safely to be sorted out.

Pindarus: Possibly the freedman by whose hand Cassius died after Philippi at his own orders.

Pisistratus: Sixth-century 'tyrant' of Athens, type of a 'benevolent despot'.

Piso: See Calpurnius and Pupius.

Plaetorius: The identity of persons of this name occurring in the Letters is doubtful.

Cn. Plancius: Befriended Cicero when Quaestor in Macedonia in 58. Curule Aedile in 54, defended by Cicero on a bribery charge in an extant speech. Last heard of in 45 as a Pompeian awaiting pardon in Corcyra.

PLATO: Fourth-century Athenian philosopher, founder of the Academy.

A. PLAUTIUS: See PLOTIUS.

*P. PLAUTIUS Hypsaeus: Leading adherent and at one time Quaestor of Pompey. Candidate for the Consulship in 53. Pompey let him be condemned on a bribery charge in 52.

PLAUTUS (T. Maccius Plautus): Early writer of Latin comedy.

A. PLOTIUS (or Plautius): City Praetor in 51. Identifiable with a Legate of Pompey in 67, who became Tribune, Curule Aedile, and probably governor of Bithynia in 49–48.

POLA: See SERVIUS Pola.

POLLA: See VALERIA.

POLLEX: Slave of Cicero.

POLLIO: See ASINIUS.

POLYBIUS: Second-century historian.

POLYCLES: Three sculptors of that name are recorded, one in the fourth century, the other two in the second.

POLYDAMAS: Senior Trojan in the *Iliad*.

A. POMPEIUS Bithynicus: Friend of Cicero, Propraetor in Sicily in 44–42. Accepted Sex. Pompeius as co-governor, who later had him executed.

*Cn. POMPEIUS Magnus: (1) Pompey the Great. *(2) Elder son of the foregoing, killed in Spain after the battle of Munda.

*Sex. POMPEIUS Magnus: Younger son of Pompey the Great. After Caesar's death revived the war in Spain, then came to terms with Lepidus. Eventually gained control of Sicily and was a thorn in Octavian's flesh until defeated in 36. Fled to the East and after further adventures was captured and executed by an officer of Antony's.

*Q. POMPEIUS Rufus: Sulla's grandson, but an associate of P. Clodius, condemned for his part as Tribune in 52 in the riots following Clodius' murder. His prosecutor was Caelius Rufus, who later befriended him when he was living in poverty in Bauli.

Cn. POMPEIUS Theophanes: Of Mytilene, a protégé of Pompey, with whom he had much influence, and author of a history of Pompey's campaigns.

POMPONIA: Sister of Atticus, married to Q. Cicero from about 70 until their divorce in 45 or 44.

T. POMPONIUS Atticus (Q. Caecilius Pomponianus Atticus): Cicero's friend and correspondent.

M. POMPONIUS Dionysius: Learned freedman of Atticus and tutor to the young Ciceros.

C. POMPTINUS: Praetor in 63, then governor of Narbonese Gaul, where he crushed a tribal revolt. Finally granted a Triumph in 54. Legate to Cicero in Cilicia.

PONTIUS: Several persons of this name occur. The following can be distinguished:

L. PONTIUS: Owner of a villa in the Trebula district, where Cicero stayed when travelling between Rome and Brundisium.

PONTIUS Aquila: Tribune in 45 and assassin of Caesar. Legate to D. Brutus in 43. Killed at Mutina.

PONTIUS Titinianus: Son by birth of the Senator Q. Titinius. Joined Caesar at Brundisium in 49.

*PORCIA: (1) Cato's sister, wife of L. Domitius Ahenobarbus. Died in 45. (2) Cato's daughter, married first to M. Bibulus, then to M. Brutus. Died, allegedly by suicide, in 43.

*C. PORCIUS Cato: As Tribune in 56 at first opposed, then supported Pompey (perhaps leagued with Crassus). Tried and acquitted in 54.

*M. PORCIUS Cato: (1) 'Of Utica'. Leader of conservative opposition to the 'First Triumvirate'. Later made common cause with Pompey against Caesar, and after Pompey's death became the life and soul of continuing resistance. Committed suicide at Utica after the republican defeat in 46. Family connections included Servilia (half-sister), her son Brutus, M. Bibulus, L. Domitius, and Hortensius. *(2) Son of the foregoing, who left Cicero and Atticus as his guardians. Killed at Philippi.

POSIDONIUS: Stoic philosopher and polymath, resident in Rhodes.

*POSTUMIA: Wife of Ser. Sulpicius Rufus.

L. (?) POSTUMIUS: Follower of Cato. As his subordinate (Quaestor?) instructed to take over Sicily in 49.

POSTUMUS: See CURTIUS.

PROCILIUS: Perhaps Tribune in 56, under prosecution in 54. May or may not be identical with the author mentioned in *Letters to Atticus* 22 (II.2).2.

PROTOGENES: Fourth-century painter.

GLOSSARY OF PERSONS

Ptolemy XII: Called 'The Piper', King of Egypt. Driven out by his subjects in 58, restored by Gabinius in 55, died in 51.

Publilia: Cicero's ward and second wife, married toward the end of 46, divorced a few months later.

Publilius: Relative, probably brother, of the above.

Publilius Syrus: Contemporary writer of mimes. A collection of maxims taken from his work survives.

Publius, Pulchellus, Pulcher: See Clodius.

*M. Pupius Piso Frugi: Friend of Cicero's youth, to whom he gave a role in his *De Finibus*. After his Consulship in 61 (severely criticized by Cicero) he disappears.

Pyrrhus: King of Epirus. Campaigned against Rome in 281–275. Wrote a treatise on tactics.

T. Quintius Scapula: Leader of a mutiny against Caesar in Spain.

L. Racilius: Tribune in 56.

Rebilus: See Caninius.

Reginus: See Antistius.

Regulus: See Livineius.

Rhint(h)on: Fourth-century writer of mock-tragedies.

L. Roscius Fabatus: Served with Caesar in Gaul. Praetor in 49 and peace intermediary. Reported dead at the battle of Forum Gallorum.

Q. Roscius Gallus: Rome's greatest comic actor, friend and client of Cicero.

T. (?) Rufrenus: Officer in Lepidus' army in 43. Apparently Tribune the following year.

Rufus: See Caelius, Mescinius, Sempronius.

*P. Rutilius Lupus: Tribune and supporter of Pompey in 56. Praetor in 49. Served under Pompey in Greece in 48.

Cn. Sallustius: Friend of Cicero and Atticus.

P. Sallustius: Perhaps brother of the above.

Q. Salvidienus Rufus: Partisan of Octavian. After a distinguished career accused of preparing to desert to Antony and committed suicide in 40.

SALVIUS: (1) Literary slave of Atticus'. (2) Influential freedman of Caesar's.

SASERNA: See HOSTILIUS.

L. SAUFEIUS: Friend of Atticus, who saved his property in the Proscriptions. A devoted Epicurean and prolific writer on the subject.

SCAEVA: See CASSIUS.

SCAEVOLA: See MUCIUS.

M. SCAPTIUS: (1) Agent of Brutus in Cilicia 51–50. (2) Presumably relative of the foregoing, looked after Brutus' interests in Cappadocia.

SCAPULA: (1) Deceased owner of an estate which Cicero wished to buy in 45. (2) See QUINTIUS.

SCAURUS: See AEMILIUS.

SCIPIO: See CAECILIUS and CORNELIUS.

C. SCRIBONIUS Curio: (1) Consul in 76, notable general and orator. Died in 53. *(2) His son, Cicero's friend and correspondent. After some variations appeared as Tribune in 50 in the role of a fervent optimate, but suddenly went over to Caesar, allegedly for a vast bribe. Led expedition to Africa in 49, where he was defeated and killed.

SCROFA: See TREMELLIUS.

M. SEIUS: Roman Knight and man of business, supporter of Caesar. Mentioned by Varro and Pliny the Elder as a noted producer of poultry, etc.

Q. SELICIUS: Friend of Lentulus Spinther, perhaps identical with a wealthy money-lender mentioned in letters to Atticus.

C. SEMPRONIUS Rufus: Acquaintance of Cicero, apparently exiled in 50 and restored by Antony after Caesar's death. Mentioned by Horace as an ex-Praetor and gourmet.

*C. SEMPRONIUS Tuditanus: The father and son (Consul in 129) of that name are the subject of one of Cicero's historical queries.

C. SEPTIMIUS: (1) Secretary to M. Bibulus in 59. (2) Praetor in 57.

SERAPIO: (1) Author of a work on mathematical geography, after Eratosthenes and perhaps before Hipparchus. (2) Owner (?) of a ship in 49.

*L. SERGIUS Catilina: Cicero's rival for the Consulship in 64. Plotted a *coup d'état* in 63, killed in battle the following year.

*SERVILIA: Mother of M. Brutus, half-sister of Cato, allegedly mistress of Caesar, and close friend of Atticus.

*M. SERVILIUS: Tried in connection with C. Claudius Pulcher's conviction in 50. The republican Tribune of 43 who later served as Legate under Cassius and Brutus may be the same.

Q. SERVILIUS: Friend of Ap. Pulcher.

*C. SERVILIUS Ahala: Ancestor of M. Brutus (through his mother and adoptive father), who as Master of the Horse in 439 killed one Sp. Maelius, suspected of plotting to become despot in Rome.

*P. SERVILIUS Isauricus: Earlier an associate of Cato and married to his niece, he joined Caesar in the Civil War and became Consul in 48. Governor of Asia 46–44. Moderate opponent of Antony after Caesar's death, but later reconciled. Consul again in 41.

*P. SERVILIUS Vatia Isauricus: Father of the above. Consul in 79 and Proconsul in Cilicia in 78-74, he gained his triumphal cognomen by operations against the Isaurian mountaineers. Died in extreme old age in 44.

SERVIUS: See SULPICIUS.

SERVIUS Pola: Professional prosecutor.

L. SESTIUS: Probably Quaestor in 44 and later a faithful follower of M. Brutus. None the less became Consul in 23 and recipient of a Horatian Ode.

P. SESTIUS: Father of the above. Quaestor in Macedonia in 62. As Tribune in 57 took a leading part in promoting Cicero's recall. Defended on charges in this connection by Cicero in 56 (speech extant). Later Praetor and Cicero's successor as governor of Cilicia in 49. Went over to Caesar after Pharsalia. Supported Cicero in 43, but kept his life and status in the thirties. A notoriously wearisome speaker.

SEXTILIUS: Four persons of this name may be distinguished in the Letters, identification of any one of them with any other being doubtful. But C. Sextilius Rufus, Quaestor (?) in Cyprus in 49, may be the Sextilius Rufus who commanded Cassius' fleet in 43; and Q. Sextilius, Milo's friend in 57, could be the Pompeian over whose expropriation Cicero waxed indignant in 44.

SEXTUS: See PEDUCAEUS and POMPEIUS.

SICCA: Friend of Cicero's, often mentioned in letters to Atticus and Terentia, perhaps a fellow-Arpinate and Cicero's 'Prefect of Engineers' in 63.

SILANUS: See JUNIUS.

P. SILIUS: Governor of Bithynia in 51–50 and owner of a property which Cicero wished to buy in 45.

SIRO: Epicurean philosopher who lived in Naples and became Virgil's teacher.

P. SITTIUS: Roman Knight, who left Italy for Further Spain and then Mauretania in 64, where, according to our sources, he became a military adventurer. In 57 condemned in absence on an unknown charge. Brought a force to join Caesar in 46 and received a principality in reward. Murdered in 44.

SOCRATES: Plato's teacher and principal speaker in his dialogues.

SOLON: Sixth-century Athenian statesman and law-giver.

SOPHOCLES: Fifth-century Athenian tragic dramatist.

C. SOSIUS: Praetor in 49.

SPARTACUS: Leader of a slave rebellion in 73–71.

SPINTHER: See CORNELIUS Lentulus.

SPURINNA: Haruspex (diviner from entrails). Warned Caesar that his life was in danger before his assassination.

L. STAIUS Murcus: Legate of Caesar's. Proconsul in Syria in 44. Active at sea on behalf of the republicans. After Philippi joined Sex. Pompeius, who eventually put him to death.

STATIUS: Slave, then freedman, of Q. Cicero.

SUFENAS: See NONIUS.

SULLA: See CORNELIUS.

*Ser. SULPICIUS Galba: Legate to C. Pomptinus, then to Caesar in Gaul. Praetor in 54. Supported Caesar in the Civil War and joined the conspiracy in 44. Fought under Pansa at the battle of Forum Gallorum. Probably killed in 43.

*Ser. SULPICIUS Rufus: (1) Friend and contemporary of Cicero's and one of the most famous of Roman jurists. Consul in 51, he worked to avoid the coming clash with Caesar, but in 49 after initial wavering joined Pompey (the common view that he remained neutral is mistaken). After Pharsalia he retired to Samos, but was appointed governor of Achaia by Caesar in

46. Died in 43 on a mission to Antony. *(2) His son. Joined Caesar's army at Brundisium in March 49, but further part in the war is unknown. After Caesar's death a republican and probably a victim of the Proscriptions.

TALNA: See JUVENTIUS.

TARCONDIMOTUS: Ruler (later king) in the Amanus mountains. Died at Actium fighting for Antony.

TERENCE (P. Terentius Afer): Second-century writer of Latin comedy.

TERENTIA: Cicero's wife from about 80 to 46.

TERENTIUS: Several persons with this name cannot be traced outside the passages where they occur.

Q. TERENTIUS Culleo: Tribune in 58 and friend of Pompey. Lepidus' officer Culleo in 43 may have been his son or a younger relative.

P. TERENTIUS Hispo: Friend of Cicero, worked for a tax-farming company (or companies) in Asia and Bithynia.

M. TERENTIUS Varro: Of Reate, the most learned and prolific author of his time. Born in 116. After a distinguished military and political career under Pompey's aegis, he gave up the republican cause after Pharsalia and became head of Caesar's new library. Narrowly escaping proscription in 43 he lived till 27 in tireless literary activity. Of his vast and varied output only a small part, and perhaps the least interesting, survives apart from fragments.

M. TERENTIUS Varro Gibba: See the recommendatory letter, 277 (XIII.10). He was Tribune in 43 and executed at Philippi.

*M. TERENTIUS Varro Lucullus: Brother by birth of L. Lucullus and an almost equally distinguished soldier. Consul in 73, triumphed for victories in the Balkans. Died not long after Lucius.

*A. TERENTIUS Varro Murena: Friend of Cicero and Ap. Pulcher.

TERTIA, TERTULLA: See JUNIA.

TESTA: See TREBATIUS.

THEMISTOCLES: Athenian leader in the Persian War of 481–479. Later exiled and took refuge with the King of Persia.

THEOPHANES: See POMPEIUS.

THEOPHRASTUS: Pupil of Aristotle and prolific writer on philosophy, politics, and natural science.

THEOPOMPUS: (1) Of Chios. Fourth-century historian noted for censoriousness. (2) Of Cnidus. Writer on mythology and friend of Caesar.

THERMUS: See MINUCIUS.

THRASYBULUS: Athenian statesman, who overthrew the oligarchy in 403.

THUCYDIDES: Fifth-century historian of the Peloponnesian War.

THYILLUS: Poet, three of whose epigrams survive in the Greek Anthology.

TIGELLIUS: A Sardinian, favourite of Caesar and later of Octavian.

TIGRANES: King of Armenia 95–c. 55.

C. TILLIUS Cimber: One of Caesar's assassins. Later as governor of Bithynia supported Brutus and Cassius. Probably died at Philippi.

TIMAEUS: Fourth–third-century historian.

TIMOLEON: Democratic leader in Sicily in the fourth century.

TIRO: See TULLIUS.

Q. TITINIUS: A wealthy Senator.

P. TITIUS: Tribune in 43 and proposer of the law establishing the Triumvirate. Died in office (other Titii crop up sporadically).

TORQUATUS: See MANLIUS.

TRABEA: Writer of Latin comedy.

TRATORIUS: Friend of Cornificius in 43.

C. TREBATIUS Testa: Of Velia. Friend and correspondent of Cicero, about twenty years his junior, recommended by him to Caesar in 54. Supported Caesar in the Civil War and lived to a ripe old age. Cicero's *Topica* is dedicated to him. Eminent jurist.

L. TREBELLIUS: As Tribune in 47 resisted Dolabella's radical economic programme, thus acquiring the cognomen 'Fides' ('Good Faith', 'Credit'). Officer under Antony in 43.

C. TREBONIUS: Tribune in 55, put through a law extending Caesar's term of command. Legate to Caesar in Gallic and Civil Wars and Praetor in 48. Governor of Further Spain 47–46. Consul-Suffect 45. Joined the conspiracy in 44. Brutally murdered by Dolabella shortly after his arrival in Asia as governor. Friend and correspondent of Cicero.

Cn. TREMELLIUS Scrofa: Praetor in the sixties and governor of
    Crete in 51–50. A leading character in Varro's dialogue *On
    Agriculture*.

TRIARIUS: See VALERIUS.

TRYPHO: See LIVINEIUS.

TUBERO: See AELIUS.

TUDITANUS: See SEMPRONIUS.

*TULLIA: Cicero's daughter. Died February 45.

L. TULLIUS: Legate to Cicero in Cilicia.

M. TULLIUS: Cicero's Secretary in Cilicia.

M. TULLIUS Cicero: (1) The orator. *(2) His son.

Q. TULLIUS Cicero: (1) Brother of the orator. (2) His son, Cicero's
    and Atticus' nephew.

TULLIUS Marcianus: He and the following accompanied young M.
    Cicero to Athens in 45. They were probably connections or
    dependants of the family.

L. TULLIUS Montanus: See the foregoing.

M. TULLIUS Tiro: Slave of Cicero, manumitted in 53, a confidential
    secretary and literary assistant. After Cicero's death devoted
    himself to propagating his work and memory.

TULLUS: See VULCATIUS.

D. TURULLIUS: Assassin of Caesar, probably Proquaestor to Tillius
    Cimber in 43. Later joined Antony and was executed by
    Octavian.

TUTIA: Considered as a possible match for the younger Quintus.

TYRANNIO: Of Amisus, originally called Theophrastus. Settled in
    Rome about 68 and became rich and well known as a scholar
    and teacher. Wrote on grammatical and literary subjects. The
    geographer Strabo was his pupil.

Paula (Polla) VALERIA: Of the Triarius family. Married D. Brutus
    in 50.

VALERIUS: (1) Called the interpreter. Probably to be distinguished
    from (2) A friend of Cicero and Trebatius, writer of mimes,
    possibly identical with the following.

L. VALERIUS: Lawyer friend of Cicero.

P. VALERIUS: (1) Businessman or tax-farmer in Cilicia in 50.(2)
    Friend at whose villa near Rhegium Cicero stayed in 44.

GLOSSARY OF PERSONS

*C. VALERIUS Flaccus: Son of the following. Served under Ap. Pulcher in 51. Killed fighting in Pompey's army at Dyrrachium in 48.

*L. VALERIUS Flaccus: Praetor in 63 and governor of Asia. Defended by Cicero in 59 in an extant speech.

*M. VALERIUS Messalla Corvinus: Son of the following. At Athens with young M. Cicero in 45. Distinguished orator and one of the great figures of the Augustan period.

*M. VALERIUS Messalla Niger: As Consul in 61 took an optimate line, but later a supporter of Pompey. Censor in 55–54, apparently died shortly before the Civil War.

*M. VALERIUS Messalla Rufus: Brother-in-law to Sulla and Hortensius' nephew, friend of Atticus and Cicero. Consul in 53. Later condemned for electoral malpractice and rehabilitated by Caesar. After Caesar's death lived in scholarly retirement to an advanced age. Wrote on augury.

C. VALERIUS Triarius: Apparently fell on the Pompeian side at Pharsalia. Cicero gave him a role in the De Finibus.

P. VALERIUS Triarius: Brother of the above.

VARRO: See TERENTIUS.

P. VATINIUS: Tribune in 59, carried through legislation on Caesar's behalf. Praetor in 55, Consul in 47, governor of Illyricum, triumphed in 42. Cicero attacked him in an extant speech, but in 54 became reconciled under pressure and defended him in court. From then on they remained on good terms.

P. VENTIDIUS Bassus: From humble beginnings rose to a Consulship (Suffect in 43) and Triumph (33). Antony's lieutenant in 43, fought for L. Antonius against Octavian in 40, as Proconsul won important successes against the Parthians.

C. VERGILIUS: Friend of Cicero, but as governor of Sicily refused him admittance in 58. Identifiable with a republican officer in Africa whose life was spared after surrender to Caesar and with a co-heir to the Scapula estate.

C. VESTORIUS: Businessman of Puteoli, friendly with Atticus and Cicero (who was apt to make fun of his lack of culture).

VETTIENUS: Businessman with whom Cicero had transactions in 49–44.

L. VETTIUS: Roman Knight from Picenum, who turned informer

against his Catilinarian associates in 63–62 and was prosecuted and imprisoned for making false charges against Caesar. Revealed or fabricated a plot against Pompey's life in 59. Died mysteriously in prison.

VETTIUS Chrysippus: an architect, freedman of the following.

VETTIUS Cyrus: a well-known architect.

VETUS: See ANTISTIUS.

L. VIBIUS Paciaecus: He and his father were prominent men in Further Spain. Served under Caesar in his final Spanish campaign.

C. VIBIUS Pansa Caetronianus: Son of one of Sulla's victims, served under Caesar in Gaul. Tribune in 51. Governed Bithynia and Cisalpine Gaul under Caesar. Consul in 43, died of wounds received in the battle of Forum Gallorum.

L. VIBULLIUS Rufus: Henchman of Pompey and his 'Prefect of Engineers' in 49.

C. VISELLIUS Varro: Cicero's cousin, son of a notable jurist and himself versed in law.

VOLUMNIA Cytheris: Freedwoman of the following and a well-known actress. Mistress of Mark Antony and allegedly the Lycoris to whom Virgil's friend Cornelius Gallus wrote love poems.

VOLUMNIUS: A Senator, perhaps identical with L. Volumnius Flaccus, bearer of a message from D. Brutus to the Senate in 43.

P. VOLUMNIUS Eutrapelus: Roman Knight and celebrated wit. After Caesar's death an adherent of Antony, probably his 'Prefect of Engineers' in 43–42.

Q. VOLUSIUS: On Cicero's staff in Cilicia.

L. VULCATIUS (or VOLCACIUS) Tullus: (1) Consul in 66. In and after the Civil War his political moderation seems to have turned into subservience to Caesar. *(2) His son, Praetor in 46 and governor of Cilicia (?) in 44. Consul with Octavian in 33.

XENO: (1) Friend and agent of Atticus in Athens. (2) Of Apollonia, commended by Atticus to Cicero in 51.

XENOCRATES: Pupil of Plato and third head of the Academy.

XENOPHON: Fifth–fourth-century Athenian historian.

ZENO: Founder of Stoicism.

GLOSSARY OF PLACES

Some names are omitted as generally familiar or explained in the notes. Italics are used for their modern equivalents.

ACHAIA: Southern Greece.

ACTIUM: Promontory on the mainland south of Corfù.

AECULANUM: Town on the Appian Way, east of Beneventum.

AEGINA: Island on the Saronic Gulf, south-west of Athens.

AEMILIAN WAY: Roman road running north-west from Ariminum through Mutina.

AENARIA (*Ischia*): Island off Naples.

AESERNIA: Town in central Italy, about 30 miles east of Arpinum.

AETOLIA: District of Greece, north-west of the Gulf of Corinth.

AFRICA: (1) The continent. (2) The Roman province, part of modern Tunisia.

ALABANDA: Town in Caria.

ALBA: (1) Alba Longa north-east of Rome (Mt Albanus = *Monte Cavi*). (2) Alba Fucens in central Italy near Lake Fucino.

ALLOBROGES: Chief tribe of Narbonese Gaul.

ALSIUM (*Palo*): Town on the coast of Etruria.

ALYZIA: Greek town south of Actium.

AMANUS: Mountain range separating Cilicia from Syria.

AMBRACIA: Town in southern Epirus.

ANAGNIA (*Anagni*): Town about 25 miles west of Arpinum.

ANTANDRUS: Town in Mysia.

ANTILIBANUS: Range of mountains in Syria.

ANTIOCH: Capital of Syria, about 40 miles west of modern Aleppo.

ANTIUM (*Anzio*): Coast town south of Rome, where Cicero owned a house.

APAMEA: Town in Phrygia.

APOLLONIA: Town on the western coast of the province of Macedonia.

APOLLONIS: Town in Asia Minor, north-east of Smyrna.

APPIA: Town in Phrygia.

APPIAN WAY: The great road linking Rome with Brundisium.

APPII FORUM: Town on the Appian Way about 40 miles from Rome.

APULIA: District in south-eastern Italy.

AQUINUM (*Aquino*): Town just south of Arpinum.

ARABIA FELIX: The Arabian peninsula.

ARADUS: Island town off the coast of Syria.

ARCADIA: Central district of the Peloponnese.

ARCANUM: Village between Aquinum and Arpinum.

ARGENTEUS (= 'Silver', *Argens*): River in Narbonese Gaul.

ARGENTEUS, PONS (= 'Silverbridge'): Bridge over the above.

ARRETIUM: *Arezzo* in Etruria.

ASIA: (1) The continent. (2) The Roman province, comprising the western part of Asia Minor.

ASTURA: Small island (joined to the mainland) off the coast south of Antium, where Cicero had a villa.

ATELLA: Town in Campania.

ATTICA: Territory of Athens.

AVENTINE: One of the Seven Hills of Rome, south of the Palatine.

BAIAE: Famous resort on the Bay of Naples, near Cumae.

BAREA: Town on the Spanish coast south of New Carthage (*Cartagena*).

BAULI: Seaside resort near Baiae.

BELLOVACI: Gallic tribe.

BENEVENTUM (*Benevento*): Important town on the Appian Way about 30 miles east of Capua.

BITHYNIA: Region in north-western Asia Minor; as a Roman province (Bithynia and Pontus) stretching much further east.

BLAUNDUS: Town in western Asia Minor about 120 miles east of Smyrna.

BOEOTIA: Greek territory north of Attica.

BONONIA: *Bologna*.

BOVILLAE: Ancient Latin town on the Appian Way about 11 miles from Rome.

BRUNDISIUM (*Brindisi*): Adriatic port in the heel of Italy.

BUTHROTUM: Town on the coast of Epirus opposite Corfù. Atticus had an estate near by.

BYLLIS: Town in Illyricum.

CAIETA (*Gaeta*): Port of Formiae.

CALACTE: Town on the northern coast of Sicily.

CALATIA: Campanian town between Capua and Beneventum.

CALES (*Calvi*): Town in northern Campania.

CALPE: Modern Cape of Gibraltar.

CAMERINUM (*Camerino*): Town in the Umbrian Apennines.

CAMPANIA: District south of Latium.

CANDAVIA: District in Illyricum (modern Albania) to the east of Dyrrachium.

CANUSIUM: Apulian town between Arpi and Brundisium.

CAPENA, PORTA: Entrance to Rome from the Appian Way.

CAPENA: Town in Etruria north-east of Veii.

CAPITOL: Highest of the Roman Hills, overlooking the Forum.

CAPPADOCIA: Kingdom in east-central Asia Minor.

CAPUA: Chief town of Campania.

CARIA: Region in south-western Asia Minor.

CARINAE: District of Rome north of the Colosseum.

CARTEIA: Spanish coast town near modern Gibraltar.

CASILINUM: Modern Capua, about 3 miles west of ancient Capua.

CASSIOPE: Town in the north-east of Corfù.

CASTRUM TRUENTINUM: Coast town about 60 miles south of Ancona.

CASTULO, Pass of: Pass in the Sierra Morena.

CATINA (*Catania*): Town on the eastern coast of Sicily.

CAUNUS: Town in Caria.

CEOS: Aegean island, one of the Cyclades.

CERAMICUS: District of Athens.

CERMALUS: A depression in the Palatine Hill, towards the Tiber.

CHAONIA: District of Epirus.

CHERSONESE: The Gallipoli peninsula.

CHIOS: Large island in the Aegean, not far from Smyrna.

CIBYRA: Town in south-western Asia Minor.

CILICIA: (1) Coastal strip in south-eastern Asia Minor. (2) Roman province comprising the whole southern coast, much of the interior, and the island of Cyprus.

CINGULUM (*Cingoli*): Inland town in Picenum.

CIRCEII: Town on the promontory west of Tarracina.

CISALPINE GAUL: 'Gaul this side of the Alps', i.e., northern Italy between the Alps and the Apennines.

CLATERNA (*Quaderna*): Town in Cisalpine Gaul, on the Aemilian Way between Bononia and Forum Cornelii.

CLITERNUM: Town in central Italy.

COLCHIS: Region bordering the south-eastern coast of the Black Sea.

COLOPHON: Town on the coast of Asia Minor near Ephesus.

COMMAGENE: Kingdom situated west of the Euphrates between Syria and Cappadocia.

COMUM (*Como*): Town on the southern shore of Lake Como, re-founded by Julius Caesar (Novum Comum).

CORCYRA (*Corfù*): Island off the coast of Epirus.

CORDUBA: *Cordova*, in southern Spain.

CORFINIUM: Chief town of the Paeligni, east of Lake Fucino.

CORYCUS: Town on the coast of Cilicia.

COSA (*Ansedonia*): Town on the coast of Etruria.

CROMMYACRIS ('Onion Cape'): Headland on the north coast of Cyprus.

CROTON: Town on the east coast of modern Calabria.

CULARO: *Grenoble*.

CUMAE (*Cuma*): Coastal town a few miles west of Naples. Cicero had a villa in its territory.

CYBISTRA: Town in the south-eastern corner of Cappadocia.

CYRRHESTICA: District of Syria, north-east of Antioch.

CYZICUS: Town on the Asiatic coast of the Propontis (*Sea of Marmora*).

DELOS: Aegean island, in the Cyclades.

DERBE: Town in Isauria.

DERTONA (*Tortona*): Town in Liguria.

DIONYSOPOLIS: Town in Phrygia.

DYRRACHIUM (*Durazzo*): Town on the western coast of the Roman province of Macedonia.

ELEUSIS: Town in Attica where the Mysteries were celebrated.

ELIS: Town in the west of the Peloponnese.

EPHESUS: On the western coast of Asia Minor, chief town of the province of Asia.

EPIDAURUS: Town on the eastern coast of the Peloponnese opposite Piraeus.

EPIPHANEA: Town in Cilicia.

EPIRUS: District of north-western Greece opposite Corfù.

EPOREDIA (*Ivrea*): Town in the foot-hills of the Pennine Alps.

EQUUS TUTICUS: Town in central Italy about 20 miles north of Beneventum (also called Equum (or Aequum) Tuticum).

ETRURIA: *Tuscany*.

FABRATERIA (VETUS and NOVA): Towns in Latium.

FALERNUM: District in northern Campania.

FICULEA: Town 5 miles north-east of Rome. Atticus had a villa between there and Nomentum (*La Mentana*).

FIRMUM (*Fermo*): Town near the Adriatic coast between Ancona and Castrum Truentinum.

FORMIAE (*Formia*): Town on the coast of Latium close to the Campanian border. Cicero had a villa near by.

FORUM CORNELIUM (or CORNELII): Town about 20 miles down the Aemilian Way east from Bononia.

FORUM GALLORUM: Village between Mutina and Bononia.

FORUM JULII (*Fréjus*): Town on the coast of Narbonese Gaul.

FORUM VOCONIUM (or VOCONII): Town in Narbonese Gaul between Pons Argenteus and Forum Julii.

FREGELLAE: Latian town destroyed in 125 and replaced by Fabrateria Nova.

FRUSINO (*Frosinone*): Latian town a few miles north-west of Fabrateria Nova.

FUNDI (*Fondi*): Latian town on the Appian Way between Tarracina and Formiae.

GADES: *Cadiz*.

GALATIA: District or kingdom in the east of Asia Minor, north of Cappadocia. The inhabitants were descended from Gaulish invaders.

GETAE: Tribe inhabiting modern Rumania.

HAEDUI: Gallic tribe.

HALAESA: Town in northern Sicily.

HALES (*Alento*): River in south-west Italy on which the town of Velia was situated.

HALICARNASSUS: Town in Caria.

HELLESPONT: The modern Dardanelles.

HERACLEA: (1) Town in Caria. (2) Town on the north coast of the Propontis (*Sea of Marmora*).

HERCULANEUM: Town near Pompeii.

HISPALIS: *Seville*.

HYDRUS (*Otranto*): Port in the heel of Italy south of Brundisium.

HYMETTUS: Mountain near Athens.

HYPAEPA: Town in Asia Minor, north-east of Smyrna.

ICONIUM (*Konya*): Town in Lycaonia.

IGUVIUM (*Gubbio*): Umbrian town on the western slope of the Apennines.

ILIUM: = Troy, near the southern entrance of the Hellespont.

ILLYRICUM: Region bordering the Adriatic from Epirus to the Gulf of Trieste.

INALPINI: Inhabitants of the Alps.

INSUBRES: Tribe of Cisalpine Gaul.

INTERAMNA (*Terni*): Town on the river Nar in Central Italy.

INTIMILII: Tribe of Liguria.

IONIA: Area on the western coast of Asia Minor settled by Ionian Greeks.

ISARA (*Isère*): River, tributary of the Rhône.

ISAURIA: Region south of Lycaonia in southern Asia Minor.

ISSUS: Cilician town on gulf of the same name in the south-eastern corner of the province.

LACEDAEMON: Another name for Sparta.

LANUVIUM: Latian town just off the Appian Way about 20 miles from Rome.

LAODICEA: (1) Town in the south-west of Phrygia. (2) Town in Syria on the coast south of Antioch.

LARINUM (*Larino*): Town in northern Apulia.

LATERIUM: Village between Arpinum and Anagnia where Q. Cicero had a property.

LATIUM: Territory to the south and east of Rome.

LAVERNIUM: Place in the neighbourhood of Formiae.

LESBOS: Large island in the northern Aegean.

LEUCAS: Town on the island of the same name between Actium and Alyzia.

LEUCATA (*Cape Ducato*): South-western extremity of the island of Leucas, south of Actium.

LILYBAEUM (*Marsala*): Town at the western end of Sicily.

LITERNUM (*Tor di Patria*): Coast town just north of Cumae.

LOCRI: Town in the toe of Italy.

LUCA (*Lucca*): Town in north-western Etruria.

LUCERIA (*Lucera*): Apulian town to the west of Arpi.

LUCRINE LAKE (*Lago Lucrino*): Lagoon adjoining the Gulf of Baiae.

LUSITANIA: Region of south-western Spain.

LYCAONIA: Region in central Asia Minor between Phrygia and Cappadocia.

LYCIA: Region on the southern coast of Asia Minor between Caria and Pamphylia.

MAGNESIA BY MT SIPYLUS: Town north-east of Smyrna.

MALEA (*Malia*): Headland at the south-eastern end of the Peloponnese.

MANTINEA: Town in Arcadia, scene of famous battle between Spartans and Thebans.

MARSI: People living near Lake Fucino in central Italy.

MASSILIA: Greek city, now Marseilles.

MEGARA: Town on the Isthmus of Corinth.

MIDAÏUM: Town in Phrygia.

MILETUS: Town on the west coast of Asia Minor, south of Ephesus.

MINTURNAE: Town a few miles south-east of Formiae.

MISENUM: Headland bounding the Bay of Naples to the north.

MOPSUHESTIA (= 'Hearth of Mopsus'): Town in the extreme east of Cilicia.

MULVIAN BRIDGE (*Ponte Molle*): Bridge across the Tiber above Rome.

MYLASA: Chief town of Caria.

MYRINA: Town on the coast north of Smyrna.

MYSIA: Region of north-western Asia Minor.

MYTILENE: Principal town of Lesbos.

NAR (*Nera*): River of central Italy.

NARBO (*Narbonne*): Roman colony in the west of Narbonese Gaul.

NARBONESE GAUL: Old Roman province in southern France.

NARES LUCANAE: Mountain pass in south-west Italy, 5 miles south-east of modern Acerno.

NARONA: Roman colony in Dalmatia.

NERVII: Tribe of north-eastern Gaul (Belgium).

NESIS (*Nisida*): Island off the coast between Puteoli and Naples.

NICAEA: Town in Bithynia.

NOLA (*Nola*): Inland town of Campania about 20 miles north-east of Capua.

NYSA: Town in Caria.

OLBIA (*Terranova*): Town in Sardinia.

OPUS: Town in Greece.

OSTIA (*Ostia*): Port of Rome.

PAESTUM (*Pesto*): Town on the western coast of Italy, south of Salerno.

PALATINE: Large hill south of the Forum, where according to tradition Rome began. A number of prominent people had houses on it, including Cicero.

PALTOS: Town on the coast of Syria, south of Laodicea.

PAMPHYLIA: Region on the south coast of Asia Minor between Lycia and Cilicia.

PANHORMUS: *Palermo*.

PAPHOS: Town in Cyprus.

PARIUM: Town on the Asiatic side of the Hellespont.

PARMA (*Parma*): Town in northern Italy.

PATRAE (*Patras*): Town on the northern coast of the Peloponnese.

PELLA: Town in Macedonia.

PELLENE: Greek town west of Sicyon.

PERGE or PERGA: Town on the coast of Pamphylia west of Side.

PESSINUS: Town in the west of Galatia.

PETRINUS: Mountain and district near Sinuessa.

PHILOMELIUM: Town in south-east Phrygia.

PHLIUS: Town in the Peloponnese.

PHRYGIA: Region in the middle of western Asia Minor.

PICENUM: Territory bordering the Adriatic south of Ancona.

PINDENISSUM: Town of the 'Free Cilicians' in the Amanus mountains.

PIRAEUS: Port of Athens.

PISAE: *Pisa*.

PISAURUM (*Pesaro*): Town on the coast of the Adriatic south of Ariminum.

PISIDIA: Region in south-west Asia Minor north of Pamphylia.

PLACENTIA (*Piacenza*): Town on the Po in northern Italy.

POLLENTIA (*Polenza*): Inland town in Liguria.

POMPEII: Town on the Bay of Naples where Cicero had a villa.

POMPTINE MARSHES: District adjoining the coast south of Rome.

PONS ARGENTEUS: See ARGENTEUS.

PONTUS: Region in north-eastern Asia Minor.

PORTA CAPENA: See CAPENA.

PRAENESTE (*Palestrina*): Latian town about 20 miles east of Rome.

PUTEOLI (*Pozzuoli*): Town east of Naples on the Bay. Cicero inherited an estate there in 45.

PYRAMUS: River in eastern Cilicia.

QUIRINAL: One of the Seven Hills of Rome.

REATE (*Rieti*): Sabine town south of Interamna.

REGIUM (*Reggio*): Town at the toe of Italy.

REGIUM (LEPIDI, *Reggio Emilia*): Town on the Aemilian Way west of Mutina.

SABINI: People of central Italy, with a reputation for old-fashioned frugality and virtue.

SACRA VIA: Street adjoining the north side of the Forum.

SALAMIS: Town in Cyprus.

SAMAROBRIVA: *Amiens*.

SAMNIUM: Region of central Italy.

SAMOS: Aegean island close to Ephesus.

SATRICUM: Place (village?) near Laterium.

SEGOVIA: Besides modern Segovia in Spain several other towns were so called.

SELEUCIA: City close to the right bank of the Tigris, near the site of ancient Babylon.

SELEUCIA PIERIA: Syrian coastal town west of Antioch.

SICYON: Greek town west of Corinth.

SIDE or SIDA: Harbour town in Pamphylia.

SIDON: Coastal town in Phoenicia (Lebanon).

SIGEUM: Town at the entrance of the Hellespont near ancient Troy.

SINUESSA (*Mondragone*): Town on the coast south of Formiae.

SIPONTUM: Coastal town in Apulia near modern Manfredonia.

SOLONIUM: Area south of the Ostian Way about 12 miles from Rome.

STABIAE: Town on the Bay of Cumae a few miles south of Pompeii.

STATIELLENSES: A Ligurian tribe on the northern slopes of the Apennines. Their chief town, Aquae Statiellae (*Acqui*), lay between Dertona and Pollentia.

SUESSA (*Sessa*): Latian town between Minturnae and Sinuessa.

SUNIUM: Promontory (and 'deme') south of Athens.

SYBOTA: Town on the coast of Epirus opposite a little archipelago of the same name between Corfù and the mainland.

SYNNADA: Town in Phrygia.

TARENTUM (*Taranto*): Town on the south coast of Italy.

TARICHEAE: Town in lower Galilee.

TARRACINA (*Terracina*): Town on the coast of Latium at the southern end of the Pontine Marshes.

TARSUS: Chief town of Cilicia proper.

TAUROMENIUM (*Taormina*): Town on the east coast of Sicily.

TAURUS: Mountain range in south-eastern Asia Minor.

TEANUM (APULUM): Town in the north of Apulia.

TEANUM (SIDICINUM, *Teano*): Inland town in Campania, a few miles south-west of Cales.

TENEDOS: Island south of the Hellespont.

THESPIAE: Town in Boeotia.

THESPROTIA: District in Epirus in which Atticus' estate was situated.

THESSALONICA: *Salonika.*

THESSALY: Region in Greece, south of Macedonia and east of Epirus.

THURII: Town near the Tarentine Gulf at the north-eastern end of the toe of Italy.

THYAMIS: River of Epirus bordering (or flowing through) Atticus' estate.

THYRREUM: Inland town east of Leucas.

TIBUR (*Tivoli*): Town in Latium 18 miles east of Rome.

TRALLES: Town in Caria.

TREBULA: The district of Trebula, near Calatia, bordered the Appian Way about 25 miles from Pompeii.

TRES TABERNAE (= 'Three Cottages'): Station on the Appian Way between Lanuvium and Forum Appii.

TUSCULUM: Latian town near modern Frascati. Cicero spent much time at his villa near by.

TYBA: Town in Cyrrhestica.

TYNDARIS (*Tindaro*): Town on the north coast of Sicily.

ULUBRAE: Small town bordering the Pontine Marshes.

UMBRIA: Region of central Italy east of Etruria.

UTICA: Chief town of the province of Africa.

VADA (*Vado*): Town on the coast of Liguria about 30 miles west of Genoa.

VARDAEI: Illyrian tribe.

VEII: Tuscan town a few miles north of Rome.

VELABRUM: District of Rome south of the Capitol.

VELIA: Town in south-western Italy south of Paestum. Also an area on the Palatine.

VELINE LAKE: Near Interamna.

VENAFRUM (*Venafro*): Town in northern Campania.

VENUSIA (*Venosa*): Town in western Apulia on the Appian Way.

VERCELLAE (*Vercelli*): Town in Cisalpine Gaul.

VESCINUM: District named from the ancient town of Vescia, on the slopes of Mt Massicus including the town of Sinuessa.

VIBO (*Bivona*): Town on the western coast of modern Calabria.

VICETINI: Inhabitants of Vicetia (*Vicenza*) in Venetia.

VIENNE (Latin VIENNA): Town in Narbonese Gaul on the east bank of the Rhône.

VOCONTII: People of Narbonese Gaul between the Rhône and the Alps.

VOLATERRAE (*Volterra*): Town in Etruria.

VOLSCI: Ancient Latin tribe. Arpinum was in their territory.

ZOSTER: Cape in Attica between Piraeus and Sunium.

GLOSSARY OF TERMS

ACADEMY (*Academia*): A hall (*gymnasium*) and park at Athens sacred to the hero Academus, in which Plato established his philosophical school. Hence Plato's school or system of philosophy, which went through various phases after his time. The terminology became confused, but Cicero recognized the 'Old' Academy of Plato and his immediate successors and the 'New' Academy of Arcesilas and Carneades, which maintained the uncertainty of all dogma and to which he himself professed to belong. In his own times this was modified by his teachers Philo of Larissa and Antiochus of Ascalon, the latter of whom claimed to represent the 'Old' Academy with a system akin to Stoicism. Cicero gave the name 'Academy' to a hall which he built on his estate at Tusculum.

AEDILE (*aedilis*): Third in rank of the regular Roman magistracies. Four at this time were elected annually, two Curule and two Plebeian. They were responsible for city administration and the holding of certain public Games. The chief magistrates in some municipalities were also so called.

ASSEMBLY: I sometimes so translate *populus* or *comitia*, as describing the Roman people convened for electoral or legislative purposes. There were several different sorts varying with the convening magistrate and the business to be done.

ATTIC(ISM): One use of the word was in connection with Roman oratory. In Cicero's time a movement principally represented by Calvus and M. Brutus favoured an austere style like that of the Athenian Lysias.

AUGUR: The priestly College of Augurs were official diviners interpreting signs (mostly from the flight and cries of wild birds or the behaviour of the Sacred Chickens) before major acts of public (and sometimes private) business. The College, like that of Pontiffs, was in practice almost a preserve of the nobility, so that for a 'new man' like Cicero membership was a coveted social distinction.

AUSPICES (*auspicia*): Divination from birds or other signs was officially necessary as a preliminary to major acts by magistrates, who were said to 'have auspices', i.e., the power of taking them.

BACCHUS' DAY (*Liberalia*): The festival of Liber Pater, commonly identified with the Greek god Dionysius or Bacchus, and Libera on 17 March. It was the usual day for a coming of age ceremony.

BOARD OF FOUR: Municipalities (not Roman colonies) were commonly governed by four principal magistrates (*quattuorviri*), divided into two pairs (*duoviri*), and a senate of *decuriones*.

BONA DEA: See GOOD GODDESS.

BOY (*puer*): Male slaves of any age were so called, as in later times.

CAMPANIAN LAND (DOMAIN – *ager Campanus*): Fertile land in Campania, originally confiscated by Rome in 211 and leased to small tenants. Caesar as Consul passed a bill (the Campanian Law) to distribute it among Pompey's veterans and the Roman poor.

CAMPUS (MARTIUS): The plain adjoining the Tiber on which assemblies of the Centuries were held, often for elections.

CENSOR: Two magistrates usually elected every five years for a tenure of eighteen months. They revised the roll of citizens, with property assessments, also the rolls of Knights and Senators, removing those deemed guilty of misconduct. They further supervised public contracts, including the lease of revenues to the tax-farmers, and issued decrees as guardians of public morals.

CENTURIES, ASSEMBLY OF (*comitia centuriata*): Form of assembly in which voting took place by 'Centuries', i.e., groups unequally composed so as to give preponderance to birth and wealth. It elected Consuls and Praetors, and voted on legislation proposed by them. The first Century to vote (*centuria praerogativa*) traditionally had a determining effect on the rest.

CENTURION: See LEGION.

COHORT: See LEGION.

COMITIAL DAYS: Days in the Roman calendar on which the popular assemblies (*comitia*) could legally be held. The Senate was normally not allowed to meet on these days.

COMITIUM: An area north of the Forum where assemblies were held.

COMMISSION, FREE or VOTIVE: See LEGATE.

COMPITALIA: See CROSSWAYS' DAY.

CONSUL: Highest of the annual Roman magistrates. Two were elected, usually in July, to take office on the following 1 January.

CONSULAR: An ex-Consul. The Consulars made up a corps of elder statesmen to whom the Senate would normally look for leadership.

CROSSWAYS' DAY (*Compitalia*): Festival in honour of the Lares Compitales (gods of the crossroads) held annually soon after the Saturnalia on a day appointed by the Praetor.

CURIATE LAW (*lex curiata*): A law passed by the Curies (*curiae*), the oldest form of Roman assembly. In Cicero's time it survived only in form, each of the thirty Curies being represented by a lictor, but still had certain legislative functions, notably the passage of laws to confirm the executive authority (*imperium*) of individual magistrates; but the precise nature of these laws is much in doubt.

CURULE CHAIR (*sella curulis*): Ivory chair, or rather stool, of state used by regular 'curule' magistrates, i.e., Consuls, Praetors, and Curule Aediles, and certain others.

DICTATOR: A supreme magistrate with quasi-regal powers appointed to deal with emergencies under the early Republic; his second-in-command, the Master of the Horse, was appointed by himself. The office was revived to legitimize the autocratic régimes of Sulla and of Julius Caesar.

EDICT: A public announcement or manifesto issued by a magistrate. The name applied to the codes issued by City Praetors and provincial governors at the beginning of their terms setting out the legal rules which they intended to follow.

EPICUREANISM: A materialistic school of philosophy named after its founder Epicurus, much in vogue among the Roman intelligentsia in Cicero's time.

EQUESTRIAN ORDER: See KNIGHTS.

ETESIAN WINDS (*etesiae*): Northerly winds which blew every year during the Dog-days.

FASCES: Bundles of rods carried by lictors in front of magistrates as a symbol of authority. Those of victorious generals were wreathed in laurel.

FLAMEN: Priest in charge of the cult of a particular deity. There were fifteen, three (those of Jupiter, Mars, and Quirinus) being superior to the rest.

FORUM: The chief square of Rome, centre of civic life.

FREEDMAN (*libertus*): A 'manumitted' slave.

GAMES (*ludi*): Gladiatorial and other shows, some recurring annually and supervised by magistrates, others put on for an occasion by private individuals. Of the former the Roman Games (*ludi Romani*) were held from 5 to 19 September, the Games of Apollo (*ludi Apollinares*) from 5 to 13 July. 'Greek Games' seem to have consisted of performances of Greek plays in the original language.

GOOD GODDESS (*Bona Dea*): A goddess whose worship was confined to women. Her yearly festival was held in the house of a Consul or Praetor and supervised by his wife.

GOWN (*toga*): Formal civilian dress of a Roman citizen. The gown of boys and curule magistrates (*toga praetexta*) had a purple hem. At sixteen or seventeen on coming of age a boy was given his White (or 'Manly') Gown (*toga pura, toga virilis*).

GREEK GAMES: See GAMES.

GREEKS: In Cicero's time the word was loosely used to include the more or less hellenized inhabitants of Western Asia and Egypt as well as those of Greece proper and the old Greek settlements elsewhere.

HONEST MEN: So I translate Cicero's *boni* ('good men', *les gens de bien*), a semi-political term for people of substance and respectability, supporters of the established order. Their opposites he calls *improbi* ('rascals').

IMPERATOR: Commander of a Roman army. But at this period the title was conferred on Generals by their soldiers after a victory and retained until they relinquished their *imperium*.

IMPERIUM: Literally 'command'; the executive authority appertaining to higher magisterial and promagisterial office.

INTERCALATION: See Appendix I(i).

INTERREGNUM: If through death or otherwise the consular office stood vacant and no patrician magistrates holding *imperium* were in office, an Interrex was appointed from among the patrician members of the Senate to exercise consular functions for five days. He was then replaced by another Interrex, and so on until new Consuls could be elected.

KNIGHTS (*equites*): In effect non-Senators of free birth possessing property over a certain level. They were regarded as forming a class of their own (*ordo equestris*) with special privileges and insignia.

LATIN FESTIVAL (*Feriae Latinae*): Movable annual festival of the Romano-Latin League held on Mt Alba. Its date was determined from year to year by the Consuls.

LECTURE HALL (*gymnasium*): The Greek gymnasium was originally a sports ground containing a *palaestra* (see below). But literature, philosophy, and music were also taught in them.

LEGATE (*legatus*): A provincial governor took several Legates, normally Senators, on his staff as deputies. Caesar in Gaul made them commanders of legions. The duties might, however, be purely nominal. The Senate could also appoint its members to 'free' or 'votive' (i.e., to discharge a vow) *legationes*, thus enabling them to travel abroad with official status. I sometimes translate with 'commission(er)'. The word can also be used for any kind of envoy.

LEGION: Roman army unit with a full complement of 6,000 men divided into ten cohorts. Each legion was officered by six Military Tribunes. Each cohort had six Centurions, the highest in rank being called *primi pili* (Chief Centurion). The ensign of a Legion was an eagle, and each cohort had its standard (*signum*).

LÈSE-MAJESTÉ (*maiestas*): The term *maiestas* covered acts 'in derogation of the majesty of the Roman People', as of magistrates or governors exceeding the bounds of their authority.

LEX CORNELIA (*de provinciis*): Law of Sulla regulating provincial administration.

LEX CURIATA: See above, CURIATE LAW.

LEX GABINIA: a law of 67 or 58 forbidding or restricting loans from Roman citizens to provincials.

LEX JULIA (*de provinciis*): Consular law of Caesar's on provincial administration.

LEX JUNIA-LICINIA: A law of 62 requiring that copies of proposed legislation be deposited in the Treasury.

LEX POMPEIA: Pompey's law against electoral corruption in 52.

LEX ROSCIA: A law of 67 assigning the first fourteen rows in the theatre to the Knights (the Senate sat below in the Orchestra).

LEX SCANTINIA: A law of uncertain date penalizing homosexual acts committed upon persons of free birth.

LIBERALIA: See BACCHUS' DAY.

LICTOR: Official attendant of persons possessing magisterial authority (*imperium*), the number varying with the rank.

LUPERCALIA: Fertility festival on 15 February held in a cave below the Palatine Hill by the Luperci. There were two Colleges of these until 45-44, when Caesar added a third called the *Luperci Iulii*.

MANUMISSION: Process of freeing a slave. This could be done either formally or informally ('between friends'), but in the latter case the master could revoke it at will.

MILE (*mille passus*): The Roman mile was 1,618 yards.

MIME (*mimus*): Type of entertainment with dancing, music, and dialogue which became highly popular in the first century B.C. It was considered more sophisticated and risqué than the Atellan Farce, which it virtually superseded.

MINERVA'S DAY (*Quinquatrus*): Festival of Minerva on 19 March.

NOBILITY: Practically, a noble (*nobilis*) at this period meant a direct descendant of a Consul in the male line. In the early Republic the Roman community was divided into patricians and plebeians, the former holding a virtual monopoly of political power. But after the Consulship was thrown open to plebeians in the fourth century many plebeian families became 'noble', and the remaining patricians were distinguished chiefly by their ineligibility to hold both Consulships in one year and for the plebeian offices of Tribune and Plebeian Aedile.

NOMENCLATOR: A slave whose duty it was to remind his master of the names of clients and acquaintances whom he happened to meet.

OPS: Roman goddess in whose temple on the Capitol Caesar deposited the state treasure.

OPTIMATES: Literally 'those belonging to the best' – the leading conservatives in the Senate and their supporters throughout the community. Sometimes the term is practically equivalent to the 'honest men' (boni), though more purely political in its implications.

OVATION: A lesser form of Triumph.

PALAESTRA: A space surrounded by colonnades, found in all gymnasia. Literally 'wrestling-school' (Greek).

PATRICIANS: See NOBILITY.

PAYMASTER-TRIBUNES (tribuni aerarii): At this time probably a class similar to the Knights but with a lower property qualification. Under the lex Aurelia of 70, juries were composed in equal numbers of Senators, Knights, and Paymaster-Tribunes.

PLEBEIANS: See NOBILITY.

PONTIFF (pontifex): These formed a priestly College in general charge of Roman religious institutions (including the Calendar), presided over by the Chief Pontiff (pontifex maximus), who was Julius Caesar from 63 until his death.

PRAETOR: Second in rank of the annual magistracies. Eight were elected at this period until Caesar increased the number to twenty. The City Praetor (praetor urbanus) was in charge of the administration of justice between Roman citizens, others presided over the standing criminal courts. After his year of office a Praetor normally went to govern a province as Propraetor or Proconsul.

PRAETORIAN COHORT (cohors praetoria): a special military unit forming a general's bodyguard.

PREFECT: Officer appointed by a magistrate (usually a provincial governor) for military or civil duties. These might be only nominal, the appointment merely conferring official status and privileges. The 'Prefect of Engineers' (*praefectus fabrum*) acted as adjutant to his chief – no longer any connection with engineers.

PROCONSUL (*pro consule*): 'Acting Consul', one who, not holding the office, exercised consular authority outside Rome by senatorial appointment. Similarly Propraetor (*pro praetore*) and Proquaestor (*pro quaestore*).

PROSCRIPTION (*proscriptio*): A procedure first employed by Sulla, then by the Triumvirs in 43. Lists of names were published, the persons thus 'proscribed' being declared outlaws and their goods confiscated. Their killers were rewarded, their protectors punished.

QUAESTOR: The first stage in the regular 'course of offices', election to which carried life-membership of the Senate. Since Sulla's time twenty were elected annually. The two City Quaestors (*quaestores urbani*) had charge of the Treasury and the Quaestors assigned to provincial governors (usually by lot) were largely concerned with finance.

QUARTAN: A fever recurring every third day; less grave therefore than a tertian, which recurred every other day.

QUIRINUS' DAY (*Quirinalia*): Festival in honour of Quirinus (the deified Romulus, founder of Rome) on 17 February.

RESOLUTION (*auctoritas*): A decree of the Senate vetoed by a Tribune was sometimes recorded under this name.

ROSTRA: The speakers' platform in the comitium, so called from the beaks (*rostra*) of captured warships which decorated it.

SATURNALIA: Festival of Saturn on 17 December, marked by merrymaking reminiscent of modern Christmas, to which it contributed some elements.

SECRETARY: I so translate (with a capital letter) Latin *scriba*. The 'scribes' were a corporation of civil servants working in the Treasury and otherwise. City magistrates and provincial governors might be assigned official Secretaries for their personal assistance. Private clerks were called *librarii*.

GLOSSARY OF TERMS

SENATE: Governing body of the Roman Republic, numbering about 600 (increased to 900 by Caesar) and composed of magistrates and ex-magistrates.

SHEPHERDS' DAY (*Parilia*): Festival of the god and goddess Pales, protectors of flocks and herds, on 21 April.

SOOTHSAYING: For *haruspicina*, an Etruscan system of divination from the entrails of sacrificial animals, from portents, and from lightning. Some of its practitioners (*haruspices*) seem to have been organized as a body of sixty and were consulted officially.

SOPHIST: A professional 'wise man', making money as a teacher and lecturer, often itinerant.

STOICISM: Philosophical school, named from the portico (*stoa*) in which its founder, Zeno of Citium (*c.* 300), taught. Cato was its most prominent Roman adherent in Cicero's time.

SUMPTUARY LAW: A series of laws during the Republic attempted to impose restrictions on luxury spending, especially on food. One was enacted by Julius Caesar in 46.

SUPPLICATION (*supplicatio*): A thanksgiving ceremony decreed by the Senate in honour of a military success, the number of days varying according to the importance of the victory. It was generally regarded as a preliminary to a Triumph.

TABLETS (*codicilli*): Wooden tablets coated with wax and fastened together with thread, used for memoranda and short notes.

TAX-FARMERS (*publicani*): Roman taxes, as on grazing-land in the provinces or excise, were largely farmed out by the Censors to private companies who bid for the right of collection. The capitalists in Rome as well as their local agents were called *publicani*. In political terms *publicani* and Knights often amount to the same thing.

TELLUS: Earth-goddess, whose temple was one of the meeting-places of the Senate.

TESTIMONIAL: Renders *laudatio* (= 'eulogy') in one of its senses. It was customary for defendants to ask prominent persons to offer witness to their good character in court either orally or in writing.

TETRARCH: Literally 'ruler over a fourth part'. In Cicero's time many minor eastern princes were called by this title.

GLOSSARY OF TERMS

TOGA: See GOWN.

TREASURY (*aerarium*): The Roman state treasury was in the temple of Saturn in the Forum, managed by the City Quaestors with the assistance of Secretaries.

TRIBE (*tribus*): A division, mainly by locality, of the Roman citizen body. The number had risen over the centuries from three to thirty-five (four of them 'urban', the rest 'rustic'). Assemblies voting by tribes (*comitia tributa*) elected magistrates below Praetor and could pass legislation proposed by Tribunes.

TRIBUNE: (1) Of the Plebs. A board of ten, originally appointed to protect plebeians from patrician high-handedness. They had wide constitutional powers, the most important being that any one of them could veto any piece of public business, including laws and senatorial decrees. They could also initiate these. They took office on 10 December. (2) Military: See LEGION. (3) See PAYMASTER-TRIBUNES.

TRIUMPH: Victory celebration by a general on his return to Rome. Permission had to be granted by the Senate.

UNIFORM: Magistrates leaving to take command of armies wore the general's red cloak (*paludamentum*) and were said to set out *paludati*.

VALUATION (*aestimatio*): Process by which a debtor's property could be transferred to his creditor in settlement. Caesar made such transfers compulsory on terms favourable to the debtor.

WEAL: The goddess Salus, who had a temple on the Quirinal Hill near Atticus' house.

MAPS

THE ROMAN

BRITAIN

R Rhine

GALLIA
COMATA

Rhone

GALLIA
NARBONENSIS

GALLIA
CISALPINA

Verona

ILLYRICUM

Massilia

Luca

R Rubicon
Ariminum

Numantia

Narbo

Albintimilium

Ilerda

Rome

FURTHER
SPAIN

NEARER
SPAIN

SARDINIA

Thurii

Sisapo

SICILY

Mylae

Rhegium

Tartessus
Gades

Munda

Leontini

Utica

Syracuse

NUMIDIA

Carthage

AFRICA

Agrigentum

Thapsus

0   100   200   300   English Miles

EMPIRE 51 B.C.

—— Boundaries of provinces
- - - Boundaries of the empire

SCYTHIANS

Borysthenes

R. Danube

BLACK SEA

PONTUS
BITHYNIA
ARMENIA
MINOR MAJOR
Zela
GALATIA
Pessinus
ASIA
Carrhae
CILICIA
R. Euphrates
Laodicea Tarsus
Side
SYRIA
Pamphylia
CYPRUS
Apamea
Citium
Paphos
CRETE

Cyrene
Alexandria
Ascalon
CYRENE
EGYPT
R. Nile

ITALY and SICILY

0   50   100   150   200 Miles

ASIA MINOR

Scales
0   40   80   120   160
English miles
0   40   80   120   160
Roman miles

GREECE AND THE
BALKANS

Scales

0   20 40 60 80 100 120 140 160
English miles

0   20 40 60 80 100 120 140 160
Roman miles

to Milvian Bridge and the North

VIA FLAMINIA

FIELD OF MARS
(CAMPUS MART(IUS))

QUIRINAL

"Sheepfold"

Theatre of
Pompey

R. Tiber

Capitol 5

CARINAE

Forum

VIA SACRA

VIA NOVA

VIA AURELIA

PALATINE

JANICULUM

AVENTINE

Porta Capena

to Arpinum and
Campania

VIA APPIA (to Campania)

VIA LATINA

1 Temple of Jupiter
2 Temple of Saturn
3 Temple of Castor
4 Senate House
5 Temple of Concord
6 Regia (official residence of High Priest)

ROME
in the late Republic